VICIOUS CIRCLES

Cultural Memory | *in the Present*

Hent de Vries, Editor

The Scene of Recalcitrance, Onerva Luoma.

VICIOUS CIRCLES

Disclosing a History of Critique

Arvi Särkelä

STANFORD UNIVERSITY PRESS
Stanford, California

Stanford University Press
Stanford, California

© 2026 by Arvi Särkelä. All rights reserved.

No part of this book may be reproduced or transmitted in any form or by any means, electronic or mechanical, including photocopying and recording, or in any information storage or retrieval system, without the prior written permission of Stanford University Press.

ISBN 978-1-5036-4541-7 (cloth)
ISBN 978-1-5036-4572-1 (paperback)
ISBN 978-1-5036-4573-8 (electronic)

Library of Congress Control Number: 2025038706

Library of Congress Cataloging-in-Publication Data available upon request.

Cover design: Daniel Benneworth-Gray
Cover art: Onerva Luoma, *Vicious Circles*

The authorized representative in the EU for product safety and compliance is: Mare Nostrum Group B.V. | Mauritskade 21D | 1091 GC Amsterdam | The Netherlands | Email address: gpsr@mare-nostrum.co.uk | KVK chamber of commerce number: 96249943

Nature centres into balls,
And her proud ephemerals,
Fast to surface and outside,
Scan the profile of the sphere;
Knew they what that signified,
A new genesis were here.

— RALPH WALDO EMERSON, "Circles"

**Livet är den trånga ringen som håller oss fången,
den osynliga kretsen, vi aldrig överträda,
livet är den nära lyckan som går oss förbi,
och tusende steg vi icke förmå oss att göra.**

*Life is the narrow ring that keeps us captive,
the invisible circle we never trespass,
life is the close happiness which passes us by,
and the thousand steps we're unable to take.*

— EDITH SÖDERGRAN, "Livet"

Contents

	Acknowledgments	xiii
	Abbreviation Key	xv
1	A Circle Around a Circle	1
	Introducing a Metaphorology of Critical Disclosure	
2	Recalcitrance to Second Nature	21
	Lovibond on Counterteleology	
3	Drawing a Vicious Circle	45
	Adorno, Emerson, and the Scene of a Disclosing Critique of Society	
4	"The Realm of Transfigured Physis Disclosed"	71
	The Young Nietzsche as a (Meta)Physician of Culture	
5	Society as Experience	105
	Adaptation and Exemplarity in Adorno and Dewey	
6	Civilization and Its Uncanniness	139
	Freud's Sense of Guilt	
7	Making Phantasies in the Wrong World	192
	Dewey, Tarde, and the Idea of a Critical Cosmology	
8	Reason and Recalcitrance	236
	Conclusions Without Closure	
	Notes	253
	Bibliography	277
	Index	295

Acknowledgments

I would like to thank Martin Hartmann, Frederick Neuhouser, and Giovanni Ventimiglia for accepting to be on my habilitation committee and reviewing the *Habilitationsschrift* that was to develop into this book. I am especially grateful to Hartmann, Michael Hampe, and Arto Laitinen for their support and close collaborations during the past five years, which I have spent on, among many other things, writing this book.

I am especially grateful to a few colleagues and friends who, in very different ways and in different phases, commented on full drafts of the manuscript. For precious advice regarding the full manuscript and its fate, I owe gratitude to Amy Allen, Steven Levine, Frederick Neuhouser, and Just Serrano. I thank Iida Rauma for particularly encouraging remarks on the last draft of the manuscript. Arto Laitinen organized a workshop on its very first full draft at Tampere University in May 2023. I am grateful for the comments I received there from him, Sauli Havu, Heikki Aleksanteri Kovalainen, Simo Pieniniemi, Corrado Piroddi, Juho Rekola, Hanna Samola, and Tuukka Tomperi. For discussing with me the very idea of this book back where it all began as a lump of bizarre intuitions in the bottom of my belly in 2019, I am grateful to Federica Gregoratto, Axel Honneth, and the late Richard J. Bernstein.

More people than I can name or remember have, in workshops or seminars, at conferences, or over a cup of coffee, given me helpful comments on drafts that went on to become chapters of this book. For such remarks, I am grateful to Borhane Blili-Hamelin, Louis Carré, Robin Celikates, Volkan Cidam, Didier Debaise, Olivier Del Fabbro, Paul Giladi, Federica Gregoratto, Michael Hampe, Martin Hartmann, Heikki Ikäheimo, Rahel Jaeggi,

Paula Keller, Hannes Kuch, Simon Kräuchi, Otto Linderborg, Onerva Luoma, Emmanuel Renault, Naoko Saito, Matteo Santarelli, Isette Schumacher, Melanie Sehgal, Titus Stahl, Heiko Stubenrauch, Tullio Viola, Jean-Baptiste Vuillerod, Robert Ziegelmann, Italo Testa, and Thomas Wallgren.

For the frontispiece of this book, I owe gratitude to Onerva Luoma. I thank Hent de Vries for considering my manuscript and including it in the series Cultural Memory in the Present. For her swift and meticulous engagement with me and my book, I thank Erica Wetter at Stanford University Press, and for helpful and precise copyediting, I thank Laura J. Vollmer. I am grateful to Marina Ruffin for help with getting the figures 1–5 right and to Jonathan Biedermann and Noah Binder for help with formatting the manuscript. While writing this book, I was constantly teaching students at the University of Lucerne and ETH Zürich, who I owe gratitude to for countless inspiring discussions.

In these six years, I have had stimulating discussions with loved ones that have not only inspired ideas in this book but given me power and courage to write them down. For such encounters, gratitude can never be enough. Yet, if it were, I would thank Borhane Blili-Hamelin, Oliver Blomqvist, Peter Borgar, Federica Gregoratto, Kennet Härmälä, Naveen Kanalu, Onerva Luoma, Vandad Neshati Malikyans, Iida Rauma, Sara Rönnqvist, Marina Ruffin, Matteo Santarelli, Andreas Särkelä, and Just Serrano.

Chapters 3 and 5 are based on and further developed from articles that I have previously published in journals. Chapter 3 is derived in part from the article "Negative Organicism: Adorno, Emerson and the Idea of a Disclosing Critique of Society," *Critical Horizons* 21, no. 3 (2020): 222–39, https://doi.org/10.1080/14409917.2020.1790752. Chapter 5 is derived in part from the article "Vicious Circles: Adorno, Dewey and Disclosing Critique of Society," *Philosophy and Social Criticism* 48, no. 10 (2022): 1369–90, https://doi.org/10.1177/01914537221117092. Chapter 4 is a heavily transformed and extended version of a chapter in a collected volume: "The (Meta)Physician of Culture: Early Nietzsche's Disclosing Critique of Forms of Life," in *Naturalism and Social Philosophy*, edited by Martin Hartmann and me (Rowman and Littlefield, 2023). Chapters 1, 2, 6, 7, and 8 are fully original to this book.

Abbreviation Key

ADORNO, THEODOR W.

AT   *Aesthetic Theory*. Edited by Gretel Adorno and Rolf Tiedemann, translated by Robert Hullot-Kentor. 1970. Continuum, 2002.

HF   *History and Freedom: Lectures 1964–1965*. Edited by Rolf Tiedemann, translated by Rodney Livingstone. Polity Press, 2006.

IS   *Introduction to Sociology*. Edited by Christoph Gödde, translated by Edmund Jephcott. Stanford University Press, 2000.

MGH   "Die menschliche Gesellschaft heute." In Adorno, *Nachgelassene Schriften*. Sec. 5, vol. 1, edited by Michael Schwarz. 1957. Suhrkamp Verlag, 2019.

MI   *Minima Moralia: Reflections from Damaged Life*. Translated by Edmund Jephcott. 1951. New Left Books, 1974.

ND   *Negative Dialectics*. Translated by E. B. Ashton. 1966. Routledge, 1973.

PETS   *Philosophical Elements of a Theory of Society: 1964*. Edited by Tobias ten Brink and Marc Phillip Nogueira, translated by Wieland Hoban. Polity Press, 2019.

PS   *Philosophie und Soziologie*. In Adorno, *Nachgelassene Schriften*. Sec. 4, vol. 6, edited by Dirk Braunstein. Suhrkamp Verlag, 2011.

S   "Society." Translated by Frederic Jameson. *Salmagundi* 10–11 ([1965] 1969): 144–53.

DEWEY, JOHN

AE   *Art as Experience.* In Dewey, *The Later Works, 1925–1953*, edited by Jo Ann Boydston. Vol. 10. 1934. Southern Illinois University Press, 2008.

DE   *Democracy and Education.* In Dewey, *The Middle Works, 1899–1924*, edited by Jo Ann Boydston. Vol. 9. 1916. Southern Illinois University Press, 2008.

EN   *Experience and Nature.* In Dewey, *The Later Works, 1925–1953*, edited by Jo Ann Boydston. Vol. 1. 1925. Southern Illinois University Press, 2008.

HNC   *Human Nature and Conduct.* In Dewey, *The Middle Works, 1899–1924*, edited by Jo Ann Boydston. Vol. 14. 1922. Southern Illinois University Press, 2008.

IPI   "The Inclusive Philosophic Idea." In Dewey, *The Later Works, 1925–1953*, edited by Jo Ann Boydston. Vol. 3. 1928. Southern Illinois University Press, 2008.

LC   *Lectures in China 1919–1920.* Translated by Robert W. Clopton and Tsuin-Chen Ou. University Press of Hawai'i, 1973.

LCN   "Lectures in Social and Political Philosophy" (notes for the lectures in China). *European Journal of Pragmatism and American Philosophy* 7, no. 2 (2015): 7–44.

LSA   *Liberalism and Social Action.* In Dewey, *The Later Works, 1925–1953*, edited by Jo Ann Boydston. Vol. 11. 1935. Southern Illinois University Press, 2008.

PP   *The Public and Its Problems.* In Dewey, *The Later Works, 1925–1953*, edited by Jo Ann Boydston. Vol. 2. 1927. Southern Illinois University Press, 2008.

UPMP   *Unmodern Philosophy and Modern Philosophy.* Edited by Philip Deen. Southern Illinois University Press, 2012.

EMERSON, RALPH WALDO

AS   "The American Scholar." In Emerson, *Essays and Lectures*, edited by Joel Porte. 1837. Library of America, 1983.

C "Circles." In Emerson, *Essays and Lectures*, edited by Joel Porte. 1841. Library of America, 1983.

E "Experience." In Emerson, *Essays and Lectures*, edited by Joel Porte. 1844. Library of America, 1983.

H "History." In Emerson, *Essays and Lectures*, edited by Joel Porte. 1841. Library of America, 1983.

N *Nature*. In Emerson, *Essays and Lectures*, edited by Joel Porte. 1936. Library of America, 1983.

OS "The Over-Soul." In Emerson, *Essays and Lectures*, edited by Joel Porte. 1841. Library of America, 1983.

P "The Poet." In Emerson, *Essays and Lectures*, edited by Joel Porte. 1844. Library of America, 1983.

SR "Self-Reliance." In Emerson, *Essays and Lectures*, edited by Joel Porte. 1841. Library of America, 1983.

FREUD, SIGMUND

BPP *Beyond the Pleasure Principle*. In Freud, *The Standard Edition of the Complete Psychological Works of Sigmund Freud*, edited by James Strachey and Anna Freud. Vol. 18. 1920. Vintage Books, 2001.

CD *Civilization and Its Discontents*. In Freud, *The Standard Edition of the Complete Psychological Works of Sigmund Freud*, edited by James Strachey and Anna Freud. Vol. 21. 1930. Vintage Books, 2001.

EI *The Ego and the Id*. In Freud, *The Standard Edition of the Complete Psychological Works of Sigmund Freud*, edited by James Strachey and Anna Freud. Vol. 19. 1923. Vintage Books, 2001.

GPAE *Group Psychology and the Analysis of the Ego*. In Freud, *The Standard Edition of the Complete Psychological Works of Sigmund Freud*, edited by James Strachey and Anna Freud. Vol. 18. 1922. Vintage Books, 2001.

MM "Mourning and Melancholia." In Freud, *The Standard Edition of the Complete Psychological Works of Sigmund Freud*, edited by James Strachey and Anna Freud. Vol. 14. 1915. Vintage Books, 2001.

OP	*An Outline of Psycho-Analysis.* In Freud, *The Standard Edition of the Complete Psychological Works of Sigmund Freud*, edited by James Strachey and Anna Freud. Vol. 23. 1940. Vintage Books, 2001.
RRWT	"Remembering, Repeating, Working-Through." In Freud, *The Standard Edition of the Complete Psychological Works of Sigmund Freud*, edited by James Strachey and Anna Freud. Vol. 12. 1914. Vintage Books, 2001.
TP	"Formulations on the Two Principles of Mental Functioning." In Freud, *The Standard Edition of the Complete Psychological Works of Sigmund Freud*, edited by James Strachey and Anna Freud. Vol. 12. 1911. Vintage Books, 2001.
U	"The Uncanny." In Freud, *The Standard Edition of the Complete Psychological Works of Sigmund Freud*, edited by James Strachey and Anna Freud. Vol. 17. 1919. Vintage Books, 2001.

LOVIBOND, SABINA

EF	*Ethical Formation.* Harvard University Press, 2002.

NIETZSCHE, FRIEDRICH

BT	*"The Birth of Tragedy" and Other Writings.* Edited by Raymond Geuss and Ronald Speirs, translated by Ronald Speirs. 1872. Cambridge University Press, 1999.
UM	*Untimely Meditations.* Edited by Daniel Breazeale, translated by R. J. Hollingdale. 1873–1876. Cambridge University Press, 2007.

TARDE, GABRIEL

LI	*Les lois de l'imitation: Étude sociologique.* In Tarde, *Œuvres de Gabriel Tarde*, edited by Éric Alliez. Sec. 2, vol. 1. 1890. Seuil, 2001.
LS	*Les lois sociales: Esquisse d'une sociologie.* In Tarde, *Œuvre de Gabriel Tarde*, edited by Éric Alliez. Vol. 4. 1895. Presses Universitaires de France, 1999.
MS	*Monadology and Sociology.* Edited and translated by Theo Lorenc. 1893. Re.press, 2012.

ONE

A Circle Around a Circle
Introducing a Metaphorology of Critical Disclosure

Things associate and create bonds that reshape the things and their associations. In a synthetic chemical reaction, two relatively simple substances associate to form a more complex substance. Simple hydrogen gas combines with simple oxygen gas, and together, they produce a complex substance: water. Our nearest galaxies associate within the Local Group of galaxies. Our own Milky Way, with its satellite galaxies, is part of the Local Group, which is a part of the Virgo supercluster—an associating component of the even greater Laniakea supercluster. Like many associative bonds, Laniakea is gravitationally weak, meaning that it will disperse. Things come and go, and so do their bonds. On Milky Way's planet Earth, reindeer are born into herds with certain associative patterns, to which the young learn to adapt, such as migration of thousands of kilometers a year. The associative life of a reindeer is heterogenous: it enters into bonds with other reindeer in the herd as well as with hydrogen-and-oxygen-produced water, irritating mosquitos, and perhaps also reindeer-herding people gazing into the Milky Way in the long and dark Arctic winter night.

Like reindeer, people are born into associative bonds, or forms of life, that precede them. Human forms of life associate with their natural environments and consist of their own associating elements, such as, importantly, people with habits, customs, impulses, quirks, interests, technologies, and phantasies. These bonds contain patterns to which individual people must adapt to in order to maintain themselves and reproduce their bonds.

People pick berries to eat and mushrooms to smoke, design clothes to keep warm and look stupendous, invent crazy dances to intensify a dull life, make trails to expand their environment, mate and date, cultivate land, and, eventually, send space probes into the Milky Way. People do not survive without association with *groups* of people. Therefore, they tend to act in ways that ensure that their forms of life remain intact. The social group grows and forms subgroups and enters into associative bonds with other social groups and eventually forms a supergroup: a society. When this happens, the habits and customs that spontaneously evolve in the group and direct the activities of its members might not secure enough stability anymore, and the society will then become, as it were, gravitationally weak. People then start to codify their habits as rules and treat them as norms and institutions so that those born into these groups later are made ready to occupy allegedly necessary social roles. People must adapt to their social environment, or their forms of life, their forms of life must adapt to the societal environment, and the society and all its elements, to its natural environment. To meet these challenges, people develop practices of inquiry—more or less formalized ways to resolve environmental indeterminacies they come to take as problems. They seek to keep their inquiries, too, stable for generations and so develop sciences of land, food, order, and drill, which they, in due course, come to term "geography," "nutritional science," "law," and "pedagogy."

Forms of life evolve in circles. People are born into associative bonds, bonds that have determinate patterns; the patterns shape people's habits, desires, impulses, and dreams in ways that tend to maintain the bonds. When these groups of people associate with each other, they form societies, more complex and cunning forms of life. As people are born into social groups that drill them and as their social groups must adapt to a perilous natural environment and a just-as-unpredictable societal environment, people find themselves under overwhelming pressure to maintain themselves and their associative bonds. It is then not surprising that their practices of inquiry, too, have a tremendous bias for continuity, for the preservation of self and society. But just as the environment is fundamentally uncontrollable, so are these inquiries. As the groups multiply and their associations diversify and society expands, recalcitrant practices emerge, and some of these aberrations become reflective too. When human associative bonds establish practices where their individual members reflect on them, some of these practices eventually will turn against the way these very bonds are structured. They react against the bonds that created them with an awareness of deviation and an interest to modify them. Their intent is *critical*. A widely shared understanding among several human forms of life takes philosophy to be such a self-reflectively deviating practice of association (although, in a remote corner of one of those forms of life, philosophy is stubbornly associated with "analysis," as opposed to "critique").

With the evolution of this particularly clever recalcitrance, cunning societal mechanisms of resisting it also evolve. The societal forms of life develop mechanisms of preserving their form by not only ignoring or violently suppressing criticism but also preemptively silencing it and turning the negation into a form of affirmation. The former mechanism makes critique seem ridiculous to begin with so that the threshold to criticize becomes unbearably high. In some circles in Germany, mentioning the extent to which the taxpayers, by enormous weapons exports to Israel, participate in producing senseless suffering in Palestine would be met by such aggressive accusations of antisemitism that the criticism is unlikely to be expressed at all.[1] But even more impressive is the latter mechanism: by it, these complex associative bonds skillfully subvert resistance into legitimation. As if by a magical spell, recalcitrance turns into applause. That Donald Trump's first presidency wasn't a complete disaster was sometimes reported as proof that American democracy "works," whereas the reasonable conclusion would rather be that his mere election was a strong enough indication that a long line of American social criticism had been right to point out that something is seriously *wrong* with American democracy. Critique of the form of life turns into an achievement of that form of life so naturally that one is tempted, with a nod to evolutionary biology, to call this a mechanism of societal exaptation.

A further, even more uncanny way such complex forms of life can sidestep criticism is by redirecting recalcitrant associative activity in such a way that it either fails to become reflective—that is, to establish itself as a practice of inquiry—or, if it does become reflective, fails to carry any effect—that is, to modify the associative bonds. In the first case, individuals' senseless social suffering fails to become critical. Society can, for example, overburden its members in various ways so that they will only ever find time to focus on their very next task ahead but never to perceive their suffering in its social environment or find time and space to express their suffering as critique. Leviathan creates a state of nature within itself, breaks its promise of peace and safety, and forces society's members to struggle against each other for artificially scarce resources—and only a lucky few will ever have time to complain. In the second case, critical inquiry fails to practically mend senseless social suffering: then, reflective recalcitrance does not become effective. Critical inquiry can, for example, be academically institutionalized as an expertise of philosophy departments at universities where sophisticated arguments for and justifications of "well ordered societies" or "the duty of the oppressed to resist their oppression" are formulated and debated, but senseless social suffering is seldom abolished by arguments and justifications. Recent research from cognitive psychology suggests that it is not primarily arguments formulated and received by rational individuals that lead to change in belief and action.[2] Rather, thinking, or critical inquiry, is a complex social process in which certain terms, ideas, and convictions emerge in associative behavior in social groups and then lead to transformations in epistemic attitudes and habitual dispositions, within which a different course of action might follow. The idea of a lonely rational individual going through and testing arguments to adopt certain beliefs and make decisions about action is, according to these findings, an intellectualist illusion. It is also a dangerous illusion since it inhibits critical inquiry from finding its place in the associative activities of the members of a form of life. Social life's circle of adaptation turns *vicious*. Society's patterns of social bonds, the societal environment, grows so overpowering that it continues into the deepest facets of the individual, whose discontent and pain is directed in various ways toward maintaining the very structure of the bonds that make her suffer senselessly.

This vicious circle is the scene of a *disclosing critique* of society. This critique is a form of social recalcitrance that seeks not primarily to *argue* against any social arrangement but to *show* how it is false and how to get out of it. Yet how, exactly, can such self-perpetuating forms of life be critically challenged? If society, the Leviathan that once promised peace and safety, has come to organize itself as an antagonistic and artificial state of nature by expanding market forms of association to nearly every sphere of social life, how can its members find sufficient conditions (time, space, power, inspiration, knowledge, poetry, and ideas) for reflective *and* effective recalcitrance? How can we break out of the vicious circle of society that destroys its own reproductive conditions and natural environment in producing piled up environmental, health, and care crises to a catastrophic extent?

1. Models of Critique: Normativist and Denaturalizing

Is there a way out of the vicious circle? This is the question of disclosing critique. It is something of a riddle since a form of life reproducing itself as a vicious circle tends to radically suppress and repress critical transformative practice. Either deviating practice cannot become reflective or reflective inquiry cannot become effective. Reflective recalcitrance then does not shift the reproductive circle of society. This, I believe, is a question as practical as it is crucial in times like ours characterized by an overwhelming number of simultaneous crises and pertinent catastrophes bundling up in ways that overburden the individuals and end up maintaining the very customs, institutions, and functional connections that caused the suffering. How can recalcitrance to these bonds become reflective and effective under these conditions?

In the contemporary philosophical debates on social critique, disclosing critique is mostly only noted in the margins and rarely taken as a viable alternative. Instead, the debate revolves around three or four "models of critique": internal, external, and immanent critiques,[3] and sometimes various types of denaturalizing critique are added to the list.[4] Internal critique judges the criticized form of life based on values already accepted by the participants of the form of life; it operates with internal criteria.[5] By contrast, external critique justifies its criticism by external criteria, which it takes to be transcendentally true; it measures a form of life by standards it holds to be objectively justified whether the actual participants agree or not.[6] Immanent critique, which is the model favored by most participants in the debate, *develops* criteria from within, which, however, have the potential to transcend the form of life; it measures its object by standards that are transformative yet linked to the way the participants lead their lives.[7] It thereby gives a more productive role to the critique that is supposed to create transformative criteria—perhaps out of the conflicts in the form of life[8]—which may not yet be apparent to the participants. Internal, external, and immanent models of critique are *normativist* models of critique insofar as they can be identified by the location of the criterion of a normative judgment upon some social object: Is the criterion applied in exercising critical judgment internal, external, or immanent to the object of judgment?

In these models, social critique is then treated as paradigmatically a form of normative judgment. Without denying the many advantages of clarifying how normative judgments matter in socially critical practice, I wish to draw attention to the narrow focus of these models. Do all forms of social critique exhibit the form of normative judgment? Clearly not. When Angela Y. Davis, in *Women, Race and Class*, tells the story of the women's movement in its American context of racial and class domination, she is not primarily passing a normative judgment. She is telling a story that uncovers the intimate ties between the antislavery campaign and the struggle for women's suffrage and the complex ways racist and classist bias divided the women's movement.[9] Thereby she *shows* that if we ever want freedom, we will have to struggle for it together. Who would dare to say this insight is not critical, that the story she tells is not a social critique? Yet Davis's story obviously *includes* many normative judgments, such as discriminating between tendencies as more or less racist. So do all forms of social critique at least include normative judgments? Also not the case! What normative judgments does Aldous Huxley's *Brave New World* or Paul Celan's *Todesfuge* or Niki de Saint Phalle's *Nanas* "include"? Are they not socially critical? But they are artworks, not philosophy! Are not Theodor W. Adorno's *Minima Moralia*, Max Horkheimer's *Dämmerung*, and Walter Benjamin's *One-Way Street* works of art? Perhaps normative judgment is neither a sufficient nor a necessary component of social critique, but, surely, it is the best path that philosophical social critique can take? But best according to what standard? Is it more efficient? This seems doubtful at least in the aforementioned situations of preemptive silencing, societal exaptation, and vicious circles: if recalcitrant, giving and asking for reasons is often silenced before it is even voiced, easily turned into applause for the democratic public or marginalized and abstracted into a remote corner of an academic debate unable to effect change in wider social life. Is it more radical? Every language game of justification rests on a complex web of habits and customs, a form of life; the more natural the appearance of these habits and customs and the more tacitly their rule is observed, the smoother the game of giving and asking for reasons will run.[10]

Recent critical social ontology has attempted to respond to these problems by analytically refining a rather plausible understanding of social critique as "debunking,"[11] which affords an alternative to normativist models of critique. Philosophical social critique is here conceptualized as a practice that exposes something that initially appears natural as constituting, in fact, a social construct and therefore a normative issue. I will thus call these "denaturalizing" models of critique. Whereas the normativist models conceive social critique primarily as normative judgment, the denaturalizing approaches understand it as a way to *enable* normative judgment. Once it has been made clear that being a woman or being queer, for example, is a social property and that "woman" and "queer" are social categories, it is revealed that the categorization and the practices involved, so the argument goes, demand justification.[12] The advantage of such denaturalization is that it creates a certain distance to the form of life by turning some previously simply habitual practice into a negotiable object of a normatively structured game of giving and asking for reasons. The individuals' adaptation to the demands of this practice must no longer be immediate, as it is now, in principle, open to them to rewrite the rules and reshape the practice. While these analyses of social critique bring enormous gains to our understanding of the normative claims of a wide variety of social movements and the normative dynamics of social domination,[13] the resulting conception of critique has, again, rather narrow limits: it gives no indication of how the results of social critique are to be made reproducible. Critiques that stop at normative negotiation are particularly prone to being embraced to death by the existing relations of domination, what Luc Boltanski has observed and called a "complex domination effect."[14] The denaturalization approach therefore leaves the question of how reflective recalcitrance can be made effective unanswered. How are the results of rational social transformation to be sustained? How do they become modes of subsequent social reproduction? This would include giving an account of their *re*naturalization, as it were,[15] of how social critique can become embodied, or "second nature"—how, in the flow of social life, the waves of recalcitrance can, to reuse Ludwig Wittgenstein's simile, shift the riverbed.[16]

In addition to these normative and denaturalizing models of critique, there are, in contemporary social philosophy, several models of genealogical critique, on the one hand, and of ideology critique, on the other. These models of social critique, which have survived the overwhelming tendency to reduce critique to normative judgment, are close relatives and occasional companions of disclosing critique—and, as such, importantly different from it. I will discuss them in due course, chiefly in the concluding chapter.

In the debates on models of critique, the possibility of a disclosing critique is sometimes mentioned but rarely discussed in detail.[17] One reason for this is surely that the existing normativist models of critique are sorted out according to the locus of their criteria (that is, whether the standard is internal, external, or immanent). Yet, in disclosing critiques, questions of criteria play a marginal role if any. However, this silence over a model of disclosing critique has been broken twice by more refined reflection. First, Axel Honneth has insightfully drawn attention to the possibility of a disclosing critique of society, which would be importantly different from the models just mentioned. Though Honneth, who is a prominent discussant in the debate on the normativist models of critique, seems to remain rather skeptical about this possibility. He identifies disclosing critique, in contrast to normative models, by its intent of "opening new horizons of meaning." In the same breath, however, he describes it as "a form of social criticism that relies on strong, context-transcending standards."[18] It remains unclear in what sense normative standards are supposed to find use in the endeavor to open new horizons of meaning—that is, in a model of critique whose intent is not primarily to judge and measure but to disclose. Similarly, it is easy to see that the intention ascribed by Honneth to disclosing critique is different from that of denaturalization. If the goal is to open new horizons of meaning, the critic cannot simply stop after having debunked an old one. As we will see in the following chapters, she must go on to deliver a redescription and care for the consequences.

The second exception to this silence over a model of disclosing critique is Sabina Lovibond's book *Ethical Formation*. Lovibond distinguishes two possible critical stances to a form of life: "determinate critique" and "counterteleology" (*EF*, pt. 3). Determinate critique demands a modification of the form of life so as to bring it into closer conformity with the morality already lived and appealed to within it. It is an internal or immanent critique: we can raise claims to the modification of parts of our form of life from within, but, like in Otto Neurath's simile of the boat that is repaired on open sea one plank at a time,[19] this form of social criticism operates as an interpretive step-by-step self-criticism of practical reason. By contrast, counterteleological critique is more radical. It is a critique "of any operation designed to assimilate to the established forms of a culture some 'matter' that lies outside them" (154). This amounts to resistance against the claims of drill and adaption as such, a critique directed against the historically evolved form of life itself. Lovibond thereby envisages the possibility of placing philosophy on the side of the "recalcitrant"—that is, of those who deviate and work in opposition to those who work to bring subjects into line with an allegedly universal form (xii, 139–41). I believe that disclosing critiques of society have this counterteleological, brazenly recalcitrant character: instead of measuring a particular form of life on a supposedly universal standard (be it external, internal, or immanent), *they challenge the allegedly universal from the perspective of a particular experience.*

Lovibond, the ethicist, is, however, far from an unconditional supporter of disclosing critique. Whereas ethics, according to her, must accommodate the determinate critique of forms of life as a standing obligation, with regard to counterteleology, she distinguishes between a quietist "philosophy proper" and a "not particularly philosophical" critical narrative of how our form of life evolved, of how we became the creatures we are (*EF*, 170–71). Social philosophy could then be understood as "prepar[ing] the way" for something like a disclosing critique of society, which, however, it "does not engage in" (171). Nevertheless, Lovibond adds that the philosophical response to the recalcitrant behavior of a disclosing critic cannot be to simply dismiss it as irrational or uncritical: the rational response involves the obligation "to put up with not knowing exactly how much of our hostility (or maladjustment) to the ethical universal could, in the end, be represented as rationally motivated" (189–90). The more or less contingent character of the evolved form of life, in other words, demands an intermittently agnostic attitude to ethical maladaptation as possibly a form of *critical* recalcitrance. Thus, Lovibond makes space in philosophy for social critique of our form of life by, on the one hand, accommodating internal and immanent social critique, whereby it appears as an extension of the morality of a form of life, and, on the other, delivering a novel standing obligation of agnosticism about recalcitrance, whereby it, as it were, turns back against the form of life that gave birth to it.

Lovibond's view is, however, committed to a specific understanding of the Wittgensteinian virtue of quietism: the philosopher leaves everything as it is. Disclosing critique of the form of life by means of a story of how we became who we are, the critical social ontology of ourselves, is a task that the social philosophers can contour but eventually will have to hand over to the participants. It is not part of "philosophy proper." By contrast, my investigation, which I would like to think of as a fellow Wittgensteinian and perhaps even a quietist one, is animated by the impulse that such talk of "philosophy proper" throws philosophy back into an uncannily slippery place, from which Wittgenstein, in one of his great achievements, brought it back to the "rough ground" of our forms of life. His appeal that philosophy "leave everything as it is" can be read as primarily a withdrawal of philosophy from the games of justification—a recalcitrant gesture in a form of life that puts the practices of claiming and justifying at its core.[20] In contrast to

Lovibond's agnosticism about the rationality of counterteleology, which I shall discuss in greater detail in the following chapter, my investigation is an experiment in embracing exemplary forms of critical recalcitrance with open arms to find out what, if anything, their own rationality could be. What, if not giving and asking for reasons, could constitute *disclosing reason*?

2. Exemplary Reconstruction

The goal of my study is primarily negative. It is to liberate philosophical social critique from a picture that keeps it captive.[21] The picture is that of social critique as *saying*. In this picture, which keeps philosophical social critique trapped in endless quarrels about its own justification, critique is a matter of passing a normative judgment. Critique measures its object, a practice, a form of life, according to normative criteria. The liberation consists in showing how social critique can also *show*.[22] And what is more, in many contexts, such as our most pressing contemporary ones, a form of critique that rather shows than says, such as a disclosing critique, is preferable. Disclosing critiques of society intend to show the way out of a vicious circle. Similarly, my intent is to show, step-by-step, that a way out of the picture is possible.

Following Wittgenstein, one is liberated from a picture by being presented not yet another picture but several alternative pictures, an "album" of sketches and stories of a whole "landscape."[23] In this study, I present various models and gestures of disclosing critique. By virtue of this method, my inquiry is antitheoretical, antisystematic, and historical.

It is antitheoretical in the rather weak sense that it does not inherently connect philosophical social critique with theory. Instead, it posits that critique is a consequence of critiquing. That is, it is always action, practice. Action always takes place in an environment and succeeds as a response to features of the environment; it adapts to them, or it adjusts them. Eventually, I will go on to suggest that critique is primarily an affair of adjusting the environment rather than adapting to it. Critique, my study takes it, is a type of recalcitrant behavior—action that resists immediate adaptation to the environment. Sometimes, under certain very exceptional conditions, critique is practiced as theory. In a very complex social environment, it may make sense to formulate a theory—that is, an inferentially structured system of propositions of (some features of) that environment—for adjusting it. Under certain even more exceptional conditions, this theory may perhaps come to take the form of a normative judgment upon that environment. That social philosophy, in the past half century, has primarily bunkered itself in this rather remote corner of critique does in no way alter the fact that critique is primarily critiquing—action by particular individuals or social groups in a social and natural environment. More important for critique than theory of critique are, consequently, the *skills to critique*. Skills can, indeed, be learned from theories. But they can also be learned from *examples* of practicing the thing one wants to learn, whether that exemplary practicing involves theory or not.

My study is, furthermore, antisystematic in a somewhat stronger sense. It does not aim at a systematic account *at all*. It does not presuppose as an ideal that a historical investigation in philosophy should result in any kind of systematic whole. This, in my view, illegitimate expectation is so deeply ingrained in the way academic philosophers read, write, and talk that I want to repeat it in italics: *in this study, I have no intent to present a unified, systematically coherent account of disclosing critique*. Given its very topic, such an attempt would be completely absurd: the only thing we know so far about disclosing critiques is that they challenge the allegedly universal from the perspective of a particular. They operate by exemplarity. Whereas normativist models of critique aim at universally justified judgments on particular practices or forms of life, disclosing critiques intend to show a way out of a false universal by means of particular *experiences*.[24] This study is, then, antisystematic in the additional sense of providing tools and seeking to develop skills for the critical disclosure of systems of thought and action.

My philosophical method is exemplary reconstruction. My intent is to excavate a history. I will reconstruct historical examples of critical disclosure, from which we, critics of today, may draw lessons for our own adventures through the overwhelmingly plural yet depressingly uniform landscapes of our contemporary forms of life. I present disclosing critique as a self-reflectively situational practice. Depending on the particular nature of the vicious circle to be disclosed, the critic must operate in a particular way. But we can learn from examples and so develop critical skills. We can, as it were, cultivate recalcitrant virtues. The goal of this study is to contribute to the cultivation of the skills of critique, which might help social recalcitrance to become reflective and effective.

This turn from saying to showing, from claims to gestures, from judgment to disclosure, is then not about turning away from critical theory but about radicalizing and strengthening it. It seeks to radicalize the project of philosophical social critique that has animated all hitherto critical theory by an excavation of its rough ground, by a renewed attention to its particulars. I believe that the aforementioned studies in cognitive psychology indicate that gestures of showing play an essential role in social processes of reflective modification of associative bonds. It is plausible that showing has more transformative power than saying. To transform means to undergo something and to do something out of it. Transformation always means "having an experience," as one of the exemplary disclosing critics in this study, John Dewey, shows (*AE*, chap. 3). The disclosing gestures examined here represent attempts to enable those addressed to have relevant experiences on their own accord.

3. Metaphors of Critique: Juridical and Poetic

This book, then, does not present an immanent critique of any of the normativist models of critique.[25] Nor does it present a theory of disclosing critique as an alternative to them. Instead, it recollects and reconstructs examples of practicing disclosing critique. Yet this procedure leaves a crucial question open: Whence to collect the examples?

Who counts as a disclosing critic, and why? It seems that I would need a criterion for singling out the relevant examples. However, no concept of disclosing critique seems readily available to function as a criterion, and I know of no author who would have laid claim on the title of the disclosing critic. If the study cannot begin by a hypothetical concept or a declared self-understanding, then what could deliver such a criterion for qualifying examples as relevant for the story?

Luckily, in the historiography of philosophy, this question has already arisen with all its might for one of its most brilliant practitioners—Hans Blumenberg. Blumenberg's metaphorology enables the disclosure of a philosophical tradition or practice by means of the study of a *metaphor*. He distinguishes two kinds of metaphors according to the roles they can take in the history of philosophy. First, metaphors can be mere "leftover elements," figurative speech that could, in that historical situation, be just as well conceptually articulated. As such, metaphors can function as decorations in philosophical prose, and they can be unmasked as unclear expressions of what could be expressed conceptually instead. But metaphor can also be a "foundational element," a ground of thinking, which, in that historical situation, *cannot* be conceptually codified. Such a metaphor resists exhaustive conceptual articulation. Instead, conceptual operations in a historical situation refer, sooner or later, to this metaphor as its underground: the metaphor *replaces* a conceptual operation, it "steps in" for a "logical 'perplexity.'" Blumenberg calls such underground metaphors "absolute metaphors."[26]

Metaphors can, then, appear both, as it were, above and below logical justification, both as a fine decoration in and as part of the rough ground of the game of giving and asking for reasons. By means of an analysis of the expressive function of absolute metaphors, Blumenberg elaborates that metaphorology "seeks to burrow down to the substructure" of a mode of thinking—for example, a critical practice. Absolute metaphors namely enable the disclosure of a space of philosophical thinking, in which conceptual operations and figurative speech can do their work; such metaphors, Blumenberg notes, "have a history in a more radical sense than concepts, for the historical transformation of a metaphor brings to light the metakinetics of the historical horizon of meaning and ways of seeing within which concepts undergo their modifications."[27] By studying the metaphorical underground, the story of a critical practice may be told. How, then, can I burrow down to the substructure of the disclosing critique of society? Whence to find its metaphor?

Now, the idea that critique is a matter of normative judgment, of giving and asking for reasons for the validity of some social arrangement, relies on a curiously *juridical* metaphoric. This metaphoric can be traced back to the perhaps most famous notion of critique in modern philosophy—namely, that of Immanuel Kant. In the "Doctrine of Method" in his *Critique of Pure Reason*, he describes critique as a court of justice: "One can regard the critique of pure reason as the true court of justice for all controversies of pure reason; for the critique is not involved in these disputes, which pertain immediately to objects, but is rather set the task of determining and judging what is lawful [*die Rechtsame*] in reason in general in accordance with the principles of its primary institution."[28] The juridical metaphor in Kant, as Raymond Geuss remarks, expresses the assumption that critique "resembles a legal procedure of some kind."[29] Like in a juridical procedure, critique is taken to settle a case with a verdict that has binding force. For Kant, "critique" means, more concretely, an inquiry by the means of reason into the limits of the proper use of reason, and thus, critique is a matter of self-legislation within these limits alone. For sure, few critical theorists would regard themselves as transferring Kant's critique of reason into social critique, as if the "critique of reason" would present an informative analogy with the "critique of society." But the interesting things to note are, first, the self-evident nature that the juridical metaphor has come to take in modern philosophy after Kant and, second, the easy path to narrowing down critique conceptually that the juridical metaphor offers.[30] A judge of a court case is not interested in just any features of whatever is put on trial but seeks from the start to construe the case such that a judgment with a binding force will come out of it. The word "critique" itself does not, however, come with any necessary connection with "judgment," "norms," "validity," "verdict," and so on. Etymologically, as κρίνειν, it is tied to *making a difference*. In ordinary language, it seems to cover an enormous variety of actions, such as turning up one's nose, giving a dissenting opinion, talking for too long about last night's theater play, or organizing a demonstration.

In his essay "Must Criticism Be Constructive?," Geuss notes that in the modern era, there is, next to the "juridical model," another model of critique—one taken by the notion in literature and the arts. In this model, "the point is not to get a single definite judgment according to narrow and focused criteria but to point things out to people, allowing them to enter into the work of art."[31] Accordingly, the critic does not try to discipline language here but to enrich it, transform it, so that recipients are put into the position of having an experience of the objects they would not have without the work of critique. The critic, on this model, then *continues* the work of art in the work of critique: in order to disclose the artwork for the recipients, she must innovate in her own language use. Rather than juridical, her work is, as it were, *poetic*.

The idea of elaborating a concept of critique as a poetic continuation of its object is by no means new in the tradition of critical theory. In fact, it seems to have been a part of the Frankfurt school's critical thought from the very beginning, appearing in Walter Benjamin's investigation of the Romantic theory of critique, *The Concept of Criticism in German Romanticism*. Critique, Benjamin observes, was for the Romantics the continuation and completion of its object, "the consummation of the work."[32] Although Benjamin carefully criticizes the Romantic conception for its formalistic and apologetic tendencies, he endorses from it the task of critique: to make the expressionless truth content of a "work" the object of experience.[33]

This book takes a non-post-Kantian path. It asks, What if we understood critique not at all in the juridical sense of judging, indictment, legislation, and condemnation but instead as a playful, creative, experimenting, and poetic activity?[34] Instead of criticizing the normativist models of critique head-on or genealogically problematizing the juridical metaphor of critique,

I will, by looking at examples, undertake experiments on the metaphorical underground of disclosing critique. The investigation departs, as it were, from an Archimedean point and, from there, tells the story of a *poetic metaphor of critique*. The Archimedean point is a passage sufficiently far away from the contemporary disputes of critical theorists. The metaphor is hopefully a long and strong enough lever to lift models of critique off their juridical ground. This study is a metaphorology of critical disclosure. It identifies a metaphor for social critique that will work as a criterion for singling out exemplary disclosing critics. It investigates metaphorically and conceptually the space disclosed by that metaphor.

What is the poetic metaphor? In this investigation, there are, initially, two of them, and they are linked, and they'll merge—but that's going way ahead of things! The investigation starts from the observation that in contemporary scholarship, the practice of disclosing critique is univocally ascribed to Theodor W. Adorno and accepts this at face value.[35] It then singles out a poetic redescription that Adorno delivers as a metaphor for the object of critique—that is, society. This metaphor is *Bannkreis*, mostly translated as "vicious circle." Adorno repeatedly uses this metaphor in his essays and lectures on social theory, where he *traces* the vicious circle of society with an uncanny effect on the recipient. The poetic redescription, as it were, helps Adorno bring out aspects of the object of critique to the recipients that they would otherwise perhaps not have experienced. However, already before Adorno, this metaphor was used by the young Friedrich Nietzsche, who, in *The Birth of Tragedy*, criticizes a form of life that is "capable of confining the individual within the smallest circle of solvable tasks" (*BT*, 85). The original German expression Nietzsche uses is "in einen . . . Kreis . . . zu bannen." A couple of years later, in the third of his *Untimely Meditations*, Nietzsche, interestingly, describes the *recalcitrance* to this form of life as "circles of culture" (*UM*, 162), which may critically disclose the form of life. In this connection, Nietzsche quotes Ralph Waldo Emerson's essay "Circles" (193).

Meanwhile in Beijing, the American philosopher John Dewey, trying to make sense of the form of reason that enables critical disclosure, quotes the same lines from Emerson as Nietzsche (LCN, 9), and he starts working on his book *Human Nature and Conduct*, in which he comes to describe society as a "vicious circle," asking, "Is there any way out?" (HNC, 88–89). Like for Adorno, who describes himself and Dewey as philosophers of openness (should we say disclosure?) in his lectures,[36] there is an uncanny feeling (of enclosure?) invoked by Dewey's metaphoric and question. In his essay "The

Uncanny," the Austrian physician Sigmund Freud exemplifies the uncanny by the experience of walking in circles (U, 327), which turns out to be a relevant feature of his critique of civilized society and surely influenced Adorno's uncanny gesture of *Bannkreis*.

The passage both Nietzsche and Dewey quote from Emerson's essay "Circles" reads,

Beware when the great God lets loose a thinker on this planet. Then all things are at risk. It is as when a conflagration has broken out in a great city, and no man knows what is safe, or where it will end. There is not a piece of science, but its flank may be turned to-morrow; there is not any literary reputation, not the so-called eternal names of fame, that may not be revised and condemned. The very hopes of man, the thought of his heart, the religion of nations, the manners and morals of mankind, are all at the mercy of one generalization. (C, 407)

The quote is Emerson's description of what it can mean if a thinker "draw[s] a circle around a circle" (405). This formulation is an initial metaphoric description of critique as disclosure. The position from which the circle around the circle is drawn, Emerson further describes, is that of the "poet" (408). "Drawing a circle around the circle" is the poetic metaphor of critique that allows disclosing the practice of disclosing critique; together with "vicious circle" as a metaphor for society, it presents an instrument for *composing a constellation*.[37]

4. Concepts as Habits of Distinguishing Similarity Classes

My hypothesis is that between Adorno's "vicious circle" and Emerson's "drawing a circle around a circle," the scene of disclosing critique can be disclosed. This scene constitutes the *excavation site* of my study. The excavation site will be opened in chapter 3. I will then, in the chapters that follow, dig through its various layers and look at the critical artifacts found at this site and reconstruct them. I do not claim that the metaphor of a circle around the circle defines disclosing critique. Surely, there can be disclosing critics out there who never even implicitly use this metaphor. But I do postulate for the purpose of historical inquiry that whoever thinks of social critique metaphorically as drawing a circle around the vicious circle *is* a disclosing critic. By burrowing down to this metaphorical substructure, my study gives such examples, from which disclosing critique may be learned. The result may not be a complete account, but it will be a definite one. It will be definitive in the sense that the metaphorological approach sketched above avoids arbitrariness in the selection of examples: disclosure as a circle around a vicious circle—this figure determines an underground tradition of philosophical social and cultural criticism from Emerson to Adorno. But it is incomplete in a way that any metaphorological investigation is incomplete: it is the conceptual analysis and poetic elaboration of a metaphor that constitutively resists conceptual codification.

Even if this history resists the expectation that it shall result in a coherent concept identifying disclosing critique, it can, conversely, not be ruled out that it will, in the end, present its result as *a* concept of disclosing critique. Naturally, that more or less likely result of this metaphorological investigation cannot be understood as a concept in the sense of identifying particulars under a universal. Rather, one may have the right to expect a concept in the less determinate sense of a class of similarities enabling a *habit of distinction*.[38] This type of concept may emerge by going through a set of examples (defined, e.g., by the trajectory of a metaphor) and reviewing the similarities and differences they display. Step-by-step, *relevant* similarities and differences in the set start to become clearer. They *repeat* with further variations. And so, gradually, a *class of similarities* is constituted.[39] So if the readers, having gone through these examples, can recognize disclosing critiques outside this particular set and distinguish them from other models of critique, they may be said to have acquired a concept of disclosing critique from this book. However, the purpose of that concept will be primarily that of cultivating skills of critique: rather than *identifying* a model of critique with strict limits, the goal of this concept, having traversed a series of variations, would be to constitute a habit of working with a cluster with fuzzy edges. What it would lack in identificatory precision, it would more than make up for in creative applicability in critical situations.

Therefore, the chapters that follow are both internally diverse and involve repetitions with difference. Chapter 3 presents the scene of disclosing critique and opens the excavation. This scene is repeated with variations in chapters 4, 5, 6, and 7. But these four chapters use the scene to develop exemplary models of disclosing critique. Each model repeats the scene of chapter 3 in a different way, thus generating new information about disclosing critique. Only chapter 4 presents one coherent model of disclosing critique. Chapters 5, 6, and 7 include two or more models, which are compared and which repeat and variegate characteristics of the model of chapter 4. The two most promising models are reconstructed in chapter 5. This way of proceeding results in many loose threads that are repeatedly followed up on and tied together. Most of the loose threads are tied together in chapter 6. The most extravagant features of the coherent model of chapter 4 are followed up on in chapter 7. Chapter 8 draws conclusions about the concept of disclosing critique. But before all of this, chapter 2 seeks to show why normative critical theorists should engage themselves with disclosing critics in the first place.

5. The Cartographer Meets Traveling Geologists at the Excavation Site

In addition to being definite, the account might also be a frustrating one for the historically interested reader since it treats these great classics of modern social philosophy—Emerson, Nietzsche, Freud, Dewey, and Adorno—as *bearers of a metaphor*; as a metaphor history, the exemplary reconstructions offered in this book cannot do justice to the whole complexity of any of these authors' work on social critique. It leaves important parts of their approaches completely out and exaggerates others—namely, those that come to light in the excavation of the metaphorical underground. Despite its exemplary method, this book is not a history of great men, such as much of our past history of philosophy has been, even in critical theory. It should also not be mistaken as the history of the reflexive stages in the development of a particular version of critical theory, like Honneth's *The Critique of Power*. Strictly speaking, it is not even a history of exemplary critics, such as Michael Walzer's *The Company of Critics*. Instead, by tracing a critical metaphor, it will give examples of a critical practice.[40]

The history that thus appears is not a linear story of the idea of drawing circles around circles. Instead, by means of conceptually disclosing the poetic metaphoric of critical disclosure, my inquiry *excavates layers* in the underground of a form of philosophizing. History appears spatially—as a sedimented second nature. The project is, as it were, geological. By this, my study, in a sense, coincides with the Greek origin of the term ἱστορία, which already in Aristotle's *History of Animals* meant "inquiry," a report on knowledge gathered. History will thus appear as *natural history*.[41] My study maps a heterogenous landscape where these previous critics have left their traces. Some of them mark still traversable paths, open for us to try out today; others are blocked or even completely barren. Some are hidden, only visible after careful archeological brushing; others are just too obvious to have caught the interest of fellow philosophers, yet they now flash before our eyes in their full dramatic diameter. Still others are fossilized in the deepest sedimented layers of its granite ground to be reached by a rock drill only. This excavation is done as a history of philosophy with the intent to inspire social critique.[42]

This said, there is an important methodological difference to be noted to Blumenberg's metaphorology. Blumenberg remarks that "the *reflective* discovery of the authentic potency of metaphorics devalues the metaphors produced in the light of that discovery as objects of metaphorology."[43] What he means by this is that once metaphor has been invented as a reflected method of philosophizing and philosophers start to produce metaphors intentionally in order to achieve something they do not believe concepts are good for, then the function of absolute metaphors changes: they do not anymore mark the unconscious underground of philosophical language games as before. Now, Emerson, Nietzsche, Freud, Dewey, and Adorno were all, for sure, reflective producers of metaphors. And this applies directly to "drawing a circle around a circle" and "vicious circle." In what sense, if any, can these words be said to constitute absolute metaphors that allow for the excavation of a way of thinking?

For Blumenberg, "absolute metaphors" are absolute in a double sense. First, they are "metaphysical" in that they metaphorize the absolute: the absolute is converted into denotations that address unverifiable and unfalsifiable yet unavoidable issues about our place in cosmos. Second, the metaphorization is absolute in that the metaphor itself is uncodifiable as it functions as the operator that discloses the horizon in which conceptualization, theorizing, and thereby also translation between metaphor and concept, figurative and nonfigurative speech, take place. For the disclosing critics, "drawing a circle around the circle" and "vicious circle" are not exactly absolute metaphors in this sense.

I suggest, in the following, that they are *negatively absolute metaphors*—again, in a double sense. First, they are not positively absolute, as Emerson, Nietzsche, Freud, Dewey, and Adorno are highly reflective about metaphors. Describing the metaphor within a philosophical practice, which is reflective about metaphorics, must then involve describing also the reflection of the metaphor in the theories produced in that practice, the role that the metaphor plays in that reflective theory according to the theorist, and the role it *really* plays. That the disclosing critics were reflective about their use of metaphors means, then, that I, as the cartographer of the landscape, must treat them as what Emerson calls "travelling geologists": "Instead of feeling poverty when we encounter a great man, let us treat the new comer like a travelling geologist, who passes through our estate, and shows us good slate, or limestone, or anthracite, in our brush pasture" (E, 489). My study must consequently map a heterogenous landscape where these previous critics have left their traces but also talk to us today as its traveling geologists with a rather high degree of awareness of what they are doing with their metaphors. As I will show in the chapters that follow, however, none of the disclosing critics fully understood the radical depth of their divergence from social critiques operating on a juridical ground. (This alone is, I believe, already an important and clarifying insight into the history of critique in the late modern period that my history of reflective metaphor can bring out.) Still, "vicious circle" and "drawing a circle around a circle" do have the function of absolute metaphors in the sense of being "foundational" rather than "leftover elements" (E, 489): they disclose the horizon in which the conceptualization, theorization, and critique of society take place. Such negatively absolute metaphors present a curious case of what Max Black calls "interaction metaphors." They neither substitute literal meaning nor remain comparisons between figurative expression and its subject; instead, they evoke a "distinct *intellectual* operation" of learning through an interaction between the implications of both the poetic expression (vicious circle) and its subject (society),[44] which, if successful, amounts to critical disclosure.

Second, "the vicious circle," as we will come to see, does indeed designate the absolute—yet as something that the metaphorical use of language itself is supposed to resist. The space of conceptual inquiry "the vicious circle" discloses is then one that entertains a *reflectively negative relation* to the "foundational" element it metaphorically posits. Aware of its metaphorical character, disclosing critique resists claiming a conceptual ground for its critical practice; instead, it regards itself as recalcitrant to the society that gave rise to it in the first place and that it regards as precarious, or even false, au fond. Because disclosing critique puts itself in relation to the absolute in this metaphorical way, my investigation will, time and again, stumble on its drive toward metaphysical speculation: it is a form of social philosophizing that includes not only social ontology but also cosmology more broadly—without ever losing sight of its critical intent. In this, if one may say, intermittent tactical Gnosticism, the ground of critical thinking is not conceptual, not even positively metaphorical, but an alienated society claiming universality, which can be initially expressed by a negatively absolute metaphor and subsequently disclosed by diverse methods, to be investigated now.

TWO

Recalcitrance to Second Nature
Lovibond on Counterteleology

> Little man, least of all,
> Among the legs of his guardians tall,
> Walked about with puzzled look.
> Him by the hand dear Nature took,
> Dearest Nature, strong and kind,
> Whispered, "Darling, never mind!
> To-morrow they will wear another face,
> The founder thou, these are thy race!"
>
> —RALPH WALDO EMERSON, "Experience"

> En fågel satt fången i en gyllene bur
> i ett vitt slott vid ett djupblått hav.
> Smäktande rosor lovade vällust och lycka.
> Och fågeln sjöng om en liten by högt uppe i bergen,
> där solen är konung och tystnaden drottning
> och där karga små blommor i lysande färger
> vittna om livet, som trotsar och består.
>
> *A bird sat captive in a golden cage*
> *in a white castle by a deep blue sea.*
> *Flattering roses promised joy and happiness.*
> *And the bird sang of a small village high up in the mountains,*
> *where sun is king and silence is queen*
> *and where barren little flowers in brilliant colors*
> *testify to life, which defies and endures.*
>
> —EDITH SÖDERGRAN, "En fången fågel"

But halt! On the journey to the excavation site, it may make sense to take a step back to get a clearer view on the distinction, appealed to in the first chapter, between normative critique and the type of "recalcitrance," which in the remainder of this book will be exemplified by disclosing critique—that unsystematizable model of critique I hope to disclose—but not "defend"—by tracing the metaphors of the "vicious circle" and "drawing a circle around a circle."

Readers with a purely historical interest in this book might want to skip this chapter. But those with a passion for systematic questions in critical theory should find it worthwhile to dwell on this distinction before digging into to the historical rough ground for inspiration. This is because it may, for these readers, be motivational to consider *why* the normative critical theorist should lend an ear to the disclosing critics in the first place, whose writings, after all, often seem helplessly outmoded, normatively implausible, or just theoretically extravagant. Why should a critical theorist perfectly at home on the metaphorical ground of judgment be expected to leap over onto that of vicious circles, if only just to learn to know it? Before delving into the historical material, I wish to address these concerns in this intermediary chapter by drawing attention to a distinction made by the contemporary feminist ethicist and critical theorist Sabina Lovibond. In her work *Ethical Formation*, she introduces a distinction between "determinate critique" and "counter-teleology," which I believe will, on the one hand, help those invested in the normative undertakings of critical theory develop a stance of their own toward the historical work to follow and, on the other, offer a particularly helpful device for making further distinctions on the excavation field, from the next chapter onward, as we start to dig and brush.

1. Ethical Formation: First and Second Nature, Raw Matter, and Form of Life

Alas, the distinction between "determinate critique" and "counter-teleology," which I hope will provide a helpful systematic background for the historical reconstruction of disclosing critique, is rather far removed from the core of Lovibond's *Ethical Formation*. In the first instance, the book elaborates a moral philosophy. In the author's own words, it presents a "practical reason approach to ethics" (*EF*, x). As much as it has important implications for critical theory, the book starts off as a systematic account of virtue ethics—an account that is cognitivist, realist, and naturalist.[1]

Lovibond's practical reason approach is in continuity with ancient, broadly Aristotelian, virtue ethics in affirming that "there is such a thing as ethical knowledge" and in conceiving this knowledge as a know-how, a practical wisdom (*φρόνησις*), grounded in good character (*ἦθος*), in the habitus, as it were, of a virtuous person (x). But it is also decisively modernist, predominantly Wittgensteinian, in *naturalizing* and *socializing* virtue and practical wisdom, which it conceives as the result of developing appropriate habits in the course of socialization into a form of life. However, it still holds that the virtuous person does not exhibit just any acquired characteristics; rather, her habituation has resulted in a certain reflective habit, a power of normative judgment, of *seriously meaning* her utterances: the intellectual virtue of being duly sensitive to the "reasons that there are" and capable of responding to the environment accordingly.[2]

The naturalizing move of Lovibond's virtue ethics consists in shifting its attention: instead of conceptualizing head-on the ideal of the virtuous person as a standard for moral judgment, her ethics reconstructs the *process* of what she calls "ethical formation"—that is, the patterns of socialization required for the upbringing of a virtuous-enough character. In fact, she rejects the idea altogether that there could be anything like a "fully autonomous theoretical account" of virtue (*EF*, 50)—that is, a theory of normative judgment that would suffice to tell individuals how to judge and act rightly in a changing environment without relying on their diverse intuitive powers. Virtue is *uncodifiable*.[3] Lovibond's moral theory is antitheoretical in the "weak" sense of accepting that theory cannot release us from the burden of modifying our habit of judgment on particular cases as they arise. Normativity—understood as pressure from the social environment on the individual to "get things right"—is based on socialization, patterns of adaptation to customs, and collective habits: it "depends on our having been initiated into certain shared practices, so that it feels natural to us, much of the time, to proceed in one way rather than another," she explains in a later essay and adds, quoting Wittgenstein, that "rule-governed behaviour is a matter of 'customs (uses, institutions).'"[4]

The thesis about the uncodifiability of the normative accedes that rational constraints have force only in the flow of a partially shared form of physical and social life, which eventually will resist conceptualization. It is only thanks to the riverbanks of habitual action molded by the "natural history" of our (however broken) form of life that we can at times see clearly what the pursuit of getting things right demands of us.[5] To claim that the normative is uncodifiable does not, however, mean denying that one could articulate certain demands for required courses of action under certain conditions. What it does rule out is that we could articulate ethical knowledge (in the form, say, of a manual or a rule book, such as the categorical imperative on some interpretations or discourse ethics) such that it would stand free of enabling conditions, such as having been socialized into a culture and having a diffuse feeling for a situation—that is, circumstances—which endow us with ethical "significance" in the first place.[6]

What the moral theorist cannot do, then, is codify ethical knowledge independently from the tacit "like-mindedness" of the social environment: a "socially constructed 'likemindedness'" of having learned a common language and received a similar upbringing and a "deeper 'likemindedness'" maintained by the traditions of those who instruct us in our first language, the spirit, as it were, of the customs "that had to be there, naturally," for us to do things with words.[7] Now, what Lovibond believes that the moral theorist *can* do is learn from the "morally exemplary person." This seems plausible: ideals and flaws, virtues and vices, wisdom and stupidity are, after all, not norms to be extracted from the mess of ordinary life but actually performed and brought before our eyes by real people. Virtue ethics, on Lovibond's rendering, invokes an "image [of the virtuous person] in the place that might otherwise have been occupied by ethical theory." The uncodifiability of virtuous persons' ethical know-how is, as it were, more than compensated by an "endless availability of real-life material from which the spirit of their thinking can be reconstructed" (*EF*, 50). The virtue ethicist can disclose the virtuous "from a position of immanence *within* linguistic practice" in a form of social life (113; emphasis original).

Such linguistic practice—that is, moral language—not only depends on uncodifiable like-mindedness in the form of life but also consists of an overwhelming plurality of things human animals do with language—things such as words, gestures, or sentences. "How many kinds of sentences are there?" Wittgenstein asks early on in *Philosophical Investigations*, answering, "There are *countless* kinds; countless different kinds of use of all the things we call 'signs,' 'words,' 'sentences.' And this diversity is not something fixed, given once for all; but new types of language, new language-games, as we may say, come into existence, and others become obsolete and get forgotten."[8] The linguistic practice from within which the virtuous can be disclosed is then in no way limited to assertive or even propositional uses of language. As an aid to tracking normativity, "explicit reason-giving" has, Lovibond remarks, a "comparatively superficial character" (*EF*, 48). In her reconstruction of ethical formation, she gives prominence to metaphor, first, by describing it in terms of "first" and "second nature":

> Human beings are a species to whom it is natural—at the level of "first," or biological, nature—to undergo initiation into a culture; this initiation . . . depends upon learning to talk and to take part in a variety of social *activities*, as envisaged by Wittgenstein under the heading of "language-games." Over time, our participation in these activities—while creating a succession of new contexts for thought and decision—gives rise to a "second," or acquired, nature. This second nature is manifested in behaviour which, though learned, is largely unreflective (like the speaking of a first language); and which, if we do make it into an object of reflection, usually produces in us a sense of inevitability. (25; emphasis original)

Lovibond associates here "first nature" with biological nature but, later in the book, also, more specifically, with "impulse," "motivational 'fragments' present in us from day one" (71). It presents, then, something *innate*, which juxtaposes it to whatever these human animals go on to learn, or acquire, from their environment. "Second nature," by contrast, presents something *acquired*, something individuals learn through initiation into the customs and institutions of a form of life, by a certain adaptation to their environment, as it were. It manifests itself in individual behavior in the shape of habits and dispositions of action. The initiation is a step-by-step affair of undergoing a series of diverse situations and thereby acquiring dispositions to respond to an environment in ways that seem, and indeed are, natural. These dispositions are predominantly unreflective and, upon extraordinary reflection, surrounded by an appearance of inevitability. For example, why do I count 8 after 7 when counting to ten, instead of, say, 7.1? Why do I walk rather than roll downhill from Zürichberg to campus downtown? Why don't we expropriate the billionaires and use their assets to combat climate change? In a certain sense, even if acquired, second nature, in any instance of ethical formation, precedes first nature: it is there, manifested in the actions of the instructors and in the shape of custom, tradition, and institution, already when the motivationally fragmented infant gasps for her first breath of the maternity clinic's moldy air.

The most important assumption that Lovibond makes about our impulsive nature is that it is our first nature to be initiated into a second: "it is characteristic of our species to supplement its 'first' nature with a 'second' one, the substance of which admits of a certain amount of historical variation;

and that this second nature comprises a certain habit of normative judgement, or a sense of 'what is a reason for what'" (*EF*, 137). Ethical formation thus has an inherently teleological character: it is its goal to implant virtue.

Lovibond brings the teleological structure of the process to the fore by a second pair of metaphors: "matter" and "form." She states, "In relation to human beings [Plato and Aristotle] posit, on one hand, an indefinite or merely potentially formbearing condition which precedes the advent of 'character' (*êthos*); on the other, a perfectly formed or finished condition which moral (*êthikê*) upbringing has to realize; and finally a process which mediates between these two by working to impose the (ideal) form of human character on the raw material presented in any particular individual. This process can be described as one of ethical formation" (55–56). Lovibond's original intervention into virtue ethics is to naturalize the metaphoric of form and matter and socialize the teleology it expresses. Whereas ancient virtue ethics, represented in *Ethical Formation* by Plato and Aristotle, focused on the ideal and morally exemplary character, Lovibond's naturalizing move is a step back, as it were, to phenomenologically describe really existing ethical formation—that is, the prevailing moral upbringing as an internalization of normative standards and intuitions for ethical significance in the process of socialization to our culture. Instead of ideologically postulating an ideal and allegedly universal psychological structure (e.g., a timelessly fixed form of human nature that incidentally turns out to be one that would be of a most instrumental disposition for the reproduction of the male-dominated slave society of the Greek city-state), Lovibond's naturalized version of the practical reason view is content "to point ... to the manifest form conferred on human action by the internalization of shared standards of conduct, and beyond that, by a diffuse feeling for ethical significance or saliency" (62).

This naturalization of form, the like-mindedness on which normativity and our pursuits of getting things right depend, paves the way for a naturalization of "the metaphor of ethical 'formation'" itself: the question of moral upbringing, in the new naturalized setting, turns into the inquiry of "whether the raw human material ... has been *turned into something*, or equipped with a 'second nature,' sufficiently in agreement with that of others" (*EF*, 62; emphasis original). The socialization of the teleology of formation, finally, consists in appreciating that the work of ethical formation is "governed by a social teleology in which one generation sets itself the goal of initiating the next into a common repository of wisdom," of what it allegedly means to get things right. The goal of formation can then be recognized as itself a "construct of upbringing" (63): rather than first, it is determinate second nature, part of the disposition of the old who see it as their task to instruct the young.

This instruction by the old has two important intended effects on the young: it should make them act *predictably* and speak *seriously*. Like Aristotle, Lovibond regards virtues analogously to technical capacities as practical *skills*—that is, as internalized habits.[9] The young start off by producing actions commanded or praised by the old. ("Now, put toothpaste on the toothbrush!"; "Tell your sister you're sorry!") Then they are expected to *imitate* the old independently. ("Oh, you're such a big girl already!") Finally, they should be able to think by themselves and react predictably to new situations as they arise. (No one tells me I'm a good boy when I figure out how to declare my taxes online.) Such initiation takes place, Lovibond summarizes, "through repetition, over a long enough period and with a sufficiently varied input of examples, of the actions characteristic of a particular skill or (moral) virtue" (*EF*, 68).

Like Nietzsche, Lovibond accedes that the goal of formation so far is to transform the young into "truly predictable" animals "with prerogative to *promise*."[10] The effect of the imitation of the old by the young is that what first presented as merely a "compliance with authority comes instead to express something inward and enduring" (*EF*, 68): ethical formation is a process of habituation which works through imitation of examples and internalization of environmental demands to produce patterns of behavior that *actually express* the normative attitudes that are expected by the social environment. It transforms the young into people who can be sufficiently *relied on* to maintain values, which are important for the continuation of the form of life, by their ways of responding to particular situations in their daily life.

However, one may ask, what is "moral" at all about this upbringing so far? How would ethical formation transcend what Lovibond at times calls "mere conditioning"?[11] How is it different from a crude reduction of these young individuals' dispositions to vehicles of self-maintenance of the form of life, for which, incidentally, Aldous Huxley, in his *Brave New World*, used the metaphor of "conditioning"?[12] This can be brought before our eyes by looking closer at what Lovibond really means by words such as "reliable" and "actually express."

Ethical formation seeks to make the young not only act predictably but also speak *seriously*. Lovibond inquires about "seriousness" as a quality of the relation of a learner to her own "words and gestures" (*EF*, 73). This way of relating to one's words and gestures is characteristically taken by others in the language game as one *really meaning* them. This discloses, on the one hand, a "scale of value" in ethical formation between a competence to represent oneself with words and gestures to the social environment and the lack of such a skill. On the other, it reveals the necessity for ethical formation to maintain "a more or less determinate boundary around the class of utterances for which, as speakers, we can properly be called to account" (74). Ethical formation draws a circle around the forms of expression it takes to respond to reason. Seriousness, the skill to really mean what one says, thus marks a social achievement, the passing of a test, as it were, in ethical formation, and it is to be set in contrast to the "mere" imitation of virtue with which it began. The practical skill of really meaning what one says has been internalized. It is an attitude the young learn to adopt, and "the lesson belongs to an extended course of instruction in *why it matters* whether this attitude is present or absent" (75).

Why should seriousness then matter? Why maintain "practical reason" as a cultural project? A first thing to note is that Lovibond does not believe that initiation into second nature overcomes first nature.[13] The mimetic impulse and the related imitative behavior that drive the young to acquire a second nature have an afterlife in seriousness: "Imitating the words and gestures of others is not . . . a clearly delimited phase of life, eventually to be superseded by another clearly delimited phase in which speech and action are strictly attributable to their ostensible subject" (*EF*, 125). Rather, mimetic patterns of behavior with their opportunistic-looking relations to ethical expressions *coexist* with the moral responsibility that Lovibond links with "really meaning." Ethical formation is not a process that can be "completed." But it is also not as if the full establishment of a second nature would be, as it were, desirable in principle but unfortunately impossible in practice due to an allegedly corrupting force of first nature. Rather, there seems to be something deeply undesirable about such a prospect. Indeed, in the essay "Ethical Upbringing," written when she was beginning to work on *Ethical Formation*, Lovibond even refers to the idea of a perfectly integrated virtuous person as an "uncanny figure."[14] Yet unless we consent to live as addressed as ideally seriously meaning our words and gestures, Lovibond argues, "we shall forfeit our participation in the kind of life to which ethical *formation* is relevant at all, and allow our status to lapse from that of recipients of upbringing to that of mere matter for conditioning"—a likewise uncanny vision (127).

As much as the prospect of becoming a virtue automaton is repulsive, so too the idea of succumbing to a mere instrument of the social environment seems to fill us with dread. There is something uncanny about the thoughts of both completing and giving up ethical formation, about the pictures of both the perfectly integrated individual moral agent and the perfectly integrated Brave New World that conditions individuals as the means for its own continuation. To extend the metaphor: there is both an *uncanniness of form* and an *uncanniness of matter*. As moralistic as it may seem, the distinction between serious and nonserious speech may be indispensable both affectively and socially—that is, it may present a contrast that "we cannot plausibly disown," on our given cultural self-understanding, without an intolerable amount of violence against the self, *and* it has become "integral to the activity of 'symbolic reproduction'" of our societies' institutional settings. For the beings we have become, the thought of not living the serious/nonserious *contrast* seems unbearable. Now that natural history has molded us to such creatures, there's no reason, Lovibond believes, for a naturalist or a historicist to be "less conscientious" in the pursuit of moral upbringing: "Perhaps we do implicitly believe we have a duty to play our part in the conservation of a certain culture of responsiveness to reasons; and perhaps the raising of this belief to consciousness will not, and should not, make it go away" (*EF*, 132).

2. Determinate Critique: Internal Normative Judgment and Advocacy of the Recalcitrant

This uncanniness may perhaps disclose something like a modern sensibility for freedom: a discomfort with the thought of a social order that seeks to undermine individuality. And this sense might produce a discontent with the very idea of ethical formation. After all, as Lovibond herself notes, her "account can be taken to call human freedom into doubt . . . by its association with an idea of the subject as a *function* or *effect* of social order" (*EF*, 134; emphasis original). However, Lovibond does not back down on the disquieting thought of the individual as a function of the social environment in a form of life. Instead, she uses it as the very background for her introduction of *social critique* into the picture. For, once formed, a serious speaker may not only speak of her peers' and her own shortcomings to act like the morally upright people their social environment expects them to be but also speak of their "possible failure to subject these very expectations to the scrutiny they deserve" (133). This conscientious objector to the expectations of the social environment believes that a failure to criticize the prevailing form of life will damn us into heteronomy, a subservience under reasons that really may be none.

But there is also the possibility of a more radical change of attitude to ethical formation. This second stance departs from the above observation that, for their project of initiating us into second nature, the old must "take advantage of the mimetic impulse that prompts us to identify ourselves ... with the people around us," that they must redirect this piece of first nature to a socially useful purpose, and, consequently, "must condemn as *recalcitrant* any behaviour that defies or subverts that purpose." This attitude holds on to the thought that first nature has an afterlife in second, and reasons that seriousness demands facing these unruly tendencies in and among us. It demands attention to what in the raw matter that went into formation remains operative without having acquired determinate form. "Such recalcitrant tendencies bear witness to the enduring presence of an *apeiron*, or formless principle, in human nature" (*EF*, 139; emphases original). By facing these tendencies, it seeks to see the established form of life under the aspect of what has evaded it.

Lovibond observes that these tendencies may turn against the form of life they are supposed to inhabit and oppose the ethical formation that condemns them. This may result in a "theoretical exercise" with the "practical interest in becoming something other than our socialization has made us up to now" (*EF*, 139). For Lovibond, an example for such a critical line of inquiry is Michel Foucault's idea of a "critical ontology of ourselves," which recollects the events that made us who we are and hopes to help us recognize ourselves as the subjects of our doing and thinking.[15]

Now, how does Lovibond accommodate such theoretical alliances with the "recalcitrant" into her practical reason view? How does the critique of ethical formation go with her account of ethical formation? How does her virtue ethics respond to the recalcitrance to virtue? Surely not with the condemning voice of the old. She namely outlines two ways in which this oppositional attitude may account for itself: "determinate critique" and "counter-teleology."

Determinate critique is, Lovibond notes, already allowed for by her practical reason approach: it arises from a critical reflection of the type exemplified above by our conscientious objector, who, as a possibly farsighted serious speaker, was worried about not only our individual failure to live up to whatever ethical formation teaches us as virtuous but also our falling short of questioning those ideals and their applications. Now, determinate critique presents the procedure of scrutinizing the reality of that ideal on its own terms: it seeks to bring the existing form of life "into closer conformity with the ideals implicit in it" (*EF*, xii). It passes an internal critical judgment on the form of life: it measures the degree to which it falls short to live up to its own ideal. Here, the critic applies her discursive powers of serious thought to the critical evaluation of the customs, institutions, and traditions from which she acquired those powers. She mobilizes her second nature against the form of life in which she was initiated into, and she does this, in her view, for the sake of that form of life. Determinate critique is progressive: it subjects the form of life to a reflective modification in order to make it better according to its own ideals.

Like John McDowell, Lovibond regards this kind of "reflective modification" of ethical formation by the young as a "standing obligation": to inherit the historically accumulated wisdom of a tradition *seriously* means for each generation to subject it to internal criticism.[16] Like McDowell, Lovibond also elaborates this reflective modification by combining the metaphor of first and second nature with the metaphoric of "Neurath's boat": determinate critique modifies the form of life as if it were a boat that must be repaired on the open sea.[17] There is no moral safe haven where it can be transformed all at once; it must be renovated, as it were, one plank at a time. As McDowell elaborates the simile, "The thought is that this application of one's ethical outlook would stand up to the outlook's own reflective self-scrutiny."[18] Recalcitrance to the current form of second nature, the determinate critic believes, must become practical with the means available in current second nature. It uses the reflective skills provided by the form of life to bring it closer to the ideals those skills were already trained for.

In contrast to McDowell, however, Lovibond goes on to give a detailed account of this procedure of critique by internal normative judgment. While she agrees with McDowellian quietism that it is not the task of philosophy to tell people how to criticize current society, she believes that it can indeed "help to sharpen the sense of some of the questions waiting to be asked when we move *outside* the bounds of philosophy" (*EF*, 137; emphasis original)—that is, it can prepare the way for a reflective encounter with the second nature with which we find ourself equipped when opposing current society. Lovibond elaborates, "The determinate critique assumes that the regime of formation actually operating within a given community—and hence the array of beliefs, attitudes, habits of inference, and other psychological attributes which that community calls 'rational'—may at any time be in need of reconstruction in order to make it more rational, or (in Platonist terms) to turn it into a more adequate realization of its 'idea.'" As can be seen by its Platonic rendering as an actualization of the community's "idea," determinate critique has little to no uneasiness with the thought of bringing life under a *form*. Its reflective modification of the social order by internal normative judgment embraces the social teleology of ethical formation—it is just that the formation should proceed more rationally by its own lights. The teleology of formation, it claims, must be reflected and redirected from within. Nevertheless, Lovibond argues, determinate critique presents a possible ally of the recalcitrant matter that has so far eluded form: it is "perfectly capable of supporting gestures, or longer-term projects, of resistance to ethical formation." It then joins forces with the recalcitrant by proposing an "alternative view of how formation ought to proceed"—one which may claim to amend the circumstances of the recalcitrant (140). A socialist determinate critic may, say, take sides with any recalcitrance to exploitation and class hegemony, a feminist determinate critic will be likely to side with recalcitrance to gender domination, an antiracist determinate critic will be disposed to embrace recalcitrance to any form of discrimination based on race or ethnicity, an anarchist determinate critic will welcome recalcitrance to a wide array of coercion and hierarchy in existing ethical formation, and so on.

Determinate critique can, then, present itself as a normativist advocate of the recalcitrant cause—the "kind of oppositional attitude which, from the standpoint of a practical reason view of ethics, is at one with the social order it opposes in its commitment to … the rationalist character ideal" (*EF*, 144). "The label '*determinate* critique' was chosen in order to mark the fact that such reflection is governed by the actual state of receptivity to reasons … which we happen to have arrived at by learning what our own society has been able to teach us about the ethical; and to record that because of this dependence on our pre-existing grasp of what counts as a (practical) reason, the resulting criticism of inherited 'morality' will proceed by pointing to certain specific flaws, identifiable on the basis of a common evaluative sensibility" (151; emphasis original). This dependence on *our* preexisting grasp on the conception of things of the old—that is, of those who have learned what there is to learn from what our society teaches about the ethical—may, however, stir discontent in some crowds of the recalcitrant youth. The price that the recalcitrant would need to pay for their alliance with the determinate critic is by no means insignificant: it is to *give up* on recalcitrance. The alliance puts them in a paradoxical situation. For as soon as recalcitrant social action envisages some social transformation, the determinate critic will enter the scene and articulate this vision as a claim to amend the form of life to the *better*. And to call the envisioned thing "better" means, at least on the determinate critic's reading, claiming that there is *reason* to prefer it to the way things stand. In seeking endorsement from a community of reasonable others, this claim, however, carries with it a positive evaluation of the like-mindedness of form, the affirmation of conformity to a criterion of correct normative judgment. In this way, the alliance will bring the recalcitrant under the pressure of normative adaptation to the form of life: they are expected to stand beside the determinate critic and appeal to the sensibility of a reasonable audience, submit to "a bit of 'second nature' created by some putative local process of formation," which they must regard as a unifying element and "which will disclose" to the old "that this reason exists" (144–45). Giving up recalcitrance may be a price too high and may therefore split the recalcitrant into the, paradoxically, *normatively* recalcitrant (the faction ready to put its oppositions in terms of normative demands) and the *ethically* recalcitrant (those who resist giving up recalcitrance).

Meanwhile, the determinate critics' advocacy of the recalcitrant is no less paradoxical. When they set out to defend the latter against the regime of ethical formation by articulating the reasons why the modification of the form of life aimed at would be better than the status quo, their advocacy will, paradoxically, depend "on the very 'forces of law and order'" that it also opposes (*EF*, 146). Such forces presumably include both rather violent institutions (such as the police and the school) and features of the relations of (re)production (such as private property or the pressure to accumulate capital). These forces, on the one hand, uphold an ethical formation that the determinate critics in their alliance oppose and, on the other, maintain the spaces of receptivity to reasons where they want the rational cogency of their articulations to be felt. In this squeeze, the rapprochement with the recalcitrant can turn out disappointing for the determinate critic as well, and she might do wisely to side with the old in the end. "So, what's your alternative to internal criticism as a nonmanipulative persuasion of the old?" the exhausted determinate critic may ask the ethically recalcitrant. Social transformation without appeal to existing reasons sounds to the determinate critics rather criminal than critical. For them, there is only ever *either* normative judgment *or* violent social clash. And in this regard, when push comes to shove, they will side with the traditional ethical rationalist. For the determinate critics, as Lovibond puts it, "despite their dissent from specific features of an existing social order—the ethically recalcitrant will be a potentially hostile principle, since it may work against the uptake of rational considerations that happen to be integral to their own project" (145).

So, to return to the extended metaphor from the end of the previous section, whereas the ethically recalcitrant may have been driven to split with the more complaisant constituents of resistance due to a sense of uncanniness of form, the determinate critics' sudden hostility may have been evoked by the shock from an uncanniness of matter.

3. Counterteleology: Ethical Recalcitrance as Social Critique?

There is, however, another kind of critic, Lovibond maintains—one whose outlook she names "counter-teleology." This different critic agrees with the determinate critic that recalcitrance, if it is to be critical, must advance to become responsive to the like-mindedness in the form of life. But she disagrees with the ethical rationalists, both their old guard and the younger wing of determinate critics, that the only options available for the recalcitrant are succumbing to shared normative criteria and violent social clash. Like the ethically recalcitrant, she worries about the price of the hope to have one's deviating thinking endorsed from an allegedly universal standpoint. And she is not appeased by that the Neurathian simile of fixing the boat on open sea, for she is not convinced that it expresses the limits for what the recalcitrant may nonviolently undertake to call the claims of existing ethical formation into question.

The emergence on the scene of these intuitions about social critique prompts Lovibond to inquire into "the possibility of some more radical development which could be realized only by a counter-teleological mode of thought" (*EF*, 149)—a possibility, however, "*not* already allowed for" by the practical reason view and its idea of a continual reflective modification of our form of life. As the name suggests, counterteleology drops the normative endorsement of social teleology and seeks to cultivate a form of thinking directed explicitly against it. Instead of embracing "form," it "tries to sympathize with the *apeiron* in its potential recalcitrance. And whereas in the determinate critique of ethical formation such sympathy comes already prepared to explain itself by pointing to some specifiable defect in existing institutions, the counter-teleological attitude revolves around the pathos of formation as such—that is, of *any* operation designed to assimilate to the established forms of a culture some 'matter' that lies outside them" (154; emphases original). Counterteleology fights the impulse of determinate critique to seek recognition of its claims from a reasonable audience, for it suspects that the determinate critics, by their quest for universal endorsement, only contribute to a continuation of the adaptation of individuals to the social environment, which the recalcitrant tendencies have succeeded to escape. Instead of pelting this project of adaptation of matter to form with further normative resources, it seeks to cultivate those impulses that have evaded the established forms of upbringing. Perhaps, its countereducation works on those aspects of our first nature, which are not mimetic but recalcitrant or just mimetic in a perverted way. Or maybe it combines parts of our second nature that are separately needed for some cultural projects endorsed by the old but condemned as transgressive in this new constellation. Or it might venture to learn from other forms of life.

Be that as it may, counterteleology points to a way out of the potentially mutually disappointing dialectic of the alliance between the recalcitrant and the determinate critics: that critical resistance to the form of life must make itself intelligible as a proposal to change the status quo to something objectively better and hence is bound to adhere to the current norm of rational receptivity, which may split the recalcitrant and push the determinate critics back into the arms of their morally upright parents. This path is disclosed by refraining from the pressure to account for oneself by a claim to universal validity. But this path raises a host of bewildering questions from the determinate critics and the old. Why ought one take any particular stance toward the ethically recalcitrant if the suggestion to do so does not provide any reason for it and ultimately questions the very commitment to giving reasons? And what would such a questioning mean? Why should anyone who accepts the authority of current ethical formation and believes in virtue and reason lend an ear to someone criticizing *such* authority? How is criticizing reason giving not a performative contradiction—does it not presuppose the very thing it opposes? "Perhaps the objector is simply confused?" (*EF*, 150).

Again, Lovibond's response to counterteleology is not to tell her readers how to practice it but to prepare the way for a rational encounter with this type of critical recalcitrance. But unlike her rational reconstruction of "determinate critique," her confrontation with "counter-teleology" is less systematic. Instead of developing further this critical attitude out of her account of ethical formation, she extracts from the recent history of French philosophy a rather limited set of examples: "In using the term 'counterteleological,' I am thinking of a family of considerations originating mainly in French philosophy of the 1960s and 1970s, but influential since then in the English-speaking world on account of the interest they have held for 'alternative' disciplines such as feminist theory, gender studies, and critical social theory insofar as this has survived the eclipse of Marxism."[19] What ties this family together in Lovibond's eyes is its focal critical concern. On her reading of these considerations, she concludes that "the central theme of counterteleological thinking appears to be that of the *violence of reason*" (*EF*, 153; emphasis original). Lovibond's reconstruction of the counterteleological attitude then follows through this literature from the idea of a violence of reason, which operates as a "critique of universalism," to an emerging ethical stance of "care for difference" (chaps. 8–9). Perhaps one could say that if the determinate critics' withdrawal from the alliance with the recalcitrant was solicited by a sense of *uncanniness of raw matter*, this family of counterteleological thinking is motivated by a sense of *uncanniness of universal form*. If the determinate critics were shocked by the prospect that the ethically recalcitrant give up on formation, the critics of universalism are repelled by what to them seems like the determinate critics' participation in the attempt to complete formation.

Lovibond's focus on this family of counterteleological thought provides, however, a rather narrow view of counterteleological thinking. *This* historical material seems at worst arbitrary and at best one-sided. Surely, one cannot reduce the recalcitrance to "any operation designed to assimilate to the established forms of a culture some 'matter' that lies outside them" (that is, the attitude she associates with counterteleology) to the opposition to "the *claims* of the universal" (that is, the critical project of Lovibond's historical material) (*EF*, 154, 151).

In the next section, I shall ask whether there might remain other avenues for philosophically defying ethical formation's project of adapting the recalcitrant. But for now, we are still left in uncertainty about Lovibond's attitude to counterteleology. Whereas the type of internal normative judgment that characterized the procedure of determinate critique was not only allowed for by practical reason but constituted a standing obligation for the virtuous person socialized in our form of life, counterteleology was "*not* already allowed for" (*EF*, 149; emphasis original). Yet *what* would be a rational attitude to the ethically recalcitrant? Surely, it would be awkward for the critical theorist to join the old guard in condemning these projects of deviation and transgression as "irrational" or "criminal," but what will she do to find out whether she may call them "critical"?

To the normative critical theorist, Lovibond recommends an "(intermittently) agnostic attitude towards the ethically 'recalcitrant,' as opposed to a policy of automatic mobilization against it" (*EF*, 192). She starts by asking, What if the recalcitrant in and among us, "simply as such," could be shown to be a "resource for *critical* thought"—that is, in some sense indispensable even for the determinate critic's project of reflective modification (186; emphasis original)? This would, Lovibond observes, quoting Adorno's *Minima Moralia*, "constitute a warning against allowing the practical reason view to be too firmly subordinated to the 'bourgeois contempt of instinct'" (*EF*, 186; *MI*, §§ 37, 60).

Insofar as the normative critical theorist understands herself as doing something other than ideal theory (a theory that claims to be in the position to give a full specification of what is to be aimed at in the way of moral and social order), she will find herself in a less-than-ideal situation where her critique must operate under conditions in which the normative resources are limited to the extent that it will not be possible to judge whether a particular instance of ethical recalcitrance is critical or criminal. That is, she lacks the normative resources to judge, once and for all, whether this instance falls short of living up to the feasible ideals of an adequate process of socialization or whether it presents a perhaps surprising praiseworthy act of resistance against an unexpectedly violent social demand. Insofar as the normative critical theorist is unable to answer this question, she must, Lovibond argues, remain open to both possibilities. Under the conditions of really existing ethical formation, the normative critical theorist must then resign herself to the "incomplete decidability" of the distinction between "good" and "bad" recalcitrance: "These 'good/bad' labels represent a contrast which the critical theorist," Lovibond writes, "would like to be able to draw in all cases" (*EF*, 189). Yet Lovibond's argument for agnosticism toward the ethically recalcitrant shows that this *cannot* succeed. For, given that we cannot *yet* know what present recalcitrant tendency will turn out as rational "after all" in a transformed normative context, the good-bad recalcitrance distinction would mean to claim "expert knowledge of the potential"—an impossible claim. Instead, Lovibond recommends the normative critical theorist accept the "element of anarchism contained in the counter-teleological attitude"— that is, the critical theorist should learn to "put up with not knowing exactly how much of our hostility (or maladjustment) to the ethical universal could, in the end, be represented as rationally motivated" and how much could not (190). She should, as it were, learn to live with the serious-nonserious contrast also as a theorist.

This argument for the critical theorist's "(intermittently) agnostic attitude" to ethical recalcitrance can be attributed to the impossibility of identifying an unproblematic normative context. Lovibond's remarks about the position of the critical theorist in her argument point to the natural limitations of the normative context in which the critical theorist must operate. *In that context*, it is often unproblematic for a well-enough-initiated virtuous critic to judge what does and what does not have practical reason on its side. However, Lovibond points out that the normative context can break down: "The suspension of some substantial part of that context . . . may create a situation in which it does indeed look presumptuous to persist in claiming that we know how to keep our judgement aligned with that of the 'exemplary practical reasoner'" (*EF*, 191–92). Such a suspension of ordinary normativity, Lovibond adds, may take place either through some "real social breakdown" or "speculatively" (192).

4. The Uncanniness of Formation: Disclosing Critique as Naturalized Counterteleology?

In the end of his nautical metaphor history, *Shipwreck with Spectator*, Blumenberg notes that Neurath's antifoundationalist simile of repairing the boat on open sea lends itself to radicalization by turning it against itself, for one might ask, Where was the ship built in the first place?[20] If there's no safe haven, our ancestors must have built it on open sea by construction material floating around. And if this is so, then two critical insights follow. First, if the ship has been built on open sea, it can, in principle, also be radically rebuilt there. Second, our ancestors must have known how to swim. The critically minded recalcitrant might then hook up to and continue the line of thought: perhaps, we have got so accustomed to this comfortable cruiser our ancestors left behind that our internal criticism is just a consequence of our having unlearned swimming? Perhaps, the catastrophe that is present society has to do with a cruiser as captivating as comfortable, one whose gears melt down, poisoning the surrounding waters out of which the travelers need to get nutrition. Perhaps we must learn to swim again? At least, we should halt the ship and start taking small dives into the water to see it sideways on.

Perhaps, then, corresponding to the normative critical theorist's intermittent agnosticism toward ethical recalcitrance, there could be the counterteleological critic's *intermittent suspension of ordinary normativity* by a speculative gesture. Such a gesture would be counterteleological in suspending the telos of current socialization, but it would still seek to appeal to a common mindedness in the form of life since it would destabilize the order of the existing reasons by *inviting* the more or less similarly socialized recipients to take a step back for the moment and *look* at the form of life from a removed, alienated perspective—to dive into the water to look at the ship sideways on.

Even though such an alienating "speculative gesture" would likely be very different from the historical mode of counterteleological thinking that Lovibond distillates under the topics of "violence of reason," "critique of universalism," and "care for difference," she does seem to disclose something like the possibility of such an alternative path of critical recalcitrance in her more systematic discussion of counterteleology. In summarizing at a one point, she refers back to counterteleological thinking as the idea that "in pointing to the historicity of the process whereby one habit of normative judgment rather than another becomes 'second nature' to us, philosophy could make us aware of new possibilities for critical reflection. The characteristic outcome of this kind of reflection [would] be a heightened consciousness of the techniques of socialization employed within one's own society: a consciousness that is apt to generate new forms of moral skepticism" (*EF*, 170–71). The naturalizing language of this passage, the employment of the metaphoric of first and second nature to counterteleology, is striking. It raises the question of whether the same naturalizing move that Lovibond applied to virtue ethics could be adopted to describe its *foil*, the counterteleological critic. Remember, the naturalizing move was that virtue ethics concentrates not on the properties of the virtuous character but instead "on the business of upbringing itself" (63)—on the production, that is, of that character. In other words, the naturalization shifted the attention of our encounter with practical reason from *form* to *formation*. Could not counterteleology make the same naturalizing move as Lovibond's teleology? What happens if counterteleology, instead of opposing abstract entities such as "reason" or "universalism," would concentrate, too, just on the "business of upbringing itself"? And could not the naturalized counterteleology itself work in the formative mode of giving examples of a form of critique challenging existing formation, as it were, as a counterformation? This naturalized counterteleology would then assumably come to do just what the name suggests: it would counter the social teleology of the form of life by retracing it step-by-step.

Interestingly, in the introduction to her *Essays on Ethics and Feminism*, Lovibond describes something like this kind of gesture as disclosing. "Modernity of thought," she writes, "if experienced to the full... should *disclose* to us the contingency of the particular package of dispositions—available at that point as the content of a possible 'second nature'"—a task she, moreover, ascribes to "critical social theory."[21]

Nonetheless, in Lovibond's own work, the status of such "speculative gestures," however naturalized, remains ambiguous, to say the least. Such naturalized counterteleology would, of course, have to operate by gestures of pointing. However, Lovibond puts in doubt their critical weight—in fact, even in terms unusually polemic for her. In the introduction just mentioned, she identifies a "difficulty with the act of pointing to deterministic (or quasi-deterministic) social processes," which is that "it does nothing, in and of itself, to equip us with an answer to the question: so what?" Here, Lovibond seems to claim that for such a gesture to be critical, it must be embedded within a determinate critique, for she goes on to say that it "presupposes something in the way of a moral position." Without such a normative grounding, she concludes, "we seem to be thrown back into the non-cognitivist exchange of rhetorical, or otherwise striking gestures—a routine that may feed satisfyingly into episodes of militant action, but that also risks lapsing into a posture of 'hip quietism.'"[22] This reminds us of the determinate critics' withdrawal from their alliance with the recalcitrant: there is no alternative beyond the game of giving and asking for reasons and violent social clash (with the less-than-enthusing addition of a hip quietism).

Yet cannot this worry be ruled out intermittently by the idea that such gestures achieve an intermittent suspension of substantial parts of the normative context—an achievement belonging to the "modernity of thought ... experienced to the full"? In the early essay "Ethical Upbringing," Lovibond goes as far as to say that "insofar as the virtuous ... habit of mind has been superimposed incuriously and with violence on the human material it encounters," the recalcitrant expression of the "underlying foreignness" of the virtuous "will have a kind of justice on its side."[23] If the expression discloses the extent to which really existing formation is an incurious and violent process ("mere conditioning"), is it then not a *critical* gesture? And if this gesture responds to an "*underlying* foreignness" of formation, has then not the sense of uncanny, which intermittently suspends ordinary normativity, a foothold a fortiori as strong as virtue and practical reason in the reality of the form of life? Remember that uncanniness, this still only vaguely indicated sense of horror, played an important role in the account of ethical formation: the act of continuing the project of ethical formation (as, e.g., in the decision of the determinate critic to withdraw from the alliance with the recalcitrant) was motivated by a sense of the uncanniness of matter. The postmodern family of counterteleological thinkers, by contrast, shared in its theoretical recalcitrance to the claims of the universal, a sense of the uncanniness of form. And, at the end of the day, our activity of upholding ethical formation as something transcending Huxleyan conditioning was motivated by the will to live the serious-nonserious contrast. The naturalized counterteleology could then be understood to respond to an underlying foreignness of formation itself—that is, to be motivated by a sense of *uncanniness of formation*, a horror that may overcome (at least some of) us in the face of the adaptation materially required and normatively expected of us by our uncompromising social environment. The "speculative gesture" could then intermittently suspend ordinary normativity by referring through this affect of uncanniness to the underlying foreignness of the formation we share. And the gesture would consist in showing, perhaps exaggeratingly, the extent to which our society as a process of socialization presents a "mere conditioning" of first to second nature. And this would, if successful, solicit the type of disclosing effect Lovibond ascribes to critical social thought.

There would even be a thin ground of agreement between normative critical theory and naturalized counterteleology. This is because such disclosing gestures do entertain a relation of immanence to the form of life by reference to a like-mindedness; this reference just does not consist in a relation of normative grounding. When the giving and asking for reasons dries up, as it were, and individuals relate to their social environment instead by something like demonstrations of how to go on—that is, ways to do things or ways to see things—such *gestures of showing*, as Lovibond herself notes at a later occasion, "will call upon a mode of understanding that exceeds the propositional." Just like I might try to show you by some demonstration how to get to the main building of ETH Zürich from Hauptbahnhof or how to dance to Beyoncé's "Cozy" with charming elegance or how to see what is alienating in Edith Södergran's use of Swedish, I could, in principle, try to communicate to you how to see the uncanny extent to which our formation amounts to mere conditioning. Such demonstrations rely on a list of skills their producers and recipients have learned from formation. Just like in the case of the exchange of reasons, demonstratives can fail by the gesture being received badly. And so Lovibond herself concludes that one "must come to terms with the role of cultural immersion in securing the intelligent uptake of a gesture of pointing."[24]

Thus, despite her occasional polemics against gestures of pointing, Lovibond's work also points to paths of making sense of a naturalized counterteleology that seeks to intermittently suspend ordinary normativity by disclosing gestures. Moreover, at times, Lovibond seems herself to evoke an uncanny feeling not just for the "form" and "matter" of social life but for formation itself. This happens, for example, when she, in a later essay, describes it as depending on conditioning: "This process [of ethical formation] depends on conditioning, but it is not one of *mere* conditioning."[25] Yet the most striking example of an uncanny suspension of ordinary normativity in Lovibond's own work is her recent interpretation of Wittgenstein's "apocalyptic view."

The interpretation refers to this seemingly bizarre fragment in Wittgenstein's *Culture and Value*: "The truly apocalyptic view of the world is that things do not repeat themselves. It is not e.g. absurd to believe that the scientific & technological age is the beginning of the end of humanity, that the idea of Great Progress is a bedazzlement, along with the idea that the truth will ultimately be known; that there is nothing good or desirable about scientific knowledge & that humanity, in seeking it, is falling into a trap. It is by no means clear that this is not how things are."[26] In her interpretation of the passage, Lovibond arrives at the idea of an engagement "with a historical moment which is such that for anyone living through it, the first step towards correct understanding of their own experience will be to *suspend the assumption* that, in general, things . . . unfold according to an intelligible pattern." The passage, she expands, is an invitation to "open up to the apocalyptic view," which would mean "to envisage the possibility of something unheard-of." The passage defamiliarizes core values of our form of life: the quest for redemption through science and technology, the desirability of progress, the goodness of knowledge. It does not raise any claims against these values or pass judgment on them by reference to shared criteria but invites the reader to see them, intermittently, as a trap. By this gesture, it suspends substantial parts of ordinary morality. And it does so by displaying an ethically recalcitrant stance, "a certain attitude of patrician distaste for twentieth-century normality."[27]

Remarkably, Lovibond links this gesture with Wittgenstein's philosophical method of describing language games. She compares Wittgenstein's address to the reader with the alienation effect of Bertolt Brecht's drama: the intention in both is to estrange the recipient from the myopia of ordinary overfamiliarity. When Wittgenstein describes language games, the reader is "made party to an 'alienated' perception of everyday phenomena."[28] The philosophical method thus discloses the familiar, the ordinary, intermittently as strange, alien. On Lovibond's reading, it is important that the philosophically induced alienation is intermittent, temporary, because otherwise the method flips to one of manipulation: it would then initiate not to an uncanny *aspect* of things but to the illusion that the way the author sees them would be more real than the ordinary perception. The philosophical intention with the alienation effect could then perhaps be described by another Wittgensteinian expression as that of "noticing an aspect"[29]—to help the recipient see the familiar as strange, not to dispense with it.

Moreover, Lovibond links this Wittgensteinian gesture of intermittently suspending ordinary normativity with disclosure, uncanniness, and social critique. The "apocalyptic view" is something the reader must rise up to: it is an aid to "disclosure," "an experience calling for openness, even against the emotional grain, to the possibility that order will *not* be maintained. . . . One has to be capable of *rising* to the 'apocalyptic view,' the view that renounces current points of reference or cognitive landmarks." This movement against the emotional grain she describes as an "exposure to the uncanny." What makes the exposure to the alien critical is precisely that it is intermittent. The critical difference, as it were, is actualized by the experience of moving freely between the familiar and the alien: "We may not be able to *remain* in the moment of the uncanny . . . , but doesn't it *make a difference* that we have experienced this moment; remembered, for example, that bits of the machinery of meaning can bend or melt or break off?" She even asserts (contrary to her repudiation of speculative gestures?) that "there is a rational impetus to this kind of reflection that is well worth maintaining."[30]

Finally, relying on Wittgenstein's philosophical self-description as a collector of reminders for particular purposes,[31] Lovibond asks, "Couldn't such 'reminders' be assembled in the service of local (concrete) projects of social criticism? Such exercise might display the radical potential of a naturalistic approach to linguistic potential—a project which, for one reason or another, remains muted in the philosophy of Wittgenstein."[32] The following chapters of this book will assemble such reminders of a naturalized counterteleology, which for reasons of limited historical selection remained muted in *Ethical*

Formation. By looking at exemplary disclosing critics, I shall survey ways of distancing us, for the time being, from our form of life to see it differently.

Lovibond shows that normative critical theorists have good reason to remain skeptical about counterteleological projects, such as disclosing critique. But she also shows that they cannot a priori discount those projects as "uncritical" either. To know whether such gestures of disclosure are criminal or critical, they must *hear them out*. The remainder of this book offers the chance to do this in the setting of a historical excavation of several layers of naturalized counterteleology.

Disclosing critique is different from the "postmodern" variants of counterteleology that Lovibond considers: its target is not universalism or value hierarchy but the uncanniness of existing ethical formation, the "conditioning" aspect of the processes of upbringing, the prevailing patterns of socialization to the allegedly universal form of social life. Indeed, as the setting of the stage of disclosing critique in the next chapter will show already, there is a naturalized form of counterteleology that astonishingly operates with the same metaphoric as Lovibond's naturalized teleology: it retraces formation from "second" to "first nature." To this excavation site, we must now finally turn.

THREE

Drawing a Vicious Circle
*Adorno, Emerson, and the Scene of
a Disclosing Critique of Society*

> En krets var dragen kring dessa ting,
> den ingen överträder.
>
> *A circle was drawn around these things,
> that no one trespasses.*
>
> —EDITH SÖDERGRAN, "Jag såg ett träd..."
>
> People wish to be settled; only as far as
> they are unsettled is there any hope for them.
>
> —RALPH WALDO EMERSON, "Circles"

As one scratches the surface of the rough ground on the excavation site asking what disclosing critique of society is or how to practice it, one will soon enough find out that the paradigmatic example of a disclosing critic is the twentieth-century German critical social theorist and composer Theodor W. Adorno.[1] If one wishes to trace the execution of this disclosing intent in Adorno's social philosophy, one then very soon encounters his curiously negative social ontology, which in manifold descriptions ascribes circularity to society. The notions of the "administered world" (*verwaltete Welt*), the "societalized society" (*vergesellschaftete Gesellschaft*), the "bedazzlement connection" (*Verblendungszusammenhang*), and the perhaps untranslatable *Bannkreis* are just some of the better known examples of Adorno's attempts to express the uncanniness of the social teleology of a form of life maintaining itself through its parts. As one digs around these concepts, a naturalistic metaphoric starts to emerge—terms such as "first" and "second nature" and even "social organism"—and, with it, a peculiar form of critical thinking that we might, following Lovibond's concept introduced in the previous chapter, hypothesize as a version of "naturalized counterteleology."

In this chapter, I will first show how Adorno figures out some of the features of his counterteleology through a critical engagement with a mode of teleological thinking in social theory—namely, social organicism. Excavating his critique of the idea of a social organism shows how his peculiar form of naturalized counterteleology emerges as a response to the question of what a genuinely critical stance to social teleology would be. But it also helps bring out the social-theoretical sophistication with which he projects circularity onto society. Second, this stance—and the disclosing force of its conception of society—comes into a clearer view when its quite surprising historical root in Ralph Waldo Emerson's idea of poetic disclosure is dug up. By two entwined metaphors—one pointing to critique, the other, to its object—the scene of a disclosing critique, a conceptual and metaphorical space for reflective recalcitrance, is brought to light. This scene will initially seem overwhelmingly complex. But it will at this stage mainly serve to determine the diameter of the excavation site, and the two metaphors will work as the leading fossils as we burrow deeper in the following chapters.

1. From Social Organicism to Negative Utopia

Let us, for the sake of experiment, define "organicism" as the teleological stance that posits the organism as an ontological principle and regards it as a self-maintaining whole reproducing itself through its parts and the parts through the whole, thereby assuming the whole to be ontologically superior to the parts. The whole is, then, sui generis, or "substance," meaning that it cannot be ontologically reduced to its parts but must be explained by independent categories. Let us then define "social organicism" as the application of this principle to the mode of existence of the social: it asserts followingly that society is an organism that reproduces itself in the way just mentioned—as it were, behind the backs of its members. Curiously, the idea of the societal organism has recently found its way back into the Frankfurt school's critical theory through Axel Honneth's organicist conception of "diseases of society" and Frederick Neuhouser's approach to social pathology diagnosis.[2] It may then not come as too far-fetched to ask whether

Adorno, the coinitiator of that tradition of social theorizing and the author of notions such as "the societalized society" and "the administered world," is a social organicist too?

To determine the extent to which Adorno's conception of society displays a teleological, organicist character, it is helpful first to recollect his debates with other authors' organicist conceptions of society. If it were possible to assess how Adorno determinately negates other organicist conceptions of society—that is, to establish what he wishes to discard and preserve from them—one would be able to better contour his stance to social teleology, if he indeed has one. Adorno discusses several social organicists in his works on social theory, such as Joseph de Maistre and Auguste Comte, as well as Herbert Spencer.[3] However, his discussions of Émile Durkheim, Aldous Huxley, and G. W. F. Hegel are the most extensive and, to some extent, the most charitable too.

1.1. Contra Durkheim

I say "to some extent" because at least the encounter with Durkheim is arguably *not* particularly charitable.[4] But let us start there anyway. Despite his rather polemical criticism of the French sociologist, Adorno initially appropriates Durkheim's social organicism as a fair empirical description of the "false state"—that is, of alienated society. In the Durkheimian societal organism, the power of all individual and particular variations is alienated into the social whole, the society, which reproduces itself in and through it. What he believes to be true in Durkheim's organicism is that it makes clear that society has not transcended its natural shape. In its "anti-ideological" moments, Durkheim's sociology presents society as a subjectless whole, a social continuation of the struggle for existence in organic nature.[5] In this respect, it gives social scientific, empirically informed support to the idea touched upon in the previous chapter that society presents an outer *second nature*.

By hypostatizing the *social* as the self-maintaining *society*, however, Adorno believes Durkheim to ontologize the empirically justified realistic diagnosis: out of a fair description of the false state, the French sociologist makes an ontological fact, an invariant structure, the substance of the social world. According to Adorno, Durkheim's organicism is, then, untrue as a social ontology: it perpetuates the natural organismic shape of the social, hypostatizes the alienated state of society.

Adorno counters that the concept of the social cannot be dissolved into that of society. Contrary to "society" stands the social life of the individuals that compose it ("d[as] Leben . . . der Individuen, aus denen sie [die Gesellschaft] sich zusammensetzt").[6] Here, Adorno takes sides with what Durkheim rejects as "individualistic sociology"[7]—namely, the process sociology of Gabriel Tarde.[8] Along with Durkheim's diametrical adversary in French sociology around 1900, Adorno takes the position that society is primarily something to be explained, not a thing that explains (see also *LS*, 124–25). It cannot be posited as a first term out of which the explanations of this new science of sociology flow but rather needs to be itself explained from the activity of its constituent elements. As Adorno elaborates this point in his lectures on *History and Freedom*, "We should not let ourselves be tempted to ontologize [society]. . . . For society itself is determined by the things of which it is composed and it therefore necessarily contains a nonsocietal dimension [*außergesellschaftliches Moment*]" (*HF*, 122; translation amended). At least counterfactually, the individuals functioning as members of the self-maintaining society can turn against society or lead their lives, as it were, with the other foot, if not outside social life, then outside the functional circles of society. As little as life can be reduced to its form, it is also wrong, Adorno believes, to ontologically dissolve the social in society.

Since Durkheim, in his *Sociological Method*, defines society as a "thing," a reality sui generis, or substance,[9] he must, in Adorno's view, blend out all social life that is effectively nonidentical to substance: deviation, variation, modification may not unfold any real consequences for the form of social life unless they are conceivable as eventual products of the societal substance. The recalcitrant—that is, those tendencies that for some reason or another evade the social teleology of society, its current patterns of socialization—are then in constant danger of being ontologically liquidated. They either constitute anomalies or cunning works of society itself. According to Adorno, Durkheim thereby does ontological injustice to his own fair empirical description of present society. Instead of sticking to his insight of the present society's natural organismic form, the French sociologist now posits it as a collective subject. This positing is baldly groundless, Adorno argues: society does not reproduce itself consciously but "blindly."[10] In his introduction to the German edition of Durkheim's *Sociology and Philosophy*, he describes this as a confusion of *second* with *first nature*[11]—metaphors handed down to him to express the acquired and the innate. What is still to be explained—namely, the socially overpowering conditions—is posited by Durkheim as primary, as subject, out of which social change is to follow, whereas Adorno indicates that society presents second nature not only in virtue of confronting us with an appearance of necessity, which Durkheim, in his view, powerfully reveals, but also in the sense of being something acquired.

Therefore, Adorno thinks that Durkheim's initially correct observation of the organismic character of contemporary society leads to a falsely harmonious, affirmative organicist social ontology that, in its apotheosis of society as substance, willingly or unwillingly, serves to maintain the false state, which it empirically expressed.[12] While Durkheim smuggles the figure of frictionless reproduction of the social whole into his sociology as the ideal of social health, Adorno, by contrast, considers this very figure as expressing a social pathology.

Let me sum up the polemic so far. The merit of Durkheim's organicism, Adorno believes, lies in its honest, empirically informed description of the false state of society: Durkheim presents the reality of the contemporary social teleology as a self-maintaining, organism-like, thing-like society, which overpowers the living individuals by displaying an appearance of necessity—as it were, a second nature. What he believes to be untrue in Durkheim, however, is a social ontology, which perpetuates this social teleology as a first nature, resulting in the glorification of societal self-maintenance. While Durkheim represents the frictionless reproduction of society, intentionally or not, as a utopia, for Adorno, it rather appears as a sign of the false state. Now, from this affirmative organicism, whose ideal is a healthy society successfully maintaining itself through its parts, we can distinguish a possibly negative organicism that would present the same condition rather as a dystopia. In criticizing Durkheim, Adorno seems to be appealing to there being something weirdly *uncanny* about the idea of a harmoniously self-maintaining society more generally. Is Adorno's way of thinking against social teleology a negative organicism?

1.2. Contra Huxley

Adorno encounters such a dystopian representation of society as an organism in Huxley's novel *Brave New World*. The novel's "World State" represents a planetary society, in which the necessity to work has been overcome by technological advance, yet class domination is artificially maintained. It replaces "Freedom, Equality, Brotherhood," the motto of the French Revolution, with "Community, Identity, Stability."[13] Interestingly, Adorno gives this emblem an organicist interpretation: "Community defines a collectivity in which each individual is unconditionally subordinated to the functioning of the whole (the question of the point of this whole is no longer permitted or even possible in the New World). Identity means the elimination of individual differences, standardization even down to biological constitution; stability, the end of all social dynamics."[14] *Brave New World* posits three dualisms, "community," "identity," and "stability," with each representing one extreme: societal reproduction instead of social transformation, suppression of differences instead of growth by them, and stability instead of dynamics.

Adorno takes Huxley to follow the empiricist tendency in Durkheim by portraying the societal organism as an outer second nature. However, the critical benefit of Huxley's organicism is that the British writer succeeds in showing how the frictionless reproduction of the "World State," more precisely, operates as an outer second nature that *shapes the inner first nature* of its composite individuals *for its own persistence*. This is what Huxley, as noted in the previous chapter, calls "conditioning": class domination is stabilized by the artificial generation of the members of the social classes—the human species industrially produced. As Adorno interprets Huxley, "The system of class relationships is made eternal and biological." The members of this society impulsively identify themselves with their functional role in the petrified division of labor. They do their job happily in a world where compulsory work has, in fact, already become technologically unnecessary. In his lecture course on philosophy and sociology, Adorno tells his students that to this extent, *Brave New World* is "prophetic" (*PS*, 238). In Huxley's negative organicism, the healthy reproduction of the societal organism appears not only as a perpetuation of class domination but also as a symmetrical *Bannkreis*—a vicious circle of second and first nature.[15] The uncanny aspect of the New World society is that it incessantly implants an inner nature in its members, who then adapt willingly and happily. Huxley's novel shows the thought of a happiness without freedom to be disconcerting.

Now, in contrast to Durkheim, Huxley's organicism is presented in the form not of theory but of a work of art, a novel. Interestingly, Adorno's essay "Aldous Huxley and Utopia" focuses on *Brave New World* as an example of what he calls a "negative utopia."[16] Later, in his *Aesthetic Theory*, Adorno returns to the concept and discusses works of Arnold Schönberg and Samuel Beckett as more thoroughgoing examples of a negative utopia (*AT*, esp. 32–33). The concept of a negative utopia is remarkably unstable in Adorno. First, it is internally unstable: it oscillates between designating "dystopia"—that is, the presentation of a radically evil society—and "utopia"—the idea of a good society. The idea is that in this oscillation this latter state, utopia, is *shown* through the former, the elaborated dystopia: the negative presentation of the false alienated state discloses the possibility of another, in which freedom *and* the pursuit of happiness count as real possibilities.[17] In a negative utopia, the utopian state is then not presented positively or concretely. It is, as it were, pointed at. In the case of *Brave New World*, Adorno believes its portrayal of the continuation of domination even after the end of scarcity, after the necessity to work has been overcome, points to the possibilities of both a total catastrophe and a free state in present society due to its technological stage. Adorno sees *Brave New World*, then, as an example of "the true consciousness of an age in which the real possibility of utopia—that given the level of productive forces the earth could here and now be paradise—converges with the possibility of total catastrophe" (33).

Second, "negative utopia" is also externally unstable: its relation to the uncanny societal organism it confronts is antinomically precarious. The need for such critical gestures of pointing to something indeterminately utopian grows with their looming impossibility: the societal organism it points to tends to swallow up such critiques and to spit them out as signs of its own legitimation. "What takes itself to be utopia remains the negation of what exists and is obedient to it. At the center of contemporary antinomies is that art must be and wants to be utopia, and the more utopia is blocked by the real functional order, the more this is true; yet at the same time art may not be utopia in order not to betray it by providing semblance and consolation" (*AT*, 33).

Any utopian gesture in the present is, Adorno believes, vulnerable to being turned into consolation for living in the wrong world. Thus, a reader of Huxley's *Brave New World* might close the book in the evening sighing, "Thank God I live in a democracy!" and then turn off the lamp to get their eight hours of sleep before getting up fresh in the morning to go to their job of controlling tickets on public transportation. The only critical reaction to this precarious position of negative utopian gestures, Adorno believes, is to not succumb to the pressure from present society to give up on utopia altogether while at the same time refraining from offering positive content for the societal organism to digest. I believe that this amounts to invoking what Freud, a decade before Huxley's negative utopia, called an "uncanny" experience (U). But we will return to that in due time.

Although Huxley exemplifies, in his novel, an organicism that is negative in the sense of evoking an uncanny feeling about the society, Adorno believes him to repeat a mistake of Durkheim's. By accepting the reality of the three aforementioned dualisms, Huxley, too, ends up ontologizing society as social substance. The author of *Brave New World* namely presents his readers with an impossible choice: societal reproduction *or* social transformation, identity *or* difference, stability *or* dynamism. These are terrorizing alternatives! Of course, Adorno would hold that society should be transformable, criticizable, but equally, forms of social life must be maintained in order for social life to go on; the social must be reproduced as society (*HF*, 97–98). Huxley's readers are thus compelled to choose between the dystopia of absolute subjection to a societal organism that reproduces itself by "conditioning" them *or* the total dissolution of the social. This is, Adorno points out, an impossible choice—a choice, as it were, between social and biological death.

Just as little as society reproduces itself as a Durkheimian collective consciousness, so little can societal self-maintenance follow from the actions of a Huxleyan "world controller." Again, Adorno stresses that the reproduction of the social whole is rather "blind"—that is, it is a nonintentional process. There is, however, also something curiously liberating about this blindness that both Huxley and Durkheim lose sight of: Adorno remarks that through the blind play of means in art, new ends can emerge that immanently transcend the given form of society and bear a transformative effect on social life. The blind and unplanned reproduction of society is, however, not harmonious. Only on the surface does it appear as a smooth autopoietic process. In fact, Adorno believes, the uncanny character of the societal organism includes that it is maintained in and through *antagonisms*. Although Huxley "gives an incisive physiognomy of total unification, he fails to decipher its symptoms as expressions of an antagonistic essence, the pressure of domination, in which the tendency to totalization is inherent."[18] The teleology of a society that has become an end in itself is not the self-movement of social substance but the *result of social antagonisms within it*. Or, as Adorno later explains to the students in his lecture course on social theory, Huxley's portrayal of the healthy societal organism as a happy society must be untrue "because cracks in this false identity appear in countless places, and because it is immediately paid for with neurosis, suffering and all conceivable phenomena of mutilation as soon as one looks even a little beneath the surface of this happy agreement" (*PETS*, 68–69). Far from harmonious, the societal organism must be conceived as a "permanence of catastrophe," to use an idea that Adorno borrows from Benjamin and often applies to characterize the constitution of social totalities.[19]

In summary, while *Brave New World* gives a richer account of the societal organism as domination—namely, in terms of a dystopian circle of second and first nature—Adorno also thinks that the negative organicist Huxley repeats a mistake of the affirmative organicist Durkheim: he, too, masks the painful antagonisms that make societal reproduction such a vicious circle in the first place. Thus, we face a further demand for a genuinely critical counterteleology: it must detach itself from all substance ontology—it should, that is, aim not at explaining the anomalous, varying, deviating from substance but, on the contrary, at tracing stability, identity, form, and order back to the antagonistic elements immanent in the society. What maintains social life in its current form is, Adorno believes, its own countless conflicts. In his view, then, counterteleology must be doubly negative: it has to, first, conceptualize the self-maintaining social whole as negativity in the sense that it presents a rather dystopian than utopian state of affairs, but, second, it must also as a social theory negate any allegedly stable positive standpoint on the social whole as substance, as sui generis, and instead grasp it as maintained by its conflicting elements. Despite its projection of a circular reproduction onto "society," Adorno's counterteleology is, then, not even negatively organicist.[20] As such, how does he approach this curiously "antagonistic" teleology of society?

1.3. Contra Hegel

It is such an antagonistic conception of the social whole that Adorno, finally, catches sight of in Hegel's *Philosophy of Right*. Two years after the essay on Huxley, Adorno identifies the idea of an antagonistic reproduction of society with Hegel's concept of organic totality:

Hegel recognized the primacy of the whole over its finite parts, which are inadequate and, in their confrontation with the whole, contradictory. But he neither derived a metaphysics from the abstract principle of totality nor glorified the whole as such.... He does not make the parts, as elements of the whole, autonomous in opposition to it; at the same time, as a critic of romanticism, he knows that the whole realizes itself only in and through the parts, only through discontinuity, alienation, and reflection.... If Hegel's whole exists at all it is only as the quintessence of the partial moments, which always point beyond themselves and are generated from one another; it does not exist as something beyond them. This is what his category of totality is intended to convey. It is incompatible with any kind of tendency to harmony.

In contrast to Durkheim and Huxley, Hegel's conception of organic totality is, ontologically speaking, not organicist anymore—it does not represent society as a self-maintaining *substance*. In other words, Hegelian totality satisfies the second of the above criteria of a critical stance to social teleology: it does not ontologize society into an entity sui generis but does instead have a story to tell about how it is maintained by its antagonistic elements. As an organic totality, Hegel's civil society, Adorno points out, does not simply reproduce *itself* but is maintained *in and through* its immanent antagonisms. It is a life process that is preserved in a more or less stable form by its internal contradictions and multiple discontinuities, which it is unable to settle and bridge: the Hegelian "civil society is an antagonistic totality. It maintains itself only in and through its antagonisms and is not able to resolve them."[21] We will have a closer look at Adorno's conceptions of both social antagonisms and antagonistic reproduction of capitalist society in chapter 5. For now, it is important to note that for Adorno, following Hegel, the "primacy" of the whole with regard to its parts is not one of substance to accidence or of an ontologically higher to an ontologically lower but of *social domination*: it is a consequence of the blind social aggregate overpowering its constituents, who, by preserving themselves, make it a reality.

This, Adorno tells the students of his introductory lecture course on dialectics, distinguishes the Hegelian organic totality from any kind of "organicist or organological thought."[22] However, even if Hegel's conception of organic totality is not anymore ontologically organicist, Adorno makes clear that it does, indeed, present yet another conception of the societal organism. The Hegelian totality, he namely adds, "is to be understood organically; the partial moments are to grow into and be interpenetrated by one another by virtue of a whole that is already inherent in every one of them."[23] Without positing a metaphysics of the subjectivity of social substance, the likes of which was in play in Durkheim and Huxley, Hegel still finds a way to conceptualize how the society as an outer second nature penetrates the individuals by shaping their inner first nature: the social whole constituted by the individuals comes to inhere in those individuals. Paradoxically, Adorno observes, once social life has been established *as* an antagonistic totality, second nature is primary, and first nature, secondary. It turns out that, as things stand, the elements are made by the whole rather than the other way around. Therefore, Adorno's Hegel, without positing society as a subject, can hold that, after all, the totality does maintain *itself*.

Now, Adorno's provocative thesis is that this conception of organic totality was posthumously materialized in the shape of the Western postwar welfare society: "Satanically, the world as grasped by the Hegelian system has only now, a hundred and fifty years later, proved itself to be a system in the literal sense, namely that of a radically societalized society."[24] Although Hegel's one-hundred-and-fifty-year-old diagnosis of the times has, according to Adorno, come true with this considerable delay, it is also untrue.[25] For the Hegelian totality, promising freedom and reconciliation in its actualization has, quite to the contrary, meant the absolute negation of freedom and reconciliation in the shape of a permanent catastrophe—the radically societalized society. Thus, Adorno believes that the concept of organic totality in Hegel has decoupled from its critical normative content.

To sum up, while Durkheim's affirmative organicism was harmonistic and uncritical, and Huxley's negative organicism, critical but harmonistic, Hegel's idea of organic totality turns out affirmative and so, in the end, insufficiently critical in embracing social teleology. A critical stance to social teleology would then have to be ontologically antagonistic, deliver an honest empirical description of present society, and present it as a negative utopia. Can such a mode of counterteleological thought be found in Adorno's social theory?

2. The Critical Concept of Society: A Disclosing Gesture

It is the suggestion, I believe, of Adorno's small essay entitled simply "Society," written just about a decade later, to contour a conception of society that presents it as antagonistic, empirically informed, and negatively utopian (S, 148). And indeed, Adorno is here trying to do justice to the results of his criticisms of Durkheim's, Huxley's, and Hegel's organicisms. Like in Huxley, the critical concept of society presents a negative utopia that evokes uncanniness about contemporary society. The negative utopia should, furthermore, not be projected into the future but be, like Durkheim's theory of society, empirically traceable in the present by the sociological production of knowledge. Finally, like in Hegel, the social totality must be comprehended as arising from its antagonistic elements.[26] The attempt is, as I would like to elaborate, to formulate a concept that is, by itself, a *disclosing gesture* too.[27]

Already in the first paragraph of the essay, Adorno consequently characterizes society as "essentially process" (S, 144). It is a natural process that maintains its form in and through its inner conflicts. This process of "societalizing" social life (*Vergesellschaftungsprozeß*) is, Adorno writes, "not something that takes place beyond the specific social conflicts and antagonisms, or in spite of them. It works through those antagonisms themselves, the latter, at the same time tearing society apart in the process" (149). Society is petrified process, a stabilized flux that maintains its shape through its antagonistic elements. As predominantly blind, nonintentional, unplanned, Adorno underlines again, society comes to form an objective "second nature" established "against its living members" (147). And this second nature, despite its blindness, preserves itself by coming to inhere in the individuals who make it reality. The criteria for a counterteleological conception of society—that is, a conception of an overpowering social whole both antagonistic and uncannily self-maintaining—seem to me to be conceptually satisfied. It remains to ask, In what sense is this concept of society critical?

Already in 1942, in his Californian exile, Adorno describes this circle of second and first nature as *Bannkreis*, a "vicious circle."[28] Two decades later, in his lectures on *History and Freedom*, he gives his students the following example of the antagonistic nature of *Bannkreis*: society shapes its members by systematically producing needs that are likewise systematically frustrated; the frustration, then, produces impulse conflicts, which, in turn, produce an agency that eventually maintains the whole (*HF*, 148–49). However, this Adornian "conditioning" is not an intentional process emanating from a Huxleyan world controller but a *naturalized* one—an outer second nature that, once social life has taken shape as an antagonistic totality, continues into individual first nature to preserve itself there. And when this has been established, the circle can be intensified by the kind of organized manipulation that he, in the excursus on "Enlightenment as Mass Deception" of the *Dialectic of Enlightenment* coauthored with Horkheimer, continues to express through a circle metaphoric: "In reality, a cycle [*Zirkel*] of manipulation and retroactive need is unifying the system ever more tightly."[29] The antagonistic totality thus comes ex post facto to preserve *itself*.

Another example for the destructive dynamics of the *Bannkreis* Adorno gives to his students is the following thought experiment: imagine that we love society not despite its violence against us but *because* of it. Adorno alludes to Anna Freud's concept of an identification with the aggressor. In her 1936 book *The Ego and the Mechanisms of Defence*, she presents the idea of an unconscious mechanism that makes a relatively impotent individual—paradigmatically, a child—identify with a more powerful individual, such as a violent adult who poses a threat that the child cannot control; to preserve herself, the child then adopts the aggression and emulates characteristics of the aggressor.³⁰ Adorno observes that the aggressor, with whom a victim comes to identify, does not need to be understood as a person but may as well be the nonintentional society whose violence its constituent members internalize (*HF*, 76). I will discuss this model in greater detail in chapter 5. What is important to note at this juncture is that Adorno's counterteleological approach portrays a society that persists *in and through resistance* against it. The internalization of the violence of a "second nature" formed "against its living members" (S, 147), Adorno describes, "sets up a catastrophic vicious circle," in which those who have an interest in changing society have already been "stamped" by its "mechanisms of identification" to the extent that they are no longer capable of resistance, because, by identification with the aggressor "society," they resist only in an "unhappy, neurotically damaged way," which tends to reinforce society as it is (*HF*, 76). Such resistance includes, among other recalcitrant tendencies, social critique. Society, as it were, "exapts" critical practices, turns them to serve its persistence in its current violent form.

This points to a rather obvious problem for any concept of society that claims to be critical. If society has become such that it can reproduce itself as a vicious circle through its inner antagonisms, how can efficient critical recalcitrance ever arise in it? How can *this* social teleology be critically challenged from within? The problem is that the society reproducing itself as a vicious circle tends not only to radically suppress critical transformative practice but also to exapt and isolate it. But the concept of society should be critical in itself. Quite the opposite seems so far the case. In what sense is Adorno's concept of society critical?

With this, I propose, we have reached the *scene of a disclosing critique of society*. Adorno describes the *Bannkreis*, again, as a circle of outer second and inner first nature: "So we come full circle. Living human individuals [*lebendige Menschen*] must act in order to change the present petrified conditions of existence, but the latter have left their mark so deeply on people, have deprived them of so much of their life and individuation, that they scarcely seem capable of the spontaneity necessary to do so" (S, 153; translation amended). Thus, the antagonistically self-maintaining *Bannkreis*, the stage of a disclosing critique of society, appears in its whole dramatic diameter as a circle of outer second and inner first nature: society continues into the innermost preintentional habitual and drive structure of the individual (see fig. 1).

So, one more time, how is Adorno's counterteleological approach to society in the face of this vicious circle to be understood as *critical*? Adorno's

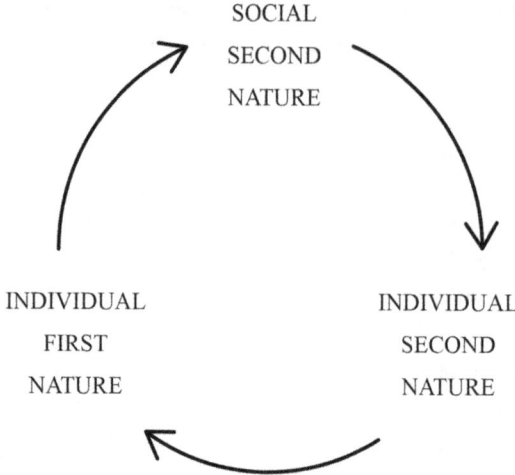

FIGURE 1. The "vicious circle" as a circle of second and first nature, as implied by Adorno. Created by the author.

answer is: "to point the vicious circle out breaks a taboo of the integral society" (S, 153). To draw the circle of outer second and inner first nature *is already the critique*.

3. A Circle Around a Circle

Adorno's counterteleology is critical by virtue of demonstrating the *Bannkreis*. What is critical here is the *disclosure* thereby effected. This becomes clearer when the origin of the idea is appreciated. The provenience of this critical gesture might be surprising. It may be traced in four steps.

First, Adorno's appropriation of Hegel's "organic totality" and his proposition that it has been posthumously—"satanically"—actualized might seem bizarre to the contemporary reader. And surely, Adorno's thesis that Hegel was wrong because he turned out to be right, which turned out to be wrong, is also intended as a provocative and critical gesture. However, the gesture seems less odd when perceived in its historical continuum, for Adorno is not inventing this way of relating to Hegel. The idea that Hegel's concept of objective spirit was actualized retrospectively and can be falsified by its own social consequences goes back to the third part of Nietzsche's *Untimely Meditations*. The young Nietzsche writes,

I understand well enough the objections the state could have raised against this whole way of looking at things so long as the fair green shoots of Hegelianism were sprouting up in every field: but now that this harvest has come to nothing, all the expectations built upon it have proved vain and all the barns remained empty—one prefers no longer to raise objections but to turn away from philosophy altogether. One now possesses power: formerly, in Hegel's time, one wanted to possess it—that is a vast distinction. Philosophy has become superfluous to the state because the state no longer needs its sanction. (*UM*, 191)

What Adorno does to the Hegelian "civil society" Nietzsche already did to the Hegelian "state": Hegel's transfiguration of his contemporary reality turned out to be prophetic as it later became reality; yet once it had been actualized, it showed itself in fact to be void of the normative significance that he had invested in it. The prophecy turned satanic.

Second, the term *Bannkreis*, a rather peculiar word to express vicious circularity, is already used by the young Nietzsche in this sense. In *The Birth of Tragedy*, he describes the new Alexandrian world he criticizes by this very term: "[The] Alexandrian type of 'Greek cheerfulness' is the cheerfulness of the theoretical man.... [I]t believes in correcting the world through knowledge, in life led by science; and it is truly capable of confining the individual within the smallest circle of solvable tasks [*in einen allerengsten Kreis von lösbaren Aufgaben zu bannen*], in the midst of which he cheerfully says to life: 'I will you: you are worth understanding'" (*BT*, 85). With its promise of happiness by the use of reason alone, the Socratism of the Alexandrian world sets up a repressive culture, which traps the individuals in a vicious circle of controlling life instead of affirming it. Without, of course, taking Nietzsche's critique of reason at face value, Horkheimer and Adorno metaphorize remarkably similarly in the *Dialectic of Enlightenment*: "The mastery of nature draws the circle [*zieht den Kreis*] in which the critique of pure reason holds thought spellbound [*in den ... bannte*]."[31]

Third, even the idea to link a circle of second and first nature with *critique* does not originally stem from the usual suspects, Georg Lukács and Walter Benjamin, to whom Adorno mostly refers when he speaks of second nature.[32] Rather, it is likely that this *circular* model of second and first nature here comes, again, from the young Nietzsche, who, in the second of his *Untimely Meditations*, describes the "critical species of history" as precisely a circle of second and first nature: "For those who employ critical history for the sake of life, there is ... a noteworthy consolation: that of knowing that this first nature was once a second nature and that every victorious second nature will become a first" (*UM*, 76–77).

Finally, the author, who influenced the young Nietzsche's circle metaphoric, was Emerson, whose essays the stateless Baselian philologist studied intensely.[33] And indeed, Emerson describes disclosure precisely as "drawing a circle around the circle" (C, 405). Now, what does this metaphor, drawing a circle around the circle, tell us about philosophical social critique?

Not unlike Adorno, Emerson regards "society" as an antagonistic whole, to which an autonomous individual must establish a certain distance of nonconformist behavior, which he calls "self-reliance": "Whoso must be a man must be a nonconformist" (SR, 261; see also *MI*, 23–24; *HF*, 55–60). Like Adorno, Emerson sees such individual recalcitrance as threatened by social teleology—more precisely, its reifying tendency to reduce individuals to organs of societal self-maintenance: "Man is metamorphosed into a thing, into many things. . . . In this distribution of functions the scholar is delegated intellect. In the right state, he is, *Man Thinking*. In the degenerate state, when the victim of society, he tends to become a mere thinker, or, still worse, the parrot of other men's thinking" (AS, 54). The moment of disclosure of such a false state, the shifting of the horizon of meaning, he describes, in his essay "Circles," as "drawing a circle" (C). And also, he notes that society's horizon of meaning can itself already constitute a circle, much like Adorno's *Bannkreis*. The gesture of a disclosing critique of society, then, constitutes "a circle around the circle" (405); in other words, it consists in drawing the circle around the circle of the reproduction of society.

So far, then, Emerson thinks like Adorno. However, Emerson's "Circles" is not primarily an essay on social theory like Adorno's "Society" is but on *poetic disclosure*: it aims at leaving a detailed record of how the circle around the vicious circle of society is drawn. The poet, he says, is "a point outside our hodiernal circle" (C, 408). The poet takes an Archimedean point—that is, an arbitrary position—outside of our form of life. From there, he sketches its limits, the horizon of meaning to be shifted. By providing us with this sketch of the limits of our form of life, the poet, Emerson continues, shatters the circle of second and first nature: "He smiles and arouses me with his shrill tones, *breaks up my whole chain of habits*, and I open my eyes to my own possibilities" (409; emphasis added). The poet frees the first-natural impulses of his addressees by disrupting their habitual behavior—that is, their individual second nature, which ties them to the outer second nature of the customs and institutions of present society.

Now, following Adorno, one might wonder how the *Bannkreis* can allow for such transformative practice as drawing a circle around itself in the way Emerson's poet intends to. How can the poet prevent that her intended critical gesture is not taken by the societal organism as either a further source of legitimation or just empty drivel? How come the poet's shrill tones aren't just idiosyncrasy already "stamped" by society? Who educates our poetic educator?

This is where Adorno, conversely, can provide a detailed record of how the circle around the circle is drawn. There are, I believe, two advantages in reading Adorno in the light of his debate with the social organicists, as I have done above. The first is that it draws attention to an important distinction in his social theory—namely, that between "the false state" and "second nature." Second nature, in Adorno, is not to be equated with the false state.[34] Or, to put it another way, "second nature" is not a purely negative concept but rather an unstable metaphor. Read along the lines I have suggested: the problem of the false state in Adorno is *not* that social processes present a second nature; his critical discussion of social organicism suggests rather that the issue is with the riddling *Bannkreis*—that is, the antagonistically maintained *vicious circle of second and first nature*.

This enables a distinction between social objectification and reification in Adorno. Second nature presents the objectified realm of social processes as habits, customs, institutions, organizations, functional connections, and societies. *Bannkreis*, by contrast, produces reification, or what Italo Testa calls "an additional objectification"; it may be understood as a "social mechanism that masks the ontological contingency, the socially produced character of certain objectifications by imposing on them an 'appearance of necessity' . . . , that is, a false appearance of being necessarily binding, immutable, invariable, and inescapable."[35] Out of social objectification, *Bannkreis* weaves reification.

That second-natural objectification is not equal to reification in Adorno becomes clear if one looks at his contribution to the sociology of organizations. The problem in contemporary society, he argues, is not too much organization but too little organization. Organizing presents a mode of social objectification, or outer second-naturalness, which can work against reification. He regards organizations as second nature yet thinks of them as emancipatory if directed rationally.[36]

This upholds what Adorno calls a "real" or "objective possibility," which can be interpreted as a counterfactual idea of a second nature that would not one-sidedly condition first nature but live plastically, learning from the variations, deviations, and recalcitrance of its members' first nature (see, e.g., *HF*, 67). This possibility is "real" or "objective" in the sense of being immanent in the form of life in which it appears. Disclosing critique, then, seeks to disclose such immanent possibilities. In doing so, it does not operate with "external standards," as is sometimes assumed.[37] Instead, it operates with an immanent dimension of the form of life, which is not, strictly speaking, normative but something to be further elaborated and articulated in the process.[38]

The second advantage of clearing the scene for the disclosing critique of society by reading Adorno in light of his discussion with the social organicists is that it led us to an initial model for how this process of disclosure can be effected: the idea of a negative utopia. The poetic redescription of the current form of life can proceed as a presentation of the false state, thereby pointing to the real possibility of another form of life. At worst, then, a society organized as *Bannkreis*, Adorno notes, reduces social recalcitrance, including poetic descriptions of its limits and its objective possibilities, either to sources of its further legitimation or to mere chance and contingency. In the first case, the redescription would come to seem like a celebration of the society, which, in virtue of having produced the poet, can be credited with the work. In the second case, it "sucks the marrow out of everything oppositional and recalcitrant, and what gets left behind is something insignificant, lacking in substance and thus a random affair" (*HF*, 96). This would eventually have the consequence of participants losing confidence that challenges to the form of life will keep occurring; *Bannkreis* erodes trust in the capacity of society to maintain critical practice.

This randomness of recalcitrance, the reduction of whatever evades the reproduction of the current form of life to mere chance, the merely contingent character that social criticism might come to take in a vicious circle, is a problem that Emerson does articulate in his conception of poetic disclosure. The poet's point "outside our hodiernal circle" is truly Archimedean in the sense of *not* being fixed—that is, not being logically determined. It is arbitrary and hypothetical. When Archimedes remarked, while explaining the principle of leverage, "Give me the place to stand, and I shall turn the earth!" he asks his addressee not for an absolute, fixed point but for a relative, hypothetical, and arbitrary one, out of which the force needed to turn the object might be generated. *Any* point at a sufficient distance will do. So when Emerson's poet asks us, "Give me a position outside our form of life, and I shall turn it!" then the appeal is to chance, contingency—in Adorno's words, a "random affair." This is, I take it, what Adorno also has in mind when he states that "chance is the form taken by freedom under a spell [*unter dem Bann*]" (*HF*, 97). Under the *Bannkreis*, there remains the appeal to objective possibility from a self-consciously random position.

More difficult to crack is the resistance to disclosure on the side of the addressees. Given the thesis of the sociologized Anna Freudian "identification with the aggressor" mentioned above, how could Emerson's poet ever provoke a transformative reaction among the recipients of the poetic gesture under the conditions of a *Bannkreis*? In order to be critically effective, Emerson argues, *my* circle must really be drawn around *yours*. This means that it really must disclose those objective possibilities of your circle, which Emerson calls your "genius" or your "higher self" (SR, passim). However, as Adorno sees it, the path to the recipient's "higher self" can be radically blocked by the identification with an aggressor society appealing, as it were, to the *lower* self so that the anger is channeled instead against the poet and her incomplete utopian-looking description of our objective possibilities: "If people really were to become fully aware that their own selves . . . belong not to them but that they are, right down to . . . their idiosyncrasies and peculiarities, . . . the negative imprint of the universal, that would involve such a fearful loss of self-esteem . . . that in all probability they would be unable to bear it" (*HF*, 74). And in his *Aesthetic Theory*, Adorno recognizes, in this repulsiveness of disclosing gestures, a core feature of the model of negative utopia: "Art is no more able than theory to concretize utopia, not even negatively. A cryptogram of the new is the image of collapse; only by virtue of the absolute negativity of collapse does art enunciate the unspeakable: utopia. In this image of collapse all the stigmata of the repulsive and loathsome in modern art gather. Through the irreconcilable renunciation of the semblance of reconciliation, art holds fast to the promise of reconciliation in the midst of the unreconciled" (*AT*, 32–33). The circle around the circle in the Adornian disclosure turns into an uncanny experience. I will discuss this problem in greater detail in chapter 6. What is important at this point is that this uncanniness of critical disclosure, I believe, explains the rather peculiar tone and style, the aesthetic quality, of Adorno's sociological writings. In such a *Bannkreis*, the recipient must first, by means of empirical knowledge of the circular character of society, be brought to the insight of her own societal determinateness. Yet, second, Adorno's exposition of this empirical knowledge is obviously exaggerated; the "administered world," the "radically societalized society," and "*Bannkreis*" itself can hardly be understood as fair and sophisticated empirical accounts of social reality. But a fair and sophisticated empirical account of social reality isn't what Adorno's negative social theory is after. Instead, it aims at disclosure. The idea is namely not to simply rub the societal determinateness of the recipient's self in her face but to also practice social theory as *an exemplary exposition of an alienation from the alienation in the false state*. The recipients of the disclosing gesture are, intermittently, brought to a distance from their ordinary myopia. Yes, the disclosing critic does expose the societal determinateness of us in the *Bannkreis*, but she also, in the very same move, draws the attention back to herself, to her exemplary way of letting herself be affected by society and of channeling that affect right back against it in a circular gesture. By means of hyperbolic, metaphoric, or otherwise poetic speech from her random position, then, she seeks to transform "the affect of powerlessness" into reflective recalcitrance against reified second nature (MGH, 213–14, 220–22; PETS, 35).

Rather than grounding or justifying social critique, drawing the circle around the vicious circle provides the recipient with an *example* of the "strenuous effort" of distancing oneself from the alienated false state by means of empirical knowledge and philosophical speculation, standing, as it were, with one foot inside and the other outside our form of life.[39] Or, as Adorno puts it in *Minima Moralia*, "Nothing less is asked of the thinker today than that he should be at every moment both within things and outside them" (*MI*, 74).

4. Two Directions of Disclosure: Decentering and Recentering Gestures

To be sure, I would not want to claim that Adorno's and Emerson's conceptions of critical disclosure are identical. In fact, I think they are, in a certain sense, the opposites of the story I am only beginning to tell: not only do they represent the two historical poles, the beginning and the end of the epoch of disclosing critique of society (1841–1969), but also, in terms of form and content, they constitute contrasting figures we will be better prepared to encounter time and again as the story unfolds. Here, in the remainder of this chapter, I would merely like to draw attention to one such contrast: Adorno and Emerson can exemplify *opposite directions of disclosure*. So far, I have been mostly clarifying what issues are at stake in Adorno's and Emerson's gestures of disclosure. But by contouring these directions of disclosure, I will retrieve a general pattern of this peculiar critical practice—a pattern, which will remain rather stable for the rest of this history. Showing, as I attempt to do now, how, in Adorno and Emerson, opposite directions of disclosure solicit each other may also help see how the idea of a disclosing critique of society can enrich contemporary critical aspirations in philosophy and perhaps even beyond.

There is namely a distinction to be made between two directions of critical disclosure: a decentering direction and a recentering.[40] The *decentering* direction of disclosure can be characterized by the creation of a disruption in the self-understanding of a form of life by means of what I have called an exemplary exposition of an alienation from the alienated state. Adorno's occasional use of the organicist vocabulary is, then, not due to his subscribing to an organicist social ontology. Rather, he takes the alienated position of a social organicist, turns its positive utopia into a negative one, and so distances himself both from the prevailing social teleology and its distance from its living members. He thus uses speculative language, a distancing style of speech, in order to help his addressees distance themselves into a reevaluation of their form of life, which initially appeared to them as self-evident—an outer second nature—but now, following his exemplary exposition, faces them in the shape of an alien, perhaps unacceptable, reality. In it, critique consists less in justification or utopian projection of values than in an *exemplary gesture*: "First of all society should be recognized as a universal block, both within men and outside them at the same time. Such knowledge, without any preconceptions as to where it might lead, would be the first condition for the spell [*Bann*] of society once to dissolve" (S, 153).

Decentering disclosure seeks, then, to provoke in its addressees the kind of rational responsiveness characteristic of what Adorno, following Hegel, calls "determinate negation." It shows them the societally determined limits of their capacity of judgment so as to push them to lift themselves up to face a contradiction that is already lived.

Emerson, by contrast, may exemplify a *recentering* direction of critical disclosure. In Emerson's description of the poet, who, from beyond our horizon, "breaks up [our] whole chain of habits" (C, 409), the decentering alienation from alienation is implied. In a later essay, "Experience," he even expresses this in terms of critical analysis: "So in this great society wide lying around us, a critical analysis would find very few spontaneous actions. It is almost all custom and gross sense. There are even a few opinions, and these seem organic in the speakers, and do not disturb the universal necessity" (E, 472). But Emerson's primary interest lies in the following move of the disclosing critic: his conception of the drawing of a circle around a circle presents the production of a new center following the shifting of the horizon, the affirmation of a higher form of life, which was so far suppressed.

What is disclosed following a decentering disclosure is the path from senseless suffering to the objective possibility of another form of life. What is disclosed following a recentering disclosure is the path from the objective possibility of another form of life to a new perspective on a higher form of life, on a society that could be more freely affirmed by its living members. Therefore, Adorno's and Emerson's exemplary disclosures are also not opposite. They present, namely, mutually soliciting forces. The Adornian alienation from alienation prepares the way for an Emersonian affirmation of a higher life. By itself, however, it claims not to know what the higher human is but only to refute the current vicious circle of the production of human nature. But it sees the establishment of an openness for that precise question as its task: "We might not know what the human being is or what is the right design for human affairs, but we do know what she ought not to be and what design is false for human affairs. Only in this determinate and concrete knowledge, is the other task, the positive, open for us."[41] The Emersonian disclosure of a new center in the old periphery claims to establish just this positive. His idea is that by inquiring into the shame, with which the poet affects us, we can creatively grasp our higher self, which was already there but blocked, rejected, suppressed, and affirm this self by reorganizing our chain of habits (SR, 259). However, this new form can only claim to be higher as long as it remains open to further challenge from Adornian decentering disclosure.

These opposing directions of critical disclosure in Adorno and Emerson explain the different (and eventually incompatible) characters of their philosophical social criticisms, along with the fact that the German philosopher works with empirical social science, while his American colleague works with poetry. To disclose the objective possibility of another form of life, Adorno must trace the vicious circle of *this* form of life. Poetry seems not to do this work; perhaps, theory can. For this reason, Adornian decentering disclosure must interrupt the philosophical prose with sociological theory, combine and even merge empirical knowledge of society with philosophical speculation in the mode of a distancing sort of speech.[42] For recentering disclosure, Emerson again needs aesthetic experience, the great work of art, the affect of shame, which accompanies the latter's reception, and the affirmation of the higher self thus disclosed. For this reason, Emersonian recentering disclosure must interrupt the philosophical prose with poetic expression—to make our petrified concepts dance.

I have exaggerated by identifying decentering disclosure with Adorno and recentering disclosure with Emerson. In reality, both directions of disclosure are present in both authors. The difference is one of emphasis and environment, as I hope to show in the following chapters. Interestingly, both authors coincide in the literary form of the essay—perhaps the privileged medium of critical disclosure in philosophy. In fact, as the following chapters will go on to indicate, it is the unity of these two directions, the decentering and the recentering of a form of life, in one and the same circular gesture that characterizes disclosing critique of society. Pointing out the vicious circle points to the objective possibility of another form of life. By this gesture, disclosing critique of society upholds Karl Marx's "wish" from his letter to Arnold Ruge "to find the new world through criticism of the old.... Even though the construction of the future and its completion for all times is not our task, what we have to accomplish at this time is all the more clear: *relentless criticism of all existing conditions.*"[43]

5. Immanence, Receptivity, and Disclosing Gestures

From scratching the surface by looking at Adorno's critique of the social organicists, we have dug us into the excavation site of this history of disclosing critique. That debate showed that Adorno does not think that the society is "like an organism." Instead of using a socio-ontological analogy for the capitalist society he sets out to critique, he metaphorically projects onto that society, this false ground of critique, the figure of a vicious circle. *Bannkreis* appears thus as a *negatively absolute metaphor*: it names the false totality and discloses a scene of critique, a metaphorical and conceptual space for reflective recalcitrance to the adaptive demands of a ground of thinking—a ground, that is, about which nothing is, at the outset, assumed to be sufficiently good or right to provide the normativity of critique.

Nevertheless, perhaps the disclosing critique of society as an articulation of the metaphor of drawing a circle around the circle might still look like external critique to some. Is it? I believe the very beginning of our excavation to show already that this would be a grave misunderstanding. Adorno's and Emerson's uses of the metaphors of the vicious circle and drawing a circle around the circle ascribe immanence to disclosing critique in at least three ways.

First, what is being disclosed are, in Adorno's words, "objective possibilities" (*HF*, 67), or, in Emerson's words, "[our] own possibilities" (*C*, 409). According to Emerson, drawing the circle around the circle is supposed to trigger an affect of "shame" in the recipient and thereby prove to be immanent to their own "genius." The poet's gesture makes me feel ashamed because I, in some sense, already know the possibilities I have been neglecting. Similarly, Adorno argues that the affect of the administered world is something each and every one of us already feels; the critic appeals to this "feeling of powerlessness" in order to violate the "taboo" of our "integral society" (MGH, 213–14; *PETS*, 35; S, 153). The critical gesture must then *hit* the form of life; the teleology of current society must be immanent to the vicious circle drawn by the critic.

Second, disclosing critique achieves its immanence in execution: the Archimedean description departs from our form of life, is relative to it, and must also become practically effective in it through the reception of the participants. Here, the disclosing critic admits her own impotence: her criticism is dependent upon reception; she sends, as Adorno puts it, a "message in a bottle."[44] But note that the reception dependency of disclosing gestures does not impair disclosing critique vis-à-vis normative models of critique. As Robin Celikates shows, whatever critical judgments the normative critical theorist may form on the basis of their theoretical knowledge "depend for their criterion of adequacy on the self-understanding of the addressees."[45] However, regarding disclosing critique, here it is important to make a distinction. Full disclosure, as it were, depends in any case on its redescription becoming practically effective in the habitual practice of its addressees. The interpretation and appropriation of a disclosing gesture is not a gratuitous addition to disclosing critique because disclosing critique demands reception for its vocation. However, even if the addressees were unable to give a correct interpretation and appropriate the gesture (whatever that would mean), the gesture can still have a real critical effect: the intermittent alienation of the addressees from the alienated state. And that, I believe, would already mark a considerable achievement of any philosophical act under a vicious circle, however intermittent and random the distance thereby produced to society.

Third, disclosure is immanent to ordinary social life. Emerson emphasizes the everyday character of disclosure: "Conversation is a game of circles" (C, 408). The aesthetic practice of shifting the horizon of meaning is already an integral part of quotidian social association. The philosophical critique of society represents a refined extension of an aesthetic aspect of the ordinary.

In Emerson's words, "The way of life is wonderful: it is by abandonment" (C, 414). The life processes, from which Adorno distinguished society as its petrified form, involves the drawing of new circles. Although Emerson's poet speaks from outside the *form* of life, she speaks from within life. Not unlike Emerson,[46] Adorno anchors the skeptical attitude necessary for critical disclosure in the ordinary. In a talk given to public officers of the state of Hesse, he remarks that "perhaps the best source for changing the world that humanity possesses at all today" is the "tradition of skepticism, of irony," which has, "in contrast to the official world of education, always been at work in that of ordinary people [*des Volkes*]."[47]

However, these qualifications of immanence do not provide an answer to the worries raised by those engaged in the debate on normativist models of critique—none of them serves to ground critical judgment. Rather, they present some of the demands of immanence for reflective and effective recalcitrance, for an objectively possible challenge to the vicious circle of society. The immanence has, then, less to do with the form of judgment than with formation, or rather *counterformation*. Education therefore marks an aspect of disclosing critique to which we must now turn, following particularly up on our discovery of the mediating figure of Nietzsche on the excavation site between the outposts of Adorno and Emerson.

But before that, let me briefly summarize the findings so far. It seems that disclosing critique of society faces at least five challenges. First, following Emerson, it must restore the continuity of disclosure between the poetry of the ordinary and that of philosophy. Second, following Adorno, it must be able to disclose not only as poetry but also as theory—namely, critical social theory—which must include the production of knowledge and hence empirical social science. Third, it must understand the curious asymmetry between the critic and the addressee only hinted at so far—as it were, its educational character. Fourth, it must transcend its two educators, Adorno and Emerson, by diagnosing why precisely the circle of societal reproduction feels uncanny and what that feeling implies. And finally, it could ontologically inquire into the conflictual tension between the process of life and the form of life implied by the appeal to organization as a nonreified form of second nature.[48]

In the following chapters, my story will excavate the reactions to these and other challenges of disclosing critique. The young Nietzsche, who read Emerson and whom Adorno read, reacts to at least three of these challenges: he anchors critical disclosure as a recalcitrant educational practice in the margins of the criticized form of life and develops a speculative account of life and its form—culture. The next chapter is devoted to his *Untimely Meditations*. The following chapter will then excavate the second layer, that of the role of social theory, by taking up Adorno's and Dewey's reactions to the challenge of disclosing by theorizing. Chapter 6 will investigate, following Freud, the uncanny feelings surrounding both the vicious circle and the drawing of a circle around it. The ontological issue will return in chapter 7, which excavates Dewey's attempt to transform, following Tarde, certain metaphysical commitments of Emersonian disclosure.

FOUR

"The Realm of Transfigured Physis Disclosed"
The Young Nietzsche as a (Meta)Physician of Culture

> I am God in nature;
> I am a weed by the wall.
>
> —RALPH WALDO EMERSON, "Circles"

> Du skall icke föra ditt hjärta till dina läppar,
> vi böra icke störa tystnadens och ensamhetens förnäma ringar,—
> vad är större att möta än en olöst gåta med sällsamma drag?
>
> *You shall not bring your heart to your lips,*
> *we shall not disturb the noble rings of silence and solitude,—*
> *what is greater to face than an unsolved riddle with curious features?*
>
> —EDITH SÖDERGRAN, "Färgernas längtan"

We have now opened the excavation site and discovered the scene of a disclosing critique of society—a scene that we will find repeated with variation in the chapters that follow. The excavation work started from the observation that Adorno, the paradigmatic example of a disclosing critic in the literature, ascribes a peculiar circularity to society, the object of his disclosing critique. It then contoured this critical concept of society by reviewing his debate with what he viewed as the social organicists' uncritical conceptions of society. It traced his critical and sometimes polemical discussion of social teleology to the point where a counterteleological conception of society started to come into view: "society" modeled as an antagonistic yet self-maintaining "vicious circle" (*Bannkreis*) of second and first nature. Soon it turned out that the curiously organicist undertones of Adorno's negative social ontology are part and parcel of a disclosing gesture. This cleared space for the hypothesis that his critique of society is primarily gestural. The place one might expect to be held by critical claims was occupied by a gesture of showing. To investigate what is at stake in this gesture of critical disclosure, it was tracked through Nietzsche back to Emerson's metaphorical expression of poetic disclosure as "drawing a circle around a circle." This helped make some initial sense of how Adorno's counterteleological concept of society is supposed to be critical: in pointing out the vicious circle of society, Adorno, too, draws a circle around the circle. The relation between Adorno's and Emerson's conceptions of critical disclosure seems still overwhelmingly complex. However, their juxtaposition immediately allowed for a distinction between two directions of critical disclosure: *decentering* and *recentering*. An important hypothesis for the rest of this study emerged too: disclosing critique of society can be understood as an exemplary and intermittent dissociation from alienated society by means of a creative association of empirical knowledge, poetic redescription, and philosophical speculation by a critic standing, as it were, with one foot inside and the other outside her form of life.

To my knowledge, Adorno refers to Emerson only twice: in the essay on Huxley's *Brave New World*,[1] discussed in the previous chapter, and in a talk he gave while touring America Houses in Germany entitled "Kultur und Culture."[2] In both texts, Emerson is merely mentioned as an example of nonconformism in America. Nietzsche, by contrast, read Emerson throughout his active life. The peak of Emerson's influence on the stateless philosopher are his *Untimely Meditations* parts 2 and 3, where he continuously paraphrases the essayist from Concord and quotes him as his "educator" in the end of part 3 (*UM*, 193). As Adorno was greatly influenced by Nietzsche and, as noted in the previous chapter, paraphrases the young Nietzsche when introducing the idea of a vicious circle (*Bannkreis*), it is safe to assume that there is a path across the landscape we are excavating leading through Nietzsche and connecting our two historical and philosophical poles, Emerson and Adorno. And indeed, Nietzsche uses and conceptually transforms Emerson's metaphor of "drawing a circle around a circle."

It can hardly be a surprise to take up Nietzsche in construing a canon of philosophical social critique. Social philosophers, in particular critical theorists, have been interested in the critical potential of his works for a long time.[3] In their varying attempts to enrich our understanding of philosophical social critique by interpreting Nietzsche, they have focused strongly on his later writings, predominantly *On the Genealogy of Morality*. Without in any way intending to deny the great value and accomplishments of the diverse perspectives that have emerged from these studies, such as the various models of genealogical critique, I will instead turn to the young Nietzsche, from whose works I will, by focusing on the metaphor of drawing a circle around the circle, excavate a so-far neglected model of disclosing critique—a model I believe to be importantly different from—yet no less valuable than—genealogical critique.[4]

Not unlike Emerson and Adorno, the young Nietzsche namely understands the critical force of philosophy in terms of its disclosing effects. It is this aspect of his *Untimely Meditations* I wish to inquire after in this chapter. I will investigate his early reflections on the critique of forms of life as an exemplary expression of "drawing circles around circles." These reflections point to a model of critique that claims less to pass a normative judgment on social life than to shift its horizon of meaning and to help transform it. Whereas the previous chapter opened the scene of disclosing critique for investigation, the present one is thus to unearth an exemplary *model* of disclosing social critique by following up on the transformations of our leading fossils, the metaphors for critical disclosure, "drawing a circle around a circle," and for society, "vicious circle." This model crystallizes into a figure of the disclosing critic: the physician of culture.

At the outset, Nietzsche can be understood to react creatively to three of the challenges for disclosing critique that emerged at the end of the last chapter: to restore the continuity of disclosure between the poetry of ordinary life and that of philosophy, to elaborate the asymmetrical relation between the critic and the addressees, and to ontologically inquire into the conflictual tension between life and its form. In *Untimely Meditations*, he both anchors the practice of disclosing critique in practices of counterformation in the margins of our form of life and includes an extravagant cosmological reflection in support of his diagnosis of a degeneration of social life. While I do not think that this cosmology is correct or particularly supportive of the important tasks of social criticism today and seriously doubt that his eventually aristocratic version of counterformation is compatible with critical aspirations, I do believe that Nietzsche's inclusion of metaphysical speculation into his practice of disclosing critique can indeed teach many lessons about critical disclosure. Challenging for us today is not so much what he says but how he says it—that is, the *way* in which he sets up, as it were, the praxis of a (meta)physician of culture.

1. The Malady of History

As a "physician of culture," the young Nietzsche diagnoses a social pathology, which he believes we all, as members of a modern form of life, suffer from.[5] In the second of his *Untimely Meditations*, *On the Uses and Disadvantages of History for Life*, he calls this pathology "the malady of history," and he conceptualizes it as a "degeneration of life": "We are all suffering from a consuming fever of history and ought at least to recognize that we are suffering from it" (*UM*, 60). Correspondingly, in the third part of *Untimely Meditations*, *Schopenhauer as Educator*, Nietzsche prognosticates his age to be a "time that really will be killed," and this killing he then specifies as meaning to become "struck out of the history of the true liberation of life" (128). It seems to me that the qualification that his time will "really" be killed and the specification that this means a lack of the "liberation of life" points to Nietzsche's serious take on naturalistic vocabulary and to him ascribing evaluative force to it. He suggests that in its crystallization into a form of life, the process of social life can literally become pathological: there is a way in which a "people" or a "culture" can degenerate (62). In both meditations, Nietzsche refers to the philosopher dealing with these pathologies as a "physician" (72, 133, 148–49, 174); her task is to offer diagnoses and prognoses in order to help cure and heal social life.

By "malady of history," Nietzsche does not refer to a merely scholarly phenomenon. Nietzsche's critique of "history" is not primarily directed against the academic discipline and not even specifically against the role this science has come to play in public discourse. Already on the first pages of the second meditation, it becomes clear that Nietzsche presents "history" as a *cosmological* category: it says something about something's place in the cosmos—namely, about human social practices as part of "life." Specifically, he contrasts such paradigmatically human social life activity with that of animals by noting humans' inability to forget (*UM*, 60–61). History operates through a specific adaptive mechanism: memory. Memory adapts the individual to the environment by the fact that the environment becomes operative in the individual. As memory, the environment imprints itself on the individual and thereby continues into its future interactions. "History" is the way in which a life process, by means of the adaptive mechanism of memory, relates back upon its past so as to redirect its movement toward a specific future. It is a particular mode of life's directedness—a mode that we would associate with processes that we characterize as distinctively social, such as a "people" or a "culture" (62). I therefore take Nietzsche's critique of "history" to present a model of social critique.

Nietzsche believes that the historicity of life comes in degrees. Although humans display a certain inability to forget, he hints at no clear conceptual discontinuity between the relatively unhistorical animal life and the relatively historical human life. The historicity that is characteristic of our social forms of life comes, as it were, creeping: following Gottfried Leibniz, Nietzsche suggests that some minimal amount of memory must be given even in the most primitive forms of life.[6] On the other hand, he emphasizes that forgetting is absolutely necessary for all living beings: "Memory revolves unwearyingly in a circle and yet is too weak and weary to take even a single leap out of this circle" (*UM*, 64). Without the ability to forget, memory would trap the living being in a vicious circle of constantly reinforcing the same environmental conditions.

"History" constitutes an aspect of the life process, of the living being's way to constitutively relate back upon itself so as to redirect its ongoing movement, but the processes of life are also driven to *break* with their past and act forward—a drive that Nietzsche calls "the unhistorical" (*UM*, 61–62). This dual demand of life is what Nietzsche invokes to reflect on in the second meditation: "This, precisely, is the proposition the reader is invited to meditate upon: *the unhistorical and the historical are necessary in equal measure for the health of an individual, of a people and of a culture*" (63; emphasis original). Life processes must be both historical and unhistorical—they must exercise both memory and forgetfulness. Living beings have to, as it were, both *adapt* to their environment and *adjust* it. It follows that there can be an "excess of history," an "oversaturation of an age with history," which leads to a collective "sleeplessness" and "rumination"—the "fever of history" (64, 83, 62, and 60).

To open up these metaphors, let's have a closer look at the young Nietzsche's conception of life.

2. *The Cosmology of Plastic Power*

Nietzsche believes that the degree to which a form of life can use history without degenerating into this vicious circle of memory is relative to its "plastic power," and he claims that all life possesses some degree of plastic power (*UM*, 62). Nietzsche may have been solicited to use the concept of plastic power by Emerson for Emerson uses it already in his first book,

Nature. There, he writes about "the plastic power of the human eye": the eye has the power to make nature into "κόσμος [cosmos], beauty." This can be understood to signify the capacity and effect of poetic redescription: "The eye is the best of artists" (*N*, 14). That the idea of plastic power is closely connected with the possibility of poetic disclosure in Emerson becomes clear in the very first sentence of the essay "Circles" where this figure of the disclosing eye returns: "The eye is the first circle; the horizon which it forms is the second; and throughout nature this primary figure is repeated without end" (C, 403). And also, in the second of Nietzsche's *Untimely Meditations*, plastic power repeats itself in all things living.

Yet what more precisely is "plastic power" in the young Nietzsche? It is (a) plastic (πλαστικός), which means that it has been shaped, designed, to be directed toward something; (b) power (*Kraft*), which means that it is itself further shaping the thing toward which it is plastic; that is, it is (c) both shaped and shaping. Both the thing that shapes it and the thing that it shapes is *life*. The shaping arises from life and works on life—that is, the living environment to which the individual living being relates itself. Life's plastic power is the capacity of a living being to redesign, to reshape, to transform itself by adjusting its environment. Or, as Nietzsche himself puts it, "I mean by plastic power the capacity to develop out of oneself in one's own way, to transform and incorporate [*einzuverleiben*] into oneself what is past and foreign, to heal wounds, to replace what has been lost, to recreate broken moulds" (*UM*, 62). The plastic power of a living being or a form of life is its capacity to use its *adaptation* to its environment for the benefit of an (active) *adjustment* of that environment. By "plastic power," Nietzsche, then, articulates something like Spinoza's *natura naturans* and *natura naturata*:[7] at every instance, nature is both creating and receiving.

Plastic power comes in degrees. All living beings and forms of life have it to some degree: they all are always plastic toward some ends, they have evolved, but they also creatively mold their environment and themselves, redirecting the process of life's evolution. Yet they do this with differing intensity. Nietzsche is a metaphysical naturalist in construing, as it were, a continuity between the "amoebae and us."[8] The criterion of this continuity is the scale of plastic power.

Early Nietzsche's cosmology of plastic power can be understood as relying on a combination of two metaphysical principles: ontological monism and modal pluralism. The idea of this combination can be traced back to the metaphysics of Spinoza. Ontological monism is the idea that all existence can be explained as expressing one principle. In Spinoza, this is famously *Deus sive natura* (God or nature) expressed as potentia (power).[9] Similarly, in early Nietzsche, the principle is nature expressed as plastic power. Modal pluralism, moreover, is the idea that there are several *ways* to express this principle; there is a plurality of modes of being the one thing. Spinoza famously claimed that there is an infinite number of modes of the one substance, which can be gradually ordered according to their degree of complexity along the two parallel attributes of extension and thinking, or body and mind, and individuated by their particular way to endeavor to persist in their own being (conatus).[10] Similarly, in early Nietzsche, there is a plurality of modes of plastic power, which can be ordered gradually according to the degree of their transformative capacity, each with its particular way to develop out of itself in its own way.

These two principles allow Nietzsche to distinguish between higher and lower forms of life according to the intensity of the plastic power they exhibit—that is, according to the degree to which their current shape allows them to shape their further activity. On the bottom end, we have forms of life whose activity predominantly serves their mere persistence, whereas the growth they display is arbitrary and minimal. For these forms of life, death means a collapse of this activity of self-maintenance and the dissolution of the plastic power that kept that unit of activity intact. On the top, we have forms of life whose activity is a creative quest for self-transformation, an expansion of the concept of what they are. Their activities not only serve the maintenance of the form but also strive to transform. This self-transformative mode of life Nietzsche calls "culture" (*UM*, 67, 78–79). Culture is the mode of life process that strives to transform itself.

Because forms of life are modes, not substances, they can climb up and down this ladder of plastic power: they can ascend to a "higher life," gaining creative freedom by a higher degree of plastic power, but they can also "degenerate," losing intensity by a lower degree of plastic power (*UM*, 75). Such degeneration is the cultural physician's model for social pathology. Correspondingly, ascendency is her model for health, growth, and the "liberation of life." Or, as Emerson puts it, "The health of the eye seems to demand a horizon" (*N*, 15).

The operation of plastic power then puts two requirements on any form of life. First, it must *sustain its shape*; otherwise, it would lose its plastic power and dissolve into a manifold of elements developing their own plastic powers. Any form of life must constantly reproduce itself in order to persist. To persist, its elements must be adapted to exercise *its* plastic power. I will call this the "requirement of self-maintenance." Second, any form of life must *modify its shape*; otherwise, it would not display plastic *power* but merely degenerate into a minimal intensity uncharacteristic of a living process. Life must evolve. Its plastic power must, to some extent, be exercised by its elements varying, deviating, and acting toward a modification of the current shape. They must, as it were, display some recalcitrance. I will call this the "requirement of self-transformation."

Both operations, the self-maintaining and the self-transforming, are necessary for Nietzsche.[11] But they can also conflict![12] The greater the plastic power of a form of life, the more effort its elements must invest into negotiating the extent to which their activity aims at maintaining or transforming its shape.[13]

3. History as Initiation into a Form of Life

Like "the plastic power of the human eye" in Emerson "forms the horizon," the young Nietzsche's "plastic power" denotes something shaped that is further shaping, something designed that is further designing, the process of life's evolutionary yet active redesigning, its self-maintaining and self-transformative operations. This implies further that, at any given point in time, any form of life must involve something *innate* as well as something *acquired*. In this context, Nietzsche takes up the Aristotelian metaphors of "first nature" and "second nature," with which Lovibond characterized social teleology in chapter 2, and out of which Adorno molded a counterteleological vicious circle in chapter 3.[14]

Like Aristotle, Nietzsche initially understands "first nature" as something innate, original, and "second nature" as something acquired, learned by initiation into a form of life. What is innate, first nature, Nietzsche associates with our "instincts" (*UM*, 76); what is acquired, second nature, he associates with our "habits" and "customs" (*Sitten*) (98); and the process of initiation he understands as that of "habituation" (*Gewöhnung*) (78). In order to continue, a form of life must then involve activities on the part of its elementary members to bring other members in line with its shape, to initiate the young to its ways—that is, practices of what Lovibond calls "formation." What Nietzsche calls "history" thus involves the instruction and education of the individual living members of a form of life so that the individual acquires its past.

However, as was already noted in the previous chapter, Nietzsche makes a crucial update with the intention to transform the Aristotelian picture of first and second nature: he says that "[every] first nature was once a second nature and that every victorious second nature will become a first" (*UM*, 76–77). First and second nature are, in Nietzsche, neither different "logical spaces," as in McDowell,[15] nor metaphors for ontological stages of nature. They are interchangeable placeholder terms for describing *phases* of a formative process of life—that is, of the operation of plastic power.[16]

Now, as plastic power, the ongoing redesigning of life operates by expressing, acquiring, and making traits innate. It constitutes a spiral-like movement of second and first nature: the customs of the form of life, the individual's social environment, find embodiment in the habits of the individual, which "inplant [*sic*]" a "new instinct" that is then expressed again in the social environment (*UM*, 76). *History* is a medium of this organic interaction: the individual acquires the past shape of the social environment, which makes itself inhere in that individual and becomes expressed through its activity as environment again. Whereas a minimum of history would hold us below the intensity of social life, hinder us from raising ourselves above the animal inside us, an excess of history would degenerate life toward mere self-maintenance of the form. The spiral of plastic power would stagnate into a vicious circle of second and first nature, the "malady of history."

Therefore, Nietzsche argues, we need history "in the service of life"—that is, we must learn to use history to relate back upon ourselves in order to reshape ourselves, an activity by us individuals to transform ourselves and our forms of life through our social environment (*UM*, 67, 75–77). Such "histories" relate back to the past to account for what has been acquired in order to give the first nature of the members of the form of life a specific shape; it habituates them to channeling their instincts according to prevailing or desirable customs. Therefore, history operates through formative practices directed at the living members of the form of life: "This path . . . leads through human brains! Through the brains of timorous and shortlived animals" (68).

Such educational practices are always socially asymmetrical. They involve power differences between the instructors and those to be instructed, the educators and those to be educated, typically between the old and the young. Thus, in a form of life maintaining itself through "history," one can distinguish an instructing and educating *core* from its *margins*. The core consists of those second nature customary and institutional arrangements that enable the established members to initiate less established members to act in accordance with a desirable continuation of the form of life. In order to emphasize the educational and socially asymmetrical character of historical reproduction, Nietzsche's calls the core "old-age" and the margins "youth" (*UM*, 115).

Here, Nietzsche famously distinguishes three ways in which individuals can realize these relationships, or, as he calls them, three "species of history": the "monumental," the "antiquarian," and the "critical." Social life must, first, maintain itself in order to go on, to continue as a life process; for this, it must, Nietzsche believes, relate back upon itself in the *antiquarian* mode to *preserve what is good*. This is established in ordinary life by *adapting* individuals to what their social environment values as desirable for the continuation of their form of life. The initiation, which this way of relating back upon itself results in, Wittgenstein will call "training" (*Abrichtung*): established partakers of a form of life bring maladapted members into line with that form by disciplining, telling, and showing them what must be done in order for it, or all that is allegedly valuable in it, to go on.[17] In the second meditation, Nietzsche, too, uses the concept of *Abrichtung* to characterize how the "old-age" pulls the "youth" toward the core of the form of life.[18] First nature is then adapted to second nature, the individual living being molded into form by habituation implanting socially desirable instincts in it: "The history of his city becomes for him the history of himself" (*UM*, 73). Thus, the antiquarian species of history responds to plastic power's requirement of self-maintenance.

But social life must, second, also grow in order to exhibit the kind of intensity that qualifies it as a characteristically social form of life; therefore, from time to time, every society, every organization of the social life process, must, Nietzsche believes, reflect its movement in the *monumental* mode so as to *inspire* its members to mold not only themselves but also their social environment. They must not only adapt to it but also *adjust* it. Importantly, this shaping process of the social environment operates by the reappropriation of examples from the history of the form of life itself. It uses its own past to inspire members to work toward a certain future movement. Here, individual living beings look back at the past of their form of life to something once acquired that now seems lost. They then *repair* their social environment by, as it were, assembling a jigsaw puzzle: in their past, they find the pieces that are missing in their current second nature. This resembles the simile of Neurath's boat self-repairing in open sea plank by plank,[19] discussed in chapter 2. Monumental history can be understood to adapt the second nature to itself without any reference external to its own past, laying out the puzzle one piece at the time. Michael Walzer, John McDowell, Sabina Lovibond, and others have called this type of self-repair "internal criticism."[20] Monumentalist educators therefore go beyond their antiquarian colleagues: whereas "training" (*Abrichtung*) works to bring the individual first nature in line with the social second nature, internal criticism evokes a more sincerely educational project in the sense of turning the attention of the individual living beings from merely adapting themselves to adjusting their common second nature according to internal demands and by means of its internal historical normative resources, such as the exemplary great deeds of the past. It adapts, as it were, the social environment to itself. Thus, monumental history responds to plastic power's requirement of growth.

However, Nietzsche believes that taken alone, each of these ways of social life to relate back upon its movement to reshape itself and its members tend to stagnate social life or even to degenerate it below the level of its characteristic plastic power. By simply one-sidedly adapting the individual living beings to their social second nature, the form of life will lose plastic power; without active individual living beings reconstructing their social environment, challenging their second nature, the form of life will stagnate to a minimum of growth.[21] And by simply solving the jigsaw puzzle of what has already been acquired, the form of life will only grow on its own account but never "out of itself," as was the demand for a form of life that would qualify as "culture"; even if monumentalist education can achieve growth, it cannot really self-transform. Nietzsche remarks that it thereby does injustice to its own past: the exemplary great deeds of the past were not the deeds of the form of life itself but of individuals challenging it by *deviating* from its customs. The only difference between antiquarian training and monumentalist education is that in the former case, the living beings work on adapting the individual beings' first nature to the second, while in the latter, they work to adapt the current second nature to its own past. Both species of history therefore constitute formative projects that enforce a *self-perpetuating circle of second and first nature*.

There is, however, a third species of history, Nietzsche tells. This is critical history. By critique, he believes, individual partakers of a form of life relate back upon the past in order to break away from it. They observe that the current form is not growing anymore—it is stagnating. Whereas antiquarian and monumental histories make the past present, *critical history makes the present past*. It kills what is already dead and thereby seeks to revive the form of life. Critical history is, I take it, the attempt to *disclose* the self-perpetuating circle of second and first nature. It does this by creating a break between the social second nature and the individual first nature and by envisioning an alternative second nature that would give life new form: "We . . . confront our inherited and hereditary nature with our knowledge, and through a new, stern discipline combat our inborn heritage and inplant [*sic*] in ourselves a new habit, a new instinct, a second nature, so that our first nature withers away" (*UM*, 76). As an educational project, disclosing critique, as it were, *initiates a new way of initiating individuals to the form of life*. It initiates a new education, a counterformation.

However, for making the present past, critical history must seek inspiration outside the prevailing form of life for it cannot rely on the exemplarity of what it once was or on its elites of instruction and institutional core. It can also not simply invoke its individual members' first nature because that is essentially the first nature of its second nature. What does this disclosing and critical education then feed on?

4. Decentering and Recentering a Form of Life

I suggest that the following part of *Untimely Meditations*, *Schopenhauer as Educator*, answers the question of what an education that makes the present past would look like—that is, for our present purposes, it contours the portrait of a disclosing critic. I believe that Nietzsche, in his third meditation, articulates the practice of critical disclosure as the creative recalcitrance of individuals and their social groups against the social environment that instructs and educates them. Paraphrasing Lovibond (*EF*, chap. 7, § 2), I shall call the stance of such individuals toward their social environment "speculative recalcitrance." I understand it as a kind of intentional deviation from a form of life that discloses its limitations and possibilities.

In the third meditation, Nietzsche returns to critical history as a peculiarly philosophical task: "If occupation with the history of past or foreign nations is of any value, it is of most value to the philosopher who wants to arrive at a just verdict . . . on the highest fate that can befall individual men or entire nations" (*UM*, 144). It is indeed *critical* history with which the philosopher engages. For she seeks to make the present past, to disclose the self-perpetuating circle of second and first nature: "The philosopher must deliberately under-assess [his own age] and, by overcoming the present in himself, also overcome it in the picture he gives of life, that is to say render it unremarkable and as it were *paint it over*" (145; emphasis added). The critical philosopher paints over the self-perpetuating circle of the current form of life. This is not only an expansion of Emerson's "drawing of a circle around a circle" as "painting it over"; it is also a paraphrasis of Hegel's statement in his infamous preface to *The Philosophy of Right* that philosophy grasps only a "shape of life grown old" and "paints its grey in grey."[22] By contrast, Nietzsche's turn of the phrase makes it the very task of the philosophical critic to *render* the current shape of life old and then to paint *over* it a picture of life—not in grey but, presumably, in multicolor!

Starting from this remark, one can recognize the two directions of disclosure abstractly distinguished and artificially kept apart in the previous chapter—now united as phases of one circular gesture. First, critical history has the austerely negative task of representing the present as a self-perpetuating circle. As a physician of culture, the philosopher diagnoses it as a degenerated form of life, a shape grown old, and intentionally exaggerates it as being, in fact, already dead. Or as Nietzsche puts it, "A historical phenomenon, known clearly and completely and resolved into a phenomenon of knowledge, is, for him who has perceived it, *dead*: for he has recognized in it the delusion, the injustice, the blind passion, and in general the whole earthly and darkening *horizon* of this phenomenon, and has thereby also understood its power in history. This power has now lost its hold over him insofar as he is knowing: but perhaps not insofar as he is living" (*UM*, 67; translation amended; emphasis added). The disclosing critic must grasp the dead shape of present life. This is a decentering movement of disclosure: she portrays her form of life from an alienating perspective, presenting it as *not livable anymore*. She aims at a disclosing effect by hauling her addresses from the "darkening horizon," the enclosed Emersonian circle, toward her own alienated position in order to jolt its core. But Nietzsche also remarks that if nothing living takes its place, what is dead can still persist by petrifaction; the individuals might go on living under the power of the old shape if the critic does not point to *new* life. Representing the present as old and exaggerating the old as dead are not enough.

Therefore, the second phase of critical disclosure consists in the positive task of disclosing new life. As we have seen in the preceding quote, the critic must also paint a picture of life over the old circle. In addition to the rather scientific job of grasping the old shape, the disclosing critic must take on the more poetic task of articulating new life: "History become pure, sovereign science would be for mankind a sort of conclusion of life [*Lebens-Abschluss*] and a settling of accounts with it. Historical education is something salutary and fruitful for the future only as the attendant of a mighty new current of life [*Lebensströmung*], of an evolving culture" (*UM*, 67; translation amended). Taken alone, history—even in its critical mode of relating back on itself to make the present past—is degenerating for life, in Nietzsche's view, because healing demands new life, something to affirm. It is not enough for the physician of culture to present a diagnosis—she must also participate in the curing. This is a recentering movement of disclosure: from an alienating perspective, the critic points at an alternative to her form of life as *something livable*. She aims at an educative effect by showing her addressees what their life could be.

It is easy to see that both tasks present the critic with a vital problem that applies to every form of external critique. For both de- and recentering the form of life, the disclosing critic seems to need a perspective from outside the present form of life, or, as Emerson puts it, "a point outside our hodiernal circle" (*C*, 408). In Nietzschean terms, the physician must speak from without the degenerating body. Yet, the reader might ask, if she speaks from the outside, how can her critique be disclosing on the inside? The systematic problem here is this. Ideally, social criticism should be compelling even to those who do not enter into discourse with the same commitments and worries as the critic. It appeals to community members' willingness to consider arguments that come with no positional preconditions. However, if the critique is the expression of an external standpoint that the addressees cannot be expected to share, it cannot meet that requirement. Why should then our physician's death certificate for the old form of life be valid for those enclosed in it? And why should her alternative be persuasive for them?

Let us start to trace Nietzsche's way of responding to this challenge by taking a step backward on the excavation site and look around! The physician of culture draws a circle of prevailing second and first nature so as to break it and paints a picture of life over it. In order to do this, she must place herself at least partly "outside" or "over" that circle. She must *dissociate* herself from the form of life she is about to disclose. Nietzsche is far from insensitive to the philosophical difficulty here. In fact, he notes that this necessary dissociation is "a difficult, indeed hardly achievable task" (*UM*, 145). What is original about his approach, however, is his description of where exactly the difficulty lies. According to the young Nietzsche, the dissociation demanded by critical disclosure is so intricate because "everything contemporary is importunate; it affects and directs the eye even when the philosopher does not want it to; and in the total accounting it will involuntarily be appraised too high" (144–45). Rather than normative or epistemological, the problem is, for Nietzsche, pragmatic through and thorough: given the self-perpetuating circularity of the current form of life, how could *any* form of social criticism be expected to come across as compelling and promising of practical success? The question turns into the following: From what exactly must the philosopher dissociate herself and to where can she withdraw in order for the critique to succeed?

Nietzsche's answer, I take it, is that she must find a position outside the self-perpetuating circle of second and first nature. This position, as we have seen, he already terms "culture" in the second meditation, and he continues to do so throughout the third. Nietzsche's term for the circle from which the philosopher must dissociate herself is "the state": "I am concerned here with a species of man whose teleology extends somewhat beyond the welfare of a state, with philosophers, and with these only in relation to a world which is again fairly independent of the welfare of a state, that of culture" (*UM*, 148). Somehow beyond the core societal organization of the form of life, the "state," from which the philosophical social critic must dissociate herself, there is, according to Nietzsche, the "fairly independent" "world" of "culture."²³

However, he immediately remarks that this world, out of which the disclosing critic shall paint over the self-perpetuating circle of second and first nature, is jeopardized by that very circle: "Now, how does the philosopher view the culture of our time? . . . [H]e almost thinks that what he is seeing are the symptoms of a total extermination and uprooting of culture" (*UM*, 148). The condition, which the philosopher seeks to criticize—that is, the degeneration of social life to mere maintenance of its form—threatens the very possibility of critique. The social environment tends to reduce even educated individuals to organs, mere means, of society's self-maintenance: "The cultured man [*der Gebildete*] has degenerated [*abgeartet*] to the greatest enemy of culture [*Bildung*], for he wants lyingly to deny the existence of the universal sickness and thus obstructs the physicians" (148–49). The self-perpetuating circle of second and first nature is the dystopian vision projected into the present of a sickness of social life, which affects not only individual components but its very *form*, a universal disease, a pathology affecting not only individual living beings but, as it were, their species. It is a *social* pathology, since it hinders the characteristic plastic power of social life operating through transformative critique from culture. It prevents the cultural physicians from operating from within by denying them their operating theater: "In the times when physicians are required the most, in times of great plagues, they are also most in peril. For where are the physicians for modern mankind who themselves stand so firmly and soundly on their feet that they are able to support others and lead them by the hand?" (133).

Here, we see the contours emerging of what Adorno later coins as *Bannkreis*, the vicious circle of a social second nature that continues into our individual first nature, thereby dismantling critique. *Bann* is Adorno's simile for those conditions that shape individuals into reinforcing a social environment that is hostile to their happiness and critical capacity. *Bannkreis* is the vicious circle by which those conditions are reproduced. Nietzsche is already well aware of the problem of *Bann*. In fact, he even uses this very word when he, in the second part of *Untimely Meditations*, tells his reader that the "supreme commandment" is to "to become mature and to flee from that paralyzing upbringing [*Erziehungsbann*] of the present age which sees its advantage in preventing your growth so as to rule and exploit you to the full while you are still immature" (*UM*, 95). Earlier in the text, Nietzsche asks what else is there anymore for the individual to do than to "turn his inspired hatred against that constraint [*Bann*], the so-called culture of his nation, so as to condemn what to him, as a living being . . . , is destructive and degrading" (82). In the third part of *Untimely Meditations*, again, he describes current cultural institutions as a vicious circle—namely, as "the rules and arrangements by means of which [the crowd] is brought to order and marches forward and through which all the solitary and recalcitrant, all who are looking for higher and more remote goals, are excommunicated [*in Bann gethan*]" (176). And, as noted in the previous chapter, he uses the concept of *Bannkreis* in *The Birth of Tragedy* (*BT*, 85) two years prior to the *Untimely Meditations* considered here. There, Nietzsche uses the expression "*in einen Kreis bannen*" to describe what the new Alexandrian world, born out of Euripides's and Socrates's tragic killing of the tragedy, does to the individual: it "rouse[s] all the passions from where they lie and *casts a spell around them*" and "*confin[es]* the individual *within* the smallest *circle* of solvable tasks" (54, 85; emphasis added; italics on the English words translating the German expression *in einen Kreis bannen*).

To sum up, Nietzsche initially reacts to the problem of external critique by expanding the scope of the difficulty: not only the outside but also the inside is problematic. If our form of life reproduces itself as a vicious circle, how can efficient critical opposition ever arise *in* it? How can a form of life, which continues into the innermost preintentional habitual and drive structure of the individual, be criticized from within? Nietzsche's uncompromising answer is that it cannot. At least not from within its institutional and educational core, the "state" and the "old-age." The critic needs a world of "culture" *beyond* the self-perpetuating circle of the state. Therefore, Nietzsche anchors "culture" in a world beyond any form of life claiming universality—in *nature*.[24]

5. Critical Cosmology

In order to map the place of culture in nature, Nietzsche turns, in his third meditation, again to cosmological speculation, which, indeed, can be read as developing further the conception of social life arising from the second meditation. Nietzsche stresses that philosophical critique demands the "belief in a metaphysical significance of culture" (*UM*, 175; see also 153, 157, 160, 173). Disclosure of the vicious circle requires a metaphysics on behalf of critique, a *critical cosmology*.

In the third meditation, Nietzsche claims that we are yet to become "men," yet to raise ourselves above the animal. As will become clearer further below and as has recently been stressed by Stanley Cavell and James Conant, "man" is here a reference to Emerson's idea of an "unattained but attainable self" to be disclosed, which Nietzsche takes himself to be staking out.[25] For a disclosing critique of society, however, the contrast concept to "man"—that is, "animality," the negativity against which the ethical aspiration strives—is the more significant here. I take it to stand for self-perpetuating circularity: the circle of second and first nature, enforced by antiquarian and monumental initiation, degenerates culture to merely self-maintaining animal life. Such a form of human social life is *culturally* dead. It means death to culture as the self-transformative mode of social life, because the individuals, who are instructed and educated to adapt to their society as their social environment, habitually reinforce it in its given shape.

Yet, one might ask, why should culture evolve in the first place? Nietzsche's metaphysical assumption is that in creatively recalcitrant individuals who strive to transform themselves and their environment, the plastic power of nature is itself seeking redemption from self-perpetuating circularity:

If all nature presses towards man, it thereby intimates that man is necessary for the redemption of nature from the curse of the life of the animal, and that in him existence at last holds up before itself a *mirror* in which life appears no longer senseless but in its metaphysical significance. Yet let us reflect: where does the animal cease, where does man begin?—man, who is nature's sole concern! As long as anyone desires life as he desires happiness he has not yet raised his eyes above the horizon of the animal, for he only desires more consciously what the animal seeks through blind impulse. But that is what we all do for the greater part of our lives: usually we fail to emerge out of animality, we ourselves are the animals whose suffering seems to be senseless. (*UM*, 157–58; emphasis added)

Here, "animality" is an expression of the self-perpetuating circle; this I take to become clear in the phrase "horizon of the animal." Antiquarian and monumental history do exercise plastic power consciously, but they still do it within the form of a merely animal life, working to continue the form of life. The universal social sickness of the self-perpetuating circle makes individuals' relation to their form of life a mere continuation of animals' relation to their species. Like animals, the members of a thus degenerated form of human social life reduce themselves to instruments of the senseless continuation of the current form of life, now as an overpowering society that maintains itself through the senseless suffering of its individual members.

That all nature presses toward man seems, however, an extravagantly essentialist and anthropocentric metaphysical claim, to say the least! Here Nietzsche's (meta)physician of culture is surely following Emerson's poet, who states that "nature has a higher end, in the production of new individuals, than security, namely, *ascension*, or, the passage of the soul into higher forms" (P, 458; emphasis original). What partly explains this bizarre proposition is the idea of plastic power and that Emerson and Nietzsche associate our truly becoming "men" with the idea of culture—that is, a self-transformative mode of life, the quest for a higher self. Plastic power presses toward the achievement of its self-transformative mode. It is nature operating as plastic power directing itself toward itself and doing this not only negatively in the mode of critical history but also affirmatively, giving itself positive form from what had been deviating content. Nietzsche unabashedly posits culture as the culmination of nature: "Culture [*Bildung*] is liberation" (*UM*, 130).

In the deviating individual of culture, "existence . . . holds up before itself a mirror": nature comes *reflectively* to itself. Nietzsche, the philologist, is utilizing the mirror—*speculum* in Latin—as the metaphor for the speculative character that the recalcitrant practice of culture takes. Culture is nature's coming to itself in a speculative mode. Culture is therefore not alien to nature but nature itself giving itself determinate forms by speculating.

This still might seem like a very dubious metaphysical outlook. However, also in formulating these extravagant claims, Nietzsche is, of note, following the Emersonian poet's advice to metaphysicians: "All the value which attaches to . . . [anyone] who introduces questionable facts into his cosmogony . . . is the certificate we have of departure from routine, and that there is a new witness" (P, 462). The extravagance is primarily gestural; it *shows* a departure from paths hitherto taken. Also, we do not need to commit ourselves to a vitalistic reading of plastic power as a life force causing nature to behave in certain ways; instead, we can read it in terms of what I would like to call a "critical cosmology," a poetically revisionist metaphysics sketched for the very purpose of critical disclosure.[26] It is a metaphysics sketched in the course of critical practice for mapping the place of critical practice in nature. The cosmology of plastic power would then situate social critique within the realm of nature as the disclosure of a natural process for itself.

In fact, one could make the case that Nietzsche's claim that nature presses toward culture turns out quasi-Darwinian. If the animality of the state reduces individuals to the mere means of its reproduction, then culture intensifies life's plastic power by taking control over its selective mechanism. This, I suggest, is Nietzsche's thought in the perhaps most disconcerting passage of the entire *Untimely Mediations*:

> How much one would like to apply to society and its goals something that can be learned from observation of any species of the animal or plant world: that *its only concern is the individual higher exemplar, the more uncommon, more powerful, more complex, more fruitful*—how much one would like to do this *if inculcated fancies as to the goal of society did not offer such tough resistance*! We ought really to have no difficulty in seeing that, *when a species has arrived at its limits and is about to go over into a higher species, the goal of its evolution lies . . . in those apparently scattered and chance existences which favourable conditions have here and there produced*; and it ought to be just as easy to understand the demand that, *because it can arrive at a conscious awareness of its goal, mankind ought to seek out and create the favourable conditions under which those great redemptive men can come into existence.* (*UM*, 161–62; emphasis added)

The challenge to the self-perpetuating circle of the form of life, the locus of its potential critical disclosure, lies in its *margins*, where favorable conditions produce deviations that might present reasonable challenges to the normative expectations embodied in its second nature. Now, Nietzsche's solution to the vicious circle that swallows up critique from within and forbids it from the outside starts from the observation that even the organic continuation of the species, and thus also the self-maintenance of a form of social life degenerated to "animality," inevitably produces "scattered and chance existences" in its margins. Every form of life relies on the *selection of arbitrary variations* as condition and consequence of its own reproduction.[27] Therefore, it is a mistake to think of forms of life as having clear boundaries defining what is inside and what remains outside. Rather, their limits are fluid. Their boundaries are potential thresholds of "go[ing] over into a higher species." They are *margins* inhabited by scattered and chance existences with a distanced perspective on the *core*.

Critical disclosure does then not need to assume a position in a clearly defined "outside" or to remain in the supposedly unproblematic "inside" of the criticized form of life. The form of life itself requires margins for its own reproduction, and from these borderlands, there is a distanced perspective on the home state and a privileged view into foreign lands.[28] The horizon is broadened from the margins.

Culture is a mode of social life that supports the overcoming of its own form by favoring conditions in its margins. A form of social life with culture is one that fosters a second nature plastic and powerful enough to identify, take on, and even support those borderland critical challenges. Taking up Emerson's idea of a "genius" to be disclosed (SR, 259), Nietzsche calls this the promotion of "an evolving culture and the procreation of genius" (*UM*, 142).

Nietzsche follows Emerson in believing that *every* individual living being is a unique variation.[29] Every individual has this potential for speculative recalcitrance that Emerson, too, calls "genius," or the "unattained but attainable self" (H, 239), yet to be disclosed by a great work of art (SR, 259). But realizing that potential, Nietzsche believes, demands a tremendous effort because the form of life itself tends to put it in *chains*—a circle! He states, "Each of us bears a productive uniqueness within him as the core of his being; and when he becomes aware of it, there appears around him a strange penumbra which is the mark of his singularity. Most find this something unendurable, because . . . a chain of toil and burdens is suspended from this uniqueness [*weil an jener Einzigkeit eine Kette von Mühen und Lasten hängt*]" (*UM*, 143). The potential of each of us to present a challenge to the current form of life is socially restricted; it is put in chains—that is, bound in the cold lifeless circle of society, which continues deep into the individual's relation to herself. "Chain" appears already in Emerson's "Circles" as a placeholder for the circle around which a circle is to be drawn, for what is to be disclosed. Recall, the poet, he writes, "*breaks up my whole chain of habits*, and I open my eyes to my own possibilities" (C, 409). In his essay "The Poet," he confesses that when reading a poem, *"my chains are to be broken. . . .* That will reconcile me to life, and renovate nature, to see trifles animated by a tendency, and to know what I am doing" (P, 451; emphasis added).

Interestingly, Adorno follows on the same note. This Nietzschean "chain of toil and burdens" resembles what he, in his sociological tracing of *Bannkreis*, calls "concretism," the socially caused inability of individuals to abstract from their immediate action context, which averts them from socially transformative action (*PETS*, 40–41). In the next chapter, I will look closer at concretism and the other sociological models by which Adorno draws a circle around the *Bannkreis*. But in the present context, it is curious enough to note the metaphorical vocabulary reminiscent of Nietzsche's *Untimely Mediations* that Adorno uses to describe concretism. It marks, he writes, the everyday social phenomenon "that the people who are given the burden, and consequently walk bent over with their heads bowed, that it has always been very hard for them to hold those heads up high . . . and see more than their immediate interests" (41). The consciousness of individuals is tied so firmly to the immediately given conditions that any critical reflection on them or attempt to reshape them becomes nearly unimaginable—it is put in chains. In contrast to Emerson and Nietzsche, however, Adorno emphasizes the lure of the chains. He thinks that these chains are so hard for the individuals to resist because they alleviate their pain of experiencing their own impotence every day, finding themselves confronted with overwhelming social powers. For this reason, Adorno is rather skeptical of the timeliness of Marx and Engels's conclusion that the workers have only their chains to lose.[30] Adorno calls this lure of the chains the "affective power" of *Bannkreis* (35). The overwhelming adaptive pressure from the social environment affects the individuals to the extent that they turn the affect into a "feeling of powerlessness" (*Gefühl der Ohnmacht*) and let it sink in (MGH, 213).

Similar to Adorno's initial description of concretism, Nietzsche describes the affect of being enclosed in this vicious circle as "suffocation" or "drowning,"[31] and the opposite movement of raising one's head above the surface to observe the stream can then be read as a metaphor for disclosure: "We feel at the same time that we are too weak to endure those moments of profoundest contemplation for very long and that we are not the mankind towards which all nature presses for its redemption: it is already much that we should raise our head above the water at all, even if only a little, and observe what stream it is in which we are so deeply immersed. And even this momentary emerging and awakening is not achieved through our own power, we have to be lifted up—and who are they who lift us?" (*UM*, 159). Each of us is a unique variation, each of us possesses a genius, a higher self yet to be disclosed. But not everyone, Nietzsche seems to say, has the plastic power to take on these affects of one's form of life and to turn them into a picture of a higher life—to be a physician of culture is an *art*. Her practice demands a particular plastic power. It requires not only the methods and knowledge of a critical historian that are necessary for the correct diagnosis; it also demands a certain sensibility for social suffering and specific skills of turning, through that sensibility, knowledge into painting.[32]

6. Critical Recalcitrance: Judging, Feeling, Painting

Nietzsche believes that the vicious circle can be broken by a speculative recalcitrance coming from the margins of a form of life and disclosing that form of life by showing an example. Yet what is speculative recalcitrance? Clearly, not all deviations from the normative expectations embodied in the second nature of a form of life are critical and disclosing. Most of them are meaningless, futile, or downright wrongful. And, as we have seen, the intention to give them transformative power is mostly put in chains by concretism. In the young Nietzsche's words, "Who are they who lift us up?" (*UM*, 159).

Nietzsche does deliver criteria for conditions that speculative recalcitrance must meet in order to count as critical rather than just criminal. The critical exemplarity, which can truly challenge the allegedly universal form of present second nature and disclose its self-perpetuating circularity, must include (a) the negativity of critical history, making the present past; (b) the positivity of a new picture of life, modifying the social environment to something that can be freely affirmed; and (c) a sensibility for social suffering, directing the negative and the positive tasks. Speculative recalcitrance is, Nietzsche believes, critical by virtue of its location in a certain conjunction of judgment, feeling, and speculation:

There is a kind of denying and destroying that is the discharge of [a] mighty longing for sanctification and salvation. . . . *All that exists that can be denied deserves to be denied*; and being truthful means: to believe in an existence that can in no way be denied and which is itself true and without falsehood. That is why the truthful man *feels* that the meaning of his activity is *metaphysical*, explicable through the *laws of another and higher life*, and in the profoundest sense *affirmative*: however much all that he does may appear to be destructive of the laws of this life and a crime against them. (*UM*, 153; emphasis added)

Here, again, the practice of the disclosing critic looks much like some sort of external critique—a critique that judges the form of life on external criteria.[33] After all, its meaning is expressed in "the laws of another and higher life." Yet this, I believe, would be a too-hasty conclusion. Note that the laws of the higher life are not the basis of a judgment upon current life: the present form of life is "denied" on *its own terms*, whereas the laws of the other life are instead "in the profoundest sense affirmative." The disclosed higher life is therefore not a normative standard for the negative judgment upon the current form of life. On the contrary, it presents a speculative hypothesis of a life worth affirming derived at through "feeling" and "denying" current life. In fact, it seems to me that Nietzsche is here in his statement that "all that exists that can be denied deserves to be denied," expanding Emerson's idea from the essay "Circles" that "every action admits of being outdone. Our life is an apprenticeship to the truth that around every circle another can be drawn" (C, 403). And Emerson, too, makes clear that the disclosing circle must be drawn *around* the criticized one: "[A man] can only be reformed by showing him a new idea which commands his own" (404).

Not only would it be misleading to represent the cultural physician's disclosing critique as an external judgment on the current form of life, but it would also be wrong to reduce her practice of critique to normative judgment as such. For following the negative judgment comes *speculation*. Nietzsche describes the speculative task as being *felt*: as a metaphysician, the physician of culture lets herself be affected by the plastic power in the form of life and channels that affect into a transformative practice. Remember that Nietzsche described the affirmative task as "painting"! Metaphysical speculation thus presents a kind of poetic redescription of life following the scientific, critical-historical refutation of the current form of life. The (meta)physician of culture is both a scientist and an artist.

Speculation grows out of the refutation with the task of lending expression to a higher life that can be freely affirmed. Because speculative recalcitrance arises from the felt senseless suffering and the immanent negation of the current form of life, the physician of culture is a disclosing critic in both negating the present form of life and affirming new life *in one and the same circular gesture*. Her refutation of the present is accompanied by the expression of a higher form of life already present yet suppressed, shoveled to the margins, as it were. This involves metaphysical speculation as an artistic enterprise. Disclosing critique may involve normative judgment but cannot be reduced to it: Nietzsche shows that it must also include feeling and speculation.

The physician of culture, Nietzsche stresses, suffers in order to overcome the suffering of the present (*UM*, 154–55). This is her peculiar plastic power: she lets herself be affected by the current social environment and channels those affects into something higher. Instead of devastation, her plastic power turns her suffering into a "longing for a stronger nature, for a healthier and simpler humanity" (146). She turns undergoing into doing, reshapes what is shaping her: "That heroism of truthfulness consists in one day ceasing to be the toy [that the eternal becoming] plays with" (155). As much as his "denial" of everything "that can be denied" anticipates Adorno's negativism, Nietzsche conceives his "educator," or the physician of culture, following the model of the "poet" found in the work of his own educator, Emerson. In Emerson, it is namely the power to both *feel* and *express* suffering of the current form of life that characterizes the poet: "The poet is the person in whom these powers are in balance, the man without impediments, who sees and handles that which others dream of, traverses the whole scale of experience, and is representative of man, in virtue of being the largest power to receive and impart" (P, 448).

Critical recalcitrance is then a specific type of individual deviation from the normative expectations crystallized in the second nature of a form of life. It requires (a) becoming aware of one's uniqueness, of the extent to which one deviates from the second nature to which the antiquarians seek to "train" us; (b) expressing this deviation in a way that truly challenges the current self-perpetuating circle of second and first nature; and (c) doing so as the member of a specific kind of community, which Nietzsche calls a "circle of culture." Let's call the first condition "self-reflexivity," the second "critical creativity," and the third "countercommunity." Becoming reflexive of one's deviation is part of dissociating oneself from the self-perpetuating circle and participating in its decentering movement (i.e., the diagnosis). Expressing this deviation is part of delivering something positive to affirm and participating in the recentering movement (i.e., the cure). Yet what does it mean to be part of a "circle of culture"?

7. Circles of Culture: Counterformation in and from the Margins

As such, disclosing critique does not, at least not necessarily, operate by reference to universal normative standards. Therefore, it also does not rely on "external standards," as Honneth assumes.[34] Instead, it is defined pragmatically: disclosing critique is defined by its disclosing effects. It can approach communicative rationality by means of an immanent negation that leads up to the expression of a particular experience from the margins of the criticized form of life, an expression of life; this refutation, and the speculation to which it gives rise, challenges the alleged universality of a form of life enclosed in a self-perpetuating circle. In other words, Nietzsche shows that instead of external universal standards, disclosing critique can operate by *marginal exemplarity*. However, to fulfill the requirement of being compelling as a form of criticism, disclosing critique relies on its disclosing effects. Eventually, as we already saw in the previous chapter, this reliance makes it constitutively dependent on its reception—that is, on the capacity of its expression to become effective in the practice of the addressees. It achieves, as it were, its rationality in execution.

Because of the reliance on reception, disclosing critique cannot be practiced alone. It is a social practice. The young Nietzsche shows with more clarity than anyone else in my canon of disclosing critique that the particular social form disclosing critique takes is that of education. Practicing critique in this educational sense presupposes recalcitrant individuals who are willing to grow beyond themselves by learning from examples. This education thus takes the shape of a *counterformation*: it educates against the education from the core of the prevailing social teleology by a cultivation of recalcitrant tendencies. On this Nietzschean view, disclosing critique requires that these "scattered chance existences" in the borderlands *organize* themselves as *countercommunities*. Expanding, again, on Emerson's metaphor, he calls such communities "circles of culture."[35]

Like antiquarian training and monumentalist internal criticism, such communities exhibit *power asymmetries* between educators and disciples. But Nietzsche is confident that this time around, the purpose of education is not primarily to adapt individuals to the environment nor to adjust it. Rather, it is to transform oneself by transforming the form of life: "Your educators can be only your liberators [*Befreier*]" (*UM*, 129). Disclosing critique of the form of life is an educational project that focuses not on the concrete universal, as do antiquarian training and monumentalist internal criticism.

By judging, feeling, and painting, it instead seeks to initiate a learning process among the members of the form of life to let themselves be compelled by a picture of life emerging from the margins. It focuses our attention toward those among us who do not conform and, more precisely, who do not conform in the specific mode of self-reflexivity and critical creativity characteristic of speculative recalcitrance.

Yet the power asymmetries in these communities must be different from those of antiquarian training and monumentalist internal criticism. Nietzsche emphasizes that in these countercommunities, the asymmetries must be shaped such that education becomes an issue of helping the recipients to elevate themselves to "culture"—that is, not primarily to adaptation but to awareness of one's own deviation and chance existence; the education is counterteleological. Like how Lovibond assumes that ethical formation must "take advantage of [a] mimetic impulse" in us (*EF*, 139; see also chapter 2), Nietzsche's idea of "nature pressing towards culture" includes the idea of an impulse in our first nature to *cultivate recalcitrance*. He also underlines that this inclination for counterformation is something we all already possess: "They long for a culture, for a transfigured *physis*" (*UM*, 145; emphasis original), and "we [already] know what culture is" (161). Having activated this inclination to education in the addressee, the disclosing critic then avoids making him "malicious and envious," and instead, she helps him to "turn his soul in another direction so that it shall not consume itself in vain longing" (160). When she has helped the recipient to turn his soul, "he will *discover* a new circle" (160; emphasis original). The discovery of what has been disclosed must be undertaken by the recipients themselves. The circle around the circle must be drawn both by the poet and the reader, as Emerson's "Circles" would have it.

In "The American Scholar," Emerson distinguishes three stages of the education of the scholar: "by nature, by books, by action" (AS, 63). Nietzsche now seems to take up Emerson's idea but by modifying it into a more social direction, only preserving the last of Emerson's stages. He namely identifies three "consecrations to culture": "love," "judgment," and "deed." I suggest that they can be read as three phases of the reception of a disclosing gesture. "Love alone," he writes, "can bestow on the soul, not only a clear, discriminating and self-contemptuous view of itself, but also the desire to look beyond itself and to seek with all its might for a higher self as yet still concealed from it." The disclosure of one's higher self proceeds through "attach[ing]" one's "heart" to an educator and "hat[ing] one's own narrowness."

Love corresponds then to the first condition for speculative recalcitrance I dubbed "self-reflexivity": becoming aware of one's uniqueness, one's recalcitrant tendencies, one's deviation from the expectations of the antiquarian trainers. "Judgment," Nietzsche continues, marks the "rediscover[y]" of the "great world of action"; one applies one's newly discovered longing for culture as "the alphabet by means of which [one] can now read off the aspirations of mankind as a whole." One passes, in other words, a critical judgment on the form of life, diagnoses it as ill, and exaggerates it as already dead. "Deed," finally, means the "struggle on behalf of culture and hostility towards those influences, habits, laws, institutions in which [one] fails to recognize [one's] goal" (*UM*, 163). The educated now goes on to actively modify the social environment as part of her own education—social transformation as part of self-transformation. Judgment and deed then correspond to the second condition of critical recalcitrance, "critical creativity," expressing one's deviation in a way that challenges the current self-perpetuating circle of second and first nature.

In becoming speculatively recalcitrant in such an educational environment, the recipients are enabled to perform the disclosure themselves. Of note, in Nietzsche, similarly to the initiation by which the form of life maintains itself (training and internal criticism), the disclosing initiation to culture is a *circle* too. In fact, this initiation *is* the "circle of culture." Through love, the individual molds her first nature, reshapes her impulses, and redirects her instincts by a new habituation, a modification of her individual second nature. Through judgment and deed, she then returns to a new social environment—that of a countercommunity. It is, however, not the old kind of initiation that pulls the margins toward the core but a new kind that *decenters* the form of life. However, Nietzsche, in his use of the metaphor of a circle around the circle, is more attentive than Emerson to the curious circumstance that the adaptive pressures of the social environment can be resisted by the same operation by which it persists: by education understood as a circle of habituation.[36]

In the initiation into a "circle of culture," the decentering movement of critical disclosure is completed. Yet how is the recentering movement of disclosure to be understood? Wherein does the affirmative aspect of this cultivation of recalcitrance lie? What shape shall the philosopher-cum-artist paint over the old grey shape of life in multicolor? What, if anything, does her "picture of life" represent? Nietzsche recognizes the urgency of these issues and seeks to respond to them: "The hardest task still remains: to say how a new *circle of duties* may be derived from this ideal and how one can proceed towards so *extravagant* a goal through a practical activity [*regelmässige Tätigkeit*]—in short, to demonstrate that this ideal *educates*" (*UM*, 156; emphasis added).

What the philosopher paints over the vicious circle is *another circle*. "The hardest task" for a disclosing critique of forms of life is to be not merely destructive and speculative but also educative. In other words, disclosing critique must go beyond the refutation of the current form of life and the painting of higher life to actually participating in the establishment of a new *form* of life—that is, a new crystallization of normative expectations in a social second nature. Like the instruction it opposes, it, too, involves *formation*, the initiation of individuals into the second nature of a form of life. It must complete the decentering education of the marginal "circle of culture" with a recentering education.[37]

That the speculative painting must amount to a "new circle of duties" means at least two things. First, what is truly transformative must also be *reproducible*. The recentering result must be a new *circle*—that is, a social second nature shaping our individual first nature with greater plastic power. As the hope of the critical historian went, "Every victorious second nature will become a first" (*UM*, 77). The difficulty is to establish this new mode of habitual and customary practice according to an *extravagant* goal, something disclosed beyond (*extra*) the path that social life has so far traversed (*vagari*). The danger is namely that the critic's "dignity and loftiness can only turn our heads and thereby exclude us from any participation in the world of action; coherent duties, the even flow of life are gone" (156). Like Emerson and Adorno, Nietzsche's disclosing critic stumbles on a robust demand for immanence. Critique must hit its target. But this relation of immanence between the critic and the object is, for Nietzsche, primarily a question of the practicality of critique—it is a predominantly pragmatic issue: the disclosed path, as extravagant as it may seem, must be *traversable*. It must express a "new circle of duties," which are fulfillable for the higher selves that this formation is to disclose in us. Counterformation must materialize in a new *form* of life—that is to say, in new habits, customs, and institutions.

Second, that new circle must establish a new normativity with some degree of antiquarian and monumental education. This is why Nietzsche describes the result of disclosure as a new circle of *duties* and emphasizes it as a *regelmässige Tätigkeit*, a "customary activity," action shaped and stabilized by modified habits. The new educational organization requires that "from that ideal image it is possible to fasten upon ourselves a chain of fulfillable duties, and that some of us already feel the weight of this *chain*" (UM, 157; emphasis added). The painting must actually be *affirmable*. The affirmability of the painting includes that the duties must be fulfillable by the higher selves of current living human beings. The disclosed form of life must be felt by some members of the current form of life, the "duties" it implies must be fulfillable by those who would be its partakers, and some of those of the current form of life must be receptive to the philosopher's disclosing education. Tellingly, as if emphasizing its second nature character, Nietzsche, to describe the new form of life, chooses the same metaphor as he used above for describing the oppressing character of the old: "chain."

By contrast, neither Adorno nor Emerson ever speaks of new chains replacing the ones broken by the poet. This is an important difference in implication, I gather, between taking the "critical theorist," the "poet," or the "educator" as figures for the disclosing critic. Whereas Nietzsche's educational recentering operates itself as a process of habituation, the Emersonian poet recenters by initiating into a new aspect: "We love the poet. . . . He unlocks our *chains*, and admits us to a *new scene*" (P, 463; emphasis added).

However, even if, for Nietzsche, the new form of life includes circular moments of antiquarian training and monumentalist internal criticism, it cannot present a *self-perpetuating* circle of second and first nature. Training and internal criticism do remain, but they lose their privileged positions in the educational organization. Instead, the new picture of life, which the physician of culture paints over the old circle, presents a *culture*—that is, a form of life that is plastic and powerful enough to embrace the creative social recalcitrance coming from such countercommunities, a life in which individual living beings are plastic and powerful enough to hang their hearts on critical educators, cultivate their recalcitrance, and challenge their form of life.

In the meantime, the countercommunity at the margin of the old form can itself serve as a lab for that new form of life. In that community, not only the negativity but also the new positivity of the self-perpetuating circularity is *felt*. The margin operates as a mediator between the old and the new center. The community, the circle of culture, channels the negative affect of the old form of life into the positive affect of a higher life, which can be expressed in speculation and established through formation. The margin then presents to the core a picture of life that claims exemplary force for the formation of social life. The circle turns into a circle of circles that shifts the horizon toward a spiral movement.

Three pragmatic demands of immanence of recentering disclosure can then be identified: (a) the new duties must be fulfillable for (the higher selves of) current individuals; (b) the coming form of life must be already felt by some (marginal) participants of the current form of life; and (c) some members of the current form of life must be receptive to disclosing counterformation.

8. Excavating the (Meta)Physician of Culture

In the second part of *Untimely Meditations*, Nietzsche presents life as a process that must both maintain a form and transform. A form of life must both reproduce itself and grow out of itself. Life can fail at each task as well as at their mediation. Then, it would either stagnate or die. Furthermore, in order to grow, in particular, the life process must both relate back to its past and break away from it. The operation of plastic power, of life relating back upon itself so as to grow out of itself and, as it were, into its new "higher self," essentially both requires and repels "history." It must both dwell on its past and let it go. It must make the past present by adapting individuals to the environment and adjusting the environment through the individuals but also make the present past by letting individuals transform the environment in the course of their self-transformation. History is the specific way a social life process relates back upon itself to design and shape itself. Because social life evolves by such practices of self-design, social criticism, to Nietzsche, has a primarily aesthetic character. The model of critique emerging from the young Nietzsche's meditations on the physician of culture amounts then not to a type of normative judgment. Although it certainly involves judgments, it cannot be reduced to critical judgment—be it internal, external, or immanent. Instead, it is a kind of design, an artistic practice, a gesture. But there is also room for science—namely, in killing the old form of life by demonstration of its suffocating circularity, its mere "animality." In the figure of the physician of culture, the scientist and the artist merge. I have suggested to read that figure as a model for the disclosing critic.

In the third part of *Untimely Meditations*, Nietzsche presents his extravagant cosmology. The (meta)physician of culture emerges from a specific type of individual deviation—namely, what I have, paraphrasing Lovibond, termed "speculative recalcitrance" in an attempt to disclose the suffocating form that social life has come to take under a self-perpetuating circle of second and first nature. This version of the vicious circle not only mediates between Emerson's "society" and Adorno's *Bannkreis* but, for Nietzsche, presents a "universal sickness." It is the alleged universal of the form of life itself that has become pathological. The task of the physician of culture is to diagnose and cure the life enclosed in that form. The cure demands preexisting receptivity for disclosure in the guise of counterformative communities. Like any physician, she can only help individuals to help themselves. By drawing the current circle in the mode of critical history and painting a new circle over it in a speculative mode, she helps her recipients to lift themselves up, but they eventually have to perform the disclosure themselves as active participants of formation in "circles of culture," or Nietzschean (rather aristocratic) countercommunities. I have suggested that Nietzsche thus takes Emerson's "drawing a circle around the circle" to present primarily an educational task: disclosing critique develops as a self-organized counterteleological cultivation of present recalcitrant tendencies. The young Nietzsche's further development of Emerson's metaphor of drawing a circle around the circle shows that disclosing critique can be conceived as a social practice whose particular social form is that of education. Nietzsche's counterformative critique of society continues Emerson's poetic disclosure.

Toward the end of the second meditation, Nietzsche says, "Only give me life, then I will create a culture for you out of it" (*UM*, 119–20). Like Emerson, Nietzsche paraphrases Archimedes: "δῶς μοι πᾷ στῶ καὶ τὰν γᾶν κινάσω" (Give me the place to stand, and I shall turn the world). That makes Nietzsche say, "Give me a position outside our form of life, and I shall transform it." Like how Emerson's poet takes "a point outside our hodiernal circle" (C, 408), Nietzsche's (meta)physician of culture seeks a position outside our horizon so as to expand our horizon. Like for Emerson and Adorno, this location has something to do with randomness and chance, but his account of that landscape is incomparably richer than that of his educator Emerson. Nietzsche believes that every form of life, no matter how vicious its circle, inevitably produces "scattered and chance existences" in its margins; it relies on the selection of arbitrary variations as condition and consequence of its persistence. Therefore, part of the surely repugnant metaphysical baggage with which early Nietzsche's example of disclosing critique comes is intended for showing that the limits of a form of life are always fluid like those of natural species—insofar as we have the chance of understanding them at least since Darwin.

Nietzsche's description of the space and practice of "drawing a circle around a circle" is richer than Emerson's but with the cost of an extravagant metaphysics. Problematic for contemporary social critique are, at least, two aspects of this critical cosmology. First is its glorification of activity and growth at the expense of, say, mimetic capacities and contemplation. Probably, disclosing critics should keep open the transformative potential of *just stopping*—that is, the possibility of, beyond any thought of growth, halting the continuation of the catastrophe that is contemporary society and only then considering alternative paths. And certainly, disclosing critics should keep in mind the human and environmental costs of any glorification of growth. The second is the blatant anthropocentrism of Nietzsche's critical cosmology. Talk of "man" as "nature's sole concern" has lost its critical force in the age of man-made mass extinction. A question Nietzsche then leaves for his own disciples in the tradition of disclosing critique is whether his insights can be held on to without speculative metaphysics or with more plausible metaphysical assumptions.

Whatever one's feelings about the young Nietzsche's metaphysics (or his aristocratic tendencies) are, it should, I believe, in no way discredit his great insight for disclosing critique that, rather than clear boundaries, forms of life have fuzzy edges—borderlands inhabited by recalcitrant tendencies and recalcitrant individuals.[38] When these individuals organize themselves in educational countercommunities and offer each other mutual aid in cultivating their recalcitrant tendencies, the form of life may be decentered, and a recentering formation might begin. From the margins, one sees beyond the center's horizon. And the higher one rises, the further it will span. Rather than his anthropocentrism or aristocratic fraternity kink, the baring of this insight rather hangs on a further assumption that Nietzsche, following Emerson, makes: we all carry a genius, a higher self to be disclosed. Curiously, this assumption becomes problematic for the disclosing critics at the end of our timeline, Dewey and Adorno, whose much more bleak uses of our leading metaphors will be mapped in the next chapter. In chapter 6, I will then investigate the fate of the Emersonian and Nietzschean assumption of a higher self by reading a reader of Nietzsche—Sigmund Freud.

Both Emerson and Nietzsche lament the lack of disclosing critics, of "poets" and "educators," in their respective time and place. "Never have moral [*sittliche*] educators been more needed," Nietzsche says, "and never has it seemed less likely they would be found" (*UM*, 133). Surprisingly, in the end of his essay on the poet, Emerson mourns, "I look in vain for the poet whom I describe" (P, 465). Emerson's statement is absolute: "the poet" does, after all, not exist. She is the description of a lack, a utopian gesture. While Emerson does not find the poet that he is describing in his essays, Nietzsche does find an educator in the end—namely, Emerson:

> Let an American tell them what a great thinker who arrives on this earth signifies as a new centre of tremendous forces. "Beware," says Emerson, "when the great God lets loose a thinker on this planet. Then all things are at risk. It is as when a conflagration has broken out in a great city, and no man knows what is safe, or where it will end. There is not any literary reputation, not the so-called eternal names of fame, that may not be revised and condemned; the things which are dear to men at this hour are so on account of the ideas which have emerged on their mental horizon, and which cause the present order of this, as a tree bears its apples. *A new degree of culture would instantly revolutionize the entire system of human pursuits.*" (*UM*, 193; emphasis original)

By the utopian description of the "poet," Emerson elevates himself to an "educator"—for Nietzsche, the (meta)physician of culture. But this, too, is a utopian figure: the character of the disclosing "educator," in the third meditation, is, for the young Nietzsche, an heir to the utopian figure of the "artistic Socrates" from *The Birth of Tragedy* (*BT*, 71)—a character who would be able to integrate art and knowledge into critical disclosing gestures that would help make social life tolerable.

How educative is Nietzsche's figure of the educator? To be sure, its history of reception belongs to the most controversial and complicated in the entire history of modern Western philosophy and evades the excavation work of a metaphor history of critical disclosure. But its aristocratic tendency of persuading the reader to adopt Nietzsche as their imaginary educator and friend is undeniable and points to Nietzsche's failure of practicing his Emersonian ideal of alienating the reader from the poet.[39] And this tendency creeps into his model of disclosing critique: he declares that, on the one hand, "your educators can be only your liberators" and, on the other, this education puts the recipient through "consecrations to culture" and in a "new chain of duties." How liberating are such educators *really*? Nevertheless, his extensions of the metaphor of drawing a circle around the circle did help generate further models of disclosing critique, some of which I will excavate in the following chapters.

Let me conclude by rephrasing four points. First, the cosmology of plastic power is nothing separate from the early Nietzsche's social criticism. In fact, it is this cosmology that allows his project of disclosing critique to proceed as the "praxis" of a physician of culture, diagnosing and curing social pathologies. Second, such speculatively recalcitrant social critique is, in his view, part and parcel of its own object—"social life." Social life is namely the kind of life that refers to critical disclosure as one of its three ways to modify its form. Third, the critical practice of the physician of culture is *immanent* in the sense of speaking from within life, responding to the requirements of plastic power, and yet it is *disclosing* too in the sense of speaking from outside the form of life, at least from outside its institutional core—that is, from an "Archimedean point" in its margins—in order to expand the concept of what we are. Fourth, as such an operator of plastic power, of life's activity of redesigning itself, social criticism has a primarily aesthetic and educational character. It aims not at judgment but rather mobilizes judgment as a phase of redesign and growth. The physician is simultaneously a scientist and an artist. Therefore, Nietzsche develops an aesthetic metaphysics for critical purposes—a critical cosmology. "Critical" does not, however, mean "negative" to Nietzsche. In contrast to his later minimalist metaphysics of the will to power,[40] the cosmology of plastic power has positive content: it develops a performative theory of nature that explains how the physician of culture, the disclosing critic, can operate from inside *and* outside her form of life.

FIVE

Society as Experience
Adaptation and Exemplarity in Adorno and Dewey

> Every ultimate fact is only the first of a new series.
> Every general law only a particular fact of some more
> general law presently to disclose itself.
>
> —RALPH WALDO EMERSON, "Circles"

> När natten kommer
> står jag på trappan och lyssnar,
> stjärnorna svärma i trädgården
> och jag står ute i mörkret.
> Hör, en stjärna föll med en klang!
> Gå icke ut i gräset med bara fötter;
> min trädgård är full av skärvor.
>
> *When night comes*
> *I stand on the threshold and listen,*
> *the stars swarm in the garden*
> *and I stand outside in the dark.*
> *Hark, a star has fallen with a clang!*
> *Do not go out into the grass with bare feet;*
> *my garden is full of splinters.*
>
> —EDITH SÖDERGRAN, "Stjärnorna"

Who needs Critical Theory? Critique is the consequence of critiquing, an activity of an organism in an environment. The young Nietzsche believed that critical history is a concrete response of a "timorous and shortlived animal" to an oppressive environment (*UM*, 68): "Only he who is oppressed by a present need [*gegenwärtige Noth*], and who wants to throw off this burden at any cost, has need [*Bedürfniss*] of critical history" (72). Even if translated here as "need," the nouns *Not* and *Bedürfnis* are used quite differently in ordinary German. *Bedürfnis* could also be translated as "requirement," "want," "necessity," or "desideratum." *Not*, by contrast, could be expressed in English as "poverty," "distress," "hardship," or "emergency." We might then say that Nietzsche believes critical history to constitute something like a requirement for a liberating response to an oppressing present distress. Max Horkheimer, in his "Traditional and Critical Theory," uses the same terms when he contrasts to traditional theory the thought of the critical theorist: "The goal at which the latter aims, namely the rational state of society, is forced upon him by present distress [*Not der Gegenwart*]."[1] However, formulating a theory seems a quite-different reaction from writing a history.

There are many ways to frame a question that could orient through the landscape of such a polycentric philosophical project as that of the Frankfurt school's critical theory. A candidate that would both seem untimely enough in our current age of umpteen emergencies and, historically, date all the way back to Horkheimer's program is, Why do social crises and catastrophes not lead to social transformation? At the heart of Adorno's response to that question lies the still only vaguely contoured idea of *Bannkreis*, which we have come to be acquainted with in the previous chapters as a gesture of pointing to a form of social life that is caught in an antagonistic yet self-perpetuating vicious circle. In particular, it seeks to show how and why individuals act in ways that stabilize social conditions that restrict their experience. Disclosing critique, as I am going to suggest in this chapter, can be found at the very core of the project of the Frankfurt school's critical theory.

I am also going to suggest that it can be found at the core of another significant tradition of twentieth-century social philosophy, too: American pragmatism—namely, in John Dewey's later social thought. I understand that these suggestions might raise some eyebrows. A long line of criticism of American pragmatism by Frankfurt school critical theorists has, despite sympathies, targeted John Dewey's social philosophy at precisely this point: he lacks, it is claimed, the theoretical means necessary for a *radical* critique of society. A Deweyan experimental method cannot, so the argument goes, be transferred to social critique because the criticized form of life can be made immune to transformative claims from within.[2] Herbert Marcuse, in his review of Dewey's *Logic*, already concluded *contra* Deweyan experimentalism that a truly critical theory must be capable of transcending given experience by reference to reason, freedom, and similar "metaphysical instances."[3] Similarly, Rahel Jaeggi—a contemporary critical theorist who, besides Hegel, takes Dewey as the most important inspiration for her model of a "critique of forms of life"—claims that there is no potential in Dewey's work for the conceptualization of "systematic learning blockages."[4]

However, Dewey does in fact formulate his approach to social critique as a response to the problem that social life might be made immune to transformative claims. In *Human Nature and Conduct*, thirty years prior to Adorno's *Bannkreis*, he conceptualizes a vicious circle in which attempts to transform social life seem to be caught and points to a way out (*HNC*, 88–91).

In this chapter, I seek to show that Adorno and Dewey share in a project at the heart of critical theory—the project of a disclosing critique of society. In different and mutually complementing ways, the Frankfurt school critical theorist and the American pragmatist point out the extent to which their contemporary societies are caught in antagonistic and painful vicious circles and thereby point to the objective possibility of another form of social life. I will first characterize the idea of a vicious circle in both authors' work. I will identify two differences between them: the first pertains to the gesture of *pointing out* the vicious circle, the other, to that of *pointing to* another form of life—that is, the different ways in which they as disclosing critics seek to decenter and recenter the form of life. The first difference is a disagreement about the role of *theory* in critical disclosure. The second difference is different; it consists not in a disagreement but in diverging attitudes toward *disclosing reason*. All of this is animated by my impression, whose plausibility I seek to show in the course of this chapter, that of all exemplary disclosing critics reconstructed in this metaphorology, Adorno and Dewey are by far the most useful for brushing a fruitful path for a disclosing critique of society today.

1. Pointing out the Vicious Circle: Adaptation and Exemplarity

At the center of Adorno's critical theory of society lies the problem of *Bann* or *Bannkreis*, which we became acquainted with in chapter 3: Why do individuals systematically act in ways that reinforce conditions that are obviously incompatible with their freedom and pursuit of happiness? Philosophically, the term *Bannkreis* is something of a protologism. The previous chapters have presented evidence that Adorno picks it up from the young

Nietzsche, who, again, expands on Emerson's metaphor for critical disclosure, "drawing a circle around a circle." But the term has a link to ordinary language too. In vernacular German, it namely denotes the sphere (*Kreis*) of influence of a person or a thing under whose spell (*Bann*) one might fall. In this sense, one could, for example, say about a student who fell under the strong influence of a teacher that *er wurde in ihren Bannkreis gezogen*. In English, one might similarly say that the student was "spellbound" by the teacher. Moreover, German law also contains the legal term *befriedeter Bezirk*, meaning a "pacified area," which marks the ground around a government institution isolated during a protest and which ordinary German language usage knows as *Bannmeile* or *Bannkreis*. Here, *Bannkreis* denotes what one in ordinary English would call a "no-protest zone." Furthermore, in Adorno's usage, *Bannkreis* also becomes closely associated with *Täufelskreis* (*circulus vitiosus*), meaning "vicious circle," and this is also how the term is mostly translated into English.

This allows an initial distinction of three semantic components of Adorno's *Bannkreis*. First, as a sphere of influence, society *attracts* the individuals, pulls them closer to itself, puts them under a spell to act in ways that are to its benefit. Second, as a pacified area, it *repels* the individuals, pushes them away from its power core, keeps them at a distance that is to its benefit. Third, as a *circulus vitiosus*, this push and pull creates a double bind that keeps the individuals reinforcing the condition that tears them apart.[5] Curiously, these three initially completely unrelated-looking semantic components of *Bannkreis* might belong together to display a critical whole—namely, the picture of a *self-perpetuating circle of painful simultaneous attraction and repulsion*.

When Adorno, in his lectures *History and Freedom*, explains *Negative Dialectic*'s *Bann* to his students (*ND*, pt. 3, chap. 2), these three semantic components of our leading metaphor seem contained. Here, he explains it as a "catastrophic vicious circle in which human beings have an objective interest in changing the world and in which this change is quite impossible without their participation. However, these mechanisms of identification have stamped themselves on people's characters to such a degree that they are quite incapable of the spontaneity and the conscious actions that would be required to bring about the necessary changes. This is because, by identifying with the course of the world, they do so in an unhappy, neurotically damaged way, which effectively leads them to reinforce the world as it is" (*HF*, 76). As we saw in chapter 3, *Bannkreis* has a predominantly gestural character. As a gesture, it points at something. To understand it, one must then turn one's attention to what is pointed at—one must *look* and ask what it *shows*. In this chapter, I want to look and see what Adorno shows by it in his sociological essays and lectures by asking what this metaphor tells us about his critical social theory.[6]

By *Bannkreis*, Adorno points at a circle of asymmetrical adaptation. Take, for example, this passage from his essay "Society": "That *adaptation* of men to social relationships and processes which constitutes history and without which it would have been difficult for the human race to survive has left its mark on them such that the very *possibility* of breaking free without terrible instinctual *conflicts* . . . has come to seem a feeble and a distant one. Men have come to be . . . *identified* in their innermost behavior patterns with their fate in modern society. . . . The process is fed by the fact that men owe their life to what is being done to them" (S, 152; emphasis added). This passage reveals four crucial features of the vicious circle: adaptation, captivity, identification, and antagonism. First, in contrast to the protological *Bannkreis*, "adaptation" is an established scientific concept that Adorno derives from evolutionary biology. The history he points at in the quoted passage is natural history: "The well adapted society is, as its historical concept urges: mere Darwinian natural history."[7] *Bannkreis* points at a nonintentional form of asymmetrical interaction between organism and environment selecting for certain intentional acts by individuals and social groups as well as certain pre- and subconscious dispositions for its persistence.

Bannkreis posits society as an overpowering *environment* that puts these *individuals*, and their *groups*, under overwhelming *adaptive pressure*: "If they want to live, then no other avenue remains but to adapt, submit themselves to the given conditions; they must negate precisely that autonomous subjectivity to which the idea of democracy appeals; they can preserve themselves only if they renounce their self."[8] The second feature is then clear enough: the vicious circle makes the individuals and groups *captive* in its reproduction. The adaptative pressure is overwhelming to the point of making the possibility of social transformation seem helplessly distant. In another socio-theoretical essay, "Theorie der Halbbildung," Adorno picks up an old polemical term of the German pedagogical tradition and calls this form of captivating adaptation "half education."[9] Instead of producing individuals capable of autonomous participation in transformative practice, action that would *adjust* the social environment, contemporary society educates only halfway: it merely *adapts* the individuals to the environment.

The third feature is that this peculiarly social form of adaptation involves *identification*: the social environment continues into the innermost layers of the individuals, reinforces itself within them by conditioning an agency that perpetuates it. This is the spell-like aspect of the vicious circle: it tends to make the individuals identify with the environment, and the overwhelming adaptive pressure on them is internalized to the extent that they surrender their quest for freedom. Society reproduces itself within and against the individual. Yet there remains, as we will see later, a *rest* of spontaneity in the individual, as it were, a leftover individuality, which also means that the identification will be conflicting and painful.

This is then the fourth feature: the identification with the violent adaptive pressure of the environment involves painful conflicts. The vicious circle is a process of adaptation where an overpowering environment continues into the most intimate facets of the individual and preserves itself there by means of *antagonisms* (*HF*, 14–15). Adorno believes that these antagonisms can be traced through the entire social fabric.[10] But he also believes that there is a *basic* antagonism, which is that between "social power and social powerlessness" (*gesellschaftliche Macht und gesellschaftliche Ohnmacht*; MGH, 218–19; *PETS*, 67)—namely, between the overpowering social environment and the individuals and social groups surviving at its mercy and to its benefit.

In section 2, I will take a closer look at *how*, in Adorno's social theory, this form of asymmetrical adaptation operates through captivity, identification, and antagonism. For now, it is enough to retain that *Bannkreis* represents the circular process of an overpowering social environment that persists by putting such an extreme adaptive pressure on individuals and social groups that they renounce their happiness and freedom for a painful form of self-preservation with which they come to identify. Like Nietzsche, Adorno sometimes uses the traditional philosophical metaphors of first and second nature to express his bleak account of social teleology: "The present social structure . . . has the character of . . . a monstrously agglomerated 'second nature'" (*IS*, 28). *Bannkreis* then involves a societal second nature that maintains itself in and through individual second nature and individual first nature.[11]

Does Adorno offer any way out of the vicious circle? As we saw in chapter 3, Adorno believes that to demonstrate the extent to which society reproduces itself as a vicious circle is already a crucial step to breaking it: "To point the vicious circle out breaks a taboo of the integral society" (S, 153). Disclosing the vicious circle is a critical gesture. The demonstration of its extent shows both how the current form of societal reproduction contradicts our dearest values, causing senseless suffering in all its phases, and that a different form of life is objectively possible. I have called the first phase of the gesture, that of pointing *out* our current society as objectively false, a decentering disclosure. Conversely, I have called the second phase, that of pointing *to* objective possibilities of another form of life, a recentering disclosure. These two strokes of "drawing a circle around a circle" seem to advance, I notice, to something like a defining characteristic of the tradition I am excavating: a disclosing critic both decenters and recenters in one critical gesture.

In chapter 3, we also saw that, by pointing the vicious circle out, Adorno distances himself in an exemplary way from the prevailing form of life to evoke an intermittent alienation among the addressees. In chapter 4, Nietzsche shows that this can be interpreted as an educational gesture to provoke variation. Such variation is a condition for the recipients to overcome socially caused unhappiness and unfreedom: only by cultivating their recalcitrant tendencies can they find their own way of growing out of themselves. The disclosing gesture is educative by virtue of showing an *example* of critical distance to society. Nietzsche located that distance to the "circles of culture" in the margins of a form of life, to what I described as counterformative communities. By contrast, Adorno practices critical disclosure in university lecture halls and the public sphere of a democratizing Federal Republic of Germany. Emerson relied on the figure of the poet, who, with her distancing form of speech, shatters the current "chain of habits" (C, 409); Nietzsche relied on the figure of the physician of culture who helps those captive in "a chain of toil and burden" to "raise [their] head[s]" (UM, 143, 159). By contrast, Adorno's disclosing gesture comes in the shape of a *theory*. Social theory, Adorno tells the students in his introductory class to sociology, "revolves essentially around the question how we are finally to break out of the vicious circle."[12] By means of theory, then, the critical social theorist *points out* the extent to which society constitutes a vicious circle and *points to* the objective possibilities of social transformations that remain. This counterteleological educative gesture of *disclosing critical theory* leaves, as it were, the door ajar so that the recipients may break out.[13]

Like Adorno, Dewey worries that in an overpowering social environment "life would petrify, society stagnate" (*HNC*, 72). In *Human Nature and Conduct*, thirty years prior to Adorno's *Bannkreis*, he calls such a stagnation of social life a "vicious circle" and, like Adorno, thematizes it in terms of a social environment's "stamping" the individual's most intimate layers (88, 76): "It seems . . . that every attempt to . . . secure fundamental reorganizations is caught in a vicious circle. For the direction of native activity depends upon acquired habits, and yet acquired habits can be modified only by redirection of impulses. Existing institutions impose their stamp, their superscription, upon impulse and instinct. They embody the modifications the latter have undergone. How then can we get leverage for changing institutions?" (88). Again, an overpowering institutional environment maintains itself within and against the individual. Dewey's vicious circle shares the same four crucial features as Adorno's: adaptation, captivity, identification, and antagonism.

For Dewey, too, the vicious circle presents, first of all, a process of asymmetrical adaptation of organism to environment. Already in the introduction to *Human Nature and Conduct*, Dewey explains that "all conduct is interaction between elements of human nature and the environment" (*HNC*, 9). Dewey goes on to give a rich account of social reproduction as a circle of custom, impulse, and habit: (a) *customs* are social second nature, our collective habits and acquired dispositions, shared among the members of a form of life, through which (b) individual first nature, our impulses, acquires social meaning; such impulses can, however, be acted upon only through (c) habits, which all individuals form as they are socialized into a form of life by customary response to their impulses (pt. 2). Social life persists as a nonintentional process, which selects for acts and dispositions among individuals and social groups. Rather than the current social environment being the result of intentional action, Dewey claims, "social institutions and expectations shape and crystallize impulses into dominant habits" (86). "No matter how accidental and irrational the circumstances of its origin, no matter how different the conditions which now exist to those under which the habit was formed, the latter persists until the environment obstinately rejects it. Habits once formed perpetuate themselves by acting unremittingly upon the native stock of activities. They stimulate, inhibit, intensify, weaken, select, concentrate and organize the latter into their own likeness. They create out of the formless void of impulses a world made in their own image" (88). The vicious circle can then, Dewey believes, be *traced* through the adaptive pressures from the social environment on habituation, which enables and conditions action by giving direction to impulses sparked in the individual by the social environment (43, fig. 2). Or, as he later writes in *The Public and Its Problems*, whereas "habits reflect ... social customs" (*PP*, 336), impulses are "reflections into the singular human being of customs" (299).

Like Adorno's *Bannkreis*, Dewey's "vicious circle" is indebted to Dar-

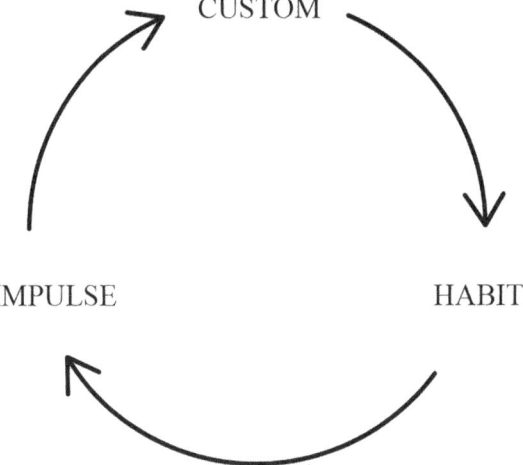

FIGURE 2. The "vicious circle" as a circular process of habituation, circling custom, habit, and impulse, as implied by Dewey. Created by the author.

winian evolutionary theory. Both Adorno and Dewey are critical of Herbert Spencer's adaptationist application of evolutionary theory to social theory.[14] However, unlike Adorno, who maintains a certain ironic adaptationism,[15] Dewey develops a competing interpretation of Darwin that claims to be, and indeed is,[16] superior to the adaptationist one. Dewey completes the concept of adaptation (of organism to environment) by that of adjustment (of the environment by the organism) and links it intrinsically with play, experimentation, and experience[17]—notions crucial for the critical projects of Adorno too.[18] In fact, during the positivism dispute in German sociology, Adorno refers to the playful and experimental character of Dewey's conception of experience: Dewey, Adorno writes, "appeals for open, unfixed, unreified thought. An experimental, not to say a playful, moment is unavoidable in such thought."[19] Again, in *Negative Dialectics*, Adorno similarly applauds Deweyan fallibilism: "In principle, philosophy can always go astray, which is the sole reason why it can go forward. This has been recognized in skepticism and in pragmatism, most recently in Dewey's wholly humane version of the latter. . . . As a corrective to the total rule of method, philosophy contains a playful element" (*ND*, 14). In both philosophers' work, the disclosure of the vicious circle is motivated by a worry about our degenerating capacity to *truly have experiences*—a power that any form of criticism presupposes.[20]

Also the Deweyan captivity in the vicious circle is to a large extent an educational problem. Like in Emerson and Nietzsche, what keeps us captive is a *chain of habits*. Yet Dewey's conception of habit is incomparably richer. He believes that all action is habitual. And all habit is based on mechanism, although mechanism does not exhaust habit. Dewey therefore introduces into our tradition a distinction within habit: what keeps us captive, puts us in chains, are *bad habits*. Bad habits are characterized by a rigid, closed mechanism that forces action into narrow and repetitive pathways. Their rigidity may then trigger the individual to try to act outside habit. But because action is only possible through enabling habits, the individual is destined, without educational effort and an accommodating environment, to be thrown back into the old habit. Good habits, by contrast, are creative: they prove to persist by enduring and expressing a great variety of diverse impulses.[21]

In explaining how society maintains itself as a vicious circle, Dewey, too, refers to mechanisms of identification. In *Liberalism and Social Action*, he claims that people tend to react to the overwhelming pressure from the social environment by "what psycho-analysis has taught us to call rationalizations" (*LSA*, 41–42). In *The Public and Its Problems*, the viciously circular "Great Society" he is disclosing rests on, among other things, an identification with "established institutions" springing from "an underlying fear of which the subject is not aware, but which leads to withdrawal from reality and to unwillingness to think things through" (*PP*, 341–42). And finally, also in Dewey, the vicious circle involves a fundamentally unstable social environment; it displays an uncontrolled *antagonistic* flux whose reproduction is "characterized chiefly by uneasiness, discontent and blind antagonistic struggles" (*HNC*, 90). Like Adorno, Dewey does not regard the vicious circle as some sort of mind game for figuring out a conceptual problem of social critique but *projects* it onto society to express its really existing alienated state: "We now live in a situation when the world seems alien rather than homelike. . . . [I]n most practical matters there is no more widespread sense than that of insecurity," he expresses his uncanny sense of contemporary capitalism in 1946 and immediately adds what this means for the critical task of philosophy: "The type of philosophy which now tries to show that all 'appearances' to the contrary the world in which we live is 'really,' fundamentally, one of fixed order, significance and worth takes on the air of theological apologetics."[22] Like Adorno, then, Dewey projects the vicious circle as a metaphoric device for thinking about a societal stability through alienating social antagonism.[23]

Also Dewey asks, "Is there any way out of the vicious circle?" (*HNC*, 89). Initially, his way out might seem to differ a great deal from Adorno's for he starts by pointing out that no social environment is "all of one piece" (90). Dewey conceives social life in a fractal way.[24] We are not simply socialized into *a* form of life or into *the* society. Society presents a form of life, which consists of *many* associating and overlapping forms of life, or *social groups*. Social groups again constitute the loci of customs and consist of associating individuals with their habits and impulses. Individuals then do not stand in an immediate relationship with the society. They never act in society. Their relationship with society is essentially mediated by the social groups that in the flow of everyday life afford them their ordinary-action context.

Each of us is, Dewey points out, socialized as a member of *many* social groups. These groups have varying interests, and they spark varying impulses in us and instill varying habits onto us.[25] They, as it were, stamp us in diverse ways: "The environment is many not one; hence, will, disposition, is plural" (*HNC*, 38). On the one hand, this makes tracing the vicious circle a complicated affair: "All of the actions of an individual bear the stamp of his community. . . . Difficulty in reading the stamp is due to variety of impressions in consequence of membership in many groups" (218). Tracing the vicious circle must involve sensibility for how the ordinary-action context of the individuals relates to their other action contexts and how it relates to the societal environment. On the other hand, this discloses a path for the critique of social groups. As we are all members of many groups, we can criticize each by resources from another. If one social group starts to reproduce as a vicious circle, we can critically disclose it with help of the example of a more freely or democratically organized group. By socialization into many groups with varying customs, we are, as it were, naturally educated to criticize. By this gesture, Dewey, like Emerson, emphasizes to his readers that exemplary critical disclosure is present in ordinary life experience. Disclosing critique is immanent to social life.

Like Emerson and Nietzsche, Dewey, too, hides a metaphoric hint at Archimedes's principle in his formulation of the vicious circle above: to point to a way out, critique namely needs "leverage." And not unlike Nietzsche, Dewey believes that this leverage, the possibility of critical disclosure, depends on the fact that forms of life do not have clear boundaries. But differently from Nietzsche who focuses on their core ("old-age") and margins ("youth"), he lays stress on their *fractal* nature—the fact that they are overlapping and consist of component forms of life (social groups) or make up greater forms of life (societies). This difference, this idea of an irreducible diversity of the social environment, allows Dewey to enter the tradition of disclosing critique of society with a remarkable innovation. He namely offers an explicit concept of *disclosing reason*. Reason, the critical leverage, is a creative collective habit arising out of the plurality and moral variability of social groups: "Reason ... becomes a custom of expectation and outlook, an active demand for reasonableness in other customs.... It arises in some exceptional circumstance out of social customs.... But when it has been generated it establishes a new custom, which is capable of exercising the most revolutionary influence upon other customs" (*HNC*, 55–56). As a reflective custom, creative collective habit, reason emerges as an arbitrary variation in the natural history of an irreducibly diverse form of life and then ex post facto serves as a means of its disclosure and adjustment.

It is precisely in the context of his discussion of the role of reason in social life that Dewey quotes exactly the same passage as Nietzsche from Emerson's "Circles." But he draws dramatically different consequences out of it. In the notes for his lectures in Beijing on social philosophy, he cites Emerson from memory: "Emerson stated the idea [of the practical efficacy of philosophy] rather intensely when he said Beware when God lets loose a thinker on the planet. All things then become fluid." And he immediately goes on to elaborate, "Thinking means the introduction of a novel and in so far incalculable factor—a deviation or departure, and an invention.... The appeal to reason that is implied is unsettling" (LCN, 9). To Dewey, the circle that Emerson's poet draws unsettles because it appeals to *reason*—the habit the poet has thanks to socialization and education in recalcitrant groups that have endowed her with the power to deviate creatively.[26] And the planet is reasonable to the extent of its ability to unsettle itself by her circle. On Dewey's reading, then, Emerson discloses reason itself as a custom of giving and receiving gestures of critical disclosure.

Dewey's gesture of pointing to the moral variability of the many social groups in ordinary life displays also an important similarity with Adorno's proposal: both agree with Emerson and Nietzsche that it is a critical distance to the form of life and the exemplarity of another way to live that enable individuals to deviate from rigid habits and develop more creative ones. Dewey's innovations are, on the one hand, to envision that the new chain of habits consists of *creative habits* that can encompass and be directed by a greater number of impulses and therefore actualize more of the potential of individuals, making them freer and happier;[27] and, on the other, to theorize the moral variability of social groups by showing that the incidence of such creative habits in *some* of these groups enables such habits also collectively as disclosing reason, a reflective custom, which allows for adjustment of the societal environment by group action. If Nietzsche already pluralized Emerson's poet into multiple educators, then Dewey *depersonalizes* the source of disclosing exemplarity: it is not necessarily an exemplary person who will help me to lift myself up, it can also be social groups that enable this by presenting to me creatively deviating social environments with exemplary power over me. Not unlike Nietzsche, Dewey, in his pedagogy, attempts to map the path to such an empowerment of the individual to "adjustment"—that is, to a transformative reshaping of the social environment (*DE*, chap. 7)—but with considerably lighter metaphysical baggage and without the aristocratic consecration of "hanging one's heart" on an educator who may or may not regard their disclosing gestures as merely intermittent.

In Dewey, the gesture of drawing a circle around the vicious circle is then also linked with the disclosure of the horizon of meaning and the cultivation of recalcitrant tendencies to resist society's pressure toward adaptation. Yet what role does theory play in the counterformation that is the disclosing critique of society?

2. Tracing the Vicious Circle: Theory as a Disclosing Gesture

Let's recapitulate this much: Adorno demonstrates the vicious circle with a theory of a basic antagonism of social power and social powerlessness, the antagonism between an overpowering society and the individuals who must adapt. Dewey, by contrast, develops a naturalized conception of reason based on an account of the moral variability of social groups due to the diversity of loci of socialization. Now, Dewey is a harsh critic of any social theorizing that postulates a conflict between individual and society. The individual, he claims, acts within *social groups*, and only the interactions between these social groups make up a society. The individual does not stand in a direct relationship with society.

Dewey's socio-theoretical account of the vicious circle is consequently group based. As he tells the audience of his lectures on social philosophy in Beijing in 1919, this type of domination can be understood as the *monopolization* of the social environment by the interests of a particular group, which puts other groups with other interests under the pressure to adapt to overpowering interests. The dominating interests become recognized as the interests of the "social whole," whereas other group interests are taken as merely "individual" (*LC*, 74–81). The dominating group is "publicly recognized," whereas the other groups have "not yet achieved such recognition."[28] Its interests then come to dominate the reproduction of society by monopolizing the power to shape the associations between social groups. In his *Lectures in China 1919–1920*, Dewey treats men of the capitalist class as this type of hegemonic group and gives women and the working classes as examples of dominated groups that struggle to "be recognized as an operating component of the larger society" (76). The interest of capital accumulation has then come to dominate the reproduction of society, whereas other social groups have been degraded to a mere means of the accumulation of capital.[29] This institutes a particular mode of association—namely, the antagonistic struggle for (artificially) scarce resources—as a universal, to which the other social groups must adapt their modes of association. Dewey believes such a group-based social theory to account sufficiently—and without recourse to an underlying conflict between the individual and society—for the vicious circle to be disclosed. And so he also later maintains in *The Public and Its Problems*, "Individuals find themselves cramped and depressed by absorption of their potentialities in some mode of association which has been institutionalized and become dominant. They may think they are clamoring for a purely personal liberty, but what they are doing is to bring into being a greater liberty to share in other associations, so that more of their individual potentialities will be released and their personal experience enriched. Life has been impoverished, not by a predominance of 'society' in general over individuality, but by a domination of one form of association . . . over other actual and possible forms" (*PP*, 356).

Adorno does, however, not postulate an *immediate* relationship between two entities, "society" and "the individual"; to him, "society" is a speculative category of mediation: it is not a fact, yet it inheres in every social fact (S, 145–46). In fact, he arrives at the antagonism between social power and social powerlessness through a careful tracing of the vicious circle as an asymmetrical adaptive process mediated by *many* types of antagonisms. And indeed, first on the list are the antagonisms *between social groups* (MGH, 192–93; *PETS*, 65–66). Second, Adorno theorizes antagonistic interactions *between sectors* of society (*PETS*, 81). A part of Adorno's story about the coexistence of rationality and irrationality in the postwar welfare society is that while these social groups are capable of acting intentionally and rationally, and the sectors constitute loci of rational planning, the *society* made up of their antagonistic interactions remains largely irrational. Third, society can involve antagonisms *within individuals* (*PETS*, 67). Society's antagonisms continue into the interactions of the individual's drives, impulses, and habits. Finally, only as a result, there emerges a picture of the basic antagonism between social power and social powerlessness—a perspective on how the societal environment overpowers individuals and their groups (MGH, 218–19; *PETS*, 67).

Like Dewey, Adorno thus distinguishes society as a nonintentional functional context from social groups that can also act intentionally (*PETS*, 22). In his lecture course *Philosophical Elements of a Theory of Society*, he, in fact, addresses the idea of group pluralism and moral variability directly. While he considers a "pluralism" of morally varying, self-organizing social groups to be a sign of a less wrong society—and to some extent even ascribes it to the prevailing one (he points to the trade unions and the student movement as examples)[30]—he claims that this diversity is not at all irreducible; it can very well be reduced, and this even tends to be the case under *Bannkreis* (127–28). Under present adaptive pressure, the antagonistic struggle for (artificially) scarce resources between social groups results in an *equalization* of their moral structure. The worry is easy to share. At universities today, students are pressured to compete for grades and credit points rather than supported to follow their impulses of curiosity to grow as individuals and develop their skills of creative recalcitrance; artists today are pressured to collect cool-looking merits on their hunt for scarce sources of funding; big farmers eat small farmers in the rural margins, yet they, too, only survive by restricting to the "cultivation" of patented crops. How much exemplary disclosing power do the associations in these groups exhibit today? Tomorrow? After one more generation of "training" new members? How morally variable are they really? What is the tendency? Adorno's worry is that as their moral variability is tendentially eliminated, the disclosing potential of group pluralism is eroded (66).

Four years later, he returns to this point in his introductory course to sociology (*IS*, 29–30). According to Adorno, to disclose precisely the connection between the moral equalization of social groups and the erosion of critical skills in the larger society, a "total theory of society" (*Theorie der Gesamtgesellschaft*) is required—a theory of the superiority of the societal environment over ordinary-action contexts (27). Now, Dewey would be more than curious and ask how to get to that superiority: How is the *tracing* expanded beyond the experiential context of action? Adorno's answer is to trace this superiority of society along the *limits of criticism* expressed in the ordinary-action context of social groups: "If one criticizes an existing social system and proposes particular improvements on the basis of this criticism, such proposals inevitably and very soon come up against a limit which cannot be understood in terms of the individual points of criticism. It can only be understood in terms of the pre-established order of society, which is extremely sensitive to changes" (49). Almost as if to give Dewey an example that the American educator would particularly appreciate, Adorno goes on to say, "For example: why does one come up against a brick wall when one tries to practice political education in a way that gives substance to the concept of democracy?" (50). So what defines society as an overpowering environment can be experienced from the inconsequentiality of the criticism expressed in the ordinary context of social groups. Adorno calls the experience of this limit "society as experience" (51). He believes that making this limit tangible as an object of experience demands a critical *theory* of society (50–51). In other words, Adorno's argument in favor of a total theory of society is that disclosing critique needs it to make the limits of critical experience in social groups *experienceable*. The theory of society is needed for disclosing society *in social groups*.

Adorno traces the vicious circle by means of what he calls "models."[31] They constitute empirically informed speculative fragments, each of which presents a particular phase of the adaptive process but also discloses it as a damaged whole. In Adorno's lectures and essays on social theory, these models are all over the place. To illustrate concretely what is at stake here, I will restrict myself to three exemplary models—examples that I believe to be closely linked—"tendency," "concretism," and "identification with the aggressor."[32]

2.1 Tendency

On a macrosociological level, Adorno models the vicious circle as "tendency" (*PETS*, 19–20). Tendencies are expressed as sets of propositions, based on social facts, about the direction in which society is evolving. Stating a tendency is an empirically informed speculative judgment: it is about the state of affairs in society and their qualitatively different outcome yet to occur. Although the assertion of a tendency necessarily goes beyond a mere assembling of social facts, it proceeds from the analysis of those facts: "Recognizing a tendency means recognizing, within the theoretical analysis of a given state, that element which qualitatively differs from this state itself,

... which means that it is not simply an extension of how the current state presents itself" (24).

The speculative aspect of stating a tendency involves the recognition of a nonidentical element—the movement of the adaptive process in a direction, which is different from its current form. To his students, Adorno gives the example of the socially effective principle of free and equal exchange: What is it *supposed* to lead to, and where does it, based on a rigorous analysis of social facts, *really* lead to (*PETS*, 20)? The model of tendency discloses how the *maintenance* of the social environment will, in fact, *modify* it.

What is the role of "tendency" in tracing the vicious circle? Judgments of tendency give an account of the dynamic of societal second nature (*PETS*, 24). The model provides social theorists with a tool for passing speculative judgments on the dynamics of a societal environment, which exerts an adaptive pressure on individuals and social groups by means of customs, institutions, and functional connections. It attempts to grasp the dynamic social environment as a movement toward what it is not. Thus, it allows the recalcitrant to speak of a social system as "not fully realized." Therefore, Adorno contends, the judgment of tendency is, as it were, always already critical: it presents society as "not the system that, according to its own concept, it should be" (27).

2.2 Concretism

Adorno borrows the term "concretism" from psychology, where it refers to an incapacity for abstraction: it marks a psychopathology of compulsively clinging to the very next task ahead, to the "concrete," as it were. By analogy, Adorno's sociological model of concretism refers to the socially caused inability of individuals "to resist their immediate interests" (*PETS*, 40), which averts them from socially transformative action. As we saw already in the previous chapter where Nietzsche anticipated this model, concretism theorizes the everyday observation "that the people who are given the burden, and consequently walk bent over with their heads bowed, that it has always been very hard for them to hold those heads up high . . . and see more than their immediate interests" (41).

Concretism is the social pathology in which the consciousness of individuals is tied so firmly to the immediately given conditions of action that any critical reflection on them and following action that would seek to adjust them become nearly unbearable burdens. They are, as it were, chained to the concrete action context of whatever social group they are associating in at that moment. In that chain of habits, critical disclosure by the example of another context of action becomes a tremendous challenge. More specifically, Adorno believes that concretism operates primarily by binding the consciousness of individuals to commodities that occupy their attention. He traces this back to a *tendency*—namely, to "the necessity for the system, in order to survive, to exert an additional pressure in every conceivable way in order to shackle people to these very consumer goods" (*PETS*, 42).

"Concretism" traces a specific phase of the vicious circle: the way the ordinary conditions of action are constantly shaped to dispose individuals to react affirmatively to the functional requirements of their social environment. In other words, it describes *social* second nature molding *individual* second nature. It illustrates, from the perspective of the individuals, how the overpowering social environment maintains itself by putting a restricting adaptive pressure on individual habituation within social groups to the point of suffocating their capacity to take a critical distance to it. It gives a tangible description of the basic antagonism as an ordinary experience of society: "The true origin [*Grund*] of this phenomenon of concretism lies much deeper.... [B]ecause of the incredible disproportion between all individuals, every individual ... and the concentrated power of society, the notion of resisting this agglomerated power seems illusory" (*PETS*, 43).

Concretism provides a partial explanation of the "inability to have [*machen*] genuine experiences": "This inability ... and the fixation on the mere objects of immediate exchange, which are affectively charged, idolized and fetishized by people, are essentially the same thing" (*PETS*, 48). The inability to really experience hollows out the kind of "experiments in living" that Dewey and Adorno believe to be essential for individuals in participating and maintaining a democratic society[33]—that is, one that really is open to critical challenges from within. Importantly, Adorno does not claim that the phenomenon of concretism makes socially transformative practice impossible. Instead, its way of disposing individuals to become resistant to genuine experiences makes social transformation *seem illusory*. For an adjustment of an overpowering environment to get off the ground, individuals need not only critical distance to their social group but some degree of theoretical consciousness—that is, the ability to make speculative judgments that point beyond the given circumstances, beyond "the concrete." Rather than eliminating such consciousness, concretism shapes the conditions of action so that the object of critique seems cognitively unattainable: "The phenomenon of concretism . . . does not prevent the objective possibility of theory formation, the incredibly complex and ramified context makes it seem opaque" (43).

Concretism strengthens half education.[34] It restrains the sort of education that takes place outside the school gates in all institutional environments of culture and that Dewey never seizes to emphasize. Without concretism's half-educating effects, Adorno claims, even the most powerless and uneducated member of society could today recognize the vicious circle; he tells his students that in contemporary society, "things are genuinely no longer so terribly complicated" (*PETS*, 43). In a talk to public officers of the state of Hesse, he lays it out with emphasis: "The reason [*Vernunft*] of every single individual would suffice to perform the rather simple thought operations for which I have developed for you some models. That people still do not accomplish this . . . does not depend on their inability to think but on the fact that they forgo thought, because the increasing insight into those contradictions . . . makes their life difficult and inflicts on them an additional suffering" (MGH, 214; my translation). Concretism makes the individual, who in principle is already educated enough to grasp the vicious circle, degenerate from that given level of critical consciousness and critical distance to functioning as a mere organ of the suffocating social environment. It does so by shaping the conditions of ordinary life to make any socially transformative action seem illusory because of the social environment's ostensibly opaque character. Adorno believes that the acceptance of the illusion of opacity is so hard to resist because it alleviates the individuals' pain of surrendering their freedom in adapting. He calls this the "affective power" of *Bannkreis* (*PETS*, 35). Adaptive pressure from the social environment affects the individuals with a "feeling of powerlessness" (*Gefühl der Ohnmacht*), the feeling of finding oneself confronted with overwhelming social powers, vis-à-vis which one's own decisions go poof (MGH, 213). It is unlikely that one raises one's head above the stream for very long if the air is unbearably hot.

Adorno underlines that this affective power awakens the feeling of powerlessness not only in those disadvantaged in society but in *every* individual. Concretism, he believes, affects the entire social fabric. That all individuals, across their varying functions in societal reproduction, are affected by the immense adaptive pressure of the social environment in roughly the same way makes an emancipatory potential explicit, for concretism is a source of solidarity: as a "phenomenon that has spread throughout society as a whole . . . this restriction to the immediate, and the decision to clench one's teeth and avoid looking beyond what is closest at all costs . . . is where we find something resembling solidarity in society as a whole" (*PETS*, 41).

Remember that Nietzsche's "chain of toil and burdens," discussed in the previous chapter, makes experiencing the "productive uniqueness," the genius that "each of us bears," "unendurable" (*UM*, 143); it suppresses the higher self. Although Adorno, unlike Emerson and Nietzsche, never explicitly appeals to a "higher self" to be disclosed, he, too, believes that something like this suppression happens in concretism. In his lecture on aesthetics from 1958 to 1959, he tells the students that there is, indeed, something like "genuine artistic talent," which he defines as "a negative ability, namely the ability to emancipate oneself from the immediacy of existence, from entanglement in the immediate purposes and velleities of life and . . . to elevate oneself." Before the words "elevate oneself," Adorno hesitates and issues a warning for "a word that one barely dares utter today, but which still has some merit." Interestingly, Adorno immediately also adds that "the one mode of behavior" that absolutely *rules out* this talent in the individual "is the concretist approach." Concretism, he elaborates, "provokes such feelings of guilt that . . . one forbids oneself to partake of the happiness that is found where one does something that cannot claim any such purpose in the business of the individual's and society's self-preservation."[35] In the next chapter, I shall investigate closer this relation of our higher self to feelings of guilt, but for now, it is worth noting that even Adorno, despite his skepticism, follows Emerson and Nietzsche in assuming something to be elevated in the individual by a gesture of critical disclosure and links this with the possibility of experiencing happiness in being creatively recalcitrant to society's adaptive demands.

The model of concretism then also discloses nonidentical moments in the vicious circle—namely, first, that of a potential for *solidarity* of all individuals damaged by its overwhelming power and, second, the promise of *happiness* in cultivating creatively one's recalcitrant tendencies. The model shifts the attention of its addressees from the next particular thing, "the concrete," to the objective possibility of a universal solidarity and individual joy *against* the alleged universality of the false society. Recognition of this solidarity is a precondition of the sort of organizing that it would take to break the vicious circle. In his theory of organization, Adorno stresses that organizing has the potential to adjust the social environment according to the needs and desires of the individuals and their groups—that is, it can constitute a mode of second nature, social objectivity, which is not reified.[36]

2.3 Identification with the Aggressor

At times, Adorno describes *Bannkreis* as a vicious circle conditioning individuals by systematically producing needs that are likewise systematically frustrated, which, then, produces impulse conflicts, which, in turn, cause individual behavior that eventually serves to reenforce the current shape of the societal environment (S, 148–49; *HF*, 76). This conditioning of individuals, Adorno suggests, works through a psychic mechanism of identification. As noted briefly in chapter 3, Adorno alludes to Anna Freud's work on an "identification with the aggressor" (IWA) when describing this destructive dynamic. In Anna Freud, IWA refers to a specific defense mechanism—namely, one by which children overcome fear through imitation: to survive, they identify with the person who violates them.[37] Now, Adorno argues that the aggressor need not always be a person but can also be the social environment whose violent adaptive pressure the individual internalizes and continues (*HF*, 76).

With this modification of IWA, Adorno wishes to turn our attention to the fact that "the adaptation required of people today apparently demands so much from them that they cannot anymore satisfy those requirements. The consequence is a certain overidentification with the state of the world, a degeneration of their critical capacity, . . . they do what in psychoanalysis once was called 'identification with the aggressor,' that is, instead of trying to change what blindly befalls them, they make themselves its advocates, and this is so because they do not experience the consciousness of possible change anymore, because the perspective in them, that there could be change at all, has already perished" (MGH, 217; my translation). The model explains how the basic antagonism between social power and social powerlessness maintains itself in and through the individual psyche by means of a defense mechanism.[38] To stay with the metaphor of second and first nature, IWA produces a painful identification of individual first nature with social second nature. It models the continuation of the social environment into the psychic structure of the individuals: society molds their drives and impulses, makes them "voluntarily affirm and even seek the forms of repression that are forced on them from without" (*PETS*, 68). The social environment besets the psychic economy by making individuals desire their own helplessness and thereby constitutes a second nature that draws a circle around their first: "The superego, the locus of conscience, not merely represents what is socially tabooed as being intrinsically evil but also irrationally combines the ancient dread of physical annihilation with the much later fear of being expelled from the social community which has come to *encircle* us in the place of nature."³⁹ Like concretism, IWA provides a partial description of the vicious circle from the perspective of individuals under an unbearable pressure to adapt to an excessively powerful social environment. But unlike concretism, it proceeds from the effects of the adaptive pressures not on habituation but on their archaic psychic structure. It also describes a more severe pathology: the individuals suffering from IWA have completely lost their capacity to resist the social environment. But the pathology is less general too: whereas Adorno holds that we all are affected by concretism, he never claims that everyone is subject to IWA. For the persistence of the vicious circle, it is enough that *many* of us are (68).

In this identification with the social environment, the adaptive pressure of concretism has already become insufferable for the individual psyche. Therefore, it is repressed. Again, Adorno alludes to the affective power of *Bannkreis*:

> As soon as the experience [of powerlessness] is turned into the "feeling of powerlessness" [*Gefühl der Ohnmacht*] the specifically psychological element has entered in, the fact that individuals, precisely, cannot experience or confront their powerlessness.... This repression of their powerlessness points not merely to the disproportion between the individual and his powers within the whole but still more to injured narcissism and the fear of realizing that they themselves go to make up the false forces of domination before which they have every reason to cringe. They have to convert the experience of helplessness into a "feeling" and let it settle psychologically in order not to think beyond it.⁴⁰

IWA results from the *repression* of the feeling of powerlessness affected by concretism: it completes half education.⁴¹ The individual has now lost her capacity to genuinely experience. The adaptation to the social environment is knitted so tightly that experiments in living may no longer be undertaken.⁴²

But again, the model also points to something nonidentical in the vicious circle. It discloses individual spontaneity as the boundary of socialization within the individual.⁴³ Social reproduction relies on it as its medium for even IWA must be enacted by concrete living beings, and the sheer pain that this identification demands of the individual shows that there is something recalcitrant in her, a leftover individuality that does not fuse with the societal power. This in turn shows that the individual resists the overpowering social environment with the same type of force through which the latter established its domination—that is, *formation*: a circle of social environment, habituation, and socialization. IWA discloses the possibility of something like Nietzschean "circles of culture" or Deweyan recalcitrant educational environments; there remains spontaneity in the individual even in the darkest hour of her adaptation. This is then perhaps the merit that the idea of a higher self still has for Adorno: the disclosed spontaneity of the painfully adapting individual is something that still can be "elevated." Like Nietzsche and Dewey, Adorno shows that critical recalcitrance is the question of a type of education, which would strengthen the individual against the power of the social environment and elevate her to the capacity of having genuine experiences, where she uses her spontaneity to adjust, or "shape" (*gestalten*),[44] her social environment—that is, *counterformation*.

2.4 Composing a Constellation: Society as Experience

Adorno's theory of society points out limits of social experience, particularly limits of the efficacy of social criticism in ordinary-action contexts within social groups. It traces how functional connections of an antagonistically structured social environment restrict social experience to the point of making their adjustment seem illusory, overwhelming, or just painful. Adorno shows, I believe, that, as part of a disclosing gesture, theory can help to grasp the conditions of alienation and so render the overcoming of those conditions possible (*PS*, 236). This tracing of the vicious circle leaves the door ajar to step with one foot outside the ordinary-action context: it enables *society as experience*. What type of critical disclosure is this?

It is a disclosure by the *composition of a constellation*. Adorno believes that "objects can be disclosed [*zu erschließen seien*] by their constellation" (*ND*, 164; translation amended). The idea is that by the construction and ordering of a plurality of models, in each of which society as a whole appears in a reduced form, the recipient can be brought to an intellectual experience of that speculative concept. This concept is itself not presentable as a theory—at least not in the traditional sense of an inferentially structured propositional whole. A theory, which instead composes a constellation, does not come with the claim to explain its object but seeks to disclose it by engaging a plurality of intellectual exercises, as it were, "hoping that it may fly open like the lock of a well-guarded safe-deposit box: in response, not to a single key or a single number, but to a combination of numbers," as Adorno metaphorizes in *Negative Dialectics* (163). What his sociological models do with the concept of society is, so to speak, encircle it to make it experienceable as if from without: "As a constellation, theoretical thought *circles* the concept it would like to unseal" (163; emphasis added). How, then, does the metaphor of a vicious circle in particular disclose as a constellation composed of models?

Remember that one of the semantic components of the word *Bannkreis* identified at the outset of this chapter was that of the sphere of influence of a person or a thing under whose spell one falls—of being spellbound, as one might say. In his 1958–1959 lecture on aesthetics, Adorno suddenly uses the term in this sense, yet not regarding capitalist society but in reference to a work of art. In answering why there should be anything like a *theoretical* reflection of art, Adorno refers to what he calls the "riddle character" of art. This is the experience, which he says he often has and believes his students may often have as well, "that one cannot understand works of art at all." Either one namely finds oneself completely inside the work of art—one is, as it were, under its spell—and the question of what the work means does not arise at all; or, through alienation, disgust, or reflection, one is thrown completely out of the artwork—"One is now," Adorno says, "outside *the sphere of influence [aus dem Bannkreis]* of art and casts one's gaze on the work; and then . . . one suddenly asks oneself abruptly: so what's it all about, what is all this?" To be able to cope with this experience, Adorno believes, *theoretical* refection of art becomes necessary.[45] The theoretical reflection on art offers a way out of the *Bannkreis* of the artwork and a way back into it. It enables aesthetic experience we would not otherwise have—the experience of coping with the riddle character of art.

I suggest that Adorno's operation with models in his sociology shows that his theory of society has a similar relation to the *Bannkreis* of society as his theory of art has to the *Bannkreis* of art. The theory enables an experience of society that we would not have without theoretical reflection. This experience is a way out of the vicious circle of society and a way back into society—society now *as experience*. In other words, the theory decenters and recenters. The theory shows a way out of the ordinary-action context, in which one acts under the spell of society, and through the tracing of the vicious circle, it enables an experience of the alienation, a way back in from the outside.

This shows, I believe, that the idea of critical theory is not dependent on the juridical model of critique. As we saw in chapter 1, its modern alternative, the poetic model of critique, derives from the world of art criticism, where the work of the critic is not understood as that of a judge who is constructing a case to pass a judgment with a binding force; instead, it is understood as that of showing the readers an informed and nuanced way to experience a work of art, a path to having an experience of their own accord that they would, however, not have had without the work of critique. What is then the experience that Adorno's critical theory of society prepares the way for?

It is a disconcerting experience on the side of the receiver, for sure. It violates our narcissism and hurts our pride as allegedly autonomous agents to experience the extent to which our action is conditioned and selected for by an overpowering, irrational social environment hostile to our freedom and pursuit of happiness. There is something uncanny about this experience of society. The theory's critical disclosure decenters our form of life: Adorno's lectures on society can then be read as a performative theory of the vicious circle of society, as drawing a circle around the circle. It presents a highly elaborate *gesture of critical disclosure*, aimed at helping his students to alienate themselves from the alienated society by taking a theoretically formed and empirically informed distanced perspective on the core. Something like the counterformation Nietzsche envisaged for the circles of culture in the margins is what Adorno seeks to practice in the lecture hall of the University of Frankfurt.

But it is also an empowering experience. Every model discloses a nonidentical moment in the vicious circle. The theory as a gesture shows that social transformation is objectively possible! Tendency shows that, by staying the same, the social environment will, in fact, change, wherefore it is also modifiable. Concretism shows that the solidarity needed for the self-organizing readjustment of the social environment is anchored in our shared restricted experience. IWA shows that the vicious circle persists by operating as that type of molding of habits and impulses, which education works on too and which can therefore also be reversed by educational measures. The theory's critical disclosure then also recenters our form of life: Adorno's tracing of the vicious circle filters out *objective possibilities* of adjusting the social environment (*HF*, 67–68.; see fig. 3 below).

Importantly, Adorno's social theory is not absolutist in the sense that Dewey criticizes: it does not postulate society as a monocausal force opposite to the individual. On the contrary, it reassembles society as a false universal by means of speculative judgments starting from the study of its effects on social experience. Adorno agrees with Dewey that such judgments arise from empirical inquiry and should be tested empirically.[46]

In *The Public and Its Problems*, Dewey does recognize such functional

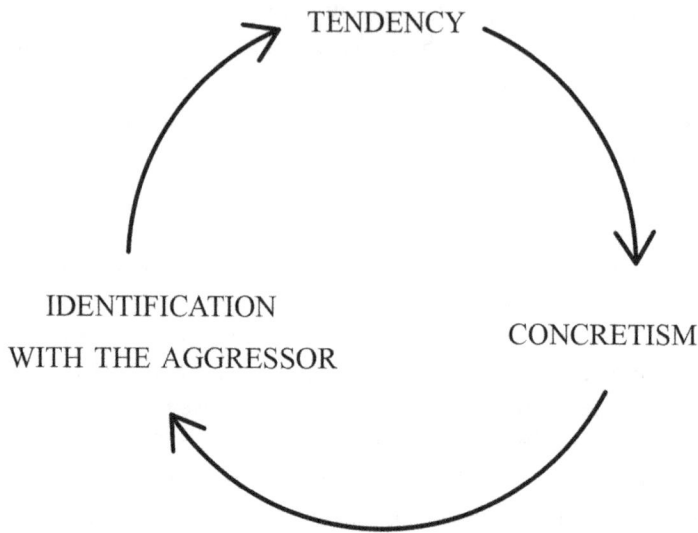

FIGURE 3. The "vicious circle" as a circle of Adorno's sociological models, such as "tendency," "concretism," and "identification with the aggressor." Created by the author.

connections: "the Great Society" that causes the diagnosed "eclipse of the public" is namely constituted by "indirect, extensive, enduring, and serious consequences of conjoint and interacting behavior" and has "formed such immense and consolidated unions in action . . . that the resultant public cannot identify and distinguish itself."[47] However, the way in which experience is restricted in a form of life need not be the consequence of a dominating "mode of association which has been institutionalized" (*PP*, 356). Adorno shows how the restriction can also be noninstitutional yet embodied. Social experience can be restricted as the consequence of a functional connection selected for in the natural history of our form of life.

Dewey observes that an "inchoate public is capable of organization only when indirect consequences are perceived, and when it is possible to project agencies which order their occurrence. At present, many consequences are felt rather than perceived; they are suffered, but they cannot be said to be known, for they are not, by those who experience them, referred to their origins" (*PP*, 317). But he never develops a theory addressing the various ways in which social domination can be embodied beyond customs and institutions. His decentering disclosure thus lacks a crucial tool for showing how indirect consequences of action can bundle up to dismantle claims to readjustment. And as long as those connections remain undisclosed, the chances are high that we keep banging our head against that "brick wall"—which Adorno warns his students of—before solving any of the problems of the public (*IS*, 50). One of Adorno's great innovations in the tradition of disclosing critique is his insight that this can only be achieved by conceiving of a second nature that is neither institutional nor merely customary but, indeed, an antagonistically structured, interconnected societal power over individuals and social groups alike, and therefore, drawing the circle around the vicious circle must involve *theoretical tracing* if it is to respond to such an environment. By mapping liminal spaces of social experience, pointing at where it is systematically restricted by current social antagonisms, Adorno's lectures on social theory develop models for precisely that type of decentering theorizing.

However, Dewey's insistence on the importance of group pluralism and moral variability for critical disclosure also draws attention to a distressing quality of Adorno's disclosing critical theory of society. In the end of his career as a professor of philosophy and sociology, he stressed the vicinity of his theory to Dewey by referring to their shared commitment to "openness": "The 'open' aspect, which I increasingly tend towards viewing as a key concept, . . . by no means comes from the philosophical tradition, although philosophers such as the American John Dewey have used the term" (*PETS*, 84). And certainly, openness toward the new is as central to Adorno's and Dewey's aesthetics as it is for their disclosing critiques of society. Yet it seems to me that there would be more room for openness in theory of society than Adorno allows for. It is, at times, astonishing to me how little openness Adorno, who designed his complete philosophy to make space for the "nonidentical" (*ND*), has for not the "new" but the "other"—in the sense of what has a different social and cultural history than western Europe. As Geuss points out, Adorno's harsh criticism of jazz and contempt for Picasso's turn to African masks for inspiration are partly consequences of his obsession with a Hegelian framework for theory.[48] Dewey's turn against Hegel was, in this regard, metaphilosophically more radical.[49] And I believe that his enthusiasm for the historical social and cultural variation of social groups offers a sort of counterpoise to Adorno's legitimate, but also theoretically over-Hegelianized, worry about equalization of the moral variability of social groups. A satisfactory account of critical disclosure cannot by theoretical operation simply ignore the disclosing potential of learning from the examples of other societies.

3. Breaking out of the Vicious Circle: Education and Organization

Despite this disagreement, which needed not be, between Dewey and Adorno regarding the status of theory in disclosing critique of society, a closer look at the "models" of Adorno's social theory also reveals a strong agreement between the two social philosophers: the way out of the vicious circle is paved by *education* and *organization*. Whereas the shared experience of the adaptive pressures in concretism points to the objective possibility of a society-wide solidarity that enables organization of group agency to adjust the social environment, IWA shows that the vicious circle can be resisted by an education that strengthens the individual against these adaptive pressures. And whereas tendency discloses the social system as fundamentally unstable and therefore susceptible to adjustment by educated and organized effort from below, concretism points to the enjoyment in cultivating one's recalcitrant tendencies—perhaps in a self-organizing social setting. This allows for an expansion of Nietzsche's "circles of culture" yet without some of his heavy metaphysical baggage and aristocratic pathos.

The experience of society discloses the extent to which the antagonistic structure of the social environment is maintained by the activities of social groups. The suffering caused by the captivity is supported by institutions, customs, and educational measures and can also be reversed by them. To put Dewey and Adorno in the language of social contract theorizing, Leviathan breaks its promise of peace and safety by maintaining a state of nature within itself. Adorno, the essayist, phrases it like this: "It is nothing less than the hypostasis of scarcity, which in its social form has now been made obviously obsolete by the very technological development to which . . . human beings are supposed to adapt [*sich anpassen*]. . . . The only adequate response to the present technical situation, which holds out the promise of wealth and abundance to men, is to organize it according to the needs of a humanity which no longer needs violence because it is its own master."[50] The Dewey of *Liberalism and Social Action* concurs: "The system that goes by the name of capitalism is a systematic manifestation of desires and purposes built up in an age of ever threatening want and now carried over into a time of ever increasing potential plenty. The conditions that generate insecurity for the many no longer spring from nature. They are found in institutions and arrangements that are within deliberate human control" (*LSA*, 43). Liberation from the captivity means adjustment of the social environment to what is already objectively possible: "Today, adaptation [*Anpassung*] to what is possible no longer means adaptation; it means making the possible real," as Adorno puts it.[51] His idea of half education is disclosing in virtue of pointing at the counterfactual of a full education—the possibility of educational practices that would consist not only in adaptation of the individuals to the environmental but, more importantly, in the adjustment of the environment by self-transforming individuals and social groups.[52]

Yet, according to both Dewey's fractal social ontology and Adorno's total social theory, *society* can only be adjusted if *social groups* are capable of transformative action. Transformative group agency again requires that individuals are able to *organize* themselves as social groups. Such groups can be critically transformative if they themselves constitute recalcitrant and exemplary social environments that serve as moral alternatives to the prevailing structure of customs. This means to *organize* social groups, particular social environments, that can adjust the larger societal environment according to the needs and desires of individuals and their groups.[53] Or, as Dewey puts it, liberation means to adjust it to "an environment in which human desire and choice count for something" (*HNC*, 9).

Whereas Adorno, in his sociology, formulates a performative theory of the overpowering societal environment, Dewey, in his pedagogy, develops a performative theory of critical social environments. Such recalcitrant and exemplary group environments present plastic second natures, educative forms of life that live through and learn from individual variation. They "foster conditions that widen the horizon of others and give them command of their own powers, so that they can find their own happiness in their own fashion" (*HNC*, 203).

The disclosing reason that Dewey derives out of the moral diversity of the social environment is also, to him, by no means a given. It demands *care*: it must be embodied and cultivated in democratically organized communities of education that constitute particular exemplary social environments in a society that has not yet experienced actual democracy (DE, 24–26). Like Adorno, Dewey understands education as "all the ways in which communities attempt to shape the disposition ... of their members" (*PP*, 360). In the circle of social reproduction, concretely in these exemplary environments, education can shift the path from individual second nature to individual first nature. In such counterformative groups, habitual dispositions can be made sensitive to a larger number of impulses by interaction with recalcitrant social environments of reflective custom.

Organization, again, can shift the path from individual first nature to societal second nature. Organizing group action mobilizes varying and unpredictable impulses of individuals for the adjustment of customs and institutions. As we saw in chapter 3, Adorno thinks that, as a counterfactual, organizations can be nonreified forms of social second nature. Similarly, Dewey, in a speech at the Conference of the People's Lobby in Washington, states with reference to the present crisis of capitalism, "This vicious circle cannot be broken by patchwork measures. It requires organization to get us out of the chaos."[54] Dewey believes that to break out of the vicious circle, experiments in organization are necessary but that not even they will be sufficient (*LSA*, 44); material conditions of societal reproduction must be transformed on a society-wide scale (62). Education and organization are then mutually conditioning: the "educational task cannot be accomplished . . . without action that effects actual change in institutions" (44). In his radio speech "Education after Auschwitz," Adorno makes a similar point: as long as the material conditions that produced fascism continue to persist, education alone will not suffice, even if it is a necessary element for its eradication.[55] As if to underline that critical disclosure must involve organizational effort, Dewey ends *The Public and Its Problems* with quoting Emerson's "Self-Reliance": "We lie, as Emerson said, in the lap of an immense intelligence. But that intelligence is dormant and its communications are broken, inarticulate and faint until it possesses the local community as its medium" (*PP*, 372; *SR*, 269).

This mutually conditioning play of education and organization is then part and parcel of social critique—that is, of what I have begun to elaborate as a recentering direction of critical disclosure. Dewey's and Adorno's great common innovation in the tradition of disclosing critique is to conceive social theory as a disclosing gesture in educational and organizational efforts. It changes, I believe, nearly everything. Recentering disclosure is not anymore merely an acquirement of a form of distancing poetic speech or speculative recalcitrance in the margins, however attractive its pull of the core. Sure, it *can* still be both. Yet in Dewey and Adorno, the recentering movement becomes a concrete part of the practice of a social critique, which is empirically informed and stretches through academic institutions to social and educational action in a broader social environment. Whereas Dewey sought to influence the educational institutions of the United States, Adorno became a leading public intellectual of a fragilely democratizing West Germany.[56] These facts, I believe, are inseparable from their disclosing critique of society. They mark their great achievements as well as their feeble attempts at recentering disclosure.

That probably the greater part of their recentering practice failed is, by all means, relevant. It discloses what I would like to call a "tragic sense of political life"—an outlook that I take to be characteristic of much of the politics of disclosing critique. Adorno and Dewey are *radical gradualists*: they recognize that the vicious circle cannot be broken by a violent revolution, nor is it likely to happen by piecemeal reform. But it must be *traced*. Already in *Dialectic of Enlightenment*, Adorno gave, with Horkheimer, expression to this tragic character of tracing the vicious circle: "Refusing to be hypnotized by the preponderant power," they write, philosophy "pursues it into all its hiding-places in the social machinery, which by its nature cannot be taken by storm, or placed under different control, but must be grasped [*begriffen*] in freedom from the spell [*Bann*] which it casts" (*DE*, 202; translation amended). It will take tremendous educational and organizational effort to actualize what has been traced as already objectively possible. As Dewey observes, "the gulf between what the actual situation makes possible and the actual state is so great that it cannot be bridged by piecemeal policies ad hoc. The process of producing the changes will be, in any case, a gradual one" (*LSA*, 45). But such educational and organizational efforts *can* be successful: as the model of tendency disclosed, the antagonistically structured social environment is susceptible to adjustment by organized and educated recalcitrance from below. In his *Introduction to Sociology*, in the spring of 1968, Adorno tells his students "that just because the present social structure . . . has the character of a monstrously agglomerated 'second nature,' even the most pitiful interventions into the existing reality can have a far greater importance—because it is almost a symbolic importance—than they might seem intrinsically to possess. I think, therefore, that we should be more sparing with the accusation of so-called reformism than may have been possible in the last century and in the early part of this" (*IS*, 28).

Adorno's and Dewey's gradualism is radical because it goes to the roots of the nature of political life under a capitalist vicious circle. The only solution to the permanent disaster, which is contemporary society, would be a revolution. Yet revolution is not a possible solution, save as gradual revolutionary transformation. The problems of contemporary capitalism are so massive that they cannot be fixed by piecemeal reform. Yet the problems of contemporary capitalism are so complex because they keep those who suffer captive; they have much more than their precious chains to lose. Adorno quips to his students, "If the workers do indeed have more to lose than their chains, then that may be painful for the theory, but it is initially very good for the workers" (*PETS*, 50). This, he believes, to be an important theoretical insight from tracing the vicious circle—an insight with important political implications. The concrete issues that then follow in his view are those of organization and education—namely, "the radical depoliticization of the trade unions . . . and . . . the lack of political training, which is tied to the problematics of political education as whole," he specifies and adds, "and if anyone does attempt such political training, they will not usually have such a good time of it" (38). In contrast to the rather aristocratic outlook of Nietzsche in the last chapter, Dewey's and Adorno's radical gradualism points to the possibility of a *democratic* politics of critical disclosure in the face of the catastrophic state of our form of life. After all, as Dewey puts it, democracy is the form of life that "will . . . not subordinate individual variations, but will encourage individual experimentation"[57]—that is, to cultivate and organize recalcitrant tendencies. The tragic sense of this outlook is to creatively affirm the situation that piecemeal reform will not resolve the issues and a "revolutionary event" is not to be expected but that education and organization is where the start must be made.[58]

To many social and political philosophers, I am sure, this intermediary result of disclosing critique of society—pointing out the extent to which contemporary social life is caught in a vicious circle and pointing to education and organization as the way out—will appear disappointingly meager. Indeed, neither Dewey nor Adorno formulate sophisticated theories of justice or the democratic constitutional state à la John Rawls or Jürgen Habermas. The reason is their observation that any constructive criticism or positive proposal, no matter how radical, can be turned into a further vehicle of the perpetuation of the catastrophe that is contemporary capitalist society. Under a vicious circle, it cannot be the task of social philosophy to formulate the principles and programs of a well-ordered society. Under a vicious circle, the task of social philosophy must be primarily and radically negative: to point out the extent of the falsehood of what *is* and thereby show what it would take to create what nonetheless still *can be*. Under a vicious circle, critique means care for the lump of reason that still remains in the thin cracks of our shattered habits.[59]

4. Care for Reason

A disclosing critique alienates us from the alienated society and shows that another form of life is objectively possible for us. A disclosing critical theory does so by tracing the limits of current social experience, which enables an experience of society as a vicious circle, pointing to education and organization as the rational means left for breaking out. The very possibility of such theoretical gestures is itself at stake. Disclosing reason must be cared for. The moral variability of our social groups it depends on is not a given. Adorno's theory of society points out its greatest threats; Dewey's theory of education shows what the care demands. No matter how poor the addressees' interpretation of the theory, merely effecting a critical distance to the society is already an act of care in the alienated society.

However, one can ask as Geuss asks following Nietzsche, "What in principle is supposed to be so bad about acting according to circumstances? Why not adapt to the circumstances? Why should not skill in adapting be as highly valued as rigid consistency of belief and action in all circumstances? Humans try to be consistent; they also try to respond to changing circumstances."[60] A disclosing critical theory does not ask people not to adapt to their environment. On the contrary, drawing a circle around the vicious circle presents an attempt to *think through* the circle of adaptation. Its observation is that people do not adapt to their environment *and adjust* it such that it correspond to the their and their groups' needs and desires. Adjustment of the circumstances presupposes, to a certain degree, the adaptation of the organism: social critique requires the survival of the critic. It takes skill and wisdom to survive in the wrong world, as Adorno shows in his *Minima Moralia*. Yet conceiving these skills and this wisdom in terms of a self-preservation to the cost of one's self would be to succumb to the vicious circle of half education.

It is curious that Adorno places such a metaphoric gesture as *Bannkreis* at the very center of his critical theory of society. What does it tell about this *theory* that its central issue—indeed, the question defining it as a *critical* theory in the sense derived from Horkheimer's program—is cast in a gesture of showing rather than in assertive claims? Theories are traditionally understood to constitute normatively structured systems of propositional claims. Critical theories are, however, not meant to constitute traditional theories. Is the gestural, showing character of *Bannkreis* then part of what makes Adorno's social theory a *critical* theory of society? I have tried to show that this is indeed so, because it gives an example of a critical distance to our form of life and the possibility of another way to live. A theory that does that in one circular gesture deserves the name of a disclosing critical theory.

To sum up, disclosing critical theory enables an experience of society. Such *critical experiences* can ignite an intentional modification of our language games, which may even continue into our habits and go on to adjust our customs and institutions (this, of course, requires education and organization). Importantly, disclosing critical theory does not modify language games by arguments alone. It unsettles by a nonassertive means of communication too—by displaying the exemplary attitude of alienating oneself from the alienated state of current society. This communication is nonassertive in the sense that it seeks, as a showing gesture, to provoke a liminal experience, the experience of society as the limit of critical experience in ordinary life. The evocation of such an experience requires theory of society, a tracing of these liminal experiences through the social fabric. It unsettles our language games, as it were, from within and below.

Dewey offers an explicit concept of disclosing reason. Such rationality arises from the diversity and moral variability of social groups—a precarious social fact that demands care. This concept of reason is more inclusive than the instrumental reason of contemporary half education, which reduces rationality to self-preservation without the preservation of self, and the alternative concept of communicative reason, which reduces rationality to the practice of exchange of assertive claims in rather exotic language games.[61] It also avoids their duality. It makes space for radical critique by the kind of creative social recalcitrance that works against our forms of life by means of exemplary critical disclosure. There is, however, no reason for a negative theory of society to be excluded from the exercise of that capacity of reason.

Dewey's pedagogy and Adorno's sociology can thus be read as presenting highly articulated gestures of philosophical social critique. They partly conflict and partly complement each other. The hypothesis emerging from this chapter is that both their agreements and disagreements are relevant for the practice of a disclosing critique of society today. In this, I believe their contributions to be incomparably more valuable than those of the other exemplary disclosing critics of my history of drawing circles around vicious circles. From Adorno, this practice gains the idea that theory of society can be a disclosing gesture, which presents an important corrective to Dewey's failure to trace the eclipse of the public. From Dewey, it gets a reminder that these theories must find ways to continue into ordinary life experience through group action for their disclosure to come full circle.

SIX

Civilization and Its Uncanniness
Freud's Sense of Guilt

> Society everywhere is in conspiracy against
> the manhood of every one of its members.
> —RALPH WALDO EMERSON, "Self-Reliance"

> Onödigt lidande,
> onödig väntan,
> världen är tom som ditt skratt.
> Stjärnorna falla—
> kalla och härliga natt.
> Kärleken ler under sömnen,
> kärleken drömmer om evighet....
> Onödig fruktan, onödig smärta,
> världen är mindre än ingenting,
> ned i djupet glider från kärlekens hand
> evighetens ring.
>
> *Unnecessary suffering,*
> *unnecessary longing,*
> *the world is empty like your laughter.*
> *The stars fall–*
> *cold and glorious night.*
> *Love smiles during sleep,*
> *love dreams of eternity....*
> *Unnecessary fear, unnecessary pain,*
> *the world is less than nothing,*
> *down into the depths slips from the hand of love*
> *the ring of eternity.*
> —EDITH SÖDERGRAN, "Stjärnenatten"

What has come to encircle the story so far is the productive, or expressive, aspect of the metaphors of "drawing a circle around a circle" and "vicious circle." Our leading fossils have lead us to excavate ways of giving a critical gesture—to investigate, as it were, the modes of production of some "work" (SR, 259), as Emerson puts it, intended to critically disclose. From the excavation site, initially defined by the diameter separating Adorno's vicious circle, as a metaphoric expression of the society to be critically disclosed, from Emerson's "drawing of a circle around the circle," as one for poetic disclosure, I have mainly reported on how Emerson, Nietzsche, Dewey, and Adorno seek to *produce* critical effects by disclosing their present forms of life. And I have done this even though already in the very beginning of the story, in chapter 3, it became evident that critical disclosure is a communicative process: for the disclosure to come full circle, it must be achieved by the recipients too. Emerson's poet discloses a higher self in the recipients by drawing a circle around their circle, which, in a sense still left open, must be drawn by the addressees again. It was this idea of poetic disclosure that Nietzsche, then, in chapter 4, socialized into an ethically recalcitrant countercultural achievement, the "circles of culture." Critical disclosure thus turned into an explicitly educational project of counterformation. In this tradition, social critique is from now on understood as recalcitrant education rather than as normative judgment. In chapter 5, finally, Adorno and Dewey sought to apply such educational projects in a much less marginal environment than envisaged by Nietzsche: the modern research university and the public sphere of highly restricted actually existing democracies. They drew empirically informed and theoretically reflected circles around their contemporary societies to provoke their contemporary counterpublics to educational and organizational group action. Even if they traced the relations of domination in society empirically by participating in sociological, psychological, and pedagogical research, they developed their theories and concepts within the metaphoric handed down to them from Emerson. Disclosing critique preserved its identity while it wandered from wilderness and periphery to the academic discourses of the twentieth-century research university. Thereby, it gave birth to disclosing critical theory.

Let me draw attention to four issues that I see emerging from the story so far. First, despite the previous chapter's acquaintance with Dewey's naturalized conception of disclosing reason, it still remains largely unclear how the envisioned understanding of social critique as education rather than as judgment could lay claim on rationality.

Second, in every chapter so far, it has been contended that something about the experience of a society reproducing as a vicious circle feels uncanny. This raises a host of questions. Why exactly should the recipient of disclosing critique perceive the circle of society as "vicious"? Why should it be experienced as problematic that society maintains its form in this way? That the form of life achieves its stability through antagonism and conflict has, after all, been applauded by generations of followers of Adam Smith and David Ricardo.[1] Is the experience of this "vicious" (*Bann, Täufel*, spell, etc.) nature of society maybe nothing other than good old superstition in a nicely and neatly rationalized package? Does disclosing critique, in the end, only appeal to emotions linked with belief in demons and witchcraft?

Third, how should the allegedly higher self disclosed in the recipient be understood? The idea of a "genius" appealed to in the recipient of disclosing critique and its critical education has been part of the tradition I am describing since its inauguration in Emerson and Nietzsche. In fact, even if Dewey never makes it explicit, it does latch on to his naturalized conception of reason: the moral variability of the many social groups allows for richer, more reflective—that is, higher—selves in the socialized members of the form of life. The idea is not even completely absent in Adorno's version of disclosing critical theory; even the most negativistic version of disclosing critique appeals to something to be "elevated" in the individual by the disclosing gesture—the negative ability to distance oneself from the society's adaptive demands. Hence, I believe this curious presupposition of a genius to be disclosed in the recipient calls for particular attention on the excavation site.

Finally, in the terrain I am mapping, we seem to hang on to the edge of an abyss separating what might in fact seem like *two* landscapes. To the attentive reader it must seem bewildering how quickly disclosing critique has shifted from the rather Romantic and poetic project of finding a form of life to affirm in Emerson and the young Nietzsche to a rather austere and sociotheoretical project of negativism in Dewey and Adorno. How can the metaphor of a circle around a circle transform conceptual shape this radically?

So far, then, I have described critical disclosure primarily from the perspective of *productive disclosure*: we have encountered various ways a critic—Emerson, Nietzsche, Dewey, or Adorno—draws a circle around the circle. In this chapter, I will reverse the perspective: I will start by describing receptive disclosure, the experience of receiving a critical gesture intended to disclose. Perhaps this will provide leads for following up on the four issues just mentioned.

Let's then take a big leap back all the way to the beginning of our story and review what Emerson says about receptive disclosure. In "Self-Reliance," he describes the experience of disclosure as the reception of a work of genius:

> A man should learn to detect and watch that gleam of light which flashes across his mind from within, more than the lustre of the firmament of bards and sages. Yet he dismisses without notice his thought, because it is his. In every work of genius we recognize our own rejected thoughts: they come back to us with a certain alienated majesty. Great works of art have no more affecting lesson for us than this. They teach us to abide by our spontaneous impression with good-humored inflexibility then most when the whole cry of voices is on the other side. Else, to-morrow a stranger will say with masterly good sense precisely what we have thought and felt all the time, and we shall be forced to take with shame our own opinion from another. (SR, 259)

The experience of disclosure is then an interaction between individuals (perhaps also groups of individuals) mediated through a great work (an artwork, a gesture) in which something familiar, something one has already "thought and felt," *returns* to the recipient. The content returning to the recipient is, moreover, in some sense, *ambivalent*: at the same time, it is familiar, something belonging to the recipient, and strange, something the recipient will be "forced to take." The reception is emotionally challenging: the *familiar* content comes with a certain greatness because it is also *strange*; it has acquired an "alienated majesty." The content is, furthermore, *both* familiar *and* strange because it consists of "thoughts" that the recipient has previously "rejected": they once were hers (perhaps, in some sense, they still are) and now, in the work, come back to her from someone else, which triggers feelings of shame. Going through such receptive experiences reflectively and repeatedly makes, finally, for an educative experience: they "teach us . . . good-humored inflexibility"—recalcitrance against the social environment.

Freud calls the quality of feeling triggered by the return of something both familiar and strange an "uncanny feeling." My hypothesis for this chapter is that to understand how the rather Romantic, affirmative, and poetic models of critical disclosure in Emerson and Nietzsche turn into the rather pragmatic, negative, and socio-theoretical models of disclosure in Dewey and Adorno, it is helpful to consider Freud's mediating role, which is, I believe, a mediation that shifts the meaning of the disclosed self and brings us closer to a naturalized conception of disclosing reason.

1. Running in Circles: The Uncanny Feeling

In fact, I believe Freud's mediating role to be so important to this story that it is worth considering it in a chapter of its own even though he, to my knowledge, never explicitly uses the metaphor of a circle around a circle. If my observation is correct, he leaves traces on the excavation site in the magnitude of a geological transformation. He tilts permanently both the conceptual space and the problem horizon opened by the metaphor. And this transformation helps understand how the rather Romantic, affirmative, and poetic conceptions of "drawing a circle around a circle" in Emerson and Nietzsche turn into the more soberly pragmatic, negative, and socio-theoretical conceptions of tracing the vicious circle in Dewey and, even more so, in Adorno. That said, I also believe that, even if Freud never may have written "circle around a circle," he *could as well* have done so: the experience of the uncanny feeling could namely be described as one. And indeed, Freud does come very close to doing just that. In exemplifying the uncanny experience, he tells the story of getting lost and finding oneself to have *run in circles*.

In his 1919 essay "The Uncanny," Freud recounts the following uncanny experience of his own:

> As I was walking, one hot summer afternoon, through the deserted streets of a provincial town in Italy which was unknown to me, I found myself in a quarter of whose character I could not long remain in doubt. Nothing but painted women were to be seen at the windows of the small houses, and I hastened to leave the narrow street at the next turning. But after having wandered about for a time without enquiring my way, I suddenly found myself back in the same street, where my presence was now beginning to excite attention. I hurried away once more, only to arrive by another *détour* at the same place yet a third time. Now, however, a feeling overcame me which I can only describe as uncanny, and I was glad enough to find myself back at the piazza I had left a short while before, without any further voyages of discovery. (U, 237; emphasis original)

The mere running in circles is surely not uncanny as such. In fact, many people, including myself, enjoy running circular jogging routes and find a peculiar, perhaps even therapeutic, satisfaction in repeating the circuit countless times. And Freud, too, recollects the experience of returning to the original piazza—a circle around the circles!—as relieving. Rather, the uncanniness seems to come with the experience of having run in circles without having realized it. Freud himself remembers that the feeling recalled "the sense of helplessness experienced in some dream-states" (237). The experience seems to be that of a bewilderment of finding ahead of oneself something that *should have been left behind*. Under exactly what conditions, then, can circles be said to be uncanny?

On the first pages of the essay, Freud initially describes the uncanny as a "quality of feeling," which lies "within the field of what is frightening," hints at its belonging to the "feelings of repulsion and distress" often neglected by aesthetics, and, like the feeling of shame that Emerson takes us to feel in experiencing the disclosing effect of a great work, takes the uncanny to "lead back to what is known of old and long familiar" (U 219–20). Now, feeling the uncanny and feeling shame are surely very different emotional responses. But that is precisely why their double analogy—of referring ambivalently back to something familiar yet strange and of being evoked in critical disclosure—is so striking and, I would add, surprising enough to merit deeper digging.

Freud continues his essay with a peculiarly long review of dictionary entries on the German word for "uncanny," *unheimlich*, and its putative antonym *heimlich*, which in English means "homely," and finds support for his hypothesis that the uncanny feeling refers to something familiar. Based on this review, he distinguishes two semantic components of "the uncanny," which I will call the homely component and the Schellingian component. The homely shade of meaning is revealed in the surprising discovery that *heimlich*, "homely," can be used, among other things, as identical with its antonym *unheimlich*, "uncanny": "What is *heimlich* thus comes to be *unheimlich*." *Heimlich*, Freud summarizes, means two quite-different things: "On the one hand it means what is familiar and agreeable, and on the other, what is concealed and kept out of sight." Even more startling to Freud is the second component: "Schelling says something which throws quite a new light on the concept of the *Unheimlich*, for which we were certainly not prepared. According to him, everything is *unheimlich* that ought to have remained secret and hidden but has come to light" (U, 224–25).

Just as its opposite *heimlich*, the "uncanny" refers to something *familiar* but *concealed*, yet as *unheimlich*, it *ought to* have remained concealed but has been *revealed*. Less surprising than this initial mess of dictionary definitions is Freud's conviction that psychoanalytic theory can help to sort it out. Psychoanalytic theory claims that anxiety is the transformed affect of a repressed impulse: if an impulse is repressed, then whatever affect belonging to it is felt as anxiety. Now, Freud believes that, among the many frightening aspects of our world, "there must be one class in which the frightening element can be shown to be something repressed which *recurs*" (U, 241; emphasis original). And *that* is the uncanny: the return of the repressed.

Repression of an impulse causes anxiety; if the affect of that impulse, despite its repression, is retriggered, then a fearful bewilderment will result, which is the uncanny feeling. As repression not only keeps or makes a wish unconscious but is also *itself* an unconscious process, the fearful feeling must indeed be bewildering and seem utterly inexplicable to the affected individual. This, Freud believes, is the "secret nature of the uncanny" for it explains how the perplexing semantic components—the familiar, the concealed, and the revealed—hang together after all: they are mutually implicated since "this uncanny is in reality nothing new or alien, but something which is familiar and old-established in the mind and which has become *alienated* from it only through the process of repression" (U, 241; emphasis added). Not unlike how the Emersonian "rejection" explained the "alienated majesty" of "what we have thought and felt all the time" (SR, 259), the Freudian "repression" explains the "alienated" character of the familiar in the uncanny feeling. Note also the semantic similarity of "the uncanny," as defined by Freud, with "disclosure": dis-closure, like the German *Er-schließung*, means "opening something that has been closed."

Freud soon introduces a further distinction that will, I believe, help explain the odd analogy between shame and uncanniness and so contribute to understanding how the Romantic, poetic disclosure of Emerson's turns into the more austere, socio-theoretical one of Dewey's and Adorno's. Freud namely identifies two different types of uncanny experience according to the element that returns. He distinguishes between uncanny feelings resulting from beliefs which have been overcome yet seem real and those caused by reinstated childhood complexes. An uncanny experience can occur, on the one hand, then, "when primitive beliefs which have been surmounted seem once more to be confirmed" and, on the other, "when infantile complexes which have been repressed are once more revived by some impression" (U, 249). The first type of the uncanny is associated with phenomena such as the "evil eye"—that is, the belief in the omnipotence of thought—or zombies—that is, the belief in the return of the dead. These are beliefs that we believe we do not hold anymore. Yet if experience at some instance seems to validate them after all, an uncanny feeling will seize us. The second type proceeds from, for example, womb phantasies or the fear of castration. These experiences refer to painful repressions in early childhood that to a large extent made us who we are. It makes, Freud thinks, a significant difference if the content of *what returns* in an uncanny experience is a (set of) belief(s) that we think we have already overcome or a repressed emotional ambivalence from our childhood.

The difference it makes is this: In the first type of uncanny experience, something actually happens that seems to confirm the content of a belief we do not hold ourselves to hold anymore. This experience is uncanny if the belief in question is "primitive" in the sense that it has already been *surmounted* in the life history of the individual or the community. Our animistic predecessors believed that inanimate things were animate, and as children, we wished that our toys could walk and talk. But our social and natural environment has since then struck us with the cold reality that this is not possible—and we have abode. Yet Freud believes that these beliefs, even if surmounted, "still exist within us" (U, 247), and they will jump at the opportunity as soon as something in the environment seems to confirm them. This gives us an uncanny feeling. *Is the silhouette in front of me on this dark street a zombie after all?* This uncanny feeling is, according to Freud, "purely an affair of 'reality-testing,' a question of the material reality of the phenomena" (248). That is, what the experience demands is a readaptation of my inner psychic life to the social and natural environment. This adaptation may or may not lead to a readjustment of that environment. *Is it a zombie? Is it not? If yes, should I fight it, or should I run? If no, should I laugh, or should I beat up the idiot who freaked me out?* Freud believes the situation to be completely different if what returns is a repressed childhood complex. When an element of the environment arouses emotional impulses that proceed from such repressed complexes, "reality testing," the question of verifying or falsifying the content of the experience as such does not arise. What must be checked is, as it were, not physical but psychic reality: "What is involved is an actual repression of some content of thought and a return of this repressed content, not a cessation of *belief in the reality* of such a content" (248–49; emphasis original). That is, the uncanny experience delivers a shock to my inner psychic life that can be taken care of only by readjusting that inner world. And that may or may not involve a habit change that would lead to my acting significantly differently in the social and natural environment.

Now, I believe this distinction between two types of uncanny experience according to the returning element helps to understand the link to Emersonian and Nietzschean shame and also how their Romantic use of circles transformed, in the stratigraphy of our excavation site, into their rather bleak application in Dewey and Adorno. Emerson's "rejected thoughts" seem namely to refer to something different than what returns in *either* of these two types of uncanny experience: at least some of those rejected thoughts seem reducible neither to repressed infantile complexes nor to primitive beliefs. What interests Emerson are the impulses, unconscious thoughts, that have been not repressed (*verdrängt*) but *suppressed* (*unterdrückt*); they have been turned down because of the adaptive pressures from the social environment ("when the whole cry of voices is on the other side" [SR, 259]). Of course, such thoughts *can* be repressed too and sometimes are if the environmental pressure is extreme (such as the behavior of the caregivers during the Oedipus complex, as Freud believes, or the violence of society in "identification with the aggressor," as Adorno believes), and they can come to seem surmounted if the educational influence of the environment convinces the individual of their "primitive" nature. Yet not all returning thoughts and feelings have been rejected in these two ways—other avenues of rejection remain. What seems to interest Emerson, in essays such as "Self-Reliance" and "Circles," are thoughts and feelings *suppressed* due to normalizing social pressures. These can then be disclosed by great works as creative variations or deviations—that is, recalcitrant tendencies—which have the potential of critically challenging the social environment. Freud would call these Emersonian unconscious thoughts "preconscious": they are "latent but capable of becoming conscious" (*EI*, 15). They are not conscious, yet there is also no *repression* in place, which would unconsciously block their path to consciousness. They are in principle—if the cry of voices were silent for a second, if concretism relaxed a little bit—up for grabs to the conscious mind.

If the unconscious content does not return from repression, there needs to be nothing particularly frightening about the reception of such Emersonian disclosure. It will rather be experienced as *shameful* as it involves the experience of the extent to which one has acted heteronomously: with shame one takes the realization that the suppression was an unnecessary adaptation to the pressures of the environment. This shame is due to the disclosure presenting the recipient something positive hitherto suppressed, a progressive phenomenon to affirm. Therefore, Emerson and Nietzsche readily postulate a higher self. However, if, as Freud observes, the disclosure hits a frightening element pertaining not to something merely suppressed ("rejected") but something *repressed* or allegedly *surmounted*, then the disclosure hits deeper. The reception will then be bewildering and deliver a shock to the psychic system. This disclosure is unlikely to bring much positive news to the recipient; instead, it will confront her with a *regressive* phenomenon. The difference in the attunement of Emersonian and Adornian disclosure, the two historical poles of our metaphorology, is partly explained by Adorno's more radical aim to reach what he takes to be the very bottom of the vicious circle of society, the repressed unconscious of the individual. For this, he uses Freudian psychoanalysis.[2] This seems plausible since the object of Freudian psychoanalysis is primarily not the unconscious mind as such but the *repressed* or "dynamic" unconscious (*EI*, 15), which can be disclosed in regressive phenomena, such as dreams or uncanny feelings—that is, experiences of its return.

Given Freud's definition of "the uncanny" as a return of the surmounted or the repressed, in what sense can circles, particularly those allegedly vicious ones of societal reproduction, be said to be uncanny? Thinking back on his own experience of running in circles Freud writes, "It is only [the] factor of involuntary repetition which surrounds what would otherwise be innocent enough with an uncanny atmosphere, and forces us the idea of something fateful and inescapable when otherwise we should have spoken only of 'chance'" (U, 237). Now, I think there is something similar in the experience of society as a vicious circle invoked by Dewey and Adorno. Returning again and again to square one, as it were, revives the superstitious belief in fate, spells, or demonic powers—that is, in the *vicious*. And so individuals in Adorno's tracing of *Bannkreis* (literally, "spell circle") act systematically, *as if under a spell* (*unterm Bann*), in a way that reinforces social conditions that are incompatible with their freedom and pursuit of happiness. To receive the tracing gesture of pointing out the vicious circle would then be an uncanny experience in the sense of the return of the *surmounted*: it revives superstitious beliefs in demons and witchcraft, such as acting under a spell or being led by a demonic power.

But I believe that Freud would think that such uncanny experiences of the spell-like character of social life, in fact, go even deeper: they can be uncanny also in the sense of the return of the *repressed*. While writing "The Uncanny," Freud was taking a break from work on another, more infamous essay, which he would finish a year later: the book *Beyond the Pleasure Principle*. There, he postulates a class of impulses operative in us that are independent of what he calls the "pleasure principle"—that is, the tendency of our impulses toward avoidance of pain and suffering. These impulses, which he subsumes under the term "the compulsion to repeat" (*BPP*, 20; originally in RRWT), are *indifferent* to our wellbeing. And indeed, already in "The Uncanny," Freud invokes the idea of repetition compulsion as an explanation for the uncanny feeling: "It is possible to recognize the dominance in the unconscious mind of a 'compulsion to repeat' proceeding from the instinctual impulses and probably inherent in the very nature of the instincts—a compulsion powerful enough to overrule the pleasure principle, lending to certain aspects of the mind their *daemonic character*...; a compulsion, too, which is responsible for a part of the course taken by the analyses of neurotic patients. All these considerations prepare us for the discovery that *whatever reminds us of this inner 'compulsion to repeat' is perceived as uncanny*" (U, 238; emphasis added). Think of it! There is something emotionally quite discomforting in sensing impulsive forces operative within oneself that are indifferent to one's own happiness and wellbeing. In *Beyond the Pleasure Principle*, too, Freud describes the ordinary emotional experience of these impulses as acting under a "daemonic power" (*BPP*, 21). Why do all my intimate relationships follow the same pattern? Why do my friendships end the same way every time? Why did Freud always break with his protégés?[3] The compulsion to repeat is, then, an unconscious force that we would rather keep as such. That is, we strongly tend to repress it—to the extent that whatever reminds us of it will be experienced as uncanny. Surely, then, having the Adornian experience of society as a vicious circle reminds us of the inner compulsion to repeat, wherefore its uncanniness would hardly come as a surprise to Freud.

This raises the question, How does experiencing such a tendency of repetition in *society*—seeing how *it*, despite the whole antagonistic flux and all the critical reactions to it in ordinary-action contexts, returns to square one every morning—relate to the uncanny experience of a force in oneself that is indifferent to one's pursuit of happiness and visible in the spell-like character of one's own ordinary life?

Perhaps a hint is given by the Freudian definition of "the uncanny" itself. The idea that the uncanny feeling arises from the return of the repressed appeared as an answer to the question of how to link the two semantic components of the homely and the Schellingian. As *heimlich*, the "uncanny" refers to something familiar but concealed, yet as *unheimlich*, it ought to have remained concealed but has been revealed. As discussed in chapter 3, Adorno sometimes presents the *Bannkreis* as identical with Hegelian "objective spirit," the idea of the "living good," the structure of a social world, which claims to offer a *home* for free and rational individuals.[4] This is clearly expressed in the provocative statement that Hegel's system has "satanically" been actualized as the shape of Western welfare society.[5] Objective spirit, the home of freedom and reason, turns into *Bannkreis* just like the homely (*heimlich*) turns into the uncanny (*unheimlich*) terror of instrumental reason. The disclosing gesture of pointing out the vicious circle would then show just how one's social world is not the *home* it claims to be but rather, just like the "compulsion to repeat," a circular process indifferent to one's pursuit of happiness. Similarly, although he famously stresses that habits are not defined by repetition, Dewey thinks that bad, rigid habits are, in fact, characterized by compulsive repetition. In a bad habit, I cannot find myself *at home*. It forces me to act in rigid pathways that I seek to avoid, but as action is impossible outside habit, that rejection only enforces the old rigid pathway anew: the attempt at difference amounts to repetition (*HNC*, 50–51). The homely becomes uncanny; yet I repeat the course of the bad habit again.

That this unhomeliness of society is an uncanny experience for the individual shows further how the loss of society as one's home is related to the experience of a loss of one's *world*:[6] when trapped in compulsive repetition, in mechanical habits, my world eventually comes to seem uncanny as a whole. Whereas I believe that the experience of one's society as uncanny is not unrelated to the experience of a loss of one's world, I do not think this study has proceeded, or indeed can proceed, far and deep enough for determining that relation positively. I take that it is this relation that Maggie Nelson points to in her poem "The World," whose first lines read,

> The world is
> reaching into
> you deeper
> and faster
> and cheaper
> than ever
> before so
> what do you
> hope for an
> afternoon
> spent alone
> with porn do
> we live in a
> world of
> bodies or
> not if the

> falling trees
> don't kill
> the chimps
> the lack of
> habitat will.[7]

Nelson presents an uncanny vertigo-like downward spiral of the *social* world continuing into *my* world as the experience of a collapse of both ego and the world. In his "Mourning and Melancholia," Freud distinguishes two responses to the experience of the loss of one's world. Such experiences can either turn into melancholia or initiate the work of mourning: "In mourning it is the world which has become poor and empty; in melancholia it is the ego itself" (MM, 246). In melancholia, the individual punishes herself for the shortcomings of her social world. The work of mourning, by contrast, bears for the individual the promise of rebuilding, as it were, her home; she reshapes her habits and becomes able to find herself to some extent to be at home in her world: "When the work of mourning is completed the ego becomes free and uninhibited again" (245).

At some point of our history, as Blumenberg's metaphorology of geometric symbolism shows,[8] the circle indeed presented a metaphorical ideal for social reproduction. The circular was the home: cosmos constituted a circle, logos was the "imitation" of that cosmic circle, and political life was to be built on logos.[9] The cosmic circle sent down to earth, as it were, a beam of imitation to shape our communities. However, the disclosing critics from Emerson via Nietzsche and Dewey to Adorno seem to show that we, at some point of our history, have surmounted the belief in a harmonious circular home, or, in Emerson's words, "Our life is an apprenticeship to the truth that around every circle another can be drawn" (C, 403). Like the pagan gods after Christianization turned into demons, the utopia of circular cosmic imitation became an uncanny dystopia. To us, the children of Emerson, there is something uncanny about any association that disallows dissociation. A necessary feature of a good-enough home has become that you can feel free both to stay and to go.

I think it is too early to clarify Freud's contribution to these issues of disclosing critique. But they do raise important questions that should be at least recorded at this junction: Does critical disclosure turn melancholia into a mourning for the loss of society as a home? Already, Nietzsche had remarked that the physician of culture should help her recipient to "turn his soul in another direction so that it shall not consume itself in vain longing" (*UM*, 160). If critical disclosure hits a frightening element of the social environment in the recipient, does it care for the triggered anxiety? How? If the receptive disclosure involves the experience of society as, indeed, unhomely and thus may be experienced as the loss of one's world, then providing the recipient a worthy space and sufficient support for mourning must be part and parcel of helping them to help themselves to alienate themselves from the alienated state of society. Does critical disclosure uncover the uncanny and care for the consequences?

2. Losing the Track: The Higher, the Lower, the Double

It seems we are stuck. The historical excavation threatens to crumble into arbitrary speculation. Let's return to the experience of receptive disclosure from another angle. The idea that the return of the repressed brought by a disclosing gesture can be uncanny seems to problematize the crucial Emersonian distinction, borrowed without reservations by the young Nietzsche, between the attained self and the "unattained but attainable self" (H, 239)—that is, the actualized self and the higher self to be attained in a receptive disclosure. The great "affecting lesson" of a disclosing gesture is that it helps the recipient to get in touch with her "genius": if the recipient can comprehend the disclosing gesture, then, in some sense, Emerson believes, its content must be something she has "thought and felt all the time"; she, as it were, already had it in her, and this "it" is her higher self. The shame she feels is, from this angle, her emotional reaction to the frustration that she had to take the content "from another" even though it was a part of her thought and she felt it all along. The aim of the disclosing gesture is then less to establish any new cognitive content than to leave the door ajar for the recipient to step up to her higher self, which *already* thinks and feels inside her.

However, Freud's essay shows that not only the return of the rejected content can be uncanny but also the very belief in a higher self. Such an agency in the soul might namely come under the suspicion of belonging to a class of uncanniness that Freud calls "the phenomenon of the 'double'" (U, 234). Such phenomena range from the uneasy feeling of hearing a friend enthusiastically bring the news that you have a doppelgänger who "looks exactly like you" or the shrug it might cause when you realize that you performed the exact same gesture (say, a wink) as someone you barely know to more intensely uncanny experiences such as catching the silhouette of an unknown person in the corner of your eye and, for a second or two, asking yourself who this unfriendly looking stranger is and realizing that the stranger is your own image in a mirror.

Freud believes that such quite-ordinary experiences of the double belong to the first type of uncanniness: they present recurrences of surmounted beliefs. "The 'double,'" he elaborates, "was originally an insurance against the destruction of the ego . . . ; and probably the 'immortal' soul was the first 'double' of the body." These beliefs, he argues, belong to a surmounted phase of both individual development and our species' natural history; they are products of the primary narcissism that characterizes the psychic life of young children and our prehistoric ancestors alike. However, having outgrown those phases of development, "the 'double' reverses its aspect. From having been an assurance of immortality, it becomes the uncanny harbinger of death" (U, 235). Having surmounted beliefs in projections out of unbounded self-love, these previously comforting figures acquire, again, a demonic character: "The quality of uncanniness can only come from the fact of the 'double' being a creation dating back to a very early mental stage, long since surmounted—a stage, incidentally, at which it wore a more friendly aspect. The 'double' has become a thing of terror" (236).

Now, the worry about the higher self to be disclosed comes from an altogether surprising thought. What one could, at least at the outset, take as an analogue for Emerson's "higher self" in Freud, the superego, might very well turn out to be an uncanny doubling. Is the higher self disclosed in receptive disclosure as an uncanny double rather than an attainable ethical ideal?

Of note, when Freud, in 1919, wrote "The Uncanny," he had not yet coined the terms "superego" or "ego ideal." However, already in "Mourning and Melancholia," written four years earlier, he had reflected on an "agency commonly known as 'conscience'" in terms continuous with his later theorizing of the ego ideal and the superego (MM, 247). When he finally theorizes it conceptually a couple of years later—first, as "ego ideal" in *Group Psychology and the Analysis of the Ego* in 1922 and, finally, in a revised form, as "superego" in *The Ego and the Id* the following year—he refers back to "Mourning and Melancholia" (*GPAE*, 109–10, 114; *EI*, 28). "The Uncanny" is then very much situated in the context of Freud's discovery of the superego, his own version of a higher self. And indeed, the Freudian superego also has a historical continuity with the Emersonian higher self. The young Nietzsche borrowed the term from Emerson; the somewhat-less-young Nietzsche transformed it into the concept of the "over man" (*Übermensch*),[10] which Freud quotes as an analogue of his "primal father," whose embodiment in the individual he claims the "ego ideal" to be (*GPAE*, 123).

Interestingly, in the discussion of the figure of the double in "The Uncanny," Freud mentions this self-observing, self-censoring, and self-punishing instance in the individual in the same terms as in "Mourning and Melancholia":

> The idea of the "double" does not necessarily disappear with the passing of primary narcissism, for it can receive fresh meaning from the later stages of the ego's development. A special agency is slowly formed there, which is able to stand over against the rest of the ego, which has the function of observing and criticizing the self and of exercising a censorship within the mind, and which we become aware of as our "conscience." ... The fact that an agency of this kind exists, which is able to treat the rest of the ego like an object—the fact, that is, that man is capable of self-observation—renders it possible to invest the old idea of a "double" with a new meaning and to ascribe a number of things to it—above all, those things which seem to self-criticism to belong to the old surmounted narcissism of earliest times. (U, 235)

This is a remarkably ambivalent passage. It allows for two divergent readings. What is, I believe, uncontroversial is that the passage argues that the formation of this self-critical psychic instance makes beliefs preceding its establishment into sources of the uncanny feeling. As will become clearer further below, the formation of the superego is, to Freud, so revolutionary a transformation in the life history of an individual that it is bound to surmount almost any preceding belief. However, the sentence "The fact that an agency of this kind exists, which is able to treat the rest of the ego like an object—the fact, that is, that man is capable of self-observation—renders it possible to invest the old idea of a 'double' with a new meaning and to ascribe a number of things to it" is open to another interpretation, one whose nutshell would be that once the superego sets itself against the ego and observes it, the individual is bound, as it were, to experience herself as her uncanny double. The superego would then, on the one hand, make the "double" into a source of uncanniness, because it surmounts the wishful projection of an external psychic life of oneself and, on the other, make itself a constant potential source of uncanniness for the ego, because it sets it as its lower double.

Does Freud mean here that the superego is a double of the ego and can be experienced by it as its uncanny double? Or does he only, less controversially, say that once the superego has been established, the double, whatever its shape, becomes an uncanny figure to the ego? These two readings are not mutually exclusive. As the idea of a higher self is so important for the practice of critical disclosure in Emerson and Nietzsche, it seems imperative to investigate the possibility that the superego, as a version of the higher self, presents an uncanny double of the ego, the attained self. Does Freud wish to point out an uncanniness of conscience, our "higher self"?

What speaks against reading the long passage above as presenting the superego as an uncanny double of the ego is that for Freud, in this phase of theory development, "conscience," the later superego, even if it can treat the ego as its object, still constitutes a *part* of the ego (MM, 247–48; U, 235–36); as the above quote goes, it is "able to treat *the rest of the ego* like an object." It is difficult to see how the ego could regard a part of itself as its external double. The reason for this is that up until 1923, Freud ascribes the function of reality testing—that is, the process of readapting one's psychic life to the environment (possibly leading to a readjustment of the environment itself)—to "conscience" or the "ego ideal" (see, e.g., *GPAE*, 114). In this case, the double could not have an uncanny effect on the ego since there would be no reality testing of the double and the surmounted belief, as the double would itself be the reality-testing instance—not to mention the even greater issue of whether reality testing can be applied to psychic reality at all, which Freud seems consequently to deny. The idea that the higher self could be an uncanny double seems to have brought us straight into a dead end.

However, from the 1923 *The Ego and the Id* onward, reality testing is definitely ascribed to the ego, whereas the superego is differentiated as a particularly intense identification with the power to observe, judge, and punish it. So let's at least have a closer look at how the superego is formed in that book and how it relates itself to the ego and the id.

First, imagine the feeblest little gizmo possible. Picture it as an undifferentiated living creature in the simplest possible form floating through space-time and colliding with objects more or less hard and sharp in its environment.[11] For the gizmo to continue in existence, it cannot allow itself to be crushed by the harder and sharper objects in the environment. Its surface, which is turned toward the environment, differentiates as an encrusted organ for the reception of stimuli. By receiving the stimuli, the gizmo can comprehend the direction as well as the hardness and sharpness of the colliding objects. And perhaps the surface can also learn to move the rest of the gizmo onto a less painful trajectory through the environment. In this allegory, the gizmo is the id, and its surface is the ego. The living individual is "a psychical id, unknown and unconscious, upon whose surface rests the ego" (*EI*, 24). As this protecting surface layer of the id, the ego is a "poor creature," a "frontier-creature," squashed between two powerful worlds—its mess of an inner world of pleasure-seeking impulses and the cold external reality of its environment (56). The ego represses impulses incompatible with the environment and reconciles other wishes to environmental demands by redirecting them or delaying gratification. The ego thus establishes and then comes to follow the rule of the "reality principle," which promises it success in the struggle for existence and overrules the "pleasure principle," the tendency to avoid pain and suffering, which continues to rule the id (TP, passim). Thus, with the reality principle, "the ego has set itself the task of self-preservation, which the id appears to neglect" (*OP*, 199).

The poor thing then struggles to mediate between the id and the environment; it tries, with one hand, to make its master id adapt to environmental demands and, with the other, to adjust the environment to accommodate at least some of the id's countless bizarre and conflicting wishes. Some of these wishes are directed at objects that the individual loves. They express her choice of love objects. Freud believes that the character of this individual is strongly influenced by the identifications the ego undergoes with beloved objects during its trajectory through the environment. Particularly intense is the effect of *lost* love objects—those who end up having a different trajectory. The ego then replaces the love object by identifying with it. Freud thinks that this is a very frequent process and supposes that "the character of the ego is a precipitate [*Niederschlag*] of abandoned object-cathexes" (*EI*, 29)—that is, its character deposes the traits of loving bonds and beloved objects as its own layers. The character of the ego is, as it were, a record of those loves. A new layer of that record emerges following what Freud calls "alteration in character": the ego adopts some features of a loved individual onto which the id had directed its libido and so makes *itself* lovable for the id; it "is trying to make good the id's loss by saying: 'Look, you can love me too—I am so like the object'" (30). To compensate for a lost beloved object, the ego makes itself lovable by imitating it; it takes on some of its lovable traits and so, to satisfy the id, changes its character.

Yet not only the ego is a poor dependent creature, but so too is (although to a lesser degree) its master id, the whole primarily unknown and unconscious individual. The id comes into the world as a helpless infant, who needs nurture and care to survive. In this emotionally difficult position of dependence, the individual develops ambivalent feelings toward the caring and nurturing elements in the environment: at times, they are warm and soft objects; at other times, cold and hard. She loves them; she hates them. Eventually, her bonds with her caregivers take an increasingly social shape as she enters other social bonds and associations. In that larger society, it is unacceptable that she could *have* her caregivers, control their trajectory, and the caregivers do not wish to be had. That larger society also demands her to form emotional bonds with other people. Psychoanalysis takes this crisis, the Oedipus complex, to mark a particularly painful and overwhelming phase for every child. It confronts her, in Jonathan Lear's words, with the question, "How do I, as a psycho-sexual being, enter society?"[12] It is an emotional crisis because the conflicting feelings of love and hate toward the caregivers are overwhelmingly confusing for the child. And it is a social crisis because the caregivers cannot be *had*. It appears between the pleasure principle and the reality principle as the conflict between the *happiness* promised by a unity with a caregiver, as it were, a return to the womb, on the one side, and the promise of *freedom* from dependence on them, on the other.

Now, Freud believes, finally, that this crisis involves the experience of a particularly intense loss of love to the extent of "permanently damag[ing]" the child (*OP*, 200). It therefore leaves a particularly deep and lasting trace in the ego: "The broad general outcome of the sexual phase dominated by the Oedipus complex may . . . be taken to be the forming of a precipitate in the ego, consisting of these two identifications in some way united with each other. This modification of the ego retains its special position; it confronts the other contents of the ego as . . . [a] super-ego" (*EI*, 34). The superego is then formed from particularly intense early childhood identifications with love objects, which leave such a deep trace in the ego that it differentiates from it, acquires a psychic life of its own, to the point of treating it as its object. The depth and differentiation of these identifications are residues of the emotional ambivalence the child felt toward the caregivers. This ambivalence toward the early love objects is recorded in the superego and transferred onto its relation to the ego: the identification is, as it were, bidden and forbidden; it "is not exhausted by the precept: 'You *ought to be* like this (like your father).' It also comprises the prohibition: 'You *may not be* like this (like your father)—that is, you may not do all that he does; some things are his prerogative'" (34). This double bind, which gives the depth to this trace in the character, is the consequence of the repression of the deep emotional ambivalence.

Importantly for our concerns, this double bind also means that, in contrast to Emerson's "unattained but attainable" higher self, the ego ideal is *not attainable* for the ego. However, even if not attainable, Freud still thinks that the superego does indeed present a higher self. It represents the most important developmental characteristics of not only the human individual but also, Freud adds, "of the species; indeed, by giving permanent expression to the influence of the parents it perpetuates the existence of the factors to which it owes its origin" (*EI*, 35). What *is* this "origin" of the superego? What is higher, and what is lower? This is Freud at his most dialectical!

Remember, in identification, to compensate for a loss, the ego offers itself to the id as a love object. Thus, the origin of the superego is the *id*! It was the id, the unknown and unconscious individual, who directed its libido toward the love objects; it was the id whose quest for pleasure had to be satisfied; it was the id to whom the ego offered itself as a compensation for that loss of satisfaction. The superego is the child of the id's unbounded love. The superego "is . . . the expression of the most powerful impulses and the most important libidinal vicissitudes of the id." Yet this time, the ego bargained with an ambivalence it could not endure: "By setting up this ego ideal, the ego has mastered the Oedipus complex and at the same time placed itself in subjection to the id. Whereas the ego is essentially the representative of the external world, of reality, the super-ego stands in contrast to it as the representative of the internal world, of the id" (*EI*, 36).

Alas, the origin of the superego is also the *environment*: the *outer* world installs itself through the internalized traits of the primary caregivers as a representative of the *inner* world *against* the ego. Freud goes as far as to claim that the superego becomes a representative of the individual's archaic heritage, a medium of extragenetic inheritance in the individual (*EI*, 35–36). Through the superego, the individual reappropriates "what biology and the vicissitudes of the human species have created in the id and left behind in it" (36). Mediated through the ambivalent relationship with the primary caregivers in the environment and the incrustation of that ambivalence as an ego ideal in the individual, she comes to reappropriate the traces that previous generations have left behind in the human body. Thus, Freud continues the topos of a victorious second nature becoming first nature, which we encountered first in Lovibond's idea of a naturalized social teleology and then in a counterteleological shape in Nietzsche, Dewey, and Adorno.[13] However, by presenting the superego as a medium, Freud suggests a *psychic* mechanism for the inheritance of acquired traits: "The experiences of the ego seem at first to be lost for inheritance; but, when they have been repeated often enough and with sufficient strength in many individuals in successive generations, they transform themselves, so to say, into experiences of the id, the impressions of which are preserved by heredity. Thus in the id, which is capable of being inherited, are harboured residues of the existences of countless egos; and, when the ego forms its super-ego out of the id, it may perhaps only be reviving shapes of former egos and be bringing them to resurrection" (38). There is, then, something uncannily circular about the working of the superego—the return of the archaic even in the highest actions of the individual. The superego not only constitutes a higher self but also represents in the self what is, as it were, the lowest: "What has belonged to the lowest part of the mental life of each of us is changed, through the formation of the ideal, into what is highest in the human mind by our scale of values" (36). Let's have a closer look then at how, in Freud, the social environment shapes the innermost psychic life of the individual. Does he present us with yet another version of the vicious circle?

I believe one can distinguish three levels of environmental shaping of the individual in Freud. On the first one, there is the individual's reappropriation, through the ego ideal, of her archaic heritage, which itself consists of traces from ancestors' repeated efforts to adapt to the environment. On this "deep" level, where "second nature" has already become "first," even the thesis of the id being the origin of the superego elaborates how the *environment* shapes the innermost psychic life of the individual: the derivation of the superego from the id "brings it into relation with the phylogenetic acquisitions of the id and makes it a reincarnation of former ego-structures which have left their precipitates behind in the id" (*EI*, 48–49). Following the formation of the superego, the individual is, as it were, predetermined to reproduce archaic adaptive patterns in her agency. Note, however, that this environmental influence comes importantly from the *past*. These psychic layers inherited from past ego structures are not a product of the *current* social environment. They may present fitness for (certain parts of) the social environment today. But that may also not be the case: if the environment has changed, they might have become *heterochronous*. The maladaptation to the social environment can then be a case of repetition, too, of the reproduction of an archaic psychic structure. The social environment may, as it were, conflict with itself in the individual, clashing with its own archaic adaptive demands. This level is what Herbert Marcuse has in mind when he later writes that "Freud's 'biologism' is social theory in a depth dimension."[14]

On the second level, the social environment can shape the individual's inner life by causing deep impulse conflicts, as exemplified above with the

Oedipus complex. On this "middle" level, it makes it unbearable for the individual not to embark on the path of the "reality principle"—that is, adaptating to the normative expectations and material conditions of the social environment. Marcuse later takes up this idea and interprets the Oedipal wish—that is, the wish to *have* a caregiver instead of *becoming* the other one—as a "protest . . . against painful, repressive freedom," a prototype of critical recalcitrance, as it were. Reestablishing a unity with "the mother" is, for Marcuse, an epitome of freedom—"freedom from want."[15] In its struggle for the mother and against the father, Marcuse believes, the sexual impulse struggles against pressure toward sublimation, against domination. Gradually, however, as the Oedipus complex evolves, freedom becomes associated with the paternal principles: "Freedom from want is sacrificed to moral and spiritual independence."[16] This discloses a promise of freedom and happiness betrayed in post-Oedipal life: the seemingly paradoxical idea of *nonrepressive self-control*—the possibility of a habitual direction of one's action that would flow from libido itself. Instead, as we saw above, in Freud, the Oedipus complex establishes the superego as an observing, criticizing, and punishing instance in the self and the nearly unchallenged rule of the reality principle for the rest of the individual's life—en route to a damaging oscillation between unhappy freedom and unfree happiness while struggling to survive in an overpowering social environment.

On the third level, once the superego has been established, it allows for an environmental shaping of the individual that is more immediately adaptive to the *current* social environment. On this "superficial" level, the superego allows environmental injunctions and restrictions to shape the individual's actions *from within*. Although Freud believes that the superego is more inert than later identifications and character changes, it remains accessible to later environmental influences. In fact, it is precisely its more rigid and resistant form that enables an environmental inner control of the individual: "It . . . preserves throughout life the character given to it by its derivation from the father-complex—namely, the capacity to stand apart from the ego and to master it. It is a memorial of the former weakness and dependence of the ego, and the mature ego remains subject to its domination. As the child was once under a compulsion to obey its parents, so the ego submits to the categorical imperative of its super-ego" (*EI*, 48). Because it constitutes a particularly inert, persistent, rigid identification, the superego enables a deeper shaping of the individual's action by the larger social environment too. It presents the social environment with, as it were, a tunnel to the ego from behind the frontlines. In the later post-Oedipal life of the individual, "the role of the father is carried on by teachers and others in authority; their injunctions and prohibitions . . . continue, in the form of conscience, to exercise the moral censorship." On this third level of environmental shaping of individual psychic life, the social environment continues into the unconscious layers of the individual and shapes its actions by moral censorship, which the maladapted ego experiences as a "sense of guilt" (*EI*, 37).

Freud insistently associates this tunnel from behind the frontlines with morality. The superego carries society as morality within the individual: "We are dealing with what may be called a 'moral' factor, a sense of guilt, which is finding its satisfaction in the illness and refuses to give up the punishment of suffering" (*EI*, 49). Morality, in Freud's view, violently presupposes that suppressing an impulse makes it go away. He agrees with other disclosing critics such as Nietzsche and Dewey that this belief is illusory. Impulses *will* be expressed; the only question is how. Morality, however, demands impulse control without caring for the consequences—that is, without providing any means for the redirection of antisocial sexual or aggressive impulses. It thus pressures the individual to turn the aggression of the id against the ego itself:

> From the point of view of instinctual control, of morality, it may be said of the id that it is totally non-moral, of the ego that it strives to be moral, and of the superego that it can be super-moral [*hypermoralisch*] and then become as *cruel* as only the id can be. It is remarkable that the more a man checks his aggressiveness towards the exterior the more severe—that is aggressive—he becomes in his ego ideal. The ordinary view sees the situation the other way round: the standard set up by the ego ideal seems to be the motive for the suppression of aggressiveness. The fact remains, however . . . : the more a man controls his aggressiveness, the more intense becomes his ideal's inclination to aggressiveness against his ego. It is like a displacement, a turning round upon his own ego. But even ordinary normal morality has a harshly restraining, *cruelly* prohibiting quality. It is from this, indeed, that the conception arises of a *higher* being who deals out punishment inexorably. (54; emphasis added)

The higher and the lower align against the ego. The higher and the lower turn out to be placeholders of the same thing; they *encircle*, so to say, the ego. In the "sense of guilt," we seem to have found at least a hint of an uncanny circularity of social teleology reminiscent of the vicious circularity of Emerson's "society" and Nietzsche's "state," anticipant of Adorno's *Bannkreis* and contemporary of Dewey's "vicious circle": the social environment shapes, through the superego, the individual's agency from within to painfully conform with its moral order. The contents of the higher layers of the self may then present all but positive ethical ideals to be attained in a critical disclosure. On the contrary, it may be their *cruelty* that is disclosed!

I will return to investigate closer this circularity in section 5. Before that, however, I would like to turn our attention to a curious detail in the passage quoted above—namely, that Freud attributes *cruelty* to both the superego and ordinary morality.

3. Drawing a Line: Morality, Cruelty, Civilized Society

On our quest for the uncanniness of the higher self, we have lost the track of its expected doubling and instead stumbled on its suspected cruelty. How come the formation of the superego, our higher self, leads to cruelty rather than to attainable ethical ideals? What could it mean, in the first place, for *morality* to be cruel? Does not cruelty designate exactly the sort of behavior that morality is supposed to prevent? I believe that Freud's statement that cruelty is the outcome of superego formation as well as a feature of ordinary morality is as difficult to appreciate as it is important for his project of critical disclosure—if he indeed has one.

The difficulty is this: appreciating Freud's choice of the adjective "cruel" (*grausam*). Why does Freud use "cruel" to designate the consequences of superego formation and a presumably prominent feature of lived morality? The contrast to another possible term may highlight the seriousness of the accusation at stake here. For instance, take "betrayal." If society demands moral behavior of its acting members (individuals and social groups) and morality is trumpeted to them as a golden path to happiness, it would be easy to understand what Freud would mean if he said that morality is a betrayal: he would simply be saying that morality, which is based on suppression of impulse, cannot lead to happiness because the only realistic conception of happiness is eventual release of impulse, or gratification, which is the exact thing that morality inhibits. Therefore, morality would mean betrayal. Now, Freud clearly thinks this is so (*CD*, chaps. 2–3). Yet cruelty is different from betrayal. Morality not only is the betrayal of a social contract promising happiness but has, *additionally*, a "harshly restraining, cruelly prohibiting quality" (*EI*, 54).

It is, as it were, understandable that the social environment demands impulse control of the individuals. It might even be acceptable, on some account of successful civilized life, that it promotes this by promising happiness, thus betraying the individuals to some necessary degree of unhappiness in their lives. But, Freud seems to ask, is it necessary for it to restrain the individual *so harshly*? If not, then the pain that the individual takes on in this, as it were, surplus impulse control amounts to *unnecessary* suffering.[17] This is, I believe, what Freud means by the cruelty of morality: it produces senseless suffering in the individuals. And his pointing out that senseless suffering presents, I further believe, a gesture of critical disclosure.

Allow me to illustrate the idea and the gesture by quoting a lengthy passage. A paradigmatic example of the cruelty of morality is what Freud, a few years later in *Civilization and Its Discontents*, thematizes as the exploitation of sexual life (*Ausbeutung des Sexuallebens*). The passage is this:

> The tendency on the part of civilization to restrict sexual life is no less clear than its other tendency to expand the cultural unit. . . . Taboos, laws and customs impose . . . restrictions, which affect both men and women. Not all civilizations go equally far in this; and the economic structure of the society also influences the amount of sexual freedom that remains. Here, as we already know, civilization is obeying the laws of economic necessity, since a large amount of the psychical energy which it uses for its own purposes has to be withdrawn from sexuality. In this respect civilization behaves towards sexuality as a people or a stratum of its population does which has subjected another one to its exploitation. Fear of a revolt by the suppressed elements drives it to stricter precautionary measures. A high-water mark in such a development has been reached in our Western European civilization. A cultural community is perfectly justified, psychologically, in starting by proscribing manifestations of the sexual life of children, for there would be no prospect of curbing the sexual lusts of adults if the ground had not been prepared for it in childhood. But such a community cannot in any way be justified in going to the length of actually *disavowing* such easily demonstrable, and, indeed, striking phenomena. As regards the sexually mature individual, the choice of an object is restricted to the opposite sex, and most extra-genital satisfactions are forbidden as perversions. The requirement, demonstrated in these prohibitions, that there shall be a single kind of sexual life for everyone, disregards the dissimilarities, whether innate or acquired, in the sexual constitution of human beings; it cuts off a fair number of them from sexual enjoyment, and so becomes the source of serious injustice. The result of such restrictive measures might be that in people who are normal—who are not prevented by their constitution—the whole of their sexual interests would flow without loss into the channels that are left open. But heterosexual genital love, which has remained exempt from outlawry, is itself restricted by further limitations, in the shape of insistence upon legitimacy and monogamy. Present-day civilization makes it plain that it will only permit sexual relationships on the basis of a

solitary, indissoluble bond between one man and one woman, and that it does not like sexuality as a source of pleasure in its own right and is only prepared to tolerate it because there is so far no substitute for it as a means of propagating the human race. (*CD*, 104–5; emphasis original)

In this passage, like in many of Dewey's and Adorno's, the social environment—the institutions and customs of society—imposes restrictions on individuals for its persistence. Freud believes this to be "perfectly justifiable." He thinks it is legitimate because civilized society needs to raise psychic energy from sexual life to maintain itself. It must *instrumentalize* the libidinal energy of the individuals. But, at some breaking point, the *extent* of the restrictions, the degree of the instrumentalization of sexuality, reverts to cruelty. The current extent of these restrictions is not necessary at all for this type of society, which Freud calls "civilization": not all civilized societies go as far as "our Western European" one, which restrains to the point of a "high-water mark"; we have already passed the breaking point. Current civilized society constitutes a social environment for its individual members that dominates them—it *exploits* them. There is an excess of adaptive demands: they transgress the limit for the suffering and unhappiness that civilized society needs for its persistence and that may be expected from individuals. There is no reproductive justification for this extent of restrictions, this demanded surplus impulse control.

The current adaptive demands then cause senseless suffering. They impose restrictions that require the individuals to give up on sexual enjoyment to an unnecessarily high degree with unnecessarily harsh sanctions and with an arbitrary distribution of tolerated sexual pleasure, which amounts to "injustice." However, instead of providing a normative theory of justice as a yardstick for some "well-ordered" civilization, Freud, in the above passage, provides his readers with a *list of examples* of socially demanded unnecessary restrictions upon individuals' sexual pursuits of happiness. For the maintenance of civilized society, it is *not* necessary that children's sexuality be disavowed, homosexuals be oppressed, extragenital sexual practices be stigmatized as perversions, monogamous intimate bonds be expected of everyone, marriage be imposed as a legal form on every lasting sexual relationship, or sex be linked with reproduction rather than, say, enjoyment or happiness. The element of cruelty, on this conception, is then not so much dependent on any identifiable cruelty-inflicting *subject* committing a moral wrong (and enjoying it). Rather, it rests on the *senselessness* of the *affected individuals' suffering*. The conception is object dependent.[18] Recognizing cruelty in this sense then requires reference to the experiences of concrete suffering individuals. Rather than some normative criterion of justice, such reference demands, in the disclosing critic, the morally cultivated cognitive habits of a more or less "wise" or "virtuous" person who can *perceive suffering* in other individuals and *trace it* through the social fabric. In chapter 4, we encountered Nietzsche, who believed that being a "physician of culture" demanded a particular "plastic power": a sensibility for social suffering and skills of "painting" that experience into a picture of a higher life. In *Civilization and Its Discontents*, the reader encounters a physician who criticizes society with the practical wisdom and theoretical tools acquired from many years of therapeutic experience with individuals suffering in that society.[19] Like Adorno will later do with considerably more conceptual nuance and empirical backing, as we saw in the previous chapter, Freud traces the suffering he encounters back to reproductive mechanisms of society.[20]

Yet what about the "painting" of a higher life that Nietzsche demands? Just as Freud's critical gesture relies little upon some positive account of justice, so does it little amount to any positive program for political reform. It may not be the task of the disclosing critic to present a detailed cultural politics that positively defines the limit of meaningful suffering. It suffices that she points out the extent to which some social suffering is senseless (decentering disclosure) and points to the objective possibility of a more meaningful social experience (recentering disclosure). Freud, the disclosing critic, certainly does not provide any concrete politics of civilization.[21] But he does satisfy the demand of disclosing critique to point to the *possibility* of such:

> When we justly find fault with the present state of our civilization for so inadequately fulfilling our demands for a plan of life that shall make us happy, and for allowing the existence of so much suffering which could probably be avoided—when, with unsparing criticism, we try to uncover the roots of its imperfection, we are undoubtedly exercising a proper right and are not showing ourselves enemies of civilization. We may expect gradually to carry through such alterations in our civilization as will better satisfy our needs and will escape our criticism. But perhaps we may also familiarize ourselves with the idea that there are difficulties attaching to the nature of civilization which will not yield to any attempt at reform. (CD, 115–16)

Freud's point is then not to *judge* the ordinary morality of civilized society as cruel according to some normative conception of a just or well-ordered society. Rather, he *shows* in what way ordinary lived morality involves and the formation of the superego enables senseless social suffering. The cruelty he points out is not an unfortunate exception in some otherwise well-ordered society; it is not an aberration, an accident. The cruelty lies at the very heart of civilized society; it lies in the way our form of life reproduces itself. Our form of life is based on the exploitation of sexuality. Our form of life is *fundamentally* cruel. He shows this by pointing out an excess: it might be necessary that sexuality should be *instrumentalized* for societal reproduction, but it is certainly not necessary that it should be *exploited*. Granted that civilization needs, for its persistence, to instrumentalize libido, it is still not necessary to make people suffer to *this* extent.

This pointing is a gesture of critical disclosure since it decenters by pointing out the cruel consequences of our morality and it recenters by pointing to the possibility of significantly less harsh societal restrictions, which would allow individuals a gentler relation to their sexuality. Like Dewey's and Adorno's, Freud's recentering gesture is rather *gradualist* than outright revolutionary: he believes that gradual adjustments of the social environment may enable a less unhappy life for the individuals. And like in Dewey and Adorno, this gradualism invokes a *tragic sense of political life*: we better not delude ourselves about the conditions under which we politically act; the nature of civilized society is not infinitely malleable.

Just how malleable a civilized society is remains an open question for a disclosing critique of society and its gradualist politics. And it certainly presents a matter of dispute, whose traces on our excavation ground certainly leap to the eye. Freud does arguably not deserve the title of a *radical* gradualist awarded to Dewey and Adorno in the previous chapter. In this contestation, Dewey, Adorno, and Marcuse criticize Freud for believing that the discontent with civilized society is our fate.[22] Remarkably, Adorno, in *Minima Moralia*, phrases this critique in a circle metaphoric: once Freud has consigned pleasure "to the repertoire of tricks for preserving the species . . . without consideration of that moment in pleasure which transcends the circle of subservience to nature [*Kreis der Naturverfallenheit*], ratio is degraded to rationalization" (*MI*, 61; translation amended; emphasis original). These authors doubt that Freud's recentering gesture is counterteleological enough: Does it have the disclosing potential to *break* the vicious circle? Is Freud, then, a theorist of the vicious circle at all?

Interestingly for our metaphor history, however, Freud brings a new possibility of *decentering* disclosure to light: the gesture of pointing out a limit.

Freud traces transgressions by the social environment in the individual: his critique of culture proceeds as an "uncovering" of the roots of individuals' senseless suffering. It traces the necessity and arbitrariness as well as the causes of current social suffering. He discloses, so to speak, *by drawing a line*. This seems continuous with our leading metaphor of drawing a circle around the circle: Freud's line can be worded as drawing the circle around the all too tight restrictions that the current social environment imposes on individuals for its own persistence.

To sum up, there was initially very little good news for a disclosing critic to take home from the previous section. First, the self appealed to in disclosing critique became ambivalent; the higher and the lower seem not anymore as easily distinguishable as originally hoped. Second, the initially promising track of the uncanny double was lost, yet, what is even worse, the suspicion that there is something uncanny about the superego is still haunting the lines of this page. Third, with this problematization of the higher self comes also a difficulty with the educator role of the disclosing critic: the educational projects of Nietzsche and Dewey cannot be successful if the educators just carry on "the role of the father." The very idea of a counterformation seems threatened. In some way, it must do justice to this ambivalence of the self to be disclosed.

Nevertheless, an unexpected gleam of light eventually shone through the shadows thrown down upon this cul-de-sac: we stumbled on a gesture of critical disclosure—critical disclosure as drawing a line. This can be understood as a branch of the metaphorical topos of drawing of a circle around the circle: tracing the narrow boundaries set for sexual play, exploration and enjoyment in this form of social life is drawing a circle around the reproductive circle of civilized society. It discloses the extent to which sexuality is exploited *and* that the circle does not need to be nearly as tight as it presently is. Thus Freud, too, is decentering and recentering: he is pointing out the senseless suffering in contemporary society and pointing to the objective possibility of another, less unhappy form of life.

Of course, it may well be that we are not anymore living in a society as sexually repressed as the Viennese of the 1920s, where Freud was writing these texts. This has been remarked on by critical theorists from Herbert Marcuse via Jessica Benjamin to Federica Gregoratto—authors who nonetheless believe that love and sexuality allow a "liminal space" for critical disclosures of social life.[23] However, although I do think it is wise to consider, at least in the form of a thought experiment, the extent to which we carry an archaic heritage from the Freudian age inside us—a habit to adapt to a perhaps materially inexistent repressive society today—it is not my concern here to defend the timeliness of Freud's analysis of civilized society. Rather, I am excavating an example of a particular disclosing gesture—a gesture of drawing a line.[24] And I still suspect this gesture must have something to do with the possibility that one's form of life can turn out uncanny.

4. Varieties of Uncanniness: The Ordinary, the Fictional, the Theoretical

We have, then, discovered a disclosing gesture in Freud. But we have lost track of the uncanny. What has Freud's pointing at the extent of our unnecessary suffering, the extent to which civilized society's moral demands switch from necessary betrayal to sheer cruelty, got to do with the uncanniness of society Dewey and Adorno seem to appeal to, and how does all this help to clarify receptive disclosure, which were the reasons I turned to Freud's role in this history anyway? We are still stuck. Back to square one: How, and why exactly, does a disclosing gesture evoke an uncanny feeling in the recipient?

Toward the end of "The Uncanny," Freud discusses two ways of evoking an uncanny experience. He distinguishes the "merely pictured" from the "actually experienced" uncanny (U, 247). On the one hand, the uncanny feeling can arise as an actually experienced distress breaking the flow of everyday life: something in the otherwise ordinary-action context elicits a return of a repressed complex or a surmounted belief. In this case, the uncanny experience is evoked by some event in ordinary life. Freud emphasizes that this ordinary variety of uncanniness is a rather rare occurrence. The "merely pictured" uncanny, by contrast, arises only when the affected person has already taken flight from the ordinary-action context into a realm of aesthetic enjoyment. The realm that Freud is particularly interested in is that of literary fiction. In this case, the uncanny feeling is evoked by an author. In fiction, the possibilities for producing uncanny experiences seem almost endless; the fictional uncanny, Freud claims, "is a much more fertile province than the uncanny in real life, for it contains the whole of the latter and something more besides, something that cannot be found in real life." Whereas the "actually experienced" uncanny takes place in the given world of ordinary life, the "pictured," Freud claims, occurs in a world that an author *makes*: "The imaginative writer . . . can select his world of representation so that it either coincides with the realities we are familiar with or departs from them in what particulars he pleases" (U, 249). To her fictional world, an author can add uncanny conditions and features that are so rare in the world of ordinary life.

With regard to the evocation of the uncanny in literature, Freud distinguishes further between fairytales and realism. No uncanniness from surmounted beliefs can arise in fantasy and fairytales because the content of the stories is not submitted to reality testing. As readers of fairytales, "we adapt our judgement to the imaginary reality imposed on us by the writer, and regard souls, spirits and ghosts as though their existence had the same validity as our own has in material reality" (U, 250). However, the return of repressed childhood complexes remains uncanny even in fairytales and fantasy since in such experiences, as we saw in section 1, reality testing does not apply anyway. So whereas talking electric creatures charging themselves in thunderstorms and obsessively reaching for the horizon surely would present an uncanny encounter in ordinary life, the Hattifatteners of Tove Jansson's *Moomin* tales are, although perhaps weird and scary, not uncanny, since they belong to the real possibilities of her world of the Moominvalley, where any inanimate being can be a talking and walking creature. The Groke, a growling lonely ghost who leaves a trail of ice behind her as she descends from her cold and lonely cottage on the Lonely Mountains to haunt the Moominvalley, on the contrary, *is* an uncanny figure since she expresses the fear of being expelled from the social community, which marks a return of the repressed emotional ambivalence toward the caregivers on whom we have all been completely dependent.

The realist writer, by contrast, makes her world *out of the ordinary world*. Unlike the author of fairytales, she "accepts . . . the conditions operating to produce uncanny feelings in real life; and everything that would have an uncanny effect in reality has it in [her] story." Realism, as it were, hauls reality testing back onboard from the ordinary action context left behind. Yet the realist writer expands the scope of possibilities for the evocation of the uncanny and increases its effect since she holds on to her aesthetic license of "bringing about events which never or very rarely happen in fact" (U, 250). She, too, is making a fictional world, but she does it primarily by adding foreign elements to a presumed ordinary world. Freud thinks of this gesture as a *deception*: the realist writer "deceives us by promising to give the sober truth, and then after all overstepping it. We react to his inventions as we would have reacted to real experiences; by the time we have seen through his trick it is already too late and the author has achieved his object." Owing to the realistic setting and prehistory of Yakov Petrovich Golyadkin's encounter with his double in Fyodor Dostoevsky's novella *The Double*, the return of the surmounted belief of the double can indeed be experienced as uncanny. By walking his readers first through the very ordinary scenes of Golyadkin's visit to the doctor's and his crashing of Klara Olsufyevna's birthday party, Dostoyevsky deceptively sets up an ordinary setting, which is also in place during the sudden appearance of Golyadkin's double in the snowstorm—and the readers only call his bluff after the uncanny has already been felt. Freud would in no way condemn Dostoyevsky for this. On the contrary, he sees deception as a constitutive feature of realist fiction (250–51).

Now, an altogether interesting question that Freud's distinction between the "experienced" uncanny and the "pictured" uncanny raises in the light of our inquiry into the practice of disclosing critique of society is this: What about the uncanny feeling aroused by *theoretical* exposition? Does theory as a disclosing gesture belong to ordinary experience or to the "merely fictional" or perhaps to a third type? Or more specifically, how should we understand the type of uncanny feeling that arises as a result of the kind of tracing theorizing encountered in Adorno's sociological essays and lectures as reconstructed exemplarily in the preceding chapter? There, disclosing critical theory not so much operated as a normatively structured system of propositional claims but rather presented as a highly elaborate gesture of pointing, step-by-step, at the uncanniness of current society. These questions become only more pertinent as we have good reason to think that Adorno knew Freud's essay on the uncanny.[25]

In order to make sense of the theoretically evoked uncanny experience of society, I suggest an extended Freudian typology where a distinction is made, first, following Freud, between the uncanny actually experienced in ordinary life and the uncanny pictured in any setting that may be taken as ordinary or not. Let's call these the *ordinary uncanny* and the *pictured uncanny*. Then, within the second type, the pictured uncanny, I suggest extending the typology by further distinguishing between *fictional* and *theoretical* subtypes: the pictured uncanny may take fictional or theoretical shape (see figure 4).

What is the criterion of the added second distinction between the subtypes fictional and theoretical? The theoretical uncanny is different from the fictional uncanny by virtue of *disallowing deception*. In contrast to more fantastic stories available to the fictional production of the uncanny, the re-

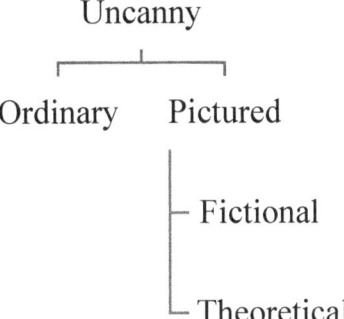

FIGURE 4. Types and subtypes of the evocation of the uncanny feeling. Created by the author.

cipient of disclosing critical theory adapts to the material reality of ordinary life—that is, she submits the content to reality testing. To this extent, the story emerging from a theoretical tracing of the vicious circle is similar to realist fiction: in contrast to the author of fairytales, both the realist author and the disclosing critical theorist *make worlds out of the real world*. Disclosing critical theory is, then, similar to realist fiction in telling a story presuming the ordinary world as its setting, thus importantly enabling reality testing as part of the reception.

However, as readers of realist fiction, we license the realist writer to *deceive* us. We are not disappointed if particular aspects of the story do not coincide with material reality. If someone protested against Virginie Despentes that Manu and Nadine of her *Baise-moi* "didn't really exist" and their murders of random men along their road trip through France "didn't really happen," we would regard it as a grave misunderstanding of realist fiction. But if we were students following Adorno's lecture course on the *Philosophical Elements of a Theory of Society* and, after a few lectures, found out that the phenomenon of concretism did not exist and that he knew it all along, we would indeed be justly disappointed. Disclosing critical theory is, then, different from realist fiction in ruling out deception as a method of evoking uncanny experiences.

Nevertheless, *disclosing* critical theory does display a further curious similarity to realist fiction, which, I believe, allows for distinguishing it more clearly from *normative* critical theory on the other side. Like the realist writer, the disclosing critical theorist claims the affective power of a storyteller. In Freud's words, "The storyteller has a peculiarly directive power over us; by means of the moods he can put us into, he is able to guide the current of our emotions, to dam it up in one direction and make it flow in another" (U, 251). A difference between normative critical theory and disclosing critical theory is, then, that the latter, as an educational project, embraces not only the social asymmetries between the educator and those to be elevated but also the affective dimensions of the communicative situation of critique as part and parcel of the practice of critique. In this regard, disclosing critical theory is different from normative critical theory but similar to realist fiction.

And here, I believe, lies the significance of the uncanny effect for disclosing critical theory. The disclosing critic evokes the uncanny as a *method of directing the affects of the recipients*. She assumes the task to guide the current of our emotions. By effecting, without deceiving, an uncanny feeling about current society, she puts the recipients in a specific mood. The mood of uncanniness is a bewilderment, a distress, a *shock*, as it were, where the recipients experience the ordinary, extraordinarily, as strange and familiar at the same time. From this mood, they can then experience the foreignness of current society to them: they can experience the alienated state as it presents itself, because the shock of the uncanny has, intermittently, brought them to a sufficient distance from it. And this distance may also bring them to experience what in themselves is recalcitrant to these bizarre adaptive demands. They have been, for the moment, alienated from the alienated state of society.

A final similarity between realist fiction and disclosing critical theory that is important to emphasize has to do with their being forms of "picturing," or what Freud elsewhere calls "phantasy making" (*das Phantasieren*). They constitute forms of thinking that involve a creative play between the reality principle and the pleasure principle. In Freud, phantasy making is a fundamental and independent form of the thought process. A few years before his essay on the uncanny, he elaborated his idea of phantasy making in his "Formulations on the Two Principles of Mental Functioning": "With the introduction of the reality principle one species of thought-activity was split off: it was kept free from reality-testing and remained subordinated to the pleasure principle alone. This is the act of *phantasy making* [*das Phantasieren*], which begins already with the play of children, and later, continued as *daydreaming*, abandons its dependence on real objects" (TP, 222; emphasis original; translation amended). "Phantasy making" is Freud's term for the thinking that escapes the rule of the reality principle—that is, the overwhelming adaptive pressures of the societal environment. It surmounts adaptive pressures on thinking. Activating instead the pleasure principle, it reaches the deepest layers of the id, thereby enabling a thinking that does not repress but embraces the traces of its archaic past—the traces of past adaptive patterns heterochronous with the current social environment. Whereas realist fiction and disclosing critical theory do submit their worlds to reality testing, their "picturing" takes a detour through phantasy making. Such surmounting of reified thinking by the force of *imaginative theorizing* involves an "experimental" and "playful moment," as Adorno noted and identified in Dewey.[26] This moment of imaginative theorizing creates a world that is to take an objective form, which then can be submitted to reality testing. Disclosing critical theory is then similar to the play of children in that it seeks contact with real objects. It involves phantasy making *through* real objects.

A crucial challenge for any form of radical social critique is to escape reproducing the conceptual structures of thinking selected for the persistence of the present social environment. The detour through the pleasure principle in phantasy making is to enable precisely this. Note that Blumenberg thinks that this is the function of metaphors in thinking too: his metaphorology was designed to "force us to reconsider the relationship between logos and the imagination." He regards the metaphoric operation of the imagination as catalyst for conceptual theorizing, an inexhaustible reserve for "transforming the universe of concepts."[27] Disclosing reason must accordingly include play and pleasure at its very core. And disclosing critical theory is, thus, similar to realist fiction, finally, by affirming as a moment of its own rationality a detour of playful phantasy making.

A skeptic might at this point ask, If disclosing critical theory may not use deception as a tool for the evocation of uncanny experiences, what may it use? I believe the list of tools to be open-ended. In the opening chapter of his *Ways of Worldmaking*, Nelson Goodman, who believes that both literary works and scientific theories are involved in "worldmaking," offers such an open list of methods that apply to world making in both the arts and the sciences.[28] Therefore, I believe it to apply also to both fictional and theoretical evocations of the uncanny.

First on his list is what he calls "composition and decomposition": artists and theorists make worlds by taking old worlds apart and then reassembling their parts into new worlds. They divide wholes into parts, partition kinds into subspecies, analyze complex processes into their constitutive components, and make distinctions; then, they reassemble them into new wholes, kinds, and processes and make connections. And crucially, Goodman notes, they give new names to the things of old worlds; they use *metaphors* to effect "double reorganization"[29]—that is, shifting a term's realm of application and relating it to the old one. So the realist writer builds her uncanny world from elements of the world of ordinary life and reorganizes it minimally to prepare the conditions for uncanny experiences. Surely, also a disclosing critical theorist can *reconstruct* society in her theory by analyzing it and putting it back together again. And in doing that, metaphors, such as "vicious circle," are a useful and permissible tool.

The second method Goodman calls "weighting": artists and theorists make worlds out of worlds by valuing some features of the old worlds as relevant or irrelevant, important or unimportant. Sometimes they just lay more or less emphasis on some elements. Such weightings need not be dichotomous; they can also involve "ratings of relevance, importance, utility, value," which "often yield hierarchies."[30] Obviously, like all social theorists, disclosing critical theorists, too, value some features of the real social world as more relevant than others, which results in hierarchies of theoretical interest. Critical theory has traditionally contrasted itself to "traditional theories" by it being self-reflective about its theoretical interest: its "weighting" has proceeded as an analysis of its own role in social life.[31]

The third is "ordering": theorists and artists build orders into their worlds. If the elements of the world are supposed to be measurable, there must be some order in it. "Orderings alter with circumstances and objectives."[32] Like how Freud's story of running in circles had a temporal order of the sequences of finding himself in the red-light district of the Italian town three times, so Adorno's models are ordered as *phases* of the vicious circle, as argued in the previous chapter. Thanks to ordering, then, the disclosing critical theorist can provide the recipient with the uncanny experience of *returning* to what should have been left behind.

"Deletion and supplementation" is Goodman's fourth method: he claims that "the making of one world out of another usually involves some extensive weeding out and filling—actual excision of some old and supply of some new material."[33] This "weeding out" sounds much less dramatic when one considers that from the map of, say, Zürich's District 5, the people, visible in the streets day and night, have been *deleted*, and the borders of the district, visible nowhere in the ordinary-world version of the district, *supplemented*. And that's great—the map is more helpful that way. Again, it will hardly be a surprise that disclosing critical theorists also delete certain elements from and supplement others to their uncanny social worlds. The question is whether their uncanny world is a good model for the disclosure of the foreignness of the ordinary. The realist writer's "deceptions" are sometimes extreme supplementations of new elements into her world—a world that was otherwise made out of the real world. Adorno is sometimes accused of underrating the significance of social movements and political institutions in his social theory.[34] But this can also be understood as a method of an uncanny world making with the intention to disclose: he is *deleting* social movements and political institutions from the ordinary world in order to disclose the foreignness of a society, whose reproduction can very well be traced without their consideration, to our needs for political self-determination (see, e.g., *PETS*, 39).

The final item on Goodman's list is the method of "deformation"[35]: artists and theorists also radically reshape parts of the old world to make a new one. Such deformations can be perceived either as corrections or distortions. Such distortions can be achieved by hyperbolic use of language. At times, Adorno, perhaps exaggeratingly, says that exaggerations are the most important aspects of a social theory.[36]

5. A Vicious Circle in the Soul: Civilized Society and the Sense of Guilt

Section 1 of this chapter showed how, for Emerson, the affect accompanying critical disclosure is that of a *shame* that helps the recipient to attain her higher self and why, after Freud, the experience of critical disclosure can turn out *uncanny*. This happens when the disclosure hits a frightening element pertaining not to some deviating mental content merely suppressed ("rejected") but to something repressed or allegedly surmounted. The reception will then deliver a shock to the psychic system of the recipient. In section 2, again, it turned out that, following Freud's metapsychology, the higher self disclosed might not be worth attaining or might not even be attainable at all: as an ego ideal, it is fundamentally ambivalent, and in civilized society, as the carrier of morality within the individual, it can be just as cruel as the id; the distinction between the higher and the lower collapses into a circle—a finding that was postponed to later investigation. Surprisingly, Freud's attribution of "cruelty" to ordinary morality and the superego revealed in the very heart of his metapsychology and cultural criticism a gesture of critical disclosure, which was roughly contoured in section 3: the gesture of drawing a line demonstrating the extent of unnecessary social suffering and the possibility of alleviating it. At this point, however, the track of the uncanny had been completely lost. Therefore, in section 4, Freud's distinction between two ways of evoking the uncanny was discussed and complemented with a third: the uncanny feeling can be effected by the circumstances of ordinary life, by artworks and by disclosing critical theories. In disclosing critical theory, evoking an uncanny feeling presents a method of directing the affects of the recipients by the use of imaginative metaphorical theorizing; disclosing critical theories are similar to realist fiction and different from normative critical theories by virtue of affirming the affective dimensions of the communicative situation of critique as part of their educational intent.

Does, then, Freud's gesture of drawing a line have anything to do with evoking the uncanny? Does he, too, apply what I have termed the "theoretical uncanny"? I believe he does! A curious—and, indeed, uncanny—aspect of his most famous work of cultural criticism, *Civilization and Its Discontents*, is that nearly every chapter starts with Freud apologizing, in one way or another, to the reader. The book begins with Freud's lament that he cannot resolve the problem of the "oceanic feeling," which his friend Romain Rolland links with religion and which Freud overlooked in his previous book *The Future of an Illusion* (CD, 64–65). Freud starts chapter 3 by apologizing to the reader that the book "has not so far taught us much that is not already common knowledge" (86). Chapter 4 begins with his complaint that the task he sets himself—that is, of clarifying how civilized society arose—"seems an immense one," and he confesses to "feel diffidence in the face of it" (99). Chapter 6 starts with an outright self-reproach: "In none of my previous writings have I had so strong a feeling as now that what I am describing is common knowledge and that I am using up paper and ink and, in due course, the compositor's and printer's work and material in order to expound things which are, in fact, self-evident" (117). The most dramatic apology is perhaps the opening passage of the final chapter, chapter 8: "Having reached the end of his journey, the author must ask his readers' forgiveness for not having been a more skillful guide and not having spared them empty stretches of road and troublesome *détours*. There is no doubt that it could have been done better. I will attempt, late in the day, to make some amends" (134). Why these recurring excuses? Why the repeated apologies?

Let me first take two steps back, though! In his two books on social philosophy following briefly after "The Uncanny," I take Freud to be struggling to theorize the psychological modi operandi of two types of social groups. I believe the idea he develops to be roughly this: the first type of social group maintains its form by *cessation* of ego ideals; the second, by their *intensification*. I will call the first type of social group a *crowd*. The second I will call *civilized society*.

Already before introducing the concept of the superego into his later metapsychology in *The Ego and the Id*, Freud had formulated the idea of ego ideals in *Group Psychology and the Analysis of the Ego* to explain how individuals are bound together in crowds. The crucial concepts by which Freud explains the psychological reproduction of a crowd are "identification" and "idealization."

The former concept is familiar from section 2. To grasp Freud's idea of the psychological reproduction of a crowd it is important first to recall that identification works as a *substitute* for what Freud calls a "libidinal object-tie"—that is, identification compensates for a lost love (*GPAE*, 108). It offsets, as it were, the diverging trajectories of the individual and an object her id wants to *have* by the ego making itself *be* like the object. Freud further believes now that identifications may be evoked whenever the individual perceives a common feature shared with another individual who is not primarily a love object and assumes that the more striking this shared feature is, the more likely it can be transformed into a new libidinal tie, as if into a love relation (107–8). Freud believes that the bond between the members of a crowd is based on an identification of this type—an identification mediated by a striking "emotional [*affektive*] common quality" (108).

Idealization, in the relevant sense here, is a tendency to resolve the tension between the ego and the superego by ascribing perfection to an external love object. The love object then "serves as a substitute for some unattained ego ideal of our own" (*GPAE*, 112). The individual loves it for qualities she previously pursued to possess herself but then gave up the quest for, perhaps because she either had set her ideal too high or was unable to deal with the inevitable double bind of the ego ideal (you must be like your father; you may not be like your father) and now, by a detour, procures by loving the object for precisely those qualities (112–13). Identificatory love offers, as it were, a looping way to possessing one's higher self without having to attain it first. Freud claims that by such an idealization of the object, "which is no longer to be distinguished from a sublimated devotion to an abstract idea, the functions allotted to the ego ideal entirely cease to operate." The self-criticism of the individual is silenced; "conscience has no application" anymore (113), and any amount of cruelty may now be carried out for the love of the object. "The whole situation can be completely summarized in a formula: *The object has been put in the place of the ego ideal*" (113; emphasis original).

Now, the formula Freud gives for the crowd combines these two psychological mechanisms of identification and idealization: the crowd is "*a number of individuals who have put one and the same object in the place of their ego ideal and have consequently identified themselves with one another in their ego*" (*GPAE*, 116; emphasis original). In a crowd, the individual members of the social group share an idealized object and thereby identify with each other. Concretely, they have replaced their higher self by a leader, or an abstract idea, and identify with each other in this devotion. A crowd is thus psychologically reproduced by cessation of the individuals' ego ideals.

How can a crowd be critically disclosed from within? How can an individual dissociate from an association like this? In the book, Freud answers these questions only in the passing. Yet interestingly, we already know the answer he gives from Dewey: a member of a group can dissociate from a crowd by virtue of being a member of many social groups! Like Dewey, Freud believes that by association in many social groups, we acquire a richer higher self, a more versatile superego and a more multilayered ego, which will possess several identifications and more resistance to idealization. It will then not so easily let its ego ideal be replaced by one love object alone. Echoing Dewey's words quoted in the previous chapter from *Human Nature and Conduct*, a book published on the other side of the Atlantic the very same year, Freud writes, "Each individual is a component part of numerous groups, he is bound by ties of identification in many directions, and he has built up his ego ideal upon the most various models. Each individual therefore has a share in numerous group minds—those of his race, of his class, of his creed, of his nationality, etc.—and he can also raise himself above them to the extent of having a scrap of independence and originality" (*GPAE*, 129). Not unlike in Dewey's idea of disclosing reason discussed in the previous chapter, Freud believes that the plurality of groups, the fact of diverse loci of socialization, not only enables the use of one social group as a (negative or positive) example for the disclosure of another but also allows the individual to "raise himself above them," transcend the specific group contexts to creative recalcitrance against their adaptive demands—the very habit that Dewey, with reference to Emerson, called "reason."

Like Adorno, however, Freud is not an unconditional supporter of group pluralism. Whereas Adorno, as shown in the previous chapter, worried about group antagonisms impoverishing the moral variability of social groups, Freud's skepticism challenges the value of pluralism *psychologically*. In *The Ego and the Id*, he asks whether a social environment with a high degree of group pluralism can become psychologically overwhelming for the individual: "If [the ego's object identifications] obtain the upper hand and become too numerous, unduly powerful and incompatible with one another, a pathological outcome will not be far off. It may come to a disruption of the ego in consequence of the different identifications becoming cut off from one another by resistances. . . . Even when things do not go so far as this, there remains the question of conflicts between the various identifications into which the ego comes apart, conflicts which cannot after all be described as entirely pathological." If the identifications in the many social groups become *too* many, *too* deep, *too* contrasting, the individual will not be able to sustain them. Freud even speculates that such might be the cause for what, in his day, was known as "multiple personality" (today, dissociative identity disorder): ideals acquired from conflicting action contexts would then take turns in seizing hold of the ego (*EI*, 30–31).

Even if Freud clearly lays more emphasis than Dewey on ego integration—that is, on the sustenance of an integrated unit of individual action—I believe the authors of these two 1922 books agree in principle: disclosing reason demands care not only for the moral variability of the many social groups but also for the internal ethical quality of every single social group too.[37] A rational social group would not demand too deep and exclusive identifications from its individual members. Had Adorno's social theory provided us with a reminder of how fragile the moral variability of social groups is, then Freud adds a further supplement to the care for disclosing reason by pointing out the limits of the individuals' psychological capacity to sustain plural layers of the ego. The care for reason, which disclosing critique both practices and relies on, applies to the socialization processes *within* any social group as much as to the associations *between* social groups.

Note that Emerson can account for the critical disclosure of this type of social group: the conscience, higher self, of an individual can be disclosed by appeal to thoughts rejected due to identification and idealization in the current action context. And so, in "Experience," he writes, "Very mortifying is the reluctant experience that some unfriendly excess or imbecility neutralizes the promise of genius. We see young men who owe us a new world . . . but . . . they lose themselves in the crowd" (E, 474). The Emersonian disclosure brings a self that is enclosed in the crowd to connect to a part of their higher self they already know from another group context but had suppressed in the crowd due to the idealizing tendency within this group. This individual would then feel ashamed of not having seen this familiar thought herself and of having now to take it from another. There is nothing particularly uncanny about this. However, I believe that the Emersonian disclosure of an ethically desirable and practically attainable higher self will not work anymore when we turn to the uncanniness of the second social group, civilized society, where conscience, the higher self, has been made into to a vehicle of societal reproduction.

In *Civilization and Its Discontents*, we namely encounter a completely different type of social group with a completely different mode of psychological reproduction and, correspondingly, a completely different disclosing gesture. Whereas the first type of association operated by cessation of ego ideals through identification and idealization, this second type of association maintains itself by *intensifying* the superego to the point of producing a repressed "sense of guilt." Freud points now to a more radical problem in dissociation form association: society keeps us tied by the force of the sense of guilt, which the ego ideals promote. In civilized society, the higher self becomes an uncanny feature of the uncanniness of society.

Freud's method in *Civilization and Its Discontents* is that of studying civilized society through the very *traces* it leaves in the character of its individual members. To Freud, civilized society is a "peculiar process which mankind undergoes" and can be traced through the character changes it produces for its persistence (*CD*, 96). Civilization uses up some of the instincts, impulses, and acquired habits of the individuals, but there are, he believes, also features in the individuals that oppose civilized society. Such *recalcitrant* tendencies include at least various dispositions for sexual pleasure, aggressive impulses, and features of the archaic heritage unfit for the current social environment. Freud asks how, by what method, civilized society takes up these adaptive challenges: "What means does civilization employ in order to inhibit the aggressiveness which opposes it, to make it harmless, to get rid of it, perhaps?" (123).

Freud believes that there are many such methods, but there is one that to him clearly appears as "the most important." This is *the sense of guilt*:

What happens in [the individual] to render his desire for aggression innocuous? Something very remarkable, which we should never have guessed and which is nevertheless quite obvious. His aggressiveness is introjected, internalized; it is . . . sent back to where it came from—that is, it is directed towards his own ego. There it is taken over by a portion of the ego, which now, in the form of "conscience," is ready to put into action against the ego the same harsh aggressiveness that the ego would have liked to satisfy upon other, extraneous individuals. The tension between the harsh super-ego and the ego that is subjected to it, is called by us the sense of guilt. (*CD*, 123)

Now, here is my final hypothesis of this chapter—a hypothesis that I hope will eventually tie together its many loose ends: the peculiar "discontent" (*Unbehagen*) with "civilized" social groups Freud diagnoses expresses itself by a *repressed sense of guilt*, and this discontent renders present civilization radically *uncanny*. The civilized society Freud traces in *Civilization and Its Discontents* presents what has, in the course of my study, been metaphorically expressed as a "vicious circle": the institutions and customs of civilized society impose restrictions on the individuals to the extent of exploiting them senselessly; these restrictions are internalized by the individuals to the point of them forbidding themselves and punishing themselves for the type of recalcitrance that could challenge the society that impedes their pursuit of happiness. Freud himself expresses this uncanniness of civilized society thus: "Civilization ... obtains mastery over the individual's dangerous desire for aggression by weakening and disarming it and by setting up an agency within him to watch over it, like a garrison in a conquered city" (123–24).

How does, then, this pacifying garrison operate? In section 2, we saw how the superego was formed, yet how exactly does the "sense of guilt" it catalyzes arise? Freud theorizes that the sense of guilt arises in two stages as a reaction to two distinct but related fears: the "fear of an authority" and the "fear of the super-ego" (*CD*, 127).

Consider this curious phenomenon: even when a person has not done anything bad but merely thinks of doing so, she may feel guilty. Why is the mere thought regarded as equal to the deed? "How is this judgment arrived at?" Why should I think there is anything bad at all in contemplating the death and destruction of the journal editor who, despite excellent reviews, desk rejected the original journal-article version of chapter 3 in clear consciousness of the fact that I would never ever act on it? Freud believes that the original motive for this thinking is "fear of loss of love." The child is constitutively dependent on the caregivers and seeks to avoid any action that would make her lose their love; with the loss of their love, she would also lose protection and be exposed to the superiority and punishment of her caregivers: "At the beginning, therefore, what is bad is whatever causes one to be threatened with loss of love. For fear of that, one must avoid it" (*CD*, 124). In the context of this fear, it also makes little difference whether one does the bad thing or merely plans it; in either case, the feared loss of love becomes real only if one gets *caught*, which is a real possibility of both acting and planning, and in either case, the reaction of the authority is imagined as the same. Freud links this fear with adult experiences of social anxiety. It continues to dispose social action in society as a general fear of authority, and eventually "the place of . . . the two parents is taken by the larger human community" (125).

However, the sense of guilt, as Freud understands it, has not arisen yet. Its further condition is the internalization of the authority as superego. Here, the distinction between doing and wishing a bad thing now collapses entirely, "since nothing can be hidden from the super-ego, not even thoughts." The ego ideals never go out on a date together for quality time to revive their relationship; the ego ideals do not leave you playing alone to do grown-up stuff in the other room; the superego doesn't even go to the toilet by itself. The superego sees everything. Yet it can be as harsh as any social authority: "The super-ego torments the sinful ego with the same feeling of anxiety and is on the watch for opportunities of getting it punished by the external world" (*CD*, 125). We thus first renounce impulses because we fear the aggression from an external authority. We then install an internal authority and control impulses for fear of it. *The authority of the social environment continues into the individual*: "The aggressiveness of conscience keeps up the aggressiveness of authority" (128).

Now, the superego may produce a peculiar pattern that was completely absent from the fear of loss of love or any later subtype of the fear of external authority. I mentioned it already when discussing Freud's metapsychology in the end of section 2, and now, it pops up again in his cultural criticism: "The more virtuous a man is, the more severe and distrustful is [his superego's] behaviour, so that ultimately it is precisely those people who have carried saintliness furthest who reproach themselves with the worst sinfulness" (*CD*, 125–26). Now, Freud believes the superego not only *continues* the authority of the social environment within the individual but also, as a sense of guilt, reverses the dynamic of its predecessor. Whereas social anxiety, the fear of authority, made the individual renounce her impulse, now, inversely, *the renunciation of impulse produces guilt*. As nothing can hide from the superego, even the mere instinct to do a bad thing provides a reason for moral punishment of the self. The sense of guilt is, as it were, a *vicious circle in the soul*: "Every renunciation of instinct now becomes a dynamic source of conscience and every fresh renunciation increases the latter's severity and intolerance.... [W]e should be tempted to defend the paradoxical statement that conscience is the result of instinctual renunciation, or that instinctual renunciation (imposed on us from without) creates conscience, which then demands further instinctual renunciation" (128–29). Civilized society presents, as it were, a vicious circle that installs a vicious circle within the individual. It is uncanny as such, and the sense of guilt is its uncanny double in the well-adapted individual (see fig. 5 below).

What remains, to come full circle, is to link Freud's insight into the vicious circularity of civilization and the sense of guilt with an uncanny gesture of critical disclosure. This gesture, I take, is Freud's recurring apology to the readers of his book. The German word for apology, *Entschuldigung*, literally translates as "de-guilting"—as it were, a confession of guilt in order to get rid of it. Yet according to the logic of the sense of guilt, the more you confess, the guiltier you turn out to feel. The explanation for Freud's compulsive-

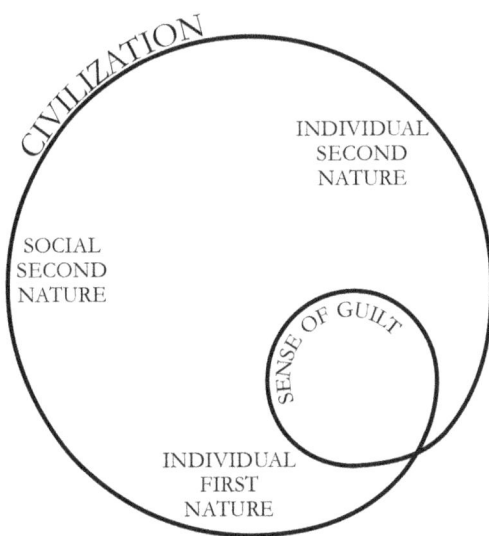

FIGURE 5. The "vicious circle" as doubling into a vicious circle of society and a vicious circle in the soul, as implied by Freud's conception of the repressed sense of guilt. Created by the author.

looking and steadily intensifying apologizing is then the simplest possible: he expresses his sense of guilt, and thus, by objectifying the operation of the vicious circle of civilized society on the soul of the author, he makes it *experienceable* to his readers.

A path to receptive disclosure is paved by the uncanny apologies as the readers are put in the position to observe how civilization violates the soul of its critic. This gesture in the context of disclosing the sense of guilt as the uncanny double of the uncanny society points, I believe, to an important insight for a disclosing critique of society: for an individual to stand up, raise her head above the stream, and offer a critical diagnosis of her culture and society means a confrontation with her own sense of guilt. What Freud then points at in these passages is what is *psychologically at stake* in taking the recalcitrant position of a disclosing critic. By this apologizing gesture, he discloses the fact that disclosing critique of society means confronting society *inside oneself*, too, in the shape of the sense of guilt. Disclosing the irrationality of the alleged universal from the perspective of a particular experience is an emotionally dissonant affair for a civilized individual.

The returning element of this uncanny gesture is the reader's own repressed societal determinateness. The sense of guilt *is* an example of repressed societal determinateness. Freud's gesture shows the extent to which that societal determination of the most civilized individuals among us is repressed. Very few of us have the habit of thinking, when struggling with feelings of guilt, of our own individual conscience as the voice of an overpowering social environment that first built a tunnel behind the frontlines and then established a garrison in the conquered city. For this reason, I even think it is irrelevant whether Freud intended this disclosing gesture consciously or not. What matters is that he provides his readers with the tools to decipher it.

Freud's disclosing gesture points, furthermore, to the sense of guilt as a vicious circle where two further vicious circles meet. To the disclosing critic, as we have seen in the preceding chapter, the society seems like a vicious circle. To society, however, it is the circle around the circle that seems vicious; it is the critic who, by her recalcitrance, is immoral and should be ashamed and feel guilt. Our two leading metaphors—"drawing a circle around a circle" and "vicious circle"—*merge*. And indeed, we can now see that they had always belonged together at the lowest and highest layers of the excavation site. Already Emerson writes in the essay "Circles," "The virtues of society are vices of the saint" (C, 411). And in "Sociology and Psychology," Adorno ties together the Huxleyan "conditioning" with the Freudian punishing instance in the self: "The coincidence of the average superego and the functional needs of a social system, namely those of its own self-perpetuation, is triumphantly achieved in Huxley's *Brave New World*."[38] In this locus, Freud discloses the sense of guilt as the uncanny double of civilized society—a vicious circle in the soul. It is an educative gesture to any reader aspiring to radically criticize their civilized form of life: prepare for struggle with its uncanny double within yourself too!

Yet what is the instance of the self that Freud is appealing to in this disclosure? What, in the end, is the fate of the "higher self" to be disclosed? Civilized society cannot be disclosed by appeal to ego ideals, like in the case of the crowd, as it is precisely the superego that promotes its exploitation of the individuals. To what psychic instance in the addressee is the cruelty of the superego, the uncanny sense of guilt, disclosed? What psychic layer is left for disclosing critique to address after its critical disclosure of the higher self as the uncanny double of alienated society?

First, I believe that Freud believes the apologizing gesture to directly address the *ego* of the reader. It asks, as it were, Can your ego take on the reality testing that the uncanniness of this double evokes? In his metapsychology, Freud theorizes that later identifications—that is, post-Oedipal layers of the ego—can be used to strengthen the ego against the despotic rule of the superego: "The ego is formed to a great extent out of identifications which take the place of abandoned cathexes by the id; ... the first of these identifications will always behave as a special agency in the ego and stand apart from the ego in the form of a super-ego, while later on, as it grows stronger, the ego may become more resistant to the influences of such identifications" (*EI*, 48). Disclosing reason demands care for a plurality of layers in the ego. Critical disclosure is then, from Freud onward, partly an uncanny exercise in uncovering the uncanny to strengthen the ego against an overpowering social environment *and* its garrison within the individual, the superego. That this exercise itself is uncanny was clear to Freud; in the "Uncanny," he notes in passing, "I should not be surprised to hear that psycho-analysis, which is concerned with laying bare these hidden forces, has itself become uncanny to many people for that specific reason" (U, 243).

Also, from this gesture toward the ego, there is a lesson to be learned on the quest for disclosing reason. By appealing to later layers of identification in it, the ego can be strengthened against the punishing voice of society in the superego. "Psycho-analysis is an instrument to enable the ego to achieve a progressive conquest of the id" (*EI*, 56). What Freud calls the ego's progressive conquest of the id is not something achieved by knowledge, explanation, justification, or arguments alone. It is not primarily cognitive. It is a practical process—a process of rehearsing, training, learning, and habituating a more autonomous ego-controlled way of living.[39] This helps understand the type of individual creative and rational recalcitrance that Nietzsche and Dewey expect to be found and further develop in the educational and organizational groups, the "circles of culture," that they envision to carry recentering disclosure.

Second, I believe there is also a more radical, hidden address to the readers in Freud—one that is even more significant for grasping the idea of a disclosing critique of society and was perhaps unconscious to Freud himself. In a way, Freud's disclosing gesture not only aims at strengthening the ego against the superego but also seeks to make new space for the *id*. Freud's metapsychology and cultural criticism show that in order for critical recalcitrance against the societal environment to become effective, it must develop methods of thinking beyond adaptive demands—that is, beyond the reality principle. Disclosing reason demands care for connections with the pleasure principle, which rules the id and its memories of the broken promises of happiness and freedom. Freud's disclosing gesture exemplifies and promotes playful and imaginative forms of thinking in its metaphorical and reflective operations. Critical disclosure is then, from Freud onward, also, to a great extent, an uncanny exercise in uncovering the uncanny to strengthen the operation of the pleasure principle in thinking to enable critical recalcitrance to transcend the present adaptive pressures—including their psychic representation, the reality principle. Bringing out the operation of the pleasure principle in a critical gesture can also be uncanny: Freud's genetic distinction between the reality principle and the pleasure principle in "Formulations on the Two Principles of Mental Functioning" shows that civilized individuals internalize not only adaptive demands as the reality principle but also the recalcitrance to them as the pleasure principle. Phantasy makes gratifying worlds. Disclosing critique uses it to trace the uncanniness of the current world and to thereby show that a different one is objectively possible.

Also from this gesture toward the id, there is then an important lesson to be learned about disclosing critique: it is different from therapy in significant ways. Whereas therapeutic practice addresses the ego in order to strengthen it, disclosing critique encourages a playful relationship between the ego and id to cultivate recalcitrant tendencies. For this reason, Freud's immediate disciples in disclosing critical theory, such as Adorno and Marcuse, tend to be very skeptical about psychoanalysis as therapy. They distinguish strictly between a recalcitrant psychoanalytic *theory* and its adaptive therapeutic practice: "While psychoanalytic theory recognizes that the sickness of the individual is ultimately caused and sustained by the sickness of this civilization," Marcuse writes, "psychoanalytic therapy aims at curing the individual so that he can continue to function as part of a sick civilization without surrendering to it altogether,"[40] and Adorno adds that this functional individual will turn out to continue the senseless suffering diagnosed by psychoanalytic theory: "Even the successful cure bears the stigma of pathologically exaggerated, self-defeating adaptation [*Anpassung*]."[41] However, whatever the aim of therapeutic practice is, according to Freud, its adaptive function is certainly not to cure us in the sense of fixing us as functions of the reproduction of society as it is. Rather, it involves, on its decentering side, learning to interrupt cyclical sets of repetition compulsions—to break vicious circles in our psychic lives (RRWT). In his cultural critique, Freud traces those circles back to a vicious circle of civilized society. For disclosing critics of society, that little difference makes worlds. On its recentering side, it involves what Freud calls an "after-education" (*Nacherziehung*), a correction of the mistakes that the parents and the social environment made in educating the individual, which, Freud emphasizes, ought always to respect the "individuality" (*Eigenart*) of the patient (*OP*, 175). The German *Eigenart* could also be translated to English as "idiosyncrasy," "peculiarity," or "quirk"—perhaps a recentering cultivation of recalcitrant tendencies, or counterformation, would then have something to learn from Freudian "after-education" after all.

Whatever the merits of the critique of psychoanalytic therapy's tendency toward adaptation or the Freudian defense against it, disclosing critics should, for sure, be careful not to draw a strict analogy between the therapist and the critic. The disanalogies are all too apparent. First, the disclosing critic has only sporadic, if any, interpersonal contact with the recipient. It follows, second, that she should not be illusioned about knowing anything at all about the "individuality" (*Eigenart*) of the recipient. That is to say, she may not assume to know how to rationally respond to the recipient's particular existential and psychological disposition. (The history of philosophy is full of unjustified generalizations of particular existential dispositions: the tendency of philosophers to project their personal psychological makeup, normally in an enormously rationalized form, onto others and even the world can probably not be overestimated.) It also follows, third, that the disclosing critic is unlikely to catch the first signs of receptive disclosure turning to what Freud calls idealization: the recipient may put the critic in the place of her superego. The critic does not have the training and the vicinity of the therapist to respond to such idealization. For these reasons, it is best for disclosing critical theory, in contrast to therapy, to remain primarily negative—that is, to avoid giving positive content about the good life of the recipients. But surely, some methods of guarding oneself against idealization remain for the disclosing critic too. And perhaps Freud's recurring apologies in *Civilization and Its Discontents* are, finally, just that: taking "care that neither the love nor the hostility" to the therapist or the cultural critic "reach[es] an extreme height," whereby his apologies would present his way of "preparing [them] in good time for these possibilities."[42]

6. What Returns?

In this chapter, I have tried to show how Freud transformed the practice of disclosing critique, the drawing of a circle around the circle of society, by drawing a circle connecting, and even subverting, the higher and the lower in us. After Freud, disclosing critique has affirmed the fall of an unproblematic higher self to be disclosed. Marcuse expresses this disillusion in *Eros and Civilization*: "The 'higher self' reigns over the domesticated impulses and aspirations of the individual, who has sacrificed and renounced his 'lower self' not only in so far as it is incompatible with civilization. . . . Freud's question—whether the higher values of culture have not been achieved at too great a cost for the individual—should be taken seriously enough to enjoin the psychoanalytic philosopher from preaching these values without revealing their forbidden content, without showing what they have *denied* to the individual."[43] What remains of the Emersonian metaphor after Freud?

What is disclosed in Emerson is the higher self, the genius; this disclosed self is, initially, unconscious: "Man is a stream whose source is hidden" (OS, 385). For Freud, too, what is disclosed in the individual is initially unconscious—the repressed sense of guilt. The Emersonian disclosure affects the recipient with a feeling of shame; she confronts content both familiar and strange, which she must take from another. After Freud, however, the disclosing confrontation with what is familiar and strange becomes primarily uncanny; disclosure hits frightening elements in the social environment, which trigger affects of repressed impulses or surmounted beliefs in the recipient. In Freud's *Civilization and Its Discontents*, these elements are linked with the repressed sense of guilt. Civilized society appears as a vicious circle—what we all already thought and felt it is but rejected—and Freud shows how it installs a vicious circle in the soul of its most civilized individual members. Yet in this uncanny gesture, Freud also appeals to our id, to a playful activation of the pleasure principle by the use of metaphorical language. So in the end, also for Freud, both the givers and the receivers of disclosing gestures are streams whose sources are hidden.

Criticizing the type of civilized society Freud is dealing with means, then, confronting not the only the society, which one faces as an outer second nature, but also the society within oneself, in one's own inner nature, the superego. It means confronting the vicious circle outside and inside oneself. Disclosing critique is not only critique from inside and outside a form of life but also critique of the form of life inside and outside the critic herself.

What we can learn from Freud for our metaphorology of disclosing critique is that the uncanny feeling accompanying disclosures of the vicious circle of society is by no means arbitrary—it is necessary and significant. An uncanny feeling is *necessarily* effected by a critical disclosure of the type of society, which reproduces senseless suffering through an uncanny double within its civilized members. It is an uncanny experience to grasp the repressed societal determinateness of oneself—that one's higher self is, at least under an aspect, the punishing voice of an overpowering social environment. The uncanny feeling is significant as a *symptom of a repression*. It is a sign that something repressed returns in an experience. Like a street sign, disclosing critical theory uses it as a medium on a path giving a hint for how to dig deeper in tracing society. It then also marks a point on a map. It can give a *direction*, as it were, to those who trace, to what it is that the current social environment has us repress. In uncovering the uncanny, disclosing critical theory is invested in tracing the repressed by means of the uncanny feeling.

On the receptive side, the uncanny feeling comes as a shock. It breaks the flow of ordinary life and enables reality testing in a situation where it would otherwise not occur. As a readaptation and a possible source of readjusting action, such reality testing might spark a process of critical social transformation—what I have described as a recentering receptive disclosure—which must go beyond the reality principle and playfully activate the pleasure principle for imaginative thinking. However, the spark to perform reality testing pertains only to the surmounted uncanny. Evoking the uncanny "theoretically" is a method of directing the affects of the recipients. By effecting, through theoretical tracing, an uncanny feeling about society, disclosing critical theory puts the recipients in a specific mood where they can have the extraordinary experience of the ordinary as strange and familiar at the same time. From this mood, they can then intermittently experience the society as the alienated state it is, because the shock of the uncanny has brought them to a sufficient distance from it. They have been, by means of the shock, alienated from alienation.

Including Freud's work on the uncanny into this history of a critical metaphor enables us to ask, in a new way, the question of what is disclosed by a disclosing critical theory: *What returns* in that theory? In Adorno, the appeal is to the "affect of *Bannkreis*," the sense of impotence in the face of the agglomerated power of society over each and every individual, which each of us feels but has repressed (see chapter 5). Why, exactly, is Adorno's disclosure uncanny? On the level of surmounted beliefs, the idea of such a social determination of the self, such tight limits to our capacity for autonomous, self-controlled agency, belongs to a heteronomous, despotic phase of our sociocultural development that, according to our self-understanding as enlightened citizens of (allegedly) liberal democratic and civilized societies, should have been surmounted. On the level of repressed childhood complexes, Freud would surely regard it as a return of the fear of castration. At times, as we saw in chapter 3, Adorno uses the simile of *Verblendungszusammenhang*, or "bedazzlement connection," to express the operation of antagonistic societal reproduction: it is not that contemporary society with its relations of domination is overwhelmingly complex; rather, its internal pressures toward competition and conflict make us *blind* to our fundamental unfreedom and the extent to which we, as individuals, participate in bringing forth conditions that put our pursuits of happiness in chains. It blinds us to the obvious, the all too familiar. In "The Uncanny," Freud remarks that "anxiety about one's eyes, the fear of going blind, is often enough a substitute for the dread of being castrated: The self-blinding of the mythical criminal, Oedipus, was simply a mitigated form of the punishment of castration" (U, 231). Adornian conceptual gestures such as *Verblendungszusammenhang* can, then, be read as mitigated forms of *Bannkreis*: the antagonistic social reproduction's bedazzling effect on us is easier to swallow than the fact of our repressed impotence in the face of the agglomerated power of a societal environment that fails to offer a good-enough home for a meaningful pursuit of happiness.

For our metaphor history, Freud's display of his struggle with his sense of guilt elucidates, furthermore, the identification of the recalcitrant with the social environment that makes them suffer. The sense of guilt presents the intensified and rationalized affect of an identification with an overpowering social environment. This raises the question of whether this form of rationalized identification with the state of society has been intensified to the point that critical recalcitrance a few decades after Freud's death encloses itself in normativist models of critique, which continue the moral and legal language of guilt into the feeble attempt to resist the society that maintains itself by perpetuating a repressed sense of guilt. If there is any truth to this worry, then disclosing critique cannot accept the language of normative critique. Instead, it must appeal not only to the ego, the instance of self-controlled agency, but also to the id, which carries with it the memory of a satisfaction of needs, the memory of childlike happiness. In this gesture, disclosing critique after Freud retains, without Emersonian Romanticism, a utopian layer upon and below its uncanniness: it points to the *possibility of a social experience, in which freedom is united with happiness*, to the Odyssean image of a "society . . . which masters itself not in order to do violence to itself and others but for the sake of reconciliation."[44] Perhaps, a form of social life that enables adaptation without any violence whatsoever will turn out to be impossible. But surely, a form of social life *can* be organized in such a way that spaces within it are enabled, established, cultivated, and maintained, in which happiness *and* freedom, forms of *nonrepressive self-control*, may be experienced in reconciliation.

SEVEN

Making Phantasies in the Wrong World
Dewey, Tarde, and the Idea of a Critical Cosmology

> A metafísica é uma consequência de estar mal disposto.
>
> *Metaphysics is a consequence of feeling sick.*
> —FERNANDO PESSOA, "Tabacaria"
>
> All things real are so by so much virtue as they contain.
> —RALPH WALDO EMERSON, "Self-Reliance"

In *Eros and Civilization*, Marcuse ascribes a disclosing effect to Freudian theory. As Freud, in his works, "traces the construction of the personality, [he] is led to dissolve the individual." By dissolving the individual "into its primary components," Freudian theory, Marcuse elaborates, "bares the sub-individual and pre-individual factors which ... actually *make* the individual: it reveals the power of the universal in and over the individuals." The tracing of the vicious circle, Marcuse suggests, operates by breaking down the alleged universal of the form of life into its constituent elements and reassembling them. Thus, the alleged universal is disclosed as, at the same time, "pre-individual," a hostile social second nature, and "sub-individual," extended into the individual's first nature. Marcuse leaves no room for doubt that this "great critical effort" is to be understood from the theory's disclosing effect: "This disclosure undermines one of the strongest ideological fortifications of modern culture—namely, the notion of the autonomous individual."[1]

This chapter will eventually provide an example of how disclosing critics can pursue a project of radical social critique without, at the outset, bunkering themselves into this ideological fortification. If social critique is to be disclosed as independent of the juridical metaphor of judging an object by giving and asking for reasons for its guilty verdict, then it can rarely make itself reliant on Kantian self-legislating autonomy or (post)monotheistic illusions of free will—both torn to pieces by Freudian psychoanalysis and Nietzschean critical history. Yet the question remains, How can social critique operate without presupposing self-legislating autonomy?

I believe this question is best addressed by, again, taking a step back on the excavation site and taking a wider look at not only how disclosing critics, as Marcuse notes, break down and reassemble their object while "drawing a circle around a circle" but also at their understanding of the metaphysical assumptions and implications of this tracing. The poetic metaphor of critique, it will appear, implies a completely different metaphysical support for social critique than the juridical metaphor. Interestingly, many users of the juridical metaphor of critique claim their justification of critique to be "post-" or "nonmetaphysical."[2] This, I believe, is not only implausible but also a striking symptom of the lack of self-reflexivity in theorizing, since it is unclear how a form of critique that is supposed to operate as judgment on its object by giving and asking for reasons would not presuppose individual autonomy and free will as much as our legal systems and their practices do. And to the extent they do this, they assume and imply a dubious idealist metaphysics. This reference to the metaphysical presuppositions of normativist models of critique is not to be misunderstood as an attempt at their refutation (Whose metaphysics would perhaps be plausible in the first place?) but taken as a remark that the mere claim to nonmetaphysical thinking offers no magical remedy to metaphysical problems. The point of metaphysical speculation, however, can hardly be to strive for plausibility. On the contrary, as the examples in this chapter will show, it can, among other things, be a drive to the distancing, alienating use of language.

This latter, non-post-metaphysical attitude to metaphysics could be exemplified by philosophers like Marx and Nietzsche or poets like Emerson and Fernando Pessoa. They all believe that people's *need* for metaphysics tends to arise in social environments that alienate them. Metaphysics is an attempt to get at a foreign and hostile, perhaps overpowering, reality. Correspondingly, one might speculate that the metaphysical need and with it metaphysics itself would disappear if the alienated state of society is overcome. They observe, however, that as things stand, we are far from such a happy estate. They agree in thinking that it would be implausible to assume that the metaphysical need had already been eradicated. Therefore, questions persist whose answers are as unverifiable and unfalsifiable as they are painfully significant for those concerned. Given this alienated state of our social world, labeling metaphysical speculation as irrational tout court seems like a harsh gesture.

This is broadly, I assume, the context in which Dewey and Tarde developed their metaphysics of social association. In this final chapter of my metaphor history of disclosing critique, I will look at how these two critical cosmologists, working with the circle metaphoric, responded to this unhappy estate. Unlike Marx but like Nietzsche, these two philosophers did namely respond by developing systematic cosmological speculations. Yet unlike Nietzsche, their speculations avoid his arbitrariness and strive to a certain rational controllability, since they let their metaphysics of association be informed and inspired by the scientific breakthroughs of their day, and they reflect critically on the social conditions of metaphysical thinking. I will first briefly characterize the attitude of disclosing critique to the tradition of Western metaphysics before I excavate an exemplary case of its critical reflection on the social conditions of speculative thinking—the case of Dewey's critique of metaphysics. I will then dig up some of the elements of an exemplary outgrowth of this critique—namely, Dewey's and Tarde's critical cosmologies—and brush them up by conceiving them as attempts at a nonrepressive type of thought aiming at critical disclosure. Finally, a postscript to the chapter will polish up a Tardean conception of recentering disclosure stumbled upon on the excavation site.

1. Disclosing Critique and Western Metaphysics: The Idea of Negatively Absolute Metaphor

Blumenberg notes that the tradition of Western metaphysics has relied on absolute metaphors. Absolute metaphors afford compensation for feeble but conscious beings for their lack of fit with a social and natural environment under whose pressures they must act intentionally to stay alive. In this environment, they always act in *situations*, which means that their intentional action is concrete and specific and must therefore be informed by a foreknowledge of their world and their place in it. Blumenberg, Dewey, and Tarde all assume that this foreknowledge is acquired, among other ways, by projecting speculations about the totality of the real onto the absolute, which then projects back a picture that helps them find their way in the perilous environment. A particularly powerful image, Blumenberg observes, has been that of a *circular cosmos*: the world was pictured as a circle, reason was the "imitation" of that cosmic circle, and the social form of life was to be built on reason as a circular home.[3] The cosmic circle sent down to earth, as it were, a beam of imitation to shape our associations. Such projecting metaphysical speculations are, of course, unfounded: they cannot be verified or falsified. Yet they are also founding: they disclose possibilities for making sense of what is experienced as senseless. Metaphysical speculation is, on this view, wishful thinking in the face of overwhelming natural or social conditions.[4]

For a metaphorology of critical disclosure, there are two important things to note about Blumenberg's metaphor history of Western metaphysics. First, the tendency of Western metaphysics was to *metaphorize the absolute*: the absolute was turned into denotations that addressed issues that were as unverifiable and unfalsifiable as they were unavoidable, since they pertained to the place of alienated human individuals in the cosmos. Second, this *metaphorization* itself was *absolute*: the circle metaphor functioned as the operator that disclosed the horizon for metaphysical speculation about our place in the cosmos, the horizon within which distinctions and translations between figurative and nonfigurative speech could take place. Metaphysics was, as it were, metaphor taken literally.

The attitude of the disclosing critics to the circle metaphoric is importantly different from this mainstream of Western metaphysics. In the essay "Circles," Emerson writes, "This natural world may be considered of as a system of concentric circles, and we now and then detect in nature slight dislocations, which apprize us that this surface on which we now stand is not fixed, but sliding" (C, 409–10). For the disclosing critics, the circle is a *negatively absolute metaphor*. And this, again, is thought of in a double sense. First, it is not positively absolute, as they all (Emerson, Nietzsche, Freud, Dewey, and Adorno) are highly reflective about metaphors. The circle metaphoric does not just appear as a perplexed substitute for theorizing when explanation runs dry; rather, it is often applied reflectively in place of explanation, justification, and reason giving as a method of showing. Still, it has the function of an absolute metaphor in being a "foundational" rather than a "leftover element" in critical practice;[5] it namely discloses the horizon in which the conceptualization, theorization, and further critique of society may take place.

Second, it designates the metaphorically expressed absolute not as the home whose grasp shall liberate us from the objectively alienated state but as an unhomely totality that the metaphorical use of language should critically disclose. The space of conceptual inquiry it discloses is then one that entertains a reflectively *negative* relation to its transitorily "foundational" element: aware of its metaphorical character, disclosing critique does not claim a conceptual ground for its critical practice; instead, it regards itself as recalcitrant to a society whose consequence it is and which it regards as precarious or even false au fond.[6]

And so their metaphysical question is different too. What becomes of metaphysical speculation based on a negatively absolute metaphor? If metaphysics is wishful thinking arising from otherwise senseless suffering and is continued in awareness of this cultural function, its question inevitably changes. In *Nature*, Emerson asks, "Why should not we enjoy an original relation to the universe?" (*N*, 7). Metaphysics as a type of phantasy making might then be worthwhile not just as a reflective symptomatology of senseless suffering but also as a way of making sense of unverifiable and unfalsifiable issues arising on the educational and organizational path to greater enjoyment. Phantasy is a necessary part of world making—particularly, in a wrong world.

2. A Social Critique of Metaphysics: Dualism as the Extension of Social Domination

How did Dewey respond to Emerson's question? Many recent and contemporary observers would rather say he didn't. On the one hand, the metaphysical aspect of Dewey's philosophy has been a source of embarrassment for several pragmatists and critical theorists who have tried to tidy up his philosophy from metaphysics, such as Richard Rorty, Hilary Putnam, and Jürgen Habermas.[7] On the other hand, postcritical philosophers invoking Dewey, such as Bruno Latour, have embarked on the project of a metaphysics of modes of existence, leaving critical intentions behind.[8]

Both trains of thought, postmetaphysical critical theory and postcritical metaphysics, assume an incommensurability of social critique and metaphysical speculation. It is therefore a pleasure to report from the excavation site that the immediate socio-critical followers of Dewey, such as Sidney Hook and John Herman Randall, emphasize the metaphysics of Dewey's *Experience and Nature*.[9] According to their pragmatic view, the question is not whether critique should allow for metaphysics but whether it gives a sincere account of its own metaphysical assumptions and implications. And the other way around, it is not the question of whether metaphysics strives for social change but whether it is conscious about its relation to social change. I believe that this third, and earliest, line of interpretation of Dewey by his immediate followers is the most promising because it recognized, avant la lettre, that his metaphysics was part and parcel of his disclosing critique of society. Indeed, in his metaphysics, Dewey continues a line of reflection on critical disclosure that we already encountered in Nietzsche's *Untimely Meditations*—the project of a *critical cosmology*.

Now, how *does* Dewey respond to Emerson's question? The latter asked, "Why should not we enjoy an original relation to the universe?" (*N*, 7). Toward the end of *Experience and Nature*, Dewey initially rephrases the question thus: "If philosophy be criticism, what is to be said of the relation of philosophy to metaphysics?" (*EN*, 308). Dewey understands the nature of metaphysical thinking in the broadly Aristotelian sense as an inquiry into existence *qua* existence, or, as he puts it, into "the generic traits manifested by existences of all kinds." Metaphysics, on this view, maps the most general modes of existence. Such an enterprise, Dewey notes, "seems to have nothing to do with criticism." Yet he comes to conclude that "any theory that detects and defines these traits is . . . but a *ground-map of the province of criticism*" (308; emphasis added). Dewey's reasons for thinking that metaphysics is socially critical are themselves partly metaphysical in nature: he believes that a sincere inquiry into modes of existence will itself reveal that metaphysics is far from socially neutral: "The very nature of the traits discovered . . . forbids such a conclusion. Qualitative individuality and constant relations, contingency and need, movement and arrest are common traits of all existence. This fact is source both of values and of their precariousness" (308). Carefully practiced, the metaphysical inquiry will, eventually, reveal itself as an effort to make sense of the experience of suffering and enjoying in a world that is socially organized and disorganized, it will discover normative pressure in the deepest layers of nature, and it will stumble on the "supreme issues: life and death" (309). Metaphysics then comes to understand itself as mapping nature as the province in which domination and critique take place.

But even more significant for our inquiry into disclosing critique of society is that Dewey's reasons for thinking that metaphysics is a "ground-map of the province of criticism" also come partly from social critique—namely, from his *social critique of metaphysics*. Dewey never tires to point out that metaphysics has social conditions and social implications. It works either as a mechanism of societal reproduction or as a force of social transformation. It follows that there are, in Dewey's view, only two kinds of metaphysics and two kinds of philosophical social critique: there is a metaphysics aware of its social conditions and social impact, and there is a metaphysics that is not, just as there is a social critique that makes an effort to investigate its metaphysical assumptions and implications and a social critique that does not. In Dewey, we seem, then, to come across a chiasmic relation between metaphysics and social critique that Adorno anticipated, as shown in the end of chapter 3: metaphysics reveals itself, on its deepest level, as socially critical, and social critique, conversely, at its most radical, in its wildest application of phantasy in resisting the adaptive pressures, as metaphysical.

Also, according to Dewey, Western metaphysics has generally been practiced unreflectively regarding its social conditions and impact. It has operated as a mechanism of societal self-preservation and provided justifications for domination; in short, it has functioned as ideology. At the outset, his critique does not directly target metaphysics as such but rather its tendency to produce *dualisms*. Dewey believes that dualisms—such as the separation between theory and practice, the ideal and the material, mind and body, culture and nature, ends and means—operate as mechanisms of social domination, predominantly class domination, producing repressive behavioral patterns in individuals.

Like Adorno,[10] Dewey believes that, since its inception in ancient Greece, Western metaphysics has been plagued by a confusion of "first" and "second nature." This confusion was, Dewey believes, the consequence of the social conditions under which metaphysical thinking first emerged. It was born in a society that had a leisure class, and it was born as the possession of that class: "Athenian philosophers were quite right in associating [its] rise ... with the emergence of a leisure class. For the existence of a class which is relieved of the burden of making a living because it can live upon the products of an inferior servile class is a socially conditioned fact." Metaphysics was enabled by releasing some people from the incumbrance of labor, of *making a living*: the members of this class, Dewey explains, had the chance, by living off the surplus labor of others, to devote themselves to the "development of ideas as ideas," to establish rationally structured language games to be played for their own sake. Yet while these rational universes of discourse seemed autonomous to the players, they remained the product of a class domination, which had become second nature: "The customs, the institutions, involved in these conditions were so settled, were so much second nature, that the philosophers were quite unaware that the leisure which made their kind of knowledge possible was a sociological phenomenon. On the contrary, they assumed that it was a proper expression of the inherent cosmological constitution of nature" (*UPMP*, 283).

Metaphysical dualisms, Dewey thinks, arise from separation between classes in ancient Greece; they are symptoms of the class division embodied in the habits, customs, and institutions of a form of social life. Dualistic separations follow from relations of domination in social life since this domination is so deeply embodied in its second nature, to which its members, including the philosophers, are initiated, that it is repeated in their metaphysical thinking too. A division maintained in habits, customs, and institutions is then subsequently *ontologized* as eternal dualisms inhering in things: second nature is confused with first, and the class structure of society is projected as the structure of the cosmos. Dewey's social critique of metaphysics seeks "to show . . . that the class-structure of society, especially low social status of workers in things necessary and useful for the maintenance of life, . . . is the source of the separation which found philosophical expression in the notion of the inherent separation of things that are merely means, means one might say 'in themselves,' and other things that are ends 'in themselves,' and that the physical conception of the 'material' in its divorce from the ideal or spiritual originated in this bifurcation" (*UPMP*, 302). Dewey's social critique of metaphysics displays the domination of one class over another as the *source* of dualisms in metaphysics—here, those between ends and means, the spiritual and the material. However, dualisms do not only follow from domination; they also "back it up" (283–85). According to Dewey, the metaphysical separation of means from ends, the ideal from the material, culture from nature, and so on ends up supporting the social conditions that brought them about. Metaphysics, then, participates in what he, in *Human Nature and Conduct*, calls the "vicious circle" of society (see chapter 5). The members of the form of life are initiated into a preexisting second nature that they take as first nature. The metaphysics that a form of life produces to preserve its relations of domination is, as it were, one of the outlines where a vicious circle of society can be deciphered. In Adornian terms, dualism can present a "model." Thus, Dewey's critique of metaphysical dualism is a disclosing critique of society by virtue of tracing a vicious circle: if social domination results in a projective phantasy making that continues the violence of that domination, then following up that connection can be a way to draw a circle around the vicious circle.

Now, Dewey does not believe that this ideological function of metaphysics, its tendency to justify class domination, is restricted to ancient Greece. On the contrary, the domination that maintains and utilizes metaphysical dualisms has persisted without significant change until his day: "The social conditions which back up the relegation of whatever is practical to a relatively degraded position exist wherever the processes of making a living are isolated from the processes of living." What has remained the same is the isolation of processes of making a living from processes of living. Dewey's posthumously published *Unmodern Philosophy and Modern Philosophy* seeks to show the extent to which our modern form of life is, after all, similar to the unmodern form of life, which in ancient Greece gave birth to metaphysics: in both, work is institutionally and habitually separated from enjoyment, satisfaction, and gratification. "The extent to which industrial operations," he explains with reference to those making a living, "have been segregated in modern times from those which constitute life, in the eulogistic sense of that word, is well exhibited in the doctrine of classical economists" (*UPMP*, 283). This seems like a reference to Marx's critique of political economy.

Following Marx's lead, such an isolation of the processes of making a living from the processes of living can be called *exploitation*.[11] Wherever one class lives off the productive and reproductive work of another, the one class exploits, and the other one is exploited.[12] In Dewey, exploitation is intimately linked with *repression*, or what he calls "postponed living." As he develops in more detail in *Art as Experience*, again paraphrasing Marx (and Engels), "The story of the . . . sharp opposition of the useful and the fine is the history of that industrial development through which so much of production has become a form of *postponed living* and so much of consumption a superimposed enjoyment of the fruits of the labor of others."[13] Isolation of the processes of making a living from the processes of living makes the isolated postpone living: exploitation produces the conditions under which individuals engaged in useful activities reschedule their enjoyment and satisfaction to a remote future or an afterlife. Metaphysical dualisms thus *continue* the social repression of society over its members as psychological repression *in* the members. How?

Now, despite these similarities, exploitation does, of course, take different forms in ancient Greece and in modern capitalism. Whereas the slave society of ancient Greece separated a class that worked and suffered senselessly, on the one side, and a class that enjoyed and contemplated (suffered meaningfully?), on the other, there evolves, according to Dewey, with modern capitalism a social second nature that pressures *all* individuals, albeit still divided in classes, to continuously postpone enjoyment to the extent of unnecessarily maintaining ways of producing, which are in themselves fundamentally unenjoyable, and ways of enjoying, which are fundamentally disappointing. On the one hand, then, Dewey observes a production that is unenjoyable and void of meaning for those involved in it:

The mass go into shops and factories in which mental submission to conditions and aims in which they do not mentally share is the rule. They may be rebellious to conditions, but they are forced to be obedient to the orders and directions that issue from the machinery they tend. They are servants, employees, not only of other persons but even more of impersonal agencies whose continual mechanical motions they must follow and to which they must accommodate themselves. Personal judgment and initiative have no organic place; their exercise would seem to be evidence of overt rebellion. Economic conditions reinforce the work of formal schooling and of much parental guidance in developing the uncritical and passive mind.[14]

The *modes of production* of modern capitalism favor *modes of instruction and socialization* that produce uncritical producers who are willing to submit to conditions in whose shaping they have no share.

On the other hand, modern capitalism brings forth *modes of reception* that are tightly restricted and fit for a perpetual postponement of enjoyment: "Useless display and luxury, the futile attempt to secure happiness through the possession of things, social position, and economic power over others, are manifestations of the restrictions of experience that exist among those who seemingly profit by the present order. Mutual fear, suspicion, and jealousy are also its products. All of these things deflect and impoverish human experience beyond any calculation."[15] Dewey makes the same observation as Horkheimer and Adorno do in the *Dialectic of Enlightenment*, written in the same year as *Unmodern Philosophy and Modern Philosophy*: "Under the given conditions, exclusion from work means mutilation.... Those at the top experience the existence with which they no longer need to concern themselves as a mere substrate, and are wholly ossified as the self which issues commands."[16] What Dewey's social critique of metaphysics seeks to disclose is the predominantly *repressive* nature of Western metaphysics: it exerts a form of additional cultural pressure on individuals to postpone enjoyment. This disclosure then also points to the *possibility* of a form of life and thought where effort would be enjoyable, and enjoyment, creative. This helps to appreciate what is, I take it, truly original about his manner of critiquing ideology. On Dewey's view, intellectual artifacts, such as metaphysical dualisms, are ideological by virtue of *extending domination* through the social fabric. Dewey's idea is that metaphysical dualisms are not just philosophical expressions of class society or merely a justificatory artifact for its maintenance but actually contribute by their repressive effect to senseless suffering in ordinary social life. This is what I would like to call his *extension thesis* about ideology. Metaphysical dualisms, as an archetype of ideological artifacts, extend the violence of the prevailing relations of domination, which brought them about through the language games of a form of life. Traditional metaphysics presents an extension of the domination and misrecognition of those engaged in the maintenance of life to other spheres of life: "When there is ... a separation of classes ... , *the materials involved in the habitual activities of the lower group share in the disesteem and contempt in which the class is held*" (*UPMP*, 289; emphasis added). The misrecognition of the dominated infects everything they touch in their activities.

Ideological artifacts extend, as it were, the line from the class structure of the second nature of the form of life to its language games causing repressive ways of talking, as it were, curving it toward a vicious circle. Dewey anchors the complete spectrum of his critiqued dualisms to this thesis of social extension of domination about ideology:

Historically, the activities of this "lower" class have to do (i) with physical things; (ii) they are carried on by bodily organs, largely manual; (iii) upon the psychological side, the senses, touch and sight, rather than ideas are the basis of control of what is done and how it is done; (iv) the activities are mainly routine, mechanically repetitious, and (v) they are performed under the direction of others and for ends in the formulation of which the workers have no share. This latter consideration is the most important one in determining the menial, quasi-servile quality of the occupations in question, and accords without a flaw with the four other traits mentioned. (*UPMP*, 289)

The domination of the working class is extended in the metaphysical dualisms of persons and things, mind and body, ideas and sense perception, spirit and mechanism, ends and means. Dewey in no way shies away from the materialistic claim that these metaphysical dualisms are the product, the consequence, of the more fundamental societal separation between the processes of living and the processes of making a living. But the metaphysical dualisms that follow, as it were, carry social domination with them as repression wherever they go. It is transported to the many language games by which ordinary life in capitalism is lived. They shape language games that the individuals play when expressing their life plans, intentions, experiences, and feelings. In this way, metaphysical dualisms *rationalize* relations of domination that cause senseless suffering in the individuals, thereby adding to that suffering.

According to Dewey, not only is the relation between class division and metaphysical dualism asymmetrical but also different dualisms have different functional value in maintaining the vicious circle. The most horrendous is the dualism between theory and practice, to which he devoted a complete book—*The Quest for Certainty*. This dualism is more detrimental to social life than any other since it functions as a systematic learning blockage. It extends the relations of domination as a separation between intellectual life, on the one side, and productive and reproductive work, on the other. Learning, however, involves trying out ideas in practice and forming new ideas based on practical consequences; if the dualism of theory and practice becomes embodied in the habits, customs, and institutions of a form of life, then there is not really much hope of overcoming the other metaphysical dualisms and class domination.[17]

In *Unmodern Philosophy and Modern Philosophy*, however, Dewey remains strictly realistic in pointing out that the social critique of metaphysics, albeit perhaps convincing some about the senselessness of these dualisms, will in no way threaten the relations of exploitation that keeps bringing them about. What it *can* do is to disclose the possibility that organizational and educational effort by recalcitrant social groups could finally bring an end to the domination that has pervaded our form of life from ancient Greece until today:

> It is not the business nor problem of philosophy to remedy the social evils which are presented in and caused by social divisions into a class that is instrumental . . . and a class that directs the productivity of others. . . . The work to be done has to be executed by all elements of society working together; it is a social problem in the deepest sense of the word social. But philosophers have a distinctive part to carry in accomplishing this work. . . . *They can point out the conditions which keep practical affairs of the highest moment upon a relatively unfree or illiberal level, since they obstruct the use and application within them of available intelligence.* (UPMP, 284–85; emphasis added)

By the disclosure of the extension of social domination into language games through metaphysical thinking, philosophy can play a part in the educational and organizational effort to break out of the vicious circle. Yet as much as Dewey opposes domination-extending traditional metaphysics, he rejects the sociological nihilism of simply debunking it. We still live in an objectively alienating form of life, and speculative attempts to get at it will make up a part of a rational reaction to it. The miserably ideological state of metaphysics, Dewey believes, does then not imply turning one's back to metaphysical suffering. Instead, the reasonable reaction would be to formulate a less miserable metaphysics, one that does justice to the objective state of a form of life that oppresses, represses, and alienates its living members. This reaction, I suggest, consists in his critical cosmology—a speculative enterprise that aids in the critique of class society and the effort to overcome it. That is to say, what is needed instead is a form of metaphysical thinking that does not already at the outset rule out the possibility of happiness and freedom by a separation of ends from means, culture from nature, mind from body.

Even if Dewey, as it were, debunks cosmology by means of sociology, this denaturalizing gesture also discloses a possibility: *pointing out* how dualisms, arising from exploitation, extend to our language games to maintain a repressive form of instruction and socialization that demands its members to postpone enjoyment at the same time *point to* the possibility of a critical and metaphysical thinking—a speculative mode of thought aiming at nonrepressive forms of social life. Thus, on the excavation site, we find ourselves back at the initially surprising idea, discovered in chapter 4 in Emerson's and the young Nietzsche's circle metaphoric, of metaphysics as a possible venue of counterteleological thinking; but this time around, we arrived here through a social critique of metaphysics.

Dewey's path to this critical thought is, first, to accept the reality of the dualism while questioning its necessity and desirability. The "intelligent critic," Dewey hints, "does not question the existence of the split," the truly existing habitual, institutional, and intellectual separation between, for example, body and mind, nature and culture, or means and ends, in the present form of life; what she does instead is "to question the desirability and the inherent necessity of the dualism involved." As hegemonic as these ways of thinking are in contemporary society, their dependence on domination and their utter undesirability can be pointed out: "The critic declines to take activities which have no significance or value in themselves as standard models for a large part, the necessary because useful part, of human action. He objects particularly to that view on the ground that it is once a reflection and 'rationalizing' justification of the condition in which the 'masses' find their activities subordinated to providing leisure and opportunity for 'higher' things to a small 'class.'" Second, the path to a critical metaphysical thinking is "directed" by a sensibility for the social suffering, the surplus impulse control, caused by the dualisms, "the injurious social . . . results or actual 'ends' of its existence" (*UPMP*, 300). Like the Nietzschean physician of culture and the Freudian cultural critic, the Deweyan critical cosmologist must possess the epistemic virtue of recognizing social suffering.

Yet how would such a critical speculative thinking operate? How would it avoid reproducing the fundamentally undesirable dualisms that it set out to critique or other modes of repressive thought that extend contemporary relations of domination into the psychic life of the individuals? Perhaps the way to avoid undesirable modes of thinking would be to think further *with* desire? Reminiscent of Freud's idea of phantasy as a form of thinking that connects with our archaic heritage and childhood's broken promises of happiness, Dewey writes in *Art as Experience*, "Through the phases of perturbation and conflict, there abides the deep-seated memory of an underlying harmony, the sense of which haunts life like the sense of being founded on a rock" (*AE*, 23). He goes on to paint with a utopian brush and express what an intellectual effort that is enjoyable and an enjoyment that is creative would look like: "When complete release [of impulse] is postponed and is arrived at finally through a succession of ordered periods of accumulation and conservation, marked off into intervals by the recurrent pauses of balance, the manifestation of emotion becomes true expression, acquiring esthetic quality—and only then" (160). Like Marcuse, Dewey seeks to envision a way of thinking that could imagine the contours of a nonrepressive form of production and consumption—a sustainable way of living socially, in which freedom and happiness can be experienced together.[18]

A part of what makes Dewey such an exemplary disclosing critic is that, like Marx and Nietzsche, he recognizes traditional Western metaphysics as ideological; yet unlike Marx, this does not make him want to leave metaphysics behind, but rather, like Nietzsche, it makes him want to reevaluate it. Like the young Nietzsche, Dewey does not attempt to simply destruct all hitherto metaphysics but rather to *transform* it into a critical cosmology. But unlike Nietzsche, his critical cosmology seeks to remain rationally controllable, initially at least by being informed by a social critique of metaphysics and seeking to appeal to a naturalized conception of disclosing reason. It seeks to evade the compulsive repetition of dualistic thinking.

In *Unmodern Philosophy and Modern Philosophy*, Dewey sets up four postulates of a naturalistic metaphysics (UMPM, 315–14). The first postulate is that experience, or culture, is a function of life. This means that the metaphysics must be naturalistic in the sense of assuming what he, in his *Logic*, calls a "continuity of the lower (less complex) and the higher (more complex) activities and forms,"[19] or, in *Experience and Nature*, what he describes as a "continuity of nature and experience" (*EN*, 8). Such a continuity requires identifying a criterion of continuity, a principle that all existence expresses. In the next section, I will investigate this as Dewey's "ontological monism."

His second postulate is that the "socio-cultural" affords the fullest expression of life. This means that the criterion of continuity must be in some sense social (*UPMP*, 315). This demands identifying different ways of satisfying the criterion of continuity. In the next section, I will investigate this as Dewey's "modal pluralism."

The third postulate is that the mental, or spiritual, is an embodied behavioral aspect of social life. This means that the social ontology in the metaphysics must be understood as incorporating and transforming nonsocial things. In the next section, I will investigate this as Dewey's surprising, and ultimately unconvincing, *scala naturae*.

The fourth postulate is that this naturalistic metaphysics must be able to function as a "necessary means or agency for systematic criticism," which Dewey regards as its "focal point" (*UPMP*, 315–16). This requires showing how the naturalistic metaphysics is to have a critical and educational effect. This I will excavate later as Dewey's contribution to what Nietzsche established as critical cosmology.

3. A Metaphysics of Social Critique: A Critical Cosmology of Associations

Dewey's initial answer to Emerson's question "Why should not we enjoy an original relation to the universe?" is, then, explanatory (*N*, 7)—because our form of life is repressively maintained by a postponement of enjoyment, which impoverishes our metaphysical imagination. Yet, perhaps, if we start with an uncompromising social critique of metaphysics, the answer continues, we might disclose the possibility of another path of speculation.

Now, I believe that, alongside Dewey, Gabriel Tarde presents a metaphysics of critical disclosure. This may be a provocative thesis for at least two reasons. The first is that today, like Dewey, Tarde is taken as the founder of postcritical social ontology,[20] but unlike Dewey, he has not at all been engaged with in critical theory.[21] Second, Tarde seems not to mention "disclosure" anywhere in his works. Yet Tarde's metaphysics is all about critical disclosure, without ever mentioning the term. In fact, it seems to me almost impossible to translate "disclosure" into Tarde's language, French. However, a disclosing intent is contained in his formulation of the task of metaphysics to show "so many variations, so many asymmetries, so many disharmonies" that repetitive reality otherwise "prevents us from seeing" (*LS*, 43; my translation). Furthermore, it makes sense to include Tarde along with Dewey, who of the two is the better critic of metaphysics, in a chapter on metaphysics in disclosing critique of society since Tarde, who influenced Dewey,[22] is arguably the better metaphysician of the two, both in terms of clarity and creativity.

Dewey and Tarde construe metaphysics of a hypothetical nature for social reasons—as ground maps, as it were. For Tarde, this is for the purposes of supporting social science; for Dewey, to support what he saw as the main task of philosophy—the criticism of social life. To do this, both authors attempted a description of the mode of existence of the province of "the social" in its wider natural environment. To both, this involved establishing the continuity as well as the difference of social processes to other modes of natural process.

This comes to be linked with a highly controversial enterprise in both authors' thought that none of their followers would ever take quite seriously—namely, the attempt of processualizing a *scala naturae*. In effect, when Tarde and Dewey are doing social ontology, they are doing more than just a provincial ontology of the social—they are also asking the cosmological question of the place of the social in nature. They are doing metaphysics, as it were, by mapping the landscape surrounding the social. Conversely, the social they conceive is "impure": the social is never quite social in the sense of a watertight compartment; it is constitutively intermixed with life and things, which it incorporates and transforms. In the sections that follow, I will attempt to show how Dewey and Tarde thought that constructing something like a "chain of beings," which might well be seen as the most conservative feature of the Western metaphysical tradition, could, in fact, contribute to the project of a radical critique of society. I will do this by focusing on two particular metaphysical assumptions Dewey and Tarde share and that we already encountered in Nietzsche's critical cosmology: ontological monism and modal pluralism.

The combination of these two metaphysical assumptions was by no means invented by any of Emerson's followers.[23] It is an old idea that can be traced back at least to Spinoza's *Ethics*. Ontological monism is the idea that all existence can be explained as expressing one principle. Spinoza believes that the one absolute substance, *deus sive natura* (God or nature), expresses itself as potentia (power).[24] As we saw in chapter 4, for the young Nietzsche, it is life expressing itself as "plastic power." Modal pluralism, again, is the idea that there are several *ways* to express this principle—in other words, there is a plurality of modes of being the one substance. Spinoza claims that there is an infinite number of modes of God or nature, which can be gradually ordered according to their degree of complexity in terms of the two parallel attributes of extension and thinking, or body and mind, and individuated by their particular way of persisting in their own being (conatus).[25] Similarly, the young Nietzsche believes that there is a plurality of modes of plastic power, which can be ordered gradually according to the degree of their transformative capacity, each with its particular way to develop out of itself. Spinoza already conceives the stipulation of a simultaneously monistic and pluralistic nature as part of an "ethics" whose goal was to disclose a path to human freedom.[26] In what follows, I would like to point to how Dewey and Tarde with their metaphysics can be seen as contributing to that emancipatory project—in terms of critical disclosure.

Now, following the postulates of his naturalistic metaphysics, Dewey must conceive of nature as transformable. For this reason, he starts *Experience and Nature* by characterizing nature as a mix of the stable and the precarious.[27] Tarde agrees; he starts his *Les lois sociales* by characterizing reality as always repeating, opposing, and adapting (*LS*, 42–43). Both believe that what is called structure, form, or substance is just a slower or more stable process with the power to direct other processes, and they describe such variations of stability and instability as constituting "rhythms of nature" (*LI*, 76; *LS*, 75–76, 78; *AE*, 152). "In truth," Dewey explains, "the universal and stable are important because they are the instrumentalities, the efficacious conditions, of the occurrence of the unique, unstable and passing" (*EN*, 96). This is much anticipated in Tarde's *Monadology and Sociology* written thirty years earlier: "Forms are only brakes and laws are only dykes erected in vain against the overflowing of revolutionary differences and civil dissensions, in which the laws and forms of tomorrow secretly take shape, and which, in spite of the yokes upon yokes they bear, in spite of chemical and vital discipline, in spite of reason, in spite of celestial mechanics, will one distant day, like the people of a nation, sweep away all barriers and from their very wreckage construct the instrument of a still higher diversity" (*MS*, 46). How then do Dewey and Tarde, these self-proclaimed metaphysical champions of variation and recalcitrance, reduce all reality to one single principle?

3.1 Ontological Monism: Association, Possession, and Adaptate

Ontological monism is the idea that there is a homogeneity of principles of existence, that all reality can be reduced to one principle. What is, then, the principle, to which Dewey and Tarde reduce all reality? What is the criterion of continuity? For Dewey, this principle is *association*: "associated... behavior is a universal characteristic of all existences" (IPI, 41). Tarde has a similar idea in mind. It is that everything that exists associates, interacts, and organizes *societies*. This is contained in the most famous proposition of *Monadology and Sociology*: "*Everything is a society*,... every phenomenon is a social fact" (*MS*, 28; emphasis original).

Tarde believes that this principle is implied in the methods and results of the empirical sciences. He suggests that the sciences always either study phenomena in association or break them down into their associating elements. Whereas Dewey's critique of metaphysics debunked cosmology by sociology, Tarde's cosmology advances to a sort of generalized sociology. Modern science identifies societies everywhere in nature: "Now, it is remarkable that science... tends strangely to generalize the concept of society. Science tells us of animal societies..., of cellular societies, and why not of atomic societies? I almost forgot to add societies of stars, solar and stellar systems," he writes, concluding, "All sciences seem destined to become branches of sociology" (*MS*, 28).

The sciences treat their objects as aggregates or as the associating elements of some aggregate. In this sense, what science assumes as real is a society or is in society. In *Les lois sociales*, Tarde traces this tendency of modern science back to those cosmic circles of ancient and medieval Western metaphysics that Blumenberg will later study as examples of absolute metaphors (*LS*, 52–53). More precisely, Tarde believes that the view that everything is a society marks a *reversal* of the "vain and false" cosmic circles (52; my translation): whereas the absolute metaphor of traditional Western metaphysics made the social imitate the cosmic, Tarde believes to be able to metaphorize the cosmic from the social—with the support of modern science. Similarly, Dewey, in his astoundingly dense metaphysical essay "The Inclusive Philosophic Idea," presents "association among things" as the general assumption scientific inquiry makes about the nature of reality: "Relation as the nerve of science correlates with association among things. This fact being noted, we observe that the qualities of things associated are displayed only in association among things, since in interactions alone are potentialities released and actualized" (IPI, 41).

Dewey and Tarde then both, as an implication of the latest developments in the sciences, propose something like a *social monism*, according to which all reality is constituted in "association" or "society." Things are associations of smaller things, and they associate with other things, becoming building blocks of bigger things. And all these things are more or less stable aggregate processes, or "societies."[28]

Tarde conceptualizes association as "possession" and defines "society"—that is, the kind of thing anything is—as "each individual's reciprocal possession ... of every other."[29] Tarde chooses the term "possession" to characterize the associations that constitute "societies" because he believes that Western metaphysics has failed due to its obsession with "being": "All philosophy hitherto has been based on the verb *Be*, the definition of which was the philosopher's stone, which all sought to discover. We may affirm that, if it had been based on the verb *Have*, many sterile debates and fruitless intellectual exertions would have been avoided." He believes that this substitution of "being" with "having" is nothing short of a revolutionary moment in the history of Western metaphysics. Starting with *having* rather than *being* has three radical consequences. First, in contrast to being, having always presupposes *another being*—the being that is *had*. Existence always involves other existence. Associations between existences are, he assumes, dynamic, reciprocal relations of possession. Second, by postulating having instead of being, existence becomes, at the outset, both internal and external: "From this principle, *I am*, all the subtlety in the world has not made it possible to deduce any existence other than my own: hence the negation of external reality. If, however, the postulate *I have* is posited as the fundamental fact, both that which *has* and that which *is had* are given inseparably at once" (*MS*, 52; emphases original). Existing happens inside and outside. Third, thinking of existence in terms of having rather than being renders existence a *gradual* affair. "Between being and non-being there is no middle term," Tarde remarks, "whereas one can have more or less" (53). Things can exist more or less (like Spinoza's potentia).

And one can be more or less in possession of a thing! Tarde namely distinguishes two kinds of possession: reciprocal and unilateral. *Unilateral pos-*

sessions are associations in which one thing dominates another, as is the case, for instance, in the relationship between master and slave or between organism and the chemical processes it utilizes for its persistence. *Reciprocal possession*, by contrast, is an association where each thing maintains itself mutually through the other, as may be the case in friendship, celestial mechanisms, or between some organs of an organism. This distinction will turn out to be of great importance when we turn to the issue of modal pluralism below.

Although Dewey often polemicizes against "monism," he does, similar to Tarde, take the idea that everything is constituted in "association," or, in other words, is "society," to establish the principle for all reality. It constitutes the disclosed continuity between things and persons, between nature and culture, from the physical through the organic to the social; in other words, association is the bridge that unites the terms of dualisms. And like Tarde, he draws the analogy between things and human societies: "Human beings illustrate the same traits of both immediate uniqueness and connection, relationship, as do other things. No more in their case than in that of atoms and physical masses is immediacy the whole of existence and therefore an obstacle to being acted upon by and affecting other things. Everything that exists in as far as it is known and knowable is in interaction with other things. It is associated, as well as solitary, single. The catching up of human individuals into association is thus no new and unprecedented fact; it is a manifestation of a *commonplace of existence*" (*EN*, 138; emphasis added). This "commonplace of existence" Dewey refers to is what Tarde calls, with reference to Leibniz, "the tendency of monads to assemble" (*MS*, 34). This agreement points to a possible disagreement between Tarde and Dewey. Tarde namely constructs his social monism as a reconstruction of Leibniz's *Monadology*, whereas Dewey's social monism is, arguably, rather Hegelian or Spinozistic.[30] This is not merely a difference in philosophical style. It expresses itself in their contrary attitudes to atomism, which Tarde, following Leibniz's lead, affirms, while Dewey remains skeptical. This disagreement can be ameliorated though perhaps not reconciled.

The issue of atomism arises for Tarde as the question of the relationship between associating elements and their aggregates—that is, "association" in the sense of "possession" and in the sense of "society." Like Leibniz infamously did two centuries before him, Tarde seems to stir confusion by treating the same thing first as an element and then as an aggregate. Humans are, for example, elements of human societies but are each also "societies" of diverse elements themselves. However, the reason for this seemingly confusing parlance is that Tarde treats "elements" and "aggregates" as placeholder concepts: what in each instance is aggregate and what is element depends on the association in question, on the given relations of unilateral and reciprocal possession. The latter determine what is an element and what is an aggregate. If we study a social group—for example, the pop group Destiny's Child—we must look at the members it *has*; the social group possesses the members rather unilaterally. And we must probably also look at the associations among these members, their reciprocal possessions. In this case, the social group is the aggregate, and the members are the elements. But we might have to, in this study, look closer at the character of one key member of the group, let's say Beyoncé. Now we break down her character into different interacting traits and look at her interactions with her peers. The former are elements she unilaterally possesses; the latter are elements she reciprocally possesses.

In other words, Tarde is not primarily interested in *beings* but in *havings*. For this reason, Tarde's reduction of aggregates to elements does not require any assumption of an *ontological* priority of some entities that are "the elements" in an absolute sense.[31] The reduction of aggregates to elements is methodological. Surprisingly, in "The Need for Social Psychology," which contains Dewey's most extensive discussion of Tarde's work, Dewey praises precisely this methodological reduction: "Tarde . . . was certainly one of the most stimulating and varied of writers, and I do not think we shall ever outgrow some of his contributions . . .—such as the necessity for reducing the gross phenomena of social life into minuter events which may then be analyzed one by one."[32] In fact, Dewey also refers to Leibniz to establish a relationship between infinitesimal elements and aggregate associations in *Experience and Nature*: "Control of beginnings and ends by means is possible only when the individual, the unique, is treated as a composite of parts, made by sequential differentiations and integrations" (*EN*, 115)—and this Dewey refers, in a footnote, to Leibniz.

Dewey then agrees with Tarde that things are aggregates constituted by elements, which are independent in the sense of not being ontologically reducible to the aggregate. They can, in other words, exert some sort of resistance to the thing whose building blocks they are. As constituents, they are always nonidentical to their constituting—as it were, *recalcitrant* to some degree to that which they constitute. Dewey's objection to atomism is not against its Tardean variant but against the commitment to the ontological priority of some entities that are declared "the elements" in an absolute sense (*EN*, 116).

In Tarde's words, one could say that both philosophers hold that the ontological explanation of things are to be found in the "infinitesimal" (*MS*, 9–15). "Infinitesimal" means that which is smaller than any identifiable entity. What is "identifiable" is based, furthermore, on the thing whose constitution is being investigated. In this sense, one might today say that the atom is something "simple" in molecular biology but something very "complex" in quantum physics—something still to be explained. The individual human person is "infinitesimal" in the ontology of human society. Dewey and Tarde claim that human societies can only be ontologically explained by reference to what to them is infinitesimal—that is, their heterogenous associating "elements," or persons and social groups. This thought leads them both to propose *fractal social ontologies*.

We encountered Dewey's fractal social ontology already in chapter 5. But Tarde is even more consistent and systematic. The radicality of Tarde's fractal conception of the social can be recognized most clearly in his conceptual creation of the "adaptate": "Agrégat signifie *adaptat*" (*LS*, 109; emphasis original). The idea is this. All associating elements *repeat*, *oppose*, and *adapt*, and in doing these things, each aggregate maintains itself as a society of elements that repeat and oppose the behavior of other elements and are adapted together. That the association, the society, is an "adaptate" means that the associating elements are adapted either to each other or together to a common function. Additionally, associations that have relations together (and each of which have adapted elements) can be coadapted, which constitutes a *higher-order adaptate*. Tarde believes that one could, in principle, go on to distinguish an infinity of orders of adaptates. But to get a fractal social ontology off the ground, he only needs two such degrees of adaptation (109–10). The first-order adaptation is that which the associating elements of a given association achieve among themselves; in this way, the pupils and the teacher of a class at school repeat and oppose their behaviors and adapt to each other, thus maintaining the class and its hierarchy from one day of school to the next—the class assembles itself as an adaptate. The second-order adaptation, again, is that which unites the association itself to the other associations that surround it—that is, to its social environment (milieu); in this way, the class can be seen to repeat and oppose and adapt to the behavior of other classes, the school administration, the opinions and worries of the parents, the pressures from the labor market, the opening hours of the local library, and various legal frameworks—the class as an adaptate in its own right adapts to its environment.

This idea of multiorder adaptates helps us understand how a fractal social ontology, avoiding organicism altogether (*LS*, 66–68), can trace the vicious circle of society. Take Dewey's vicious circle from chapter 5. Here, the third-order adaptate—society—presents a social second nature (customs, institutions, functional connections) that exercises overwhelming adaptive pressures on its associating elements—social groups—by putting them in antagonistic relations ("opposition") to each other that pressure them to imitate ("repeat") whatever promises survival on the market. By this adaptive pressure, the second-order adaptates—social groups—are impoverished in the moral variability of their customs and repeat the antagonistic structure of the third-order adaptate by putting an overwhelming adaptive pressure (what Adorno refers to as the process of "concretism") on their associating elements, the habits and impulses of the individuals, who, as first-order adaptates are thereby tilted to act outside rigid habit just to find themselves back in the old habit and so end up affirming the third-order adaptate that makes them suffer senselessly. Finally, this third-order adaptate—society—must adapt to *its* environment constituting a fourth-order adaptate (society and its natural environment), which reflects back on its internal adaptive pressures (think of the pressures the current metabolic rift puts on societal reproduction). And so we have come full circle. Turning explicitly against Durkheim, like we recorded Adorno did in chapter 3, Tarde declares, "Instead of explaining the small by the large, the detail by the gross, I explain the similarities of the whole by the accumulation of elementary actions, the large by the small, the gross by the detail" (63n1; my translation). In other words, fractal social ontology helps *trace* the vicious circle.[33]

Tarde and Dewey share two arguments for the hypothesis of social monism. The first one is epistemological: they find that social monism is implied in scientific practices. Their metaphysics is therefore naturalistic also in the sense that it does not wish to dictate methods and assumptions to science but, on the contrary, asks what successful scientific inquiries assume and imply about the nature of reality. But there is also an ethical argument for social monism in both authors' works: we should embrace this implication of science because it corresponds to and even expands on the way we live as human beings. We *are* "societies" by virtue of each of us having a body with various organs, impulses, habits, and vocabularies that we are unable to fully control, and we live and become the creatures we are *in* "societies," such as our families, trade unions, dancing classes, reading groups, the European Union, or Switzerland. In this sense, Dewey characterizes his metaphysics as that of the "common man."[34] We are, at every instance of our life, adaptates in adaptates: partly integrated first-order adaptates under the pressure to adapt to higher-order adaptates. If we affirm our society-likeness, the relative integration of ourselves, and transform our social environment to accommodate such loosely integrated adaptates, we may lead less repressive lives and coexperience freedom and happiness. Like Spinoza, Dewey and Tarde develop monisms to help us lead less meaningless lives: they believe that the perspective of "association" is something we are bodily and culturally immediately acquainted with, although we easily (are made to) forget it. And once we recognize that science, too, operates with this metaphysics (although scientists might easily forget it), it will become easier for us, they believe, to utilize science for life.

3.2 Modal Pluralism: Associational Fields

Dewey and Tarde distinguish several *modes* of association. "Association barely by itself," Dewey remarks, "is a wholly formal category. It acquires content only by considering the different forms of association which constitute the material of experience" (IPI, 43). The identification of such a form of association places some modes of existence in a certain region or "province" of what Dewey calls "the existential scheme of things" (49). The theory of these modes of association constitutes what I will call their *cosmology*: their attempt to distinguish something like stages or levels of reality. Dewey calls these types "degrees" or "special modes" or "fields" of reality (IPI, esp. 42 and 44; *EN*, esp. 208–10). Tarde calls them "worlds" or "orders" (*MS*, esp. 29, 48). In what follows, I will call them *associational fields*. For both authors, the speculation on associational fields predominantly involves asking the question of the place of the *social* in the cosmos, of mapping the landscape of the social. Each field constitutes the conceptual space of a regional ontology, and so Dewey and Tarde imagine them to deliver a physical ontology, an organic ontology, and a social ontology. But we will also see that these ontologies are not only closely linked but, more importantly, continuous and intertwined. Therefore, mapping these fields by combining a social monism with a modal pluralism involves establishing the identity and nonidentity of different modes of association as well as the ways in which one associational field grows out of another. "The gist of our problem," as Dewey states, "consists in deciding which of these forms presents the broader and fuller range of associations."[35]

Dewey's and Tarde's social monism is so thin that it is almost nonexistent. In the end, existence is assumed to be homogeneous only on account of it always involving associated behavior of some elements. It is a minimal monism: "Association in general is but a matrix," Dewey explains, adding that "its filling is the facts of association actually displayed in nature. Indeed, the category of association is but a highly abstract notation of what is formally common to the special modes" (IPI, 44). What associational fields do Dewey and Tarde then draw on their maps?

They identify the same three associational fields: the physical, the organic, and the social.[36] In a certain parlance, each of these fields can be characterized by its distinct *mechanism*. All associations, then, operate through some mechanism. Dewey states that "all life operates through a mechanism" (*HNC*, 51), and Tarde identifies "the social mechanism, the vital mechanism, the stellar mechanism, or the molecular mechanism" (*MS*, 47). This should not be confused with the clearly mistaken corollary that either of them would defend a mechanistic metaphysics. "Mechanism" needs not mean more than the constitution of an operational aggregate, an adaptate, doing something in the world by elements associating in a more or less regular manner. The idea is that on all associational fields, we can identify things by the *way* in which they operate and break them down to their associating elements. These elements possess each other reciprocally, while the entity maintained by their association possesses them unilaterally. Another way to put this is that the associational fields are distinguished by the consequences their elementary associations produce on an aggregate level and then incorporate in their ongoing activity. The adaptate, as it were, moves in circles. As Dewey puts it, the association of things confers upon their "assembly and its constituents . . . new properties" (*EN*, 138), whose complexity, stability, and freedom distinguish the mode from other ones, and "the higher the form of life the more complex, sure and flexible is the mechanism" (*HNC*, 51).

Whereas physical processes in Dewey are characterized by association, in which the reactions of the elements prepare the conditions to which their further associating behavior reacts,[37] Tarde describes their circulation as "waves" (*ondulation*) (*LS*, 48). In both cases, the general idea is, I take it, that the physical association displays a circulation, in which the association goes on without regard to the quality of the consequences. Organic processes are, for Dewey and Tarde, characterized by growth and decay of the association between organism and environment; the organism grows until it eventually stagnates and dies. In an organic process, Dewey specifies, "a connected continuity of acts is effected in which preceding ones prepare the conditions under which later ones occur." In contrast to physical processes, in organic life, this "chain of cause and effects" has a "cumulative continuity, or else death ensues."[38] Therefore, organic life is characterized by *habitual* action and reaction. Habit is an incorporation of previous actions and their consequences in an associating organism (*HNC*, 50–51). Similarly, Tarde believes that the vital mechanisms are "habit or inheritance," both being instances of what he calls "conformity to the precedent" (*LS*, 51; my translation). In both Dewey and Tarde, organic processes can then be characterized by a more intricate and intense circulation of elements and adaptate: the association of the elements produces cumulative consequences that are, as it were, incorporated in subsequent action. Importantly, both hold that self-maintenance, or self-preservation, is not the end of organic processes but rather a means for growth. In this, they agree with Alfred North Whitehead, who once quipped that "the art of persistence is to be dead."[39] Organisms, as it were, trade off persistence for growth in intensity.

Although Dewey and Tarde surely disagree on many details in social ontology (and perhaps even more so in physical and organic ontologies), importantly, they both agree with Nietzsche that the social form of association has an aesthetic or transformative character: it unfolds as a *shaping and receiving of things*, as a creative process (see chapter 3). In Dewey's terminology, social associations have their characteristic rhythm of effort and enjoyment (*AE*, 62–63). Social association cannot be conceptualized as an affair between persons only but always involves other elements too—for example, physical things. Social associations have an aesthetic character in involving a mutual give-and-take, production and reception, where the production reflects reception, and the reception reflects production (17–18). Similarly, in Tarde, the fundamental social fact is *imitation*, which is never purely normative and intersubjective but operates through productive exemplarity and receptive variation of an example, both constituting phases of an "imitational beam" (*LS*, 69–71), which spreads the variation in varying ways through the social fabric. This imitational beam must be embodied, must involve things, because it always spreads through some media (59–61). In Dewey's words, social associations "take up and incorporate within themselves things associated in the narrower way which we term the physical" (*IPI*, 47).

But social associations also take up and incorporate within themselves organic elements. Both authors single out *habits* as the central media of sociality, and they conceive habits as constitutively both mechanical *and* creative. Habits make surprising variations of the imitational beam or the exemplary behavior into a more or less stable mechanism, which maintains the activity with minute variation (*LS*, 59–60). I will get back to this in the postscript to this chapter. For now, it is important merely to record that social associations are, in Dewey and Tarde, embodied in habit *and* take up variations of habit. Social associations are, then, characterized by intricate and intense circulations of habits and physical things.

Now, Dewey as surprisingly as emphatically holds that the social can be ranked as *higher* than the other fields: social associations, he writes in *Experience and Nature*, present a "culmination of nature" (*EN*, 157). In "The Inclusive Philosophic Idea," he maintains that in "a comparison of definite types of association, the social, in its human sense, is the richest, fullest, and most delicately subtle of any mode actually experienced" and that social phenomena constitute "the widest and most intricate scale of the generic trait of associated behavior" (IPI, 44, 47). Tarde is no less enthused than Dewey by the social mode of existence:

> We must . . . look to the social world to see monads laid bare, grasping each other in the intimacy of their transitory characters, each fully unfolded before the other, in the other, by the other. This is the relation par excellence, the paradigm of possession of which all others are only sketches or reflections. By persuasion, by love and hate, by personal prestige, by common beliefs and desires, or by the mutual chain of contract, in a kind of tightly knit network which extends indefinitely, social elements hold each other or pull each other in a thousand ways, and from their competition the marvels of civilization are born. (*MS*, 56)

Even if Tarde never uses such terminology as "the culmination of nature," he still agrees with Dewey's idea of the social as the "inclusive philosophic idea" insofar as it attributes not only methodological but also ontological priority to the social in the human sense. The "possessive" relations of social agents who can relate with "ideas" to objects, he believes, extensionally transcend all "possessive" relations in the physical and organic fields: persons operating with ideas enjoy a "special dominion of the world" (55). Whereas a celestial body can possess only so many other celestial bodies in their gravitational field, already microbes can, by means of cooperation, possess a much greater organism by infection. Possession by means of gestures, concepts, and ideas in social association go way beyond what can be established in the other two associational fields. Only in social associations, then, can we ask Emerson's question and, eventually, come to enjoy an original relation to the universe.

3.3 A Chain of Havings to Break the Chain of Habits?

But wait! Is it not a curious finding that Dewey—who, with such an intense vigor, critiqued traditional metaphysics for its reproduction of their society's class structure in the imagination—should now himself set up a hierarchy in nature, a *great chain of beings*?[40] Does he not repeat what he criticized in his own imaginative inquiry whose "focal point" was to amount to a nonrepressive method of critical thought? How is his own cosmological hierarchy not yet another naturalization of social hierarchy? Does he continue, after all, Nietzsche's anthropocentrism of "man" as "nature's sole concern"?

To be sure, in *Unmodern Philosophy and Modern Philosophy*, Dewey blasts a relentless critique of the Aristotelian hierarchization of nature. More precisely, the critique is directed against the idea that species of existence lower in rank may be said to be *a condition but not a constituent* of higher species: just like vegetable life would, in this picture, be a condition of animal life, the slave's work would be the condition of the philosopher's leisure, but just like no vegetable can bring the animal into existence, the slave can have no share in philosophy (*UPMP*, 297–303).

In Dewey's view, however, the chief mistake of Aristotle is not that he assumes divisions and hierarchies in nature. Rather, his mistake is to conceptualize the divisions as categories sui generis and the hierarchy as structured by an external end, telos: "Stated in terms of means and ends, the principle involved in the kind of hierarchical arrangement assumed by Aristotle to exist in Nature is that there is a kind of means which are wholly external to the ends of which they are the conditions" (*UPMP*, 298). However, if the cosmological hierarchy can be understood as not one of substances, essences, or species of beings but of modes of association, associational fields growing out of each other, then the need for an external end of nature is unmasked as merely satisfying needs of domination in society: "If things, events, in and of themselves are neither means nor ends, but become one or other or both, under the influence of the social conditions which determine prevailing customs of use and enjoyment, the primary problem is creation of social conditions in which productive activities are such as to be intrinsically rewarding and refreshing and final consummatory activities are such as to be also productive. . . . The problem is one of social arrangements in their economic aspect" (303). In Dewey's view, the metaphysical problem is then not whether there is hierarchy in nature; the problem is how to conceptualize this hierarchy without extending into metaphysics the repressive social conditions that prevail and instead provide a conceptualization supportive of the quest for nonrepressive forms of effort and enjoyment (the establishment of which is, in the end, a task for collective educational and organizational effort) by itself cultivating a nonrepressive form of thinking, a self-reflexive phantasy making. This implies, for the critical cosmologist, the charge of conceptualizing the hierarchy without reified categories sui generis and without a final end. Positively, the task is then to construct an open-ended *scala naturae* without a final term—as it were, a rhythmic crescendo of associational fields. This would be a hypothetical, stipulated cosmology to aid in bringing about a state of social associations, a social adaptate, in which production is enjoyable and reception can be creative. This conceptualization would consist in an imaginative world making in which nonrepressive self-control is not excluded at the outset but kept alive as a real possibility for the associated behavior of suffering elements. It would also already be an attempt at practicing nonrepressive self-control: as there is no external or final end regulating the conceptualization, the work of the metaphysician becomes a playful association of means. And indeed, there is something quite childlike about Tarde's and Dewey's speculations. Perhaps the task of their reader is to take on that regression as a quest for nonrepressive modes of thought—a radical detour to the pleasure principle in an attempt to think beyond the reality principle, the internalized relation of adaptation.

Dewey and Tarde agree that there is a continuity from physical via organic to social associations. And they also agree on the identity criteria (repetitions and variations of associations). But there is also some agreement about the criteria for the nonidentity of the associational fields. Dewey often refers to a growth in the complexity, stability, and freedom of associations (*HNC*, 51; *EN*, 200–207; IPI, 42–44). Tarde sometimes refers to the difference in degree as one of increasingly heterogenous environments (*LI*, 77–78). Of note, growth in *heterogeneity* does not presuppose growth in *complexity* or vice versa. In some moods, Tarde does, in fact, explicitly reject the idea that social associations are more complex than physical or organic ones. However, in other moods, he says, like Dewey, that the organic is more complex and freer than the physical, and the social, more complex and freer than the organic. He further argues that the more complex and free processes instrumentalize the less complex and free processes (*LI*, 94).

Despite these differences, the drive of both Dewey and Tarde is to conceptualize modal immanent transcendence. On the one hand, this means telling the story of how a higher associational field was stabilized by associations on a lower level; this would be a *diachronic* perspective on the cosmological hierarchy, in which Dewey's cosmological selectionism becomes central. On the other hand, the fields, once established, cannot be conceived as "pure" in the sense of consisting only of their characteristic associating elements (as, for example, in the idea that human society would consist of norm-governed associations of persons only); this would be a *synchronic* perspective on cosmological hierarchy, in which Tarde's concept of unilateral possession becomes central.

Let's start with the diachronic perspective. Dewey seems to endorse a type of cosmological selectionism: in this picture, a higher mode of association transcends a lower one by evolving as a by-product of the latter associations. These leftovers then stabilize to reorganize the associations that produced it as its material. This is how Dewey, for example, reconstructs the genesis of social life: it evolves first as a by-product of organic associations that have come to utilize "signaling acts," which then produce the possibility of reacting to such an act *as a sign*, which, if reflected back, enables participation—that is, social association.[41] In Tarde, the issue is more ambiguous. It might be possible to read him as a selectionist too; sometimes, he even alludes explicitly to a selectionist view. However, in the first pages of the final and concluding chapter of *Les lois de l'imitation*, it becomes clear that Tarde oscillates between two models.

The first model is to postulate a *universal desire to repeat and spread*. Tarde postulates an original cosmological force that evolves from the physical mode of repetition via the organic mode of habit and inheritance to its social mode, imitation. This "desire" can be given several interpretations. It is an idea that, in the tradition of process metaphysics, can, again, be traced back all the way to Spinoza's *Ethics*, the principle of conatus.[42] Tarde's contemporaries gave it other names. The young Nietzsche named it "plastic power" (see chapter 4). Charles Sanders Peirce called it "agape."[43] Henri Bergson called it "élan vital."[44] In a footnote in the beginning of the last chapter of *Les lois de l'imitation*, Tarde indeed comes close to Peirce's agapism in playing with the idea of conceiving universal repetition as "love" (*LI*, 419).

The second model is closer to Dewey's view. Tarde plays with the idea of a *universal natural selection of variations in repetition*. Dewey clearly takes his getting rid of postulated "original forces," such as those assumed in Tarde's first model, by means of a cosmologically extended Darwinian selectionism as one of his greatest achievements in the field of metaphysics.[45] This is hardly Tarde's dominating view though. However, earlier in *Les lois de l'imitation* (*LI*, 205–6), he hints at something like a unilateral possession of the lower mode by the higher mode. Interestingly, in this phase of his life, he had not yet developed the concept of unilateral possession, which later figures prominently in *Monadology and Sociology*. Instead, he here uses the terms "domination" and "control." The cosmologically higher is that which has come to dominate or control the lower. He introduces ontological content or "substance" to the three modes of association: the content organized, or controlled, by social processes of imitation is "belief" and "desire"; the substance organized by organic processes of inheritance is "creative and functional life-forces"; the substance organized by waves are "molecular and motor forces." Tarde also introduces the notion of a hyperphysical world of "energy" here. The idea is that the mode of processes of the lower associational field produces the substance to be organized of the higher associational field in a "virtual" shape. Consequently, the physical waves mold functional life forces out of molecular and motor forces; the organic processes of inheritance and habit, again, mold primitive forms of belief and desire out of the creative and functional life forces, and, finally, belief and desire are then molded to ideas and volition in social processes. "Substance" is, on each associational field, the *unintended consequence of associations* on a lower field. Each mode of association organizes its own substance out of the unorganized leftovers of the substance organized by the lower mode. This would come considerably closer to Dewey's view that social associations evolved as a by-product of organic associations.[46]

This brings us to the *synchronic* perspective on the hierarchy of associational fields. Tarde suggests that a *scala naturae* can be constructed by replacing final ends with an immanent asymmetry of unilateral possessions.[47] Tarde turns the chain of beings into *a chain of havings*! The key to Tarde's suggestion is the *asymmetrical continuity* between reciprocal and unilateral possessions (*MS*, 54–59). In *Monadology and Sociology*, he summarizes, "Unilateral possession and reciprocal possession are . . . necessarily united. But the latter is superior to the former" (56). The idea is that every possession is to some degree reciprocal, but not every reciprocal association is unilateral.

If a possession were fully unilateral, there would be nothing possessed since there would be no opposition and hence no other existence to existentially constrain the possessing; there would be nothing to be *had*. This means that no associating element can be completely absorbed in its role of producing the adaptate whose element it is. Therefore, all associating elements are to some degree nonidentical to their societies. They always constitute, however minimally, a locus of recalcitrance. In Tarde's words, they

always belong only by one aspect of their being to the world they constitute, and by other aspects escape it. This world would not exist without them; without the world, conversely, the elements would still be something. The attributes which each element possesses in virtue of its incorporation into its regiment do not form the whole of its nature; it has other tendencies and other instincts which come to it from its other regimentations; and, moreover . . . , still others which come to it from its basic nature, from itself, from its own fundamental substance which is the basis of its struggle against the collective power of which it forms a part. (47; emphasis added)

A molecule, let's say of water, that is an element of an organic body of a person associating socially, let's say of Beyoncé performing "Cozy" on stage, belongs then at once to three "worlds": the chemical, the organic, and the social (48). And these worlds are hostile to each other since the organic is constituted by unilaterally possessing the chemical, and the chemical resists reduction to it, just like the organic is controlled by the social and resists reduction to it (all of which Beyoncé interestingly thematizes in "Cozy," a song that impressively explores, by the limited methods of popular music, the possibility of nonrepressive self-control). This relative independence of the chemical is expressed in phenomena such as illness and death, and the relative independence of the organic, in our impulsive nature. Similarly, social entities are constituted by organic and physical elements that resist their unilateral possession by the social. If these "social elements" were purely social, "it would follow that societies . . . would exist without change for all eternity" (47). Social associations are never quite social and thus are constantly haunted by recalcitrant tendencies within them.

Now, as he turns the chain of beings into a chain of havings by constructing the cosmological hierarchy as unilateral possession, Tarde avoids extending social relations of domination into metaphysical phantasy making by external final ends. Remember that not only does he describe unilateral possession as "control" and "domination," but the former was originally formulated in those social terms. Instead of turning a blind eye to what Dewey calls "the social problem" at the bottom of metaphysics, Tarde traces the social problem, the normative pressure to repress and adapt to domination, through the associational fields of nature, very much like Dewey's social critique of metaphysics traces its extension in metaphysical thinking. Tarde's cosmology of possession discloses normative pressure to adaptation as taking place *in nature all the way down*. The vicious circle of society appears then as an extension of the circulations of natural adaptates. But the idea of unilateral possession not only enables cosmology without final ends. Positively, it keeps the possibility of happy and free adaptates alive. Tarde never excludes the possibility of the element's nonrepressive self-control; instead, he shows that the many modes of opposition, or recalcitrance, go all the way down in nature too. In this simultaneous decentering and recentering movement, Tarde's metaphysics of possession itself displays the creative recalcitrance of a disclosing gesture.

4. Phantasy Making in the Wrong World: Critical Cosmology as Creative Recalcitrance

Dewey's and Tarde's solution to the ideological excesses of Western metaphysics is neither to wait for the revolution to overcome the alienated state that causes the metaphysical need nor to let their language of critique be domesticated to correspond to the repressive standards of allegedly nonmetaphysical theorizing. Instead, they seek to develop a metaphysics conscious of its social conditions and social consequences, a metaphysics that can critique its social conditions and embrace its social implications, a metaphysics, finally, that cultivates a nonrepressive form of thinking: a critical cosmology.

With the Tardean distinction between unilateral and reciprocal possessions, one can observe the contours of such a model of critical cosmology taking shape. It opens the horizon of a cosmological circulation available for the disclosing critics to utilize the negatively absolute metaphor of vicious circles avoiding both Nietzschean metaphysical arbitrariness and the tendency of Western metaphysics to extend domination. By disclosing how both the normative pressure to adapt and the recalcitrance to it go all the way down in nature, Dewey's and Tarde's associationist metaphysics provides an alternative to the intentionalist paradigms in social ontology, which are often assumed by normativist models of critique.[48] In Dewey and Tarde, the social is constitutively mediated by life and things. Social associations incorporate and transform them: they constantly utilize them as their media, and so social associations are embodied in habits and technology. Social associations are habitually constituted and, as such, are only sometimes normatively codifiable. But because social adaptates are never quite social, there is always a source of recalcitrance in their elements, which belong by other aspects of their being to other worlds. These other aspects, such as our impulses and erratic habitual variations, our heterochronous archaic heritage and suppressed memories of childhood happiness, may, perhaps, by educational and organizational efforts, develop into creative recalcitrance with disclosing force—they may, perhaps, be "elevated." We, too, are elements that may oppose our adaptates effectively due to belonging by only one aspect of our being to the wrong world. Like Emerson's poet, each element stands both inside and outside its adaptate.

Reflecting its own content, this metaphysics is itself critical in displaying an exemplary disclosure from inside and outside its form of life. It serves as a medium of critical disclosure: informed by science, with a sensibility for poetry and an eye on ordinary language, critical cosmology delivers alienating speech that can affect the recipients to alienate themselves from alienating language games. Metaphysical thinking, on this view, can function as a phantasy making informed by science, inspired by poetry, and oriented toward ordinary language and so can exemplify a form of criticizing that might escape the adaptive rationality of the reality principle while remaining rationally controllable.

The rational controllability of critical cosmology is different from that of a disclosing critical *theory*. Whereas disclosing critical theory, as we saw in chapters 5 and 6, submits itself to reality testing, critical cosmology does not, as its content is unverifiable. Whereas disclosing critical theory makes society experienceable by tracing its vicious circle, critical cosmology starts from reality-tested content and uses it as means of a playful phantasy making in concepts and metaphors. Critical cosmology and disclosing critical theory are different models of critical disclosure.

Against such an ambition, contemporary critics of metaphysical thinking have claimed that metaphysics presents an untenable "sideways-on view" of mind and world.[49] It is true that it *involves* a "sideways-on view," but from Dewey and Tarde, we can learn that it cannot be reduced to that only. It is a sideways view *on us ourselves*, starting from within our form of social life, to which we belong with one aspect of our being, and returning to it. Metaphysical speculation can be a critical practice taking a detour. It might seem extravagant, but that's literally its point. Why should philosophy not be extravagant? As Michael Hampe remarks, the intent to critically disclose our forms of life has, indeed, been an integral part of the metaphysical tradition: "The speculative aspect of the metaphysical tradition is to a large extent (not universally) the result of a quest for a distanced standpoint from which human thought and action can be viewed as clearly as possible and in its far-reaching ramifications. It is, moreover, the attempt to make conceivable, in rudiments, new forms of life through new forms of speech; at least insofar as the old forms of speech and life lose their self-evidence and necessity through the distancing and centrifugal speech of philosophy."[50] As Nietzsche already showed in chapter 4, if critique aspires to effective recalcitrance against prevailing customs, it cannot operate with prevailing vocabularies and methods—that is, with the tools of the second nature it resists. It needs a deviating form of speech, as it were, a poetic position outside the circle to draw a circle around it. Not all metaphysics is either empty hubris or symbolic violence. Dewey, for one, shows that not all metaphysics is about the quest for absolute certainty. In *Experience and Nature*, he remarks about common sense that "its organs of criticism are for the most part half-judgments, uncriticized products of custom, chance circumstance and vested interests. Hence common sense when it begins to reflect upon its own convictions easily falls a victim to traditional theories; *and the vicious circle begins over again*" (*EN*, 318; emphasis added). Effective recalcitrance must be creative too: if it is to help break out of the vicious circle, it cannot endorse its language. In linguistically mediated association, recalcitrance can take the form of a *dissociating type of speech*. The strangeness of metaphysical language, its uncanniness to the reader, its distance to scientific and ordinary vocabularies, and, not to forget, its childlike playfulness all can be methods of critical disclosure—expressions of recalcitrant forms of thinking in provincial tongues that mobilize the poetic powers of human language against the gravitational pull of a vicious circle of society hostile to us lower-degree adaptates with our recalcitrant tendencies.

To be sure, whatever dissociating speech the inquiry of the critical cosmologist produces, it must be receivable in the form of life critiqued: critical cosmology must be practiced with one eye on ordinary language. Yet the basic idea of a fractal social ontology that "everything is a society," as foreign as it may seem, is, perhaps, not applicable in contemporary society but surely receivable in ordinary life. At least some of us do experience ourselves as only partially integrated adaptates in social association with other partially integrated adaptates. And for many of us, it surely feels more liberating to think of oneself as that than as a self-legislating free will with moral responsibility for every single impulse. (However, I do not know how far this experience may be generalized.)

To sum up, critical cosmology's dissociating speech can seek to take the position of Emerson's poet outside the circle of society and give an alienating description of its alienated state. It shows the extraordinariness of the ordinary and the ordinariness of the extraordinary—the extent to which our lives are alienated and the nearly immediate affinity of experiencing oneself as a "society." The shock of its dissociating use of language appeals to the imagination. It makes a split within us experienceable—the split between what is attained, an adaptate of senseless suffering, and what might be attainable, an adaptate of enjoyment and creativity. And it shows itself as an example of cultivating a recalcitrant, nonrepressive way of thinking, as *counterteleology*.

Dewey believes that metaphysics can be a phase of a gesture of critical disclosure. In *Unmodern Philosophy and Modern Philosophy*, he describes the procedure as follows: "The more detailed exposition of the opinion will cover three matters. First, a statement of the connections existing between material and ideal and subject matter in culture as culture. Secondly, discussion of the phases of the historic conditions of the split between lower and higher social functions in their direct affect upon philosophical formulations; third, a discussion of the issue from the standpoint of any naturalism consonant with present-day knowledge" (*UPMP*, 289). On Dewey's view, the critical cosmologist, then, starts like the Nietzschean physician of culture and the Freudian cultural critic with a critical diagnosis of the times studying the symptoms of current social suffering. She then provides a critical genealogy of the metaphysical assumptions and implications that serve the ideological function of maintaining the relations of domination, providing, as it were, a symptomatology. She reacts by formulating a metaphysics not of domination but of emancipation—that is, an account of a transformable and self-transformative nature that keeps the possibility of nonrepressive self-control open.

One is tempted to ask, though, Did Dewey not forget the final step of the procedure—the *counterformation*? How can the recalcitrant cosmology itself extend to the practices of the prevailing form of life? How can the dissociating speech of the critical cosmologist partake in the educational and organizational effort of recentering disclosure? Can Tarde, once again, jump to the rescue?

5. Imitational Circulation of Hesitation: A Tardean Postscript

Indeed, I believe he can! Remember, in Tarde, association—on whatever associational field—always involves *repetition, opposition,* and *adaptation.* These three concepts express universal "aspects" of reality (*LS*, 43): "These are," he expands, "the three terms of a circular series, capable of turning endlessly" (102; my translation).

In the *social* version of this circular series, the repetitive aspect is *imitation.* Tardean imitation is, I believe, best understood as habit taking (*LS*, 59–60, 109–10): in imitating, an associating individual takes on a habitual trait of another. Importantly, the habitual trait is given by an individual who is different from the habit taker; they always have, to some extent, different habitual and drive structures. Therefore, imitation is not copying: repetition always presupposes difference; imitation is only possible between individuals who are unique. In imitation, the trait that is taken on also therefore always changes to some extent, because it adjusts to the habitual dispositions and drive structures of the habit-taking individual. And if that individual is then imitated by a further associating individual, the habitual trait taken on this time will, again, not be exactly the same as in the first imitational sequence but will change a little bit again as it adjusts to the habitual dispositions and drive structures of this third individual. This series of social repetition of minute habitual variations is what Tarde calls an "imitational beam" (*rayon imitatif*) (69–70; my translation).

Imitational beams propagate from the particularity of some associating individual's behavior: the habit taker imitates a habit giver. A habitual variation takes the character of an *example*, circulates in the social group, and is gradually consolidated into a custom, or social second nature. The totality of such imitational beams that flow from an initiator whose example has spread is what Tarde calls an "imitational radiation" (*rayonnement imitatif*) (*LS*, 87; my translation). Social life, Tarde further elaborates, is made up of a dense and messy interweaving (*entrecroisement touffu*) of imitational radiations, between which the interferences are innumerable and succeed or fail at consolidation into collective habit (87). In principle, however, Tarde goes on to propose, there is a tendency of such a social variation to spread into the initiator's social environment *as a circle*, "the tendency of an example, once launched, in a certain social group, to spread according to a geometric progression, if this group remains homogeneous" (69; my translation). This is reminiscent of Emerson's line in *Nature*: "Throw a stone into the stream, and the circles that propagate themselves are the beautiful type of all influence" (*N*, 21).

This tendency of imitation to geometrical progression is, however, most often hindered by obstacles of various kinds. It is quite rare, Tarde observes on various social statistics, that an imitational beam of a habitual variation draws a perfect circle (*LS*, 69). Some of the resistances come from the diversity of climate and geography, but these are not the strongest; the foremost obstacle that stops an imitational radiation and its consolidation into a custom is another similarly expansive imitational radiation that meets it on its way and interferes with it. Tarde calls these obstacles "social oppositions" (chap. 2). Every time, according to Tarde, that I hesitate between, say, two ways of speaking or two ideas or two beliefs or two ways of dressing, an interference of imitational beams takes place in me—imitational beams that have spread to me from sources mostly barren to me and often extremely distinct from each other in space and time (69–70). The interferences of the imitational beams are not all mutual hindrances, however; on the contrary, Tarde believes that they often form alliances and serve to accelerate or to amplify each other. This then results in a more intense imitational radiation. Sometimes, such coalescing imitational beams result in the occasion of "a geniality which is born from their meeting and their combination in a brain" (71), like, for example, how imitational beams from Hegel and Marx, from Nietzsche and Freud, from Kafka and Kraus, and from Mahler and Schönberg all coalesce in Adorno's *Aesthetic Theory*.

But before looking closer at Tarde's conception of geniality, let's ask him what happens when imitational beams do conflict. How is this conflict resolved? What are the influences that decide? Tarde distinguishes two modes of such resolution: "the logical" and "the extralogical" (*LS*, 70; see also *LI*, chaps. 5–7). Some conflicts between an imitational beam and its opposition are resolved by reasonable discussion or creative deliberation where a critical distance both to the prevailing habit and the variation is taken. Others are resolved by given habits, customs, institutions, and functional connections just swallowing up the variation and its imitations into the channels of prevailing societal reproduction. Tarde adds, however, that these latter, "extralogical" resolutions are, in fact, logical, too, in a certain sense of the word, "because, when, between two examples, the plebeian blindly chooses that of patrician, the rural that of the urban, the provincial that of the Parisian . . . , the imitation, as blind as it is, is moved in sum by a presumption of the superiority attached to the example according to its appearance of social authority" (*LS*, 70; my translation). This is what Tarde calls "the cascade of imitation from top to bottom of the social scale" (70; my translation). The "core" of the form of life pulls the "margin," as the one-year-younger Nietzsche had observed twenty years earlier in his *Untimely Meditations*. Exemplarity is channeled by social second nature.

These two models for the resolution of conflicts between habitual disposition and imitational radiation can, I believe, be more extensively understood as *social mechanisms of selection*. Thus, the question of conflict resolution between imitational beams could be rephrased as follows: Which imitational beam is selected, and how does the selective mechanism work? When imitational beams collide in the imitational radiation, each can be, as it were, selected for the form of social life either logically or extralogically— that is, by some type of critically distanced perspective or blindly. In reality, the selection is, I assume, sometimes a combination of both and always blind to some extent. Take the selection of the imitational beam emanating from Charles Darwin's theory of natural selection. This is a rather extreme example of a "logical" selection. The theory has, after all, been the topic of some of the most intense public and academic debates in history from its original publication in 1859 until today. Still, a likely contributing cause for the selection of the theory of the evolution of species by natural selection of inherited variations that increase the individual's ability to compete, survive, and reproduce was, and is, the structure of our overpowering societal environment that likewise pressures *us* to compete, survive, and reproduce. Conversely, beyond its specific sectors of human knowledge, Darwinism had widespread and uncontrollable influence in politics, the economy, and culture—an influence that was surely blindly selected for the most part for the persistence of relations of domination in society (despite its revolutionarily liberating observation that species change by individual variation and deviation, which could make one think instead that those relations of domination, for the benefit of which Darwinism was selected, could change too).

To sum up, a habitual variation is received as an example and constitutes an imitational beam in a social association. Because the imitated trait is embodied as a habit in the initiator, it will spread through several imitational beams in the habit giver's many social groups, and perhaps some of her beams will eventually intersect, producing an imitational radiation. Some imitational radiations are selected rather logically; others, rather extralogically. The extralogical selection mechanism has its own logic of domination: it tends to select in favor of the preservation of the hierarchies in the current form of life. A form of social life can then, on Tarde's account, be traced along the selections of the many intersecting imitational radiations of its associations.

Tarde calls the elementary form of social *opposition* "hesitation." Social opposition, he exemplifies, takes place every time an individual "hesitates between adopting or rejecting a new model which offers itself to her, a new locution, a new rite, a new idea, a new school of art, a new conduct." The ordinary course of action is interrupted by the conflict between an imitational beam and an established habit. The individual stops, hesitates. Hesitation, Tarde expounds, is "this small internal battle, which is reproduced in millions of copies at each moment of the life of a people, is the infinitesimal and infinitely fertile opposition of history" (*LS*, 79–80; all my translation).

And so, I might ask, when confronted with Darwinism, should I adopt its consequences? In what sense and in which spheres of life? What do I do with my religious beliefs? I might, like Dewey, hesitate and oppose *social* Darwinism while emphatically affirming the idea of the evolution of species by the natural selection of inherited traits as a metaphysically and culturally liberating idea.[51] Or, I might, like Adorno, hesitate, take a step back, and use it, ironically, as a model for culture and society instead (*ND*, pt. 3, chap. 2). Or to take a more "extralogical" example, when in my habit of discussing the horrifying future of civilized social life on this planet, I might hesitate and ask, Do I say "climate change" or "climate catastrophe"? I'd probably do better in hesitating to continue an imitational radiation from the Republican lobbyist Frank Lutz, who, if Latour is right,[52] replaced "global warming" with "climate change" in a depoliticizing gesture. Yet what are the consequences of circulating "climate catastrophe" in my social associations? Do I thereby discourage my fellow associating elements from taking transformative action by implying that the cause is already lost, or do I rather contribute to a realistic understanding of the situation in which we act?

Now, *hesitation* would, then, surely be the form that the critical recalcitrance, which disclosing critique appeals to and exemplifies, takes within the individual: the critic hesitates before an overpowering social environment to continue its adaptive demands in her own action. But Tardean hesitation can also consist of an opposition against a new variation, against recalcitrance, in favor of the powers that be: as we saw Adorno problematize in chapter 3, the recipient of the disclosing gesture might not at all want Emerson's poet to "break up [her] whole chain of habits" (C, 409).

If an imitational beam contradicts the habits of the individual, hits on hesitation in her, and she receives it "logically," Tarde points out, then one of three things will happen. One, the hesitator allows herself to be moved completely in the direction of the imitational beam; she undergoes a habit change and abandons her contradicting way of thinking and acting. In this case, there is next to no internal struggle; the imitational beam celebrates, as it were, a victory without combat (*LS*, 88). In her, the imitational beam then takes one more step, and she contributes her slight variation to the theme. So, I might, for instance, read Steven Jay Gould's *The Structure of Evolutionary Theory*, let myself be completely convinced by its interpretation of Darwinian evolution, and drop all my contradicting old Darwinian habits of thinking after giving it some thought.

Two, the hesitator reacts against the gesture, the foreign idea or habit that offends her, and affirms or wants all the more energetically what she was already affirming and wanting. In this case of repelling the example, there is a disturbance in her, an intimate struggle, and this disorder, too, Tarde believes, may spread contagiously, because it is an overexcitement and not a paralysis of the individual. From there, a faction in the association splits off (*LS*, 88–89). So I might later read, say, Richard Dawkins's *The Selfish Gene*, feel utterly offended by its vulgar gene-centered view on evolution and its unreflective extension outside a genetic evolutionary theory's specific sector of human knowledge, and stick even firmer than before to more liberal readings of Darwinian theory.

Three, the hesitator undergoes only "half the influence" of the imitational beam. This reaction receives the beam as what Tarde calls "the shock" (*le choc*). The shock is followed by a lessening of its more or less hindered and paralyzing force, out of which a new variation of habit results by an alienated distance both to her own habit and the odd new imitational beam (*LS*, 88). So I might even later come across Dewey's essay "The Influence of Darwinism on Philosophy" and start seeing Darwinian theory's idea that small variations in *individuals* make *universals* change as an astonishingly liberating and powerful idea that jolts various parts of my life experience to the extent that I will, step-by-step, readjust my habits of thinking and acting.

Now, I believe that disclosing critique of society aims at this third and last type of hesitation. Disclosing critical gestures aspire, partly by uncanny means, to cause a *hesitation shock* in the recipients that, for the moment, alienates them from the alienated state of society. Disclosing critics, albeit most often faced with the second type of hesitation, are not after convincing the recipient. They do not request the hesitator to follow the critic instead of their own habit but to take a critical distance to the vicious circle inside and outside themselves and consider the objective possibility of happiness and freedom in its place, whatever that be taken to mean. At least, they do not wish the recipient to follow them in the sense of agreeing with their claims or their theory. They are not judges, and their critiques do not come with binding verdicts. If they wish the addressee to follow them in anything, then that would be in the cultivation of a *habit of hesitation* itself.

Remember that hesitation, as the elementary form of social opposition, hindered the imitational radiation to form a perfect circle. Tarde understands habit as repetition of the self, imitation as repetition of other, and the imitational beam as collective habituation (*LS*, 59–60). In imitating, the associating individual adjusts her habitual disposition both externally, to the behaviors of others and the adaptate whose part she is, as well as internally, to her other habits and character traits. Now, the *hesitation shock* interrupts habit and collective habituation. But hesitation can become habit too: it can be cultivated as a reflective habit in the individual. In fact, in passing, Tarde mentions such a peculiar habit and names it: "skepticism" is hesitation that has become habitual (90). And remember, it was the "skepticism" of the ordinary that Adorno, in chapter 3, regarded as "perhaps the best source for changing the world that humanity possesses at all today."[53]

If hesitation can, as "skepticism," be made into a habit, then it can also be *imitated*. If it can be imitated, then it can spread as an imitational beam and lead to imitational radiation. If the imitational radiation is successful, it will *consolidate skepticism into a custom*, into second nature of a social group. If this is the case, we have a Nietzschean circle of culture with Deweyan disclosing reason in place: a reflectively recalcitrant social group that, by force of the reflective collective habit, can also act collectively. We have *effective and reflective critical recalcitrance* (see fig. 6 below).

Now, such a counterformation can both *host* disclosing gestures (the custom of hesitation supports their production and enables their reception) and *spread* their radiation into the wider society (the custom of hesitation is an embodied collective habit that makes collective action possible and is, as such, able to be imitated). No question, such counterformative radiation will be resisted by the current social second nature with its cascade of imitation

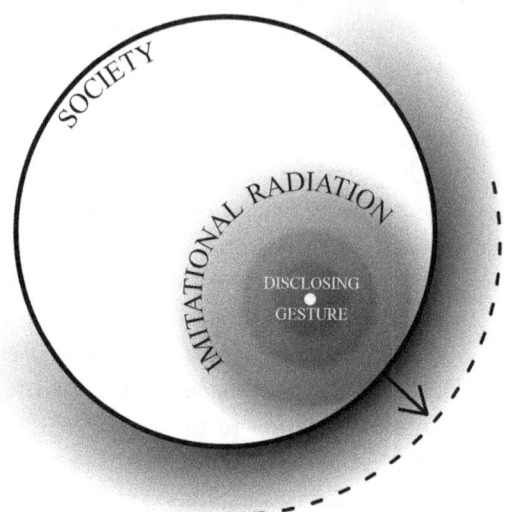

FIGURE 6. The "vicious circle" being broken by a disclosing gesture that gets imitated as a habit of hesitation, as implied by Tarde. Created by the author.

from the top to the bottom. But the *hesitation shock* can alienate the recipient from the extralogical flow of imitation. Such a shock can be affected by evocation of the uncanny feeling, which in turn can direct the appeal to the recipient's recalcitrant tendencies and activate the creative thinking of imagination.

Such an imitational radiation against the cascade from the top to the bottom would, of course, as Adorno and Dewey show, take educational and organizational effort. In his "The Meaning of Working Through the Past," Adorno envisages something like this type of imitational radiation in education and organization against fascism in postwar West Germany. Admitting at the outset that "such a pedagogy in practice will probably reach in general only those people who are open to it anyway and who therefore are hardly susceptible to fascism," he adds, "On the other hand, it is certainly not at all superfluous to fortify this group with enlightened instruction against the non-public opinion. On the contrary, one could easily imagine that from this group something like cadres could develop, whose influence in the most diverse contexts would then finally reach the whole of society, and the chances for this are all the more favorable, the more conscious the cadres become."[54]

On this emerging view of disclosing reason, being reasonable includes possessing a great variety of habits, including the reflective habit of hesitating among them and the external pressures of imitational habit taking, and it includes becoming a skilled hesitator. Geniality, Tarde maintains, is a consequence of the accumulation of such exercises in hesitation: "We can see accentuated, by the very fact of these innumerable psychological oppositions of which the life of any social individual is composed, her individual originality, her own genius" (*LS*, 80; my translation). Geniality is then also about happening to find oneself in the intersection of fruitful imitational beams, in a unique position of imitational radiation—that is, finding oneself under the lucky *constellation* of many good educators in many good circles of culture.

Having a higher self, on this view, involves having good examples and the space to digest them. The genius a disclosing gesture appeals to is then neither a transcendent moral instance in the individual nor an unattained but immanently attainable ethical ideal in her. And it is most definitely not a self-legislating, responsible free will. Rather, it is an acquired and cultivated skill of relating to one's own habitual disposition and drive structure as well as to external influence in varied and creative ways. It is the hesitant elevation of the spontaneity in the painfully adapted individual. Tarde's ontology of imitation can be received as an attempt to make sense of social critique without presupposing free will and self-legislating autonomy. Instead of self-legislating normativity, the inner-worldly loci of critique are the innumerable instances of recalcitrance to adaptation in the individual that can be cultivated as the habit of hesitation and experienced as "I am a society."

EIGHT

Reason and Recalcitrance
Conclusions Without Closure

> The people fancy they hate poetry,
> and they are all poets and mystics!
> —RALPH WALDO EMERSON, "The Poet"

1. The Outcome of the History and Its Moral

At the outset of the investigation, I said that this book is antitheoretical, antisystematic, and historical. I have, correspondingly, not aimed at presenting an alternative critical theory or a systematic account of disclosing critique. But has this history at least contoured a *concept* of disclosing critique?

In *Philosophical Investigations*, Wittgenstein asks, "How would we explain to someone what a game is?" and he answers that he supposes that "we'd describe games" and then add, "This and similar things are called 'games.'" We can, Wittgenstein believes, *look* at examples and *see* what a concept means. This is, I hope, what the reader has experienced from my report from the excavation site that is a scene of disclosing critique. In this sense, I have indeed disclosed a concept of disclosing critique—a concept that is as open as is a landscape. Wittgenstein adds, "We don't know the boundaries [of a concept] because none have been drawn.... [W]e can draw a boundary for a special purpose. Does it take this to make the concept usable? Not at all! Except perhaps for that special purpose."[1] The gesture of this investigation lies somewhere between the two extremes in Wittgenstein's implied spectrum of concepts—that is, between those that have boundaries drawn around them for a special purpose and those that do not. I have *sketched the contours* around the usage of a negatively absolute metaphor to show how to make sense of a practice of the radical critique of society—a practice that does not submit itself to prevailing social normativity or the form of the concept afforded by the form of life it critiques. There are the contours of *an* open concept of disclosing critique in this book covering *many* examples of a critical disclosure that is always invoked for a special purpose and from a particular experience.

Does this make the concept usable for the special purpose of a critique of contemporary society, for a disclosing critique today? That depends on what it is used for in such a situation more precisely. My intention has been to historically contour a concept that would be useful as a source of inspiration and as an education of critical skills—as it were, as a *cultivation of recalcitrant virtues*. However, as I believe this history shows, disclosing critique of society is radically situational; its concept is the consequence of critiquing. Eventually, the concept of a disclosing critique of contemporary society can only be the result of that very critiquing.

There are striking similarities in the types of disclosing critique I have mapped and which I hope to have sufficiently pointed out by investigating the excavation site disclosed by the leading fossils, "drawing a circle around the circle" and "vicious circle." First of all, the excavation has shown that disclosing critique is a type of critical gesture: it points out a vicious circle and points to a way out. In all exemplary cases, I thus stumbled on *decentering* and *recentering* directions of the disclosing gesture. Indeed, my study points to this unifying characteristic of a disclosing critique of society: a disclosing critique decenters and recenters a form of life in one circular gesture. Second, none of the exemplary gestures reconstructed conformed to normative judgment. Sure, they all involved normative judgments in some form. I am not suggesting that disclosing critique is a nonnormative critique (whatever that would mean). But it is a practice of social critique that does not assume the form of normative judgment but rather of an educative gesture. Even where it contains judgments, disclosing critique is not played in the (rather exotic) language game of objective judgment. Instead, it seeks to change the rules of these games by initiating a *counterformation*. All the exemplary gestures of critical disclosure therefore assumed something recalcitrant to be "elevated" in the addressee (a higher self, sexual and aggressive impulses, spontaneity, our adaptate character, etc.), and this something was assumed to be in one way or another *recalcitrant* to current patterns of socialization. Most of these models then went on to point to some version of a combination of education and organization as the way out of the vicious circle. Third, all the exemplary gestures were reflective about the fact that this appeal to the addressees makes disclosing critique fundamentally *dependent on reception*. This prompted the more refined versions of disclosing critique to seek to disclose a *disclosing form of reason*. Whereas this disclosure in Adorno was very careful not to say anything positive about it, Dewey and Freud pointed more concretely to its glimpses in the pluralism of ordinary life and our capacity for phantasy making, and let's not forget that Tarde fantastically suggested a model for it under the name of skepticism, whose ordinary version Adorno already pointed to as the best source for social transformation. Last on this list (which could perhaps be continued) is the *sensibility for senseless social suffering*, which in all these models seems to direct their decentering and recentering movements. Now, such a sensibility cannot be understood as a "criterion of critique." It is a critical skill, a habit to be cultivated, and the cultivation of it would be one of the educative tasks of disclosing critique in its *care for reason*.

Despite these similarities, the attempt was not to formulate a theory, a normatively structed system of propositions, or a sharply outlined concept of disclosing critique. I have given examples that, I believe, may, negatively, liberate us from the narrow picture of social critique in the normativism that has kept critical theory captive for too long and, positively, liberate us to try disclosing critiques of society again.

Instead of a theory, then, this book gives examples of a practice. But it also exemplifies that practice by practicing it itself, as it were, once removed: the metaphor history presented here sought to disclose disclosing critique. It did perhaps not draw a circle around a circle, but it did identify a circle of users of a negatively absolute metaphor—a "circle of culture," as the young Nietzsche would have called it—and it contoured it. By telling a story that traced the poetic metaphor of critique as a circle around a circle, it sought to disclose this practice of critique by giving examples of more or less successful attempts at practicing it. Sometimes, the excavation found objects utterly useless, such as the young Nietzsche's positive metaphysics of "plastic power," which in the arbitrariness of its content displayed nothing but a curiosity to record by the "travelling geologist." Sometimes, the excavation revealed objects helplessly outdated but nonetheless interesting and worth following up on, such as Nietzsche's *method* of critical cosmology, which was then rediscovered in enhanced shape in Dewey and Tarde. At yet other times, the excavation made definite findings, revealing real treasures to carefully package, bring back home, and hand over to the practicing social critics, such as Adorno's and Dewey's conceptions of social *theory* as a disclosing *gesture*. Finally, there were times when the investigation dug deeper in the excavation site stretching between Emerson and Adorno just to better get at the connections among the layers in the ground to see what was hidden in these treasures, such as looking with an almost-obsessed patience into the uncanny with Freud.

With these merits, one might perhaps even see the investigation as a contribution to disclosing critical theory—provided such an enterprise would ever again get off the excavation ground. Without itself having the shape of a theory, the story it tells might contain valuable insights into the stakes of critical theorizing that aims at disclosure. In this chapter, I wish to conclude by pointing at those insights that seem to me most crucial for any attempt at revitalizing this at first widely neglected and now long forgotten practice of philosophical social critique.

2. Philosophy and Its History as Critical Disclosures

As a reminder, another way to put this would be that the investigation was not theoretical but rather historical. I have told a story of critiquing, which gives examples of a set of alternatives to the current obsession with normative judgment and denaturalization in philosophical social criticism—a set that was delimited by the usages of two metaphors that merged and that was shown to contain internal resemblances, commonalities, and connections. At the outset, I posited that social critique is a consequence of critiquing—a curious thing that peculiar individual organisms (or groups of them) may do in an environment that puts them under conflicting adaptive stress. I have mapped the landscape through the examples of some such individual responses to particularly restrictive environments in modern capitalism. My focus has, on several accounts, been extremely restricted too. First, I have said almost nothing about the biographies of these individuals. Even worse is that I have rarely given more than anecdotal evidence about the asphyxiating environments they were responding to! And the worst thing of all is that I have said so little about *what* these critics were criticizing. That is to say, my story is neither an intellectual biography, a history of an idea, a cultural history of philosophy, nor a rational reconstruction. Instead, my focus was the rather limited one of metaphorological exemplary reconstruction. On top of that, it was much more limited than the metaphorological focus of Blumenberg, who sought to disclose epochs in the history of philosophy. My attempt was, by contrast, to contour a *practice* of philosophical critique of society by telling the story of a metaphor, "drawing a circle around a circle," which, on its curious trajectory from Emerson via Nietzsche and Freud and through a detour with Tarde to Dewey and Adorno, came to embrace a metaphor for society and its critique alike as "vicious circles."

I believe Emerson, Nietzsche, Dewey, and Adorno were right to hesitate to think of philosophy as a science or to subsume philosophy under an academic discipline. At times I, for one, struggle to make sense of the place given to or taken by philosophers at contemporary research universities. What's their research input? What's the output? How is any of these bizarre things they do empirically controllable? *History* of philosophy, however, seems different from its object of study in this regard. It is a self-evident discipline of the humanities just as the history of art, the history of science, or the history of technology. While I believe that philosophy, which often is constitutively fused with the ethical and existential sensibility of the individual practicing it, is seldom worthwhile as abstracted from its history, the history of philosophy is in a different way subject to the methodological norms of a scholarly community and hence controllable by its critical scrutiny.

In this investigation, I have sought to follow such rules by applying them creatively. I have used the tools of metaphorology on an artifact they were not originally designed for. With the toolkit of metaphor history, Blumenberg responded to a concrete problem of his immediate scholarly environment: predominantly, the methodological shortcomings of conceptual history of philosophy. By contrast, my investigation has, by using its toolkit, developed the *history of negatively absolute metaphors*. There remain similarities. Both the history of absolute metaphors and that of negatively absolute metaphors seek to disclose something predominantly nonconceptual by predominantly conceptual means. Whether an absolute metaphor is unconsciously projected on the blank screen of "reality," like in the case of Blumenberg's objects of study, or reflectively applied in order to disclose a space for radical critique of a social reality that is experienced as false, the ground of the practice itself fundamentally escapes conceptual codification in the given historical situation. And thus, it will also necessarily fail to satisfy several standards of conceptual precision. But one can excavate it by exemplifying the many practical reactions that have taken place on it; one can point out relevant features, compare consequences, investigate assumptions and implications, and speculate about their possibilities. The practices are receptive to disclosure by their metaphoric relation to the ground they place themselves on.

The investigation, itself at times operating by metaphors, such as "ground" and "excavation site," posited "history" rather spatially. The story told by these methods did not result in anything like a report of a temporal sequence of events. Rather, history appeared as a multilayered space, in which connections between the layers were followed up, traced, and displayed. This was an affordance of the occasion: accepting the scene of disclosing critique as its excavation site, history appeared predominantly as sedimented second nature.

Now, philosophy as a not exhaustively scientific or scholarly practice can surely learn from the scholarly enterprise of a history of philosophy. This is perhaps less surprising as it might seem. For *pointing to texts* can be a philosophically significant critical gesture, showing what has been lost in contemporary discourse by using, as it were, the archaic as a means of cultivating recalcitrant tendencies. The regressive digging on the excavation site then resembles the play of a child on the beach who gasps at the weird things around her (a particularly flat stone, an enchanting shell, and what is this—dry seaweed?), picks them up, brings them to the grown-ups, and gleefully cries, "Look!"

This commits me, at the end, to ask what philosophy, or more concretely philosophical social criticism, can learn from this story? First of all, I believe it would be a grave mistake to draw the conclusion that my inquiry implied that it is necessary to criticize in this way (whatever "this" would be taken to mean—I have shown many related ways to criticize). Rather, I think that philosophers, and others too, can by hearing out this story come to see that *it is possible, realistically, to criticize in ways like these*, and therefore, it is *not necessary* to stay trapped in the juridical picture. To summarize some of the socio-philosophical implications of this excavation, it may be helpful to compare disclosing critique to three forms of philosophical social critique that have, after the end of my story around 1970, escaped the pressure to reduce critique to its narrow juridical model and survived against the odds: genealogical critique, the critique of ideology, and critical imagination.

3. Genealogy, Ideology, and Critical Imagination

Genealogical critique and the critique of ideology are different from disclosing critique, but they can, in certain critical situations and under certain social conditions, be part of the decentering direction of a disclosing gesture.

Like disclosing critique, genealogical critique, escapes, as Raymond Geuss notes, the "juridical metaphor";[2] in fact, the circumstance of which a critique gets caught in a juridical metaphoric is a particularly interesting finding for genealogical critique. However, critical genealogy does not resort to a reflective metaphoric, as disclosing critique does, to disclose an alternative language game of critique. Genealogy is more straightforwardly methodological: it relies on an understanding of critique as a way to "question" and "problematize" something.[3] In genealogical critiques, this "something," interestingly, always involves the self-evident assumptions of a form of social life and how it shapes "subjectivity," "identity," or "the self."[4] This is, obviously, very similar to disclosing critical theory's drive to trace the vicious circle: both follow up on how the second nature of the form of life, as it were, shapes the first nature of its members. In genealogical critique, the method of tracing is historical: "To offer a genealogy," Geuss defines, "is to provide a historical dissolution of self-evident identities."[5] Genealogical critique problematizes by tracing how a specific historical process shaped subjects to become what they are.

Genealogy, then, provides a method of tracing features of identity and normativity in the vicious circle. And as such, it is one of several imaginable methods that a disclosing critic can rely on as she traces the vicious circle: genealogical critique can be a decentering gesture of disclosure. Depending on the situation, the disclosing critic may reasonably resort to tracing the vicious circle historically by giving a genealogical account. And to be sure, disclosing critics, in fact, have often been remarkably inclined to do so. In Nietzsche, Freud, Dewey, and Adorno, it should be rather easy for an investigation of the relationship between genealogy and disclosing critique to identify genealogical elements in the decentering directions of their disclosing gestures.[6]

The relationship between disclosing critique and the critique of ideology is more ambivalent. On the one hand, just like it can include a critical genealogy, disclosing critique can also include a critique of ideology. As we saw in chapter 7, Dewey's social critique of metaphysics is not only an application of critique of ideology but develops original insights into it: Dewey's extension thesis of metaphysical dualisms shows that critique of ideology is not only compatible with a disclosing critique of society but also disclosing critics have something to contribute to it.

In *Philosophy and Real Politics*, Geuss defines an ideology as "a set of beliefs, attitudes, preferences that are distorted as a result of the operation of specific relations of power," and he stresses that "the distortion will characteristically take the form of presenting these beliefs, desires, etc., as inherently connected with some universal interest, when in fact they are subservient to particular interests."[7] Ideology critique as well, then, sets up a relation among the relations of power in a form of life, perhaps as embodied in its second nature, shaping beliefs and attitudes of the individuals for it to appear as necessary and in universal interest. Like disclosing critique, the critique of ideology seeks to challenge an appearance of universality. Therefore, the critique of ideology can play a role in a disclosing critique of society. Depending, again, on the situation, it can make a fruitful and even crucial contribution—namely, that of tracing a necessary phase of that particular vicious circle, the distortion of the attitudes of those whose activity turns out to maintain a hostile second nature. And as such, it, too, can be a helpful phase of the decentering direction of a disclosing gesture.

However, this phase may not always be significant, and so the critique of ideology is not always relevant. The attitudes may, for example, not be distorted by ideology but *diverted* by concretism, as we saw in chapter 4. On the other hand, then, it is part of the self-understanding of disclosing critics that ideology critique is a seriously limited approach. The vicious circle does not present merely "false consciousness" or "distorted beliefs and attitudes," although those can very well constitute a phase of its reproduction. Dewey regarded dualistic beliefs as *extensions* of domination: the beliefs were not external means to the ends of the powers that be but a continuation in language games of the violence of material domination—first in the language games of socially detached Greek philosophers, which then cast, as it were, an imitational beam to ordinary language from the top to the bottom of the social scale, as Tarde would say.

But there is an even more radical divergence between disclosing critique and the critique of ideology. Disclosing critics do not assume that there needs to be "false consciousness" or "distorted beliefs and attitudes" in place *at all* in a vicious circle. Adorno, for one, accepts a version of the thesis of a death of ideologies. Ideologies have lost their bite in postwar welfare societies; he tells his students that "ideology today merges to an ever greater degree with the image of reality as it actually is" (*PETS*, 72). If "what actually is" means a free and happy form of social life, this waning of its ideological distortion would, of course, be good news. But as this is far from being the state of things, Adorno sees the end of ideology as a threat to critique: as ideology loses its justificatory function in society and degenerates to a mere decoration of crude adaptive pressure, critique loses leverage. As long as ideologies are distorted pictures of reality, they at least provide resources for a radical critique that points out the extent to which a society fails to live up to the picture it gives of itself—they reveal, as it were, broken promises. Under the present vicious circle, however, Adorno believes there really to be no veil to be lifted. Rather than ideology, the current form of domination is characterized by a "veil of veillessness" (*Schleier der Schleierlosigkeit*)—the overwhelming adaptive pressure from the societal environment has become self-justificatory (*PS*, 234–35). The waning power of ideologies does, then, not lead to emancipation, because domination becomes sheer second nature. A consequence of the declining power of justificatory ideologies is the naturalization of both social domination and social critique. I believe that Adorno's disclosing critical theory, as it is found in his lectures and essays on social theory, responds to this particular vicious circle.

Adorno's observation is that under the *Bannkreis* of present society, ideology takes a *complementary* rather than a justificatory role (*PS*, 251). It adds something allegedly hopeful to a second-natural social reality, which does not itself ask for justification anymore in any substantial issue. This situation can be observed in how the relations of domination maintain themselves even if they are sheerly obvious to everyone involved. Take the peer-review system of publication. No academic philosopher I know really believes in an ideology justifying this system of publication. No one believes that it produces clearer concepts, original thinking, creative new ideas, deeper understanding, resolutions to problems, dissolution of riddles, critical disclosures, or whatever anyone takes to be the desirable outcome of philosophizing. If anything like that ever appears in a peer-reviewed publication, it is pure luck or it is because that is what writing philosophy is about anyway—or maybe it even happened *despite* the system. Still, we keep maintaining the system from one day to the other. Is it not purely an overwhelming pressure from the social environment that makes us reproduce it in our habits?

With the end of ideology, society's claim to reason is eroded. A vicious circle maintains itself without the type of seemingly rational justification that ideologies would deliver. The critique of ideology loses its radicality if it only attacks complementary decorations as it cannot point to values that society really claims for itself anymore. The question that haunts these lines is this: What happens in a society that doesn't rely on justification in any of its substantial issues, if all critique is reduced to judgment and adaptation to normative standards?

An answer to that question has been given by Richard Rorty, who has suggested a third contemporary type of social critique, which, in the last decades, has resisted the temptation to become a form of normative judgment. Like disclosing critique, Rorty's "radical critique" affirms that there are situations in which social critique cannot rely on criteria internal in the practices of the current linguistic community. In Rorty's view, this is so because these criteria are the criteria of the oppressors, and the demands of the oppressed expressed in this language will come across as "crazy." A radical critique of society, he argues, "can only take the form of imagining a community whose linguistic and other practices are different from our own." Imagination is for radical critique, he stresses, "the only recourse."[8]

The disclosing critics would worry that taking the "form of imagination" cut radical critique short, reducing it to a merely arbitrary exercise in poetic recentering. Disclosing critique of society is different from Rortyan "radical critique" in its initial negativism. It assumes that imagination is *not* "the only recourse" since pointing out the falsity of what is does not presuppose the acceptance of the criteria of the oppressor: one can use negative pictures, such as that of a vicious circle, to evoke an uncanny sense of the foreignness of the contemporary form of life and thereby intermittently establish a critical distance to the oppressing state. It is in that intermittent state of alienation from alienation where the work of a critical phantasy making can begin. Disclosing critique is, then, characterized by a decentering move that sets the ground for the recentering imagination. To paraphrase Marx, relentless critique paves the way for an imagination that is radical. Whereas ideology critique and genealogical critique are possible methods of a disclosing critique in its decentering move, Rortyan "radical critique" shares with it a recentering direction but stands on a completely different ground.

To sum up, while anti-ideological, disclosing critique is different from the critique of ideology, it neither seeks to justify anything at all in the prevailing social orders nor is in the business of adding hope to the hopeless social reality of our times. Regarding justification, its objective is purely negative. In contrast to giving hope, it points at objective possibilities in the present form of life. In addition to the decentering direction it shares with genealogical critique and the critique of ideology, it has a *recentering* direction. Disclosing critique is, then, different from both genealogical critique and ideology critique by virtue of its inherent educative drive to *care for reason*.

4. Complying, Bluffing, and Disclosing

This reliance on poetry and imagination might raise a worry. Does not the poetic, imaginative, and playful nature of disclosing critique imply some kind of esotericism? Does not its use of a language that the benighted masses and mummified academic philosophers have trouble understanding lead to some sort of elitism? An attraction of the juridical model of critique, which the disclosing critics reject, is surely that it generally conceives of itself as instituting a tribunal of judgment that is accessible to all rational beings (whatever that is taken to mean). Perhaps it is no accident, after all, that three of the exemplary disclosing critics—Emerson, Nietzsche, and Adorno—are frequently called out by my colleagues as prone to adopting elitist ways of speaking. There might be a danger, then, that disclosing critique, in order to have effects in the social world, must depend on charismatic figures to create and interpret its metaphors to their *followers*.[9]

To his credit, Nietzsche explicitly acknowledges that the educational practices that disclosing critique relies on always involve power asymmetries between the critic and the audience she addresses—like all other instruction in society. But he goes even further: he suggests a quasi-institutional form for these power differences ("circles of culture"), where they acquire a rather aristocratic shape ("consecrations to culture"), which is surely more than is necessary for the cultivation of recalcitrant tendencies. To the young Nietzsche's defense, he seems to think of these forms as occasional: disclosing critique should, in the end, undo the power asymmetries it feeds on; it should alienate the recipient from the critic. There is, however, good reason to doubt that Nietzsche was successful in this.[10] Nevertheless, Dewey and Freud both note that critical disclosure does not necessarily rely on exemplary individuals at all (charismatic or not) since exemplary social groups can play this role, too, and are, in fact, more important as it is by virtue of the membership in a plurality of diverse groups that individuals can come to critically disclose in the first place. Still, there are two varieties of the issue of elitist esotericism that surely give cause to worry. I shall call them the "compliance problem" and the "bluffing problem."

The compliance problem arises from the doubt that, rather than serious purposiveness to transform society, the behavior of the recipient of a disclosing gesture might exhibit passive compliance—for instance, to the charisma of the critic. She would, then, not so much try to participate in a critique of society (as would be the intent of a recentering move of critical disclosure) as allow herself to be brought, as it were, under an *ethical appearance* of belonging to the critics. In short, instead of critical recalcitrance, the recipient's participation in the disclosure might be that of adaptive compliance.

This certainly points to a real problem. For disclosing critique is dependent on rational receptivity for disclosing gestures, or, as Dewey and Adorno would emphasize, for *really having experiences*. In a form of life, for example, where authoritarian-personality structures are widespread, there is not much receptivity for disclosure left but instead a lot of receptivity for claims to compliance. To be sure, disclosing gestures are prone to be mistaken for such claims. And where this is the case, they fail to be critical. Already since Nietzsche, a large portion of the metacritical self-reflection of disclosing critique concerns precisely the question of how, by what methods, the disclosing critic can alienate the recipient not only from the alienated society but also from the critic herself. This reflection must surely be intensified in disclosing critical *theory*, which, due to its participation in the theory business, evokes the association that it might, like normative theories, be out to convince and convert. That disclosing critical theory has not been more vocal about this reflection, more explicit about the gap that separates its intent from that of normative theories, must count as one of its greatest philosophical failures. By this neglect, it has contributed to the misunderstanding of its various disclosing gestures as normative arguments, as "moves" in a game of giving and asking for reasons. Disclosing critical theory has, in other words, suffered from a certain lack of methodological self-awareness regarding its difference from normative critical theory.

That said, the worry about producing adaptive compliance in place of critical recalcitrance will not go away. To say, however, that this worry *can* be made to go away means succumbing to manipulation and making oneself into an enemy of critique. To fight the illusion that we could, once and for all, draw a clear line between recalcitrance that is critical and recalcitrance that is criminal, one may, to speak with Tarde, spread the circulation of the habit of hesitation. This is what I have suggested disclosing critics of society, in fact, do in their best moments.

The bluffing problem arises from the worry that it is not clear that the critic's way of speaking is really something "higher" than the recipient's, that there is "something there" from which to learn. Perhaps, nothing real is disclosed at all. Perhaps, the critic is not only confused but actively bluffing. This problem presupposes that there is something as determinate as concepts "out there" in reality waiting to be pointed at by a disclosing gesture. It assumes that disclosing critique seeks to show something that could be *said* as well. There is a problem with the bluffing problem: it implicitly credits the social reality with a degree of determinacy equal to that of the concepts with which it wishes to compare it. Moreover, the bluffing problem presupposes that the disclosing critical theorist would be intending to convince or convert the recipient. Some disclosing critical theorists surely do try to convince their recipients by normatively binding arguments. Yet this is not disclosing critical theory. This is simply due to the circumstance that some disclosing critics (for example, Dewey and Adorno) have normative projects of critique, too, next to their disclosing critique. At any rate, showing a way out of the vicious circle and displaying a recalcitrant way of thinking are categorially different from convincing by arguments.

However, here, in a deeper layer of the bluffing worry, the disclosing critic does face a serious problem. In a form of life that affords place of pride to competing and winning, it is difficult to make oneself understood if winning a game is not what one is after. And so it is not easy to avoid one's attempts at critical disclosure being misunderstood as claims to be right if critique is assumed at the outset to constitute a game of reasons where the best argument wins. Wittgenstein urges, "Do not forget that a poem, even though it is composed in the language of information, is not used in the language-game of giving information."[11] By analogy, even if critiques often contain normative judgments, they may not always be at home in the language game of giving and asking for reasons.

5. Care for Reason in a Catastrophic Culture

If any positive critical proposal might bounce back from the societal environment as an extension of its violence, then the critical task of philosophy cannot be to formulate positive ideals but rather is to remain uncompromisingly negative and become a relentless critic of all those obstacles to experience that constitute present society and point out the lump of reason in our shattered habits and customs where education and organization can still work toward readjustment. Yet present society has developed such a tremendous capacity for turning criticism into applause, making even the critique of ideology miss its target, that it seems necessary to ask, at the very end, whether even disclosing critique can be successful. Is there any chance for reflective recalcitrance to become effective today? May we still assume that lump of reason out there in our customs? In Adorno's words, is there anything left to "elevate"?

Since Adorno's day, neoliberalism has probably eroded the claim of rationality in society even further.[12] Going back to the debate between Dewey's democratic socialism and Walter Lippmann's new liberalism, Barbara Stiegler concretely shows how one variant of disclosing critique failed in the face of neoliberalism, which she insightfully deciphers as an austere politics of adaptation: Dewey lost, and Lippmann won.[13] In her view, neoliberalism consists of an artificial production of states of nature in society. If the Leviathan that once promised peace and safety has come to organize itself by disintegrating itself into antagonistic states of nature by expanding market forms of association to nearly every sphere of social life, which send imitational radiation to even further ones, how can its members find sufficient conditions for reflective and effective critical recalcitrance?

Adorno points out that as the adaptive pressures become more transparent and the rule of particular interests become more obvious, society becomes more accessible to certain types of critical insight (MGH; *PS*, 204–5). In an administered world, the invisible hand becomes visible. In a certain sense, the prospects of a disclosing critique are not lost with the erosion of society's claim to reason since a disclosing critique of society doesn't justify anything. It doesn't measure society. It doesn't present a program for reform. Whereas under a vicious circle, any such justification or program can be turned into a further vehicle of the perpetuation of the catastrophe that is contemporary society, a disclosing critique seeks, in one circular gesture, to alienate us, intermittently, from the alienated society instead and show that another form of life is objectively possible. It does so by tracing the limits of current social experience, which enables an experience of society, pointing to education and organization as the nonviolent means left for breaking out. But it does also not rule out the possibility of a catastrophic world in which nonviolent reactions to the violence of society become impossible.

All disclosing critique is new critique. And it is always dependent on an *audience* who is perhaps not prepared but at least *able* to experience something new and receive a disclosing gesture. (If it is able but not prepared, the critique will evoke an uncanny experience.) Yet the audience will only assemble if there is *space* for it to do so. I doubt that there is much place for disclosing critique in present society—at least, not so much in academic philosophy, which has made critical theory a formalized subdiscipline of a philosophical discipline that places itself next to empirical and hermeneutic sciences ruled by a fundamentally adapting system of peer-reviewed publication in research, of hunting and accounting for credit points in teaching, of a constant flux of imperatives in administration and with a wider social environment deeply suspicious of academic institutions and even education in general. Disclosing critics have, however, never expected gifts from the society they criticize. As we can learn from Emerson's reaction to the America of his time and Adorno's to the Germany of his, when there is no place for it, disclosing critique has made space for itself. When there is no space left for disclosing critique in the present time, one thing left to do to help make that space is to recollect the wonderful period of reflective, yet eventually ineffective, critical recalcitrance in philosophy between 1840 and 1970. In telling that story, I wish not to succumb to nostalgia but to point to the *possibility* of disclosing critique as a concrete critical practice. This practice, I believe, failed all along. Disclosing critique never rose to the reflective *and effective* recalcitrance it aspired to. Why this reflective recalcitrance failed to become effective is a question for a social and cultural history of recent philosophy.[14] But from an exemplary reconstruction of it, as in the preceding chapters, we can learn that it is possible to fail again. And failing in the care for reason is infinitely better than not trying at all.

In fact, I believe assessing the preceding chapters as indicative of the idea that a disclosing critique of society could be a complete success is incoherent: in a form of life that is false au fond, the disclosing gesture can be neither performed nor received in any complete sense, and if the form of life were not false, then there would not be any need for its critical disclosure. Disclosing critics will not enter the contemporary scene to "fix" our form of life. What, then, could its care for reason mean for us today?

Today, the catastrophic state of society is obvious in a sense that was not present for the disclosing critics between 1840 and 1970. In his day, Adorno still had to scratch the surface layer of the welfare state to disclose the catastrophic vicinity of total catastrophe. Today, after five decades of neoliberal destruction of social safety nets, in the wake of a pandemic, with unpredictable oligarchs in "control" of the nuclear arsenal, and in the midst of an ecological catastrophe, there is not much left to scratch.

Today, the catastrophic state of society extends, to apply Tarde's concepts, beyond the lower-order adaptate of society to the higher-order adaptate of society and its natural environment, which one might name "culture." We find ourselves in a new historical constellation of nature and culture: a contradiction between the continuation of our capitalist form of life and the survival of humanity as we know it.[15] This affects any model of critical cosmology disclosing critics might seek to develop—the anthropocentrism and growth hubris of Nietzsche's physician of culture, which may still haunt even the Tardean chain of havings, have probably completely lost their critical force in the Anthropocene. But it also marks an unforeseen challenge for the social ontology of disclosing critique insofar as it should be able to conceive of education and organization as the way out of catastrophe. Today, we find ourselves completely unable to react collectively to this planetary emergency.[16] The fact that global warming has reached the point of no return indicates that the ecological disaster that we are facing is not merely a crisis; it is, to use Adorno's expression, a permanent catastrophe, a mutation of our society's relationship with its natural environment—that is, of our culture. Unlike the permanent catastrophe Adorno was thinking of, however, our current one may not lend itself to administrative perpetuation. Franck Fischbach has recently characterized this situation in its significance for critical theory as a transition from the old choice of "socialism or barbarity" to the present one of "capital or earth (*terre*)," adding, "Whereas the latter option may not bring socialism, the former will certainly lead to barbarity."[17]

Adorno once remarked that culture means care; it derives from the Latin *colere*, which originally meant the activity of the farmer, the *agricola*—that is, a certain way of relating to nature: the *care for nature*.[18] The fact that we set different relations to nature, that we have different forms of life, different ways of caring for nature within and without us, means, as Dewey shows, a chance for us, by mutual criticism, to come to terms with ourselves, to grow by reconciling ourselves with something different than ourselves. If culture means care of nature, then perhaps reason, following Freud and Dewey, could be understood as care of the relationship between culture and nature, inside and outside us. Reason would mean a coming to terms with oneself and each other as natural and cultural beings. Disclosing reason then promises a nonviolent mode of cultural transformation, the possibility of transforming our lives with care, the possibility to put a nonrepressive end to repression, the possibility of a life without anxiety.

It is written on the face of current society that it is brutally failing in this regard. There are two options: we can either ignore the fact that global warming has reached the point of no return—that is, try to suppress the fact that our culture will change, try to, as it were, "engineer" ourselves into a new form of life—or we can go about this change reflectively, react to the catastrophe creatively, go through our mutation with care. One such reaction has been to formulate normative theories about climate justice. While I would never want to imply that there is anything unreasonable about cultivating our ethical intuitions in a systematic way, there seems to be little to no evidence from over two millennia of moral teaching that normative theories are an effective way to change human action. Another attempt at a creative reaction has been to create a completely new vocabulary for nature and culture by speculative means.[19] A disclosing critique today would find it easy to agree that we need a radically new beginning. However, the disclosing critics teach us that a radically new beginning cannot mean suppressing the past. Such reactions end with implausible and abstract vocabularies that cannot be continued in ordinary language nor offer guidance in everyday life. They will be either powerless or violent in the face of prevailing habits and customs. Therefore, suppressing the past isn't radical at all; it is superficial. By contrast, the disclosing critics have shown us that one can proceed negatively by tracing the prevailing forms of life, debunking the metaphysical assumptions of their vocabularies, and using imagination to point to the possibility of another form of life. No culture can be created from scratch; new forms of life are assembled from the fragments of old forms of life. Reacting with care means being sensitive to the needs and powers our forms of life have developed, redigesting our histories from the perspective of the catastrophe that is the adaptate of present culture, and using imagination in a form of thinking that seeks to put an end to senseless suffering. The disclosing critics have shown us that we can only react critically from preexisting habits by cultivating their recalcitrant tendencies and redirecting them playfully from the point of view of the catastrophe to that of the objective possibilities it affords.

We do not know what reason would look like in a sustainable form of social life that could be freely and happily affirmed by its associating elements. But we can still critically disclose what it amounts to in the not-yet—and far-from—free and happy society we live in today, and, while doing that, we might catch a glimpse of the former.

Notes

Chapter 1
1. For an account of preemptive silencing, see Laitinen, "Social Pathologies."
2. Mercier and Sperber, *Enigma of Reason*; Sloman and Fernbach, *Knowledge Illusion*.
3. Honneth, "Reconstructive Social Criticism"; Celikates, *Critique as Social Practice*; Jaeggi, *Critique of Forms*; Stahl, *Immanente Kritik*.
4. Haslanger, *Resisting Reality*, esp. chap. 3; Ásta, *Categories We Live By*.
5. A famous example of internal critique is Michael Walzer's interpretive approach to social criticism; see Walzer *Interpretation and Social Criticism*; Walzer, *Company of Critics*. For an analysis of the potentials and limits of this approach in the context of contemporary critical theory, see Hartmann, "Biblical Prophets."
6. John Rawls's theory of justice, which distinguishes methodologically between ideal theory and nonideal theory, is sometimes taken as an example of the external critique of society; see Rawl, *Theory of Justice*, 7–8, 215–16, 308–9. For an analysis of this approach in the context of critical theory, see Schaub, "Incompleteness of Ideal Theory."
7. For a famous recent example of the immanent critique of society, which seeks to apply immanent critique in an ambitious and impressively detailed normative reconstruction of our democratic form of life, see Honneth, *Freedom's Right*. For more methodological analyses of immanent critique, see Jaeggi, *Critique of Forms*; Stahl *Immanente Kritik*.
8. This, at least, is Rahel Jaeggi's suggestion; see Jaeggi, *Critique of Forms*.
9. Davis, *Women, Race and Class*.
10. For more detailed criticisms of normativist models of social critique, see Guess, *Philosophy and Real Politics*; Vogelmann, "Measuring, Disrupting, Emancipating"; Särkelä, *Immanente Kritik*; Allen, *Critique on the Couch*, chap. 5; Freyenhagen, "Pro-

fessor Habermas." For a distinction between normativism and naturalism in social philosophy, see Särkelä and Laitinen, "Between Normativism and Naturalism."

11. Haslanger, *Resisting Reality*; Ásta, *Categories We Live By*.
12. Ásta, *Categories We Live By*, 36.
13. Exemplified by Haslanger, "Racism."
14. Boltanski, *On Critique*, 128; see also Geuss, *Changing the Subject*, 201–2.
15. Gregoratto et al., "Critical Naturalism."
16. Wittgenstein, *On Certainty*, §§ 96–97.
17. Notable exceptions include Bohman, "Welterschließung und radikale Kritik"; Honneth, "Disclosing Critique of Society"; Kompridis, *Critique and Disclosure*; Lara, *Politics of Disclosure*.
18. Honneth, "Disclosing Critique of Society," 51.
19. Neurath, "Anti-Spengler," 199–200.
20. Wittgenstein, *Philosophical Investigations*, §§ 107, 124.
21. Wittgenstein, *Philosophical Investigations*, §§ 115, 309.
22. Wittgenstein distinguishes categorically between "saying" and "showing": "What *can* be shown, *cannot* be said"; see Wittgenstein, *Tractatus logico-philosophicus* 4.1212; emphasis original.
23. Wittgenstein, *Tractatus logico-philosophicus* 3–4.
24. In recent critical theory, Alessandro Ferrara has strongly emphasized the role of exemplarity in the philosophical critique of society, and by that, he has developed the normativist model of critique further by relying on Kant's third critique. However, his treatment of critical exemplarity remains within the model of normative critique, or what he calls the "paradigm of judgment," which is what disclosing critique, as contoured here, seeks to challenge. See Ferrara, *Force of the Example*.
25. For such a critique, see Särkelä, *Immanente Kritik*.
26. Blumenberg, *Paradigms for a Metaphorology*, 3, 5.
27. Blumenberg, *Paradigms for a Metaphorology*, 5.
28. Kant, *Critique of Pure Reason*, A751/B779.
29. Geuss, "Genealogy as Critique," 154.
30. For a thorough problematization of a legalistic vocabulary of critique, see Loick, *Juridismus*. For a relativization and contextualization of a judging conception of philosophy more generally, see Hampe, *Erkenntnis und Praxis*, 198–204. On the practice of philosophical critique in particular, see Vogelmann, "Measuring, Disrupting, Emancipating."
31. Geuss, "Must Criticism Be Constructive?," 88.
32. W. Benjamin, *Concept of Criticism*, 177.
33. W. Benjamin, "Goethe's Elective Affinities," 340–41.
34. There are many family resemblances between my distinction between normative critical theories that aim at judgment and disclosing critiques that rather focus on experimentation, on the one hand, and the more general distinctions between two types of *philosophies* made by Richard Rorty and Michael Hampe, on the other. Between "systematic" and "edifying" philosophies, see Rorty, *Philosophy*,

365–72; between "doctrinal" and "nondoctrinal" philosophy, see Hampe, *What Philosophy Is For*, 2–3. The disclosing critics of my study are among both Rorty's and Hampe's favorite examples of edifying, or nondoctrinary, philosophers. But there are, at least, three important differences between Rorty's and Hampe's distinctions and mine to be kept in mind. First, disclosing critique, insofar as it is expressed philosophically at all, presents at most a subtype of edifying, nondoctrinary philosophizing for it belongs to the group of edifying, nondoctrinary philosophies that *criticize* (one can imagine other edifying philosophical things to do than critique, such as, e.g., cultivating wisdom). Second, the disclosing critics are a socially critical type of edifying, nondoctrinal philosophers who proceed *negatively* by a certain critical gesture. Third, this critical gesture presents in disclosing critique of society primarily a reaction to an alienated state of *society*; so, in contrast to edifying philosophies in Rorty (but not so much to nondoctrinary philosophies in Hampe), disclosing critiques do not mainly react to systematic philosophies, not even to normative critical theories, but to a false social world. However, only the third difference may disqualify disclosing critiques as edifying philosophies in Rorty's sense—depending on how strictly one takes his condition that edifying philosophies should react to systematic philosophies (is it an intention? does it present an entry condition?).

35. See, e.g., Bohman, "Welterschließung und radikale Kritik"; Kompridis, "Über Welterschließung"; Kompridis, *Critique and Disclosure*; Honneth "Disclosing Critique of Society"; Müller-Doohm, *Adorno*, i; Freyenhagen, "Objective Reason."

36. Adorno, "On the Logic," 113; *PETS*, 84.

37. The idea of constellation will be discussed more carefully in chapter 5. The methodological concept of constellation was introduced by Benjamin as a method of reconfiguration; see W. Benjamin, *German Trauerspiel*, 10–11. Adorno takes it up very early as a method of "grouping and trial arrangement"; see Adorno, "Die Aktualität der Philosophie," 131.

38. On concepts as habits of distinction, see Ros, *Begründung und Begriff*.

39. For a recent, more detailed suggestion of how concept may be understood as similarity classes, see Forster and Hampe, "Classes as Clusters."

40. The closest relative of this book is perhaps Blumenberg's *Shipwreck with Spectator*. It does not exactly present a metaphor history of social critique such as the one I am suggesting but rather a history of a metaphor of existence with implications for "cultural criticism" (*Kulturkritik*); see Blumenberg, *Shipwreck with Spectator*, 8–9.

41. Särkelä, "Anpassung und Erschließung."

42. For exemplary studies in history of philosophy with the intent to inspire critical theory, see Walzer, *Company of Critics*; Neuhouser, *Hegel's Social Theory*; Neuhouser, *Diagnosing Social Pathologies*; Saar, *Die Immanenz der Macht*.

43. Blumenberg, *Paradigms for a Metaphorology*, 3; emphasis original.

44. Black, "Metaphor," 292–93; emphasis original.

Chapter 2

1. In her reply to Hans-Johann Glock's criticism of her "anti-anti-realist" reading of Wittgenstein, Lovibond remarks that her work is intended to respond not only to problems of normative ethics in the analytical tradition but likewise to "those of critical theory." Lovibond, "Wittgenstein and Moral Realism," 25; Glock, "Wittgensteinian Anti-Anti-Realism." I fear the following representation of Lovibond's thinking will be guilty of the opposite deformation: a certain neglect of her original insights in normative ethics.

2. Lovibond, introduction, 83.

3. On the uncodifiability thesis, see also McDowell, "Virtue and Reason," 57–58; Diamond, *Realistic Spirit*.

4. Lovibond, "Between Tradition and Criticism," 97–98; Wittgenstein, *Philosophical Investigations*, § 199.

5. *EF*, 63; Wittgenstein, *Philosophical Investigations*, § 415; see also Särkelä, "Anpassung und Erschließung."

6. Lovibond, "Between Tradition and Criticism," 105; Diamond, *Realistic Spirit*, 325.

7. *EF*, 50–51; see also Lovibond, "Between Tradition and Criticism," 114.

8. Wittgenstein, *Philosophical Investigations*, § 23; emphasis original.

9. *EF*, 68–69; see also Aristotle, *Nicomachean Ethics*, bk. 2, chap. 1.

10. *EF*, 68–69; see also Nietzsche, *Genealogy of Morality*, essay 2, §§ 1–2; emphasis original.

11. *EF*, 127; see also Lovibond, "Practical Reason," 82.

12. Huxley, *Brave New World*.

13. On the difference between accounts of first and second nature that conceive of second nature as overcoming the first and those that assume that such an overcoming has never taken place, see Testa, "Criticism from Within Nature."

14. Lovibond, "Ethical Upbringing," 132.

15. *EF*, 138–39; Foucault, "What Is Enlightenment?," 45–46.

16. *EF*, 151, 172, 192; McDowell, *Mind and World*, 125–26.

17. *EF*, 136, 148–49; McDowell, *Mind and World*, 81.

18. McDowell, *Mind and World*, 81.

19. *EF*, 152. The exemplary counterteleological critics Lovibond is considering as members of this family are Jacques Derrida, Michel Foucault, Jean-François Lyotard, Richard Rorty, Rosi Braidotti, and Paul Feyerabend. At times, Lovibond seems additionally to consider Friedrich Nietzsche as something like a godfather of them all; see Lovibond, "Feminism and Postmodernism"; *EF*, 179–80. At other times, she seems to think that this family should not entertain such an intimate bond with him; see Lovibond, "Selflessness." (It is, of course, no contradiction to hold both views.)

20. Blumenberg, *Shipwreck with Spectator*, 76–79.

21. Lovibond, introduction, 6; emphasis added.

22. Lovibond, introduction, 7.

23. Lovibond, "Ethical Upbringing," 144.
24. Lovibond, "Between Tradition and Criticism," 108.
25. Lovibond, "Practical Reason," 82; emphasis original.
26. Wittgenstein, *Culture and Value*, 64.
27. Lovibond, "Wittgenstein, Tolstoy," 44–45.
28. Lovibond, "Wittgenstein, Tolstoy," 47.
29. Wittgenstein, *Philosophical Investigations*, "Philosophy of Psychology—a Fragment" [previously known as "Part 2"], §§ 111–364.
30. Lovibond, "Wittgenstein, Tolstoy," 49, 51–52; emphases original.
31. Wittgenstein, *Philosophical Investigations*, § 127.
32. Lovibond, "'Sickness of a Time,'" 66.

Chapter 3

1. See, e.g., Bohman, "Welterschließung und radikale Kritik"; Kompridis, "Über Welterschließung"; Kompridis, *Critique and Disclosure*; Honneth, "Disclosing Critique of Society"; Müller-Doohm, *Adorno*, i; Freyenhagen, "Objective Reason."
2. Honneth, "Diseases of Society"; Neuhouser, *Diagnosing Social Pathologies*; see also Honneth, *Idea of Socialism*, chap. 4. For detailed criticisms of that conception, see Freyenhagen, "Honneth on Social Pathologies"; Särkelä and Laitinen, "Between Normativism and Naturalism"; see also Laitinen and Särkelä, "Four Conceptions."
3. For Adorno's discussion of de Maistre and Comte, see Adorno, "Über Statik"; *HF*, 24. For his discussion of Spencer, see *PS*, 42–43.
4. For more charitable and nuanced readings of the critical potential of Durkheimian social organicism and social pathology diagnosis, see Neuhouser, *Diagnosing Social Pathologies*, chaps. 7–10; Carré, "Naturalism to Social Vitalism."
5. Adorno, "Einleitung," 13; *HF*, 117.
6. Adorno, "Einleitung," 41.
7. Adorno, "Einleitung," 41; Durkheim, *Sociology and Philosophy*, 12–14.
8. On Adorno's relationship to process ontologies of the social, see Renault, "Processual Social Ontology"; Särkelä, *Immanente Kritik*, chap. 5, sec. 1. For an alternative reading of Adorno's critique of Durkheim focusing on the political dimensions in his work instead of the socio-ontological issue at stake here, see Christ, "Critique of Politics." I will return to discuss Tarde and his socio-ontological alternative to social organicism in chapter 7.
9. Durkheim, *Sociological Method*, 29.
10. Adorno, "Kulturkritik und Gesellschaft," 16.
11. Adorno, "Einleitung," 13.
12. Adorno, "Einleitung," 13.
13. Huxley, *Brave New World*, 1.
14. Adorno, "Aldous Huxley and Utopia," 98.
15. Adorno, "Aldous Huxley and Utopia," 100, 113. On first and second nature in Adorno more generally, see Testa, "Criticism from Within Nature"; Hogh and König, "Bestimmte Unbestimmbarkeit."

16. Adorno, "Aldous Huxley and Utopia," esp. 113.
17. On the notion of a "negative utopia" in Adorno, see also Geuss, "Art and Criticism," 171–73.
18. Adorno, "Aldous Huxley and Utopia," 112–113.
19. E.g., *HF*, 92. See also W. Benjamin, "Concept of History," § 9.
20. Hereby, I wish to take back the idea I entertained in my article on Adorno's "negative organicism" that there is a "doubly negative organicism" emerging from Adorno's critical discussion of the social organicists; see Särkelä, "Negative Organicism." My thought back then was that although Adorno himself never coins the term "negative organicism," it could still be useful to think of the attitude I described with it as analogous with what he elsewhere calls his "negative universal history." See, e.g., *HF*, chaps. 9–10. Where the latter idea animates his discussions of the philosophy of history, the former directs his social theory, or so my thought was. In both cases, I believed, Adorno can be observed to proceed from an immanent criticism of what to him must be an obvious case of a highly ideological standpoint, universal history and social organicism, to preserving the reality of that idea in drawing a circle around it. But now, on the basis of various discussions following my publication of that article, I think that this term only causes unnecessary confusion. Instead, I now investigate Adorno's negatively utopian gesture hypothetically under the rubric of "counterteleology"—an open term for ethically recalcitrant thinking about social teleology borrowed from Lovibond (see chapter 2).
21. Adorno, "Aspects of Hegel's Philosophy," 4, 28; latter translation amended.
22. Adorno, *Introduction to Dialectics*, 22.
23. Adorno, "Aspects of Hegel's Philosophy," 27.
24. Adorno, "Aspects of Hegel's Philosophy," 27.
25. To do justice to the complexity of Adorno's attempt to think against Hegel using Hegel's social ontology would be beyond the scope of the present topic. For more detailed recent interpretations of Adorno's attempt to go beyond Hegel with Hegel, see O'Connor, "Adorno's Reconception"; Finlayson, "Origins of Immanent Criticism"; Sommer, *Das Konzept*; Bernstein, "'Our Amphibian Problem'"; Moir, "Speculation, Dialectic and Critique." With regard to the question of social wholes, see Blili-Hamelin and Särkelä, "Unsocial Society."
26. Strictly speaking, the antagonistic character of totalities in Hegel and Adorno is *not* the same. On antagonistic totalities in Hegel, see Blili-Hamelin, "Topography," chap. 5. For a comparison of social antagonisms in Hegel and Adorno, see Blili-Hamelin and Särkelä, "Unsocial Society."
27. Adorno writes in a letter to Max Horkheimer, "Our stuff [*unsere Sachen*] will have to become more and more such *gestures from concepts* [*Gesten aus Begriffen*] and less and less theory in the conventional sense. Only that the whole work of the concept is needed for this." Adorno to Horkheimer, August 21, 1941, in Horkheimer, *Gesammelte Schriften*, 153; emphasis added; my translation.
28. Adorno, "Thesen über Bedürfnis," 396.
29. Horkheimer and Adorno, *Dialectic of Enlightenment*, 95.

30. A. Freud, *Ego*, 109–11. Although Adorno always attributes the notion of the mechanism of an identification with the aggressor to Anna Freud, in reality, the idea comes from Sándor Ferenczi, who presented it four years earlier; see Ferenczi, "Confusion of the Tongues."

31. Horkheimer and Adorno *Dialectic of Enlightenment*, 19.

32. E.g., Adorno, "Idea of Natural-History"; *ND*, pt. 3, chap. 2; *HF*, chaps. 12–13. This is not to say that Benjamin would not play a significant part in this metaphoric ground. Benjamin uses the term *Bannkreis* in important points of his works, most strikingly when introducing the important idea of divine violence: "Since . . . every conceivable solution to human problems, not to speak of deliverance from the confines [*Bannkreis*] of all the world-historical conditions of existence obtaining hitherto, remains impossible if violence is totally excluded in principle, the question necessarily arises as to what kinds of violence exist other than all those envisaged by legal theory." W. Benjamin, "Critique of Violence," 247.

33. See Nietzsche, *Twilight of the Idols*, 198–99.

34. This is my only disagreement with Italo Testa's pathbreaking article on Adorno's negative social ontology; see Testa, "Ontology."

35. Testa, "Ontology," 295.

36. Adorno, "Individuum und Organisation."

37. See, e.g., Honneth, "Disclosing Critique of Society."

38. By "not, strictly speaking, normative," I mean that what is disclosed cannot be presupposed as already *codified* in the sense of presenting a norm or a bundle of norms, which could then be used by the critic as a normative contrast to the object of critique. That said, a critical disclosure of the object might lead to an ex post facto codification of a piece of societal second nature such that it then can be rendered useful in a "more strictly normative" critical project. That, perhaps more advanced, project would, however, not anymore be that of a primarily disclosing critique of society. Another conceptual strategy, an alternative to this Emersonian "counterteleological view," on the disclosure of "objective possibilities" articulated here is, to my mind, the more Aristotelian one presented by Fabian Freyenhagen; see, respectively, Losurdo, *Nietzsche, the Aristocratic Rebel*; Freyenhagen, *Adorno's Practical Philosophy*.

39. For "strenuous effort," see Hegel, *Phenomenology of Spirit*, § 58.

40. To a certain extent, my suggestion follows that of Kompridis, who makes the distinction between decentering and centering disclosure; see Kompridis, "Über Welterschließung," 536–37. However, looking at the issue with Adorno and Emerson, his notion must be reverted, as Emerson's centering disclosure, in some sense, is conceived as one of reflecting the movement of the decentering disclosure typical of Adorno. In that sense, it involves the "shattering" of a decentering disclosure and serves to establish a *new* center of an already shifted circle.

41. Adorno, "Individuum und Organisation," 456; my translation.

42. On the role of the sociological production of knowledge in critical disclosure, see Renault, "Critical Theory, Social Critique."

43. Marx to Ruge, September 1843, in Marx, *Writings of the Young Marx*, 212; emphasis original.

44. Adorno, *Philosophy of New Music*, 102. The simile of the message in a bottle may, in fact, stem from Horkheimer. It first appears in a letter of his to Salka Vierteil in 1939; at around the same time, though, Adorno uses it for the first time in the above cited *Philosophy of New Music*, which he drafted from 1940 to 1941. Müller-Doohm, *Adorno*, 400–401, 423.

45. Celikates, *Critique as Social Practice*, 151.

46. The Emersonian treatment of skepticism has been elaborated with great sophistication by Stanley Cavell; see Cavell, *Conditions Handsome and Unhandsome*, esp. chap. 1.

47. MGH, 215; see also Adorno, "Free Time."

48. Such a social ontology of disclosing critique cannot, of course, be an ontology of invariant structures ("substance ontology") like the one implied in Durkheim and Huxley. It would rather have to be an ontology that makes space for the self-decentering and self-recentering of social life—that is, for radical social transformation. But since Adorno tends to identify all ontology with substance ontology of invariant structures, this would seem like a highly paradoxical undertaking to him, as noted in Testa, "Ontology." My story will later deal with this issue with reference to other disclosing critics. But there might be a way to dig with Adorno too. One could namely try to affirm that paradox and to reconceive the contradiction between sociality and ontology by taking "social ontology" as a *chiasmus*—that is, as a critical gesture that merges two concepts that initially seem contradictory into a term that exerts critical power by expanding the meaning of both terms. Famous Adornian examples of such disclosing chiasms are "natural history," "culture industry," and "myth and enlightenment." See Rose, *Melancholy Science*, 18–19; Särkelä, "Anpassung und Erschließung." Such chiasmi initiate, much like Max Black's "interaction metaphors," an interaction between two terms that make for an intellectual experience that cannot be translated into conceptuality; see Black, "Metaphor," 285–91. Taken as a chiasmus, the very concept of social ontology, like Adorno asked of the concept of society, might itself be possible *as* a critically disclosing gesture.

Chapter 4

1. Adorno, "Kulturkritik und Gesellschaft," 95.

2. Adorno, "Kultur und Culture," 167–68.

3. See, e.g., Deleuze, *Nietzsche and Philosophy*; Foucault, "Nietzsche, Genealogy, History"; Butler, *Psychic Life of Power*; Geuss, "Genealogy as Critique"; Owen, "Criticism and Captivity"; Saar, "Genealogy and Subjectivity"; Saar, "Understanding Genealogy."

4. I will return to discuss genealogical critique in chapter 8.

5. On social pathologies, see Honneth, "Pathologies of the Social"; Honneth, "Reconstructive Social Criticism"; Honneth, "Diseases of Society"; Freyenhagen, "Honneth on Social Pathologies"; Hirvonen, "Ontology of Social Pathologies";

Laitinen, "Social Pathologies"; Laitinen and Särkelä, "Analyzing Conceptions"; Laitinen and Särkelä, "Four Conceptions"; Neuhouser, "Hegel on Social Ontology"; Neuhouser, *Diagnosing Social Pathologies*; Särkelä, "Degeneration of Associated Life"; Särkelä and Laitinen, "Between Normativism and Naturalism"; Zurn, "Social Pathologies." On Nietzsche's diagnosis of social pathologies in his later works, see Neuhouser, "Nietzsche on Spiritual Illness."

6. Leibniz maintains that not all beings have souls but that those that do have memory: "On appelle *Ames* seulement celles dont le perception est... accompagnée de memoire." Leibniz, *Monadology*, § 19.

7. Spinoza, *Ethics*, pt. 1, prop. 29.

8. Rorty, "Dewey," 295–96.

9. Spinoza, *Ethics*, pt. 1, prop. 11.

10. Spinoza, *Ethics*, pt. 1, prop. 10, pt. 2, prop. 13, pt. 3, prop. 7.

11. Stiegler, "1880"; Thomä, "'Falling in Love.'"

12. I have previously formulated a more nuanced account of this tension between reproductive and transformative requirements of social life; see Särkelä, *Immanente Kritik*, esp. pt. 3. Frederick Neuhouser has recently very similarly characterized this tension in terms of human social life's "function" of "integrating the ends of life with those of freedom." Neuhouser, *Diagnosing Social Pathologies*, 347.

13. The reader might wonder, Where does life's plastic power come from? Is plastic power some kind of a vitalistic life force, a power-causing growth, as it were, from behind the life process? Or is it a feature of life processes that has been selected? Often Nietzsche is read as a vitalist; see Danto, *Nietzsche as Philosopher*; Deleuze, *Nietzsche and Philosophy*; Richardson, *Nietzsche's System*; Schacht, *Nietzsche*. Life is then characterized by a particular kind of force driving its development and growth. Plastic power would be a kind of Bergsonian élan vital, the principle of a basic ontology of life. It has been suggested that the later Nietzsche's notion of "will to power" ought to be read as such a cosmic life force; see Deleuze, *Nietzsche and Philosophy*; Richardson, *Nietzsche's System*. This is a highly problematic conception. First, today, we know that we can explain evolutionary processes without postulating any vital forces pushing life processes forward. This explanation relies on the mechanism of a natural selection of arbitrary variation in individuals. Second, as Donovan Miyasaki points out, the vitalistic reading "clearly oversteps the boundaries of Nietzsche's naturalism by treating the will to power as a metaphysical substance: a force that is self-identical and underlies all changeable, sensible properties"; see Miyasaki, "Will to Power," 257. It is also possible not to read Nietzsche's "plastic power" in the vitalistic sense of a "life force" lurking behind and causing the movement of the life process. The advantage of early Nietzsche's aesthetic metaphysics of plastic power is that its rather poetic expression allows for a less vitalistic reading too. Plastic power could thus be something itself designed by the process of life's evolution. In this reading, *plastic power has evolved*. It presents a characteristic of life that has been selected. Its concept describes the way in which a process, which is living, relates back upon itself so as to maintain itself by growing. It poetically describes a mode of process in the

world that constantly deals with the contrasting drives to both maintain its form and transform. For this reason, I believe, Nietzsche qualifies plastic power as a "develop[ing] out of oneself"; see *UM*, 62. The important thing to note is that "plastic power" would then be *ontologically* basic for life yet *genetically* secondary to natural selection. John Richardson has developed both readings with regard to the "will to power"—i.e., as a basic ontological operator in *Nietzsche's System* and as a selected trait in *Nietzsche's New Darwinism*. A question is whether the selectionist view could accommodate the basic ontology view. Then the kind of growth that "plastic power" describes would be something selected as basic for life; its selection would not make it ontologically less basic. Whereas interpreters from both camps tend to ascribe some sort of vitalism to Nietzsche at the outset and only disagree as to the extent to which this can be amended to Darwinism, Barbara Stiegler instead reads Nietzsche here as struggling with a topic that later becomes pivotal *within* Darwinian evolutionary theory itself, as scholars such as Richard Lewontin and Stephen Jay Gould come to stress the activity of organisms—i.e., the evolved power of individual living beings to construct their environment; see Stiegler, *"Il faut s'adapter."* In fact, this became rather quickly an issue within Darwinian philosophy: already John Dewey developed a thorough reading of Darwin stressing the need to both get rid of original forces and conceive of individual living beings as creative with regard to their environments; see Dewey, "Influence of Darwinism"; Dewey, "Need for a Recovery"; see also Särkelä, "Der Einfluss." A similar conception of Darwinian evolution was later developed in Whitehead, *Function of Reason*.

14. On the significance of "first" and "second nature" for contemporary social philosophy, see *EF*; Testa, "Criticism from Within Nature."

15. McDowell, *Mind and World*.

16. For a helpful articulation of the idea of "first" and "second nature" as interchangeable placeholder concepts in Dewey, see Testa, "Dewey." James Conant attempts a socio-philosophical extension of Nietzsche's moral perfectionism that also works with the concepts of first and second nature. Surprisingly, Conant—who, in his impressive reading of Nietzsche's moral perfectionism, focuses on the third essay in *Untimely Meditations*—completely ignores Nietzsche's conception of first and second nature in the second essay in *Untimely Meditations* and disregards the processual placeholding character of first and second nature. Instead, Conant's socio-philosophical extension of Nietzsche's perfectionism starts with the idea that Nietzsche asks about the possible perfection not only of individual persons but also of entire forms of life. Conant, *Friedrich Nietzsche*, 337–38. This overlooks, however, the disclosing intent in early Nietzsche's social philosophy: the cultural physician's task is less to perfect a given form of life than to help the individuals to challenge and eventually transform their own form of life.

17. Wittgenstein, *Foundations of Mathematics*, §§ 22, 46; see also Hampe, *What Philosophy Is For*, 72–80.

18. *UM*, 97, 115. Hollingdale translates this as "train[ing] up" and, confusingly, as "adjustment." Ibid.

19. Neurath, "Anti-Spengler," 199–200; McDowell, *Mind and World*, chap. 4, § 7; *EF*, chap. 7, § 1.

20. Walzer, *Interpretation and Social Criticism*; McDowell, *Mind and World*; *EF*.

21. Stiegler, "1880"; see also Stiegler, *Nietzsche*.

22. Hegel, *Philosophy of Right*, 16.

23. Nietzsche seems here to refer to Richard Wagner's conception of the state. Wagner believed that people's needs and desires were repressed by "the State" and that his music could make the recipients aware of those repressed impulses, hence listening to his music would be a transformative experience to them; see Wagner, *Opera and Drama*, pt. 2, chaps. 2–3.

24. Somewhat similarly in the contemporary debate, Luc Boltanski distinguishes between "reality" and "world": whereas reality exhibits a more or less determinate order, which social critique might ontologically challenge, the world is more or less chaotic and indeterminate. Social criticism can ontologically challenge social reality by assembling elements from the world. Boltanski, *On Critique*, 57–61.

25. H, 239; Cavell, *Emerson's Transcendental Etudes*, chap. 12; Cavell, *Cities of Words*, chap. 11; Conant, "Nietzsche's Perfectionism." For a critique of their moral-perfectionist interpretations of Nietzsche, see Lemm, "Is Nietzsche a Perfectionist?"

26. Peter Strawson distinguishes between "descriptive" and "revisionary" metaphysics: whereas descriptive metaphysics merely describes the "structure of our thought about the world," revisionary metaphysics tries to "produce a better structure." Strawson, *Individuals*, 9. I'm not sure if the distinction as such is coherent, as description without revision seems hardly imaginable, and the preference for a "better structure" might not fit the cases of revisionary metaphysics. However, a historian of philosophy might surely distinguish between descriptive and revisionary *claims* in metaphysics: authors who *claim* to be merely describing and those who *want* to intervene into our modes of thinking by their engagement with metaphysics. The young Nietzsche belongs to the second category, which he exemplifies as a particularly poetic case.

27. Stiegler writes, "Without the maladapted, who take the risk of experimenting with other ways of living, there would never be evolution." Stiegler, "1880," 71.

28. The decentering disclosure liberates from what David Owen terms "restricted consciousness" by the example of such a marginal perspective. Owen, "Criticism and Captivity," 216. However, by virtue of also including recentering disclosure, disclosing critique is a more encompassing critical project than Owen's account of genealogy as a criticism of restricted consciousness. There have been several interesting attempts to theorize the idea of such disclosing gestures from the margins in recent social philosophy. To begin with, Deleuze and Félix Guattari's idea of a *littérature mineure* elaborates one version of such marginal disclosure; see Deleuze and Guattari, *Kafka*. Naomi Scheman offers a lucid and sophisticated account of what she calls "privileged marginality" in her work on Wittgenstein's

"forms of life"; see Scheman, "Forms of Life." Guillaume Le Blanc has developed a historiographical approach to countercultural philosophical critique, which seems very promising for studying such critical gestures in detail; see Le Blanc, *Philosophie comme contre-culture*.

29. *PETS*, 38, 49–50. Cavell and Conant point out the great extent to which Nietzsche, on this point, follows Emerson; see Cavell, *Emerson's Transcendental Etudes*, chaps. 7 and 12; Cavell, *Cities of Words*, chap. 11; Conant, "Nietzsche's Perfectionism."

30. *The Communist Manifesto* ends with the following sentences: "The proletarians have nothing to lose but their chains. They have a world to win. Working men of all countries, unite!" Marx and Engels, *Communist Manifesto*, 102.

31. On asphyxiation as a metaphorical net of social critique, see Särkelä, *Immanente Kritik*, pt. 3.

32. For the role that the category of social suffering can play in social critique, see Renault, *Social Suffering*.

33. Honneth, "Reconstructive Social Criticism"; Stahl, *Immanente Kritik*, 26–30; Jaeggi, *Critique of Forms*, 177–78.

34. Honneth, "Disclosing Critique of Society."

35. In her criticism of both Rawls's and Cavell's interpretations of the third essay in *Untimely Meditations*, Vanessa Lemm emphasizes this critical and agonistic character of (the circles of) culture: "The aim of culture is to criticize given institutionalized forms of social and political life and eventually to overcome them, fostering freer forms of life, both on the level of the individual and on the level of social and political organization." Lemm, "Is Nietzsche a Perfectionist?," 14. Interestingly, the idea of the disclosing effect of such countercommunities has recently become a topic of critical theorizing in two very different ways: while Raymond Geuss's idea of "xenomorphs" takes the shape of a narrative gesture with an intended disclosing effect, in Daniel Loick's *Die Überlegenheit der Unterlegenen*, it takes the form of an elaborate theory of countercommunities. An important difference between the latter conception and Nietzsche's "circles of culture" is that Loick partly defines (probably to the advantage of his conception) countercommunities by their *oppressed* position in the form of life, whereas the status of being oppressed (understood as something different from being marginalized) seems completely absent in the young Nietzsche's rather aristocratic conception. See, respectively, Geuss, *Not Thinking Like a Liberal*, 165; Loick, *Die Überlegenheit der Unterlegenen*, 16.

36. In "Experience," Emerson writes,

> In liberated moments, we know that a new picture of life and duty is already possible; the elements already exist in many minds around you, of a doctrine of life which shall transcend any written record we have. The new statement will comprise the skepticism, as well as the faiths of society, and out of unbeliefs a creed shall be formed. For, skepticisms are not gratuitous or lawless, but are the limitations of the affirmative statement, and the new philosophy must take them in, and make affirmations outside of them, just as much as it must include the oldest beliefs. (E, 487)

This Emersonian idealism of disclosure being completed by a liberating experience of reconciliation of the old and new is, to my mind, completely absent in Nietzsche's *Untimely Meditations*. Nietzsche's view of recentering disclosure is educational and materialistic: it is a question of transforming the form of life, adjusting the social environment, by *habituation*—as I wish to indicate on the few following pages.

37. An ongoing example for a turn from de- to recentering disclosure could be Greta Thunberg and the Fridays for Future movement. Thunberg's example helps to disclose an enclosure in our current form of life, to elevate others to participants in the movement that tends to function as an educative antiauthoritarian community. It remains to be seen whether she will succeed in recentering our form of life. Dieter Thomä has developed the model of the "democratic hero," which I believe is helpful for studying these types of disclosures; see Thomä, *Warum Demokratien Helden brauchen*.

38. This I take to be a significant contrast to Emersonian Romanticism of wilderness. For a critique, see Hampe, *Die Wildnis*, chap. 1.

39. Lovibond, "Nietzsche on Distance."

40. Miyasaki, "Will to Power."

Chapter 5

1. Horkheimer, "Traditional and Critical Theory," 216–17.
2. Hartmann, "Vertiefung der Erfahrung"; Särkelä, "American Pragmatism."
3. Marcuse, "John Dewey," 226.
4. Jaeggi, *Critique of Forms*, chap. 9 passim.
5. The aspect of attraction and repulsion is expressed in Horkheimer and Adorno's use of *Bannkreis* in the first excursus of *Dialectic of Enlightenment* when he describes Odysseus in the hands of Polyphemus as "within the sphere controlled by the rock-hurling giant [*im Bannkreis der schleudernden Hände des Riesen*]." Horkheimer and Adorno, *Dialectic of Enlightenment*, 53.
6. As I already denoted in chapter 1, this metaphorological way of looking has the unfortunate consequence that the richness and complexity of the theory and its theorist will be extremely reduced. In what follows, I will *not* attempt a rational reconstruction of Adorno's (or Dewey's) social theory. Instead, the excavation work of this metaphor history of critical disclosure has reached a point at which the role of a *critical theory of society* as (part of) a disclosing gesture becomes a significant issue to be investigated. Therefore, the following pages look at the socio-theoretical conceptual space disclosed by the metaphoric of "drawing a circle around a vicious circle."
7. Adorno, "Theorie der Halbbildung," 96; my translation.
8. Adorno, "Working Through the Past," 98.
9. Adorno, "Theorie der Halbbildung," passim.
10. Blili-Hamelin and Särkelä, "Unsocial Society."
11. E.g., Adorno, "Idea of Natural-History"; *ND*, pt. 3, chap. 2; *HF*, chaps. 13–14;

see also Pensky, "Natural History"; Honneth, "Capitalist Form of Life"; Särkelä, "Anpassung und Erschließung"; Testa, "Criticism from Within Nature"; Testa, "Ontology."

12. IS, 14. Similar formulations stemming from Adorno that link the enterprise of social theory with breaking the *Bann* can be found in the introductory chapter of the sociology textbook of the Frankfurt Institute for Social Research; see, e.g., Institut für Sozialforschung, *Soziologische Exkurse*, 18.

13. One may get a sense of the importance of education for Adorno's and Horkheimer's conception of critique from these lines from this birthday letter from Horkheimer to Adorno on the latter's sixty-fifth anniversary: "All your efforts to educate an enlightened, nonconformist youth . . . belong to the highest that exists in terms of intellectual resistance to the course of the administered world." Horkheimer to Adorno, September 11, 1968, in Müller-Doohm, *Adorno*, 713–14; my translation.

14. *PS*, 42–43; Dewey, *Quest for Certainty*, 52–53.

15. Adorno, "Theorie der Halbbildung," 96.

16. Dewey, "Influence of Darwinism"; Särkelä, "Der Einfluss"; Pearce, *Pragmatism's Evolution*.

17. Stiegler, *"Il faut s'adapter."*

18. For a state-of-the-art study on Adorno's concept of nature, see Vuillerod, *Theodor W. Adorno*.

19. Adorno, "On the Logic," 113.

20. *ND*, 28–43; *AE*, chap. 3. For a more detailed account of Adorno's reception of Dewey, see Särkelä, "American Pragmatism," 151–53.

21. *HNC*, 50–51. See also Levine, "Hegel, Dewey and Habits."

22. Dewey, "Introduction to *Problems of Men*," 169.

23. I thank Martin Hartmann for explicitly expressing to me the apparently widespread doubt that Dewey would ever evoke an uncanny feeling for society. I hope the passage quoted above demonstrates that evocation clearly enough.

24. Särkelä, "Das andere Leben."

25. *LC*, chap. 4; see also Honneth and Särkelä, "Anerkennung als assoziiertes Leben."

26. On the connections between Dewey and Emerson, see Saito, *Gleam of Light*. For a systematic attempt at spelling out this creativity, see Joas, *Creativity of Action*.

27. Dewey, "Philosophies of Freedom."

28. *LC*, 76; see also Särkelä, "Ein Drama in drei Akten."

29. Särkelä, *Immanente Kritik*, 372–76; Gregoratto and Särkelä, "Social Reproduction Feminism."

30. For the example of the trade unions, see *PETS*, 127–28. For that of the student movement, see Adorno, "Spätkapitalismus oder Industriegesellschaft?," 368.

31. The idea of thinking in models dates all the way back to his inaugural lecture; see Adorno, "Die Aktualität der Philosophie." And this stayed with him throughout his philosophical life.

32. For a further contextualization of these models, see Blili-Hamelin and Särkelä, "Unsocial Society."
33. Regarding the quote, see Mill, *On Liberty*, 122, 144.
34. Adorno, "Theorie der Halbbildung," 116.
35. Adorno, *Aesthetics*, 31.
36. Adorno, "Individuum und Organisation."
37. A. Freud, *Ego*, 109–21.
38. Adorno, "Sociology and Psychology," pt. 2, 87.
39. Adorno, "Sociology and Psychology," pt. 1, 71; emphasis added.
40. Adorno, "Sociology and Psychology," pt. 2, 89; translation amended.
41. Adorno, "Theorie der Halbbildung," 119–20.
42. For a systematic and more elaborated account of this model in Adorno, including an attempt to think it further under current neoliberal conditions, see Gandesha, "'Identifying with the Aggressor.'"
43. Adorno, "Sociology and Psychology," pt. 2, 92.
44. Adorno, "Theorie der Halbbildung," 121–22.
45. Adorno, *Aesthetics*, 35–36; emphasis added.
46. *PP*, 314; see also Adorno, "On the Logic"; *PP*, 362.
47. See also Stiegler, *"Il faut s'adapter,"* 133–40.
48. Geuss, "Art and Criticism," 177–78.
49. Särkelä, *Immanente Kritik*.
50. Adorno, "Veblen's Attack on Culture," 92.
51. Adorno, "Veblen's Attack on Culture," 92; translation amended.
52. Adorno, "Theorie der Halbbildung."
53. Adorno, "Thesen über Bedürfnis."
54. Dewey, "America's Public Ownership Program," 285.
55. Adorno, "Education after Auschwitz," 192–93.
56. Like Dewey, Adorno, too, was engaged in political education and educational reform; see, e.g., Adorno, "Zur Demokratisierung"; see also Müller-Doohm, *Adorno*, 568–75.
57. Dewey and Tufts, *Ethics*, 433.
58. On Adorno's politics, see also Freyenhagen, "Adorno's Politics." On Dewey's account of revolution and radical social change, see Renault, "Événement." For a realistic Deweyan account of education and organization, see Serrano, *Democratization*. The sense of tragedy in Dewey's political philosophy has been a topic from his day to ours; see Hook, *Metaphysics of Pragmatism*; Glaude, *In a Shade of Blue*.
59. In the notes for his lectures on social philosophy in China, Dewey writes, "Thinking arises... only in the thin cracks of solid habits, and only with great difficulty penetrates the resistant mass." LCN, 8.
60. Geuss, *Changing the Subject*, 193.
61. Habermas, *Theory of Communicative Action*, pt. 3.

Chapter 6

1. Foley, *Adam's Fallacy*.
2. Adorno, "Kulturkritik und Gesellschaft"; Adorno, "Aldous Huxley and Utopia"; see also Kotkavirta, "Adorno ja psykoanalyysi"; Fong, *Death and Mastery*, chap. 4.
3. For Freud's own examples, see *BPP*, 21–22.
4. Hegel, *Philosophy of Right*, § 142; see also Neuhouser, *Hegel's Social Theory*, chaps. 4–5.
5. Adorno, "Aspects of Hegel's Philosophy," 27.
6. Cavell, *In Quest of the Ordinary*, chap. 6.
7. Nelson, *Shiner*, 9.
8. Blumenberg, *Paradigms for a Metaphorology*, chap. 10.
9. Blumenberg, *Paradigms for a Metaphorology*, 118.
10. Cavell, *Emerson's Transcendental Etudes*, chap. 12; Conant, "Nietzsche's Perfectionism."
11. In *Beyond the Pleasure Principle*, Freud calls this impecunious thing the "vesicle" (*das Bläschen*); see *BPP*, 26–27.
12. Lear, *Freud*, 179.
13. Joel Whitebook insightfully elaborates Freudian psychoanalysis in the broadly Hegelian context of "first" and "second nature," but his focus is on Hegel and Freud as "theorists . . . of the transition from [first] to [second nature]"; Whitebook, "First and Second Nature," 383. For the theme of critical disclosure, the more interesting aspect, as noted in chapter 4, is the Nietzschean dimension in Freud's thinking of first and second nature—namely, the continuation of second nature in the first.
14. Marcuse, *Eros and Civilization*, 5–6. One can probably not overstate the importance of this Freudian influence on disclosing critical theory. The recognition of this continuation of the social environment into the biological makeup of the individual was the crucial factor in Adorno's and Marcuse's vehement rejections of the sociopsychological neo-Freudian revisionisms of Erich Fromm and Karen Horney. Adding socio-theoretical elements to Freud's metapsychology, they believe, was not only superfluous, since the latter was already deeply social, but *uncritical*, since it hypostatized the social environment against the individual. The possibility of a disclosing critique of society, tracing the vicious circularity of environment and individual, was then blocked from the outset. The demise of disclosing critique in critical theory after 1970 is paralleled by the rejection of Freudian drive theory by the authors setting the tone after Adorno and Marcuse. See Adorno, "Die revidierte Psychoanalyse"; Marcuse, *Eros and Civilization*, 5–7, 238–74. For an overview of the issues at stake, see Whitebook, *Perversion and Utopia*; for a recent debate in this vain, see Honneth, "Facetten des vorsozialen Selbst"; Whitebook, "Wechselseitige Anerkennung." Recently, Benjamin Fong and Amy Allen have sought to take Adorno's and Marcuse's challenges seriously. At times, their proposals seem to me to indicate that something like a disclosing intent might be at work in their psycho-

analytic reconceptions of social critique; see Fong, *Death and Mastery*, chaps. 1, 4, 5; Allen, *Critique on the Couch*, esp. chap. 5.

15. Marcuse, *Eros and Civilization*, 269.

16. Marcuse, *Eros and Civilization*, 270.

17. The term "surplus impulse control" introduced here is similar to Marcuse's concept of surplus repression in *Eros and Civilization* (see, e.g., 35), and both terms can, I take it, be used interchangeably in many contexts. But whereas my "surplus impulse control" is introduced merely as a heuristic tool for making sense of a philosophically significant gesture in Freud's metapsychology and cultural criticism, Marcuse's "surplus repression" is an ambitious socio-theoretical concept with a historicophilosophical backing and a theoretical, eventually utopian, intent.

18. In his famous essay "Of Cruelty," Michel de Montaigne describes cruelty as involving putting oneself in the power position of the perpetrator, a sort of "identification with the aggressor," to speak following Anna Freud and Adorno (see previous chapter), and a specific aggressive impulse, the "instinct of inhumanity" (*l'instinct de l'inhumanité*). Montaigne, "Of Cruelty," esp. 383–86. For a contemporary reading along these lines, see Hampe, *Die Dritte Aufklärung*, chap. 3.

19. An interesting model for the type of wisdom implied in Freud's critique of culture has been reconstructed by John Forrester. He suggests that psychoanalytic theory is produced as a kind of "thinking in cases"; see Forrester, "If p, Then What?" The theory itself then displays a practical wisdom in virtue of running on exemplarity. The Oedipus complex would be, as it were, the original case, and every new analysand of Freud's would, with her particular recalcitrant tendencies, constitute a further case enriching the theoretical account. Every new case would deliver wisdom: theoretical tools *and* a larger sensitivity for the particularities of the cases to come. See also Guggenheim et al., *Im Medium des Unbewussten*, chap. 1.

20. Freud's diagnosis of culture is, then, not *only* a cultural-critical outcome of years of experience of psychoanalytic practice; it is also a part of the theory of that practice: the shape of our civilization is what to a considerable extent makes his clients suffer, and hence, theoretical claims about culture build a part of the etiology of psychoanalytic theory; see, e.g., *OP*, 185.

21. Freud was, however, an enormous *source of influence* in this regard. For Freud's influence on the (counter)cultural politics of the twentieth century, see Zaretsky, *Political Freud*.

22. For Dewey, see *HNC*, 106–7; for Adorno, see *MI*, 58–66; Adorno, "Sociology and Psychology," e.g., pt. 1, 68; Adorno, "Sociology and Psychology," pt. 2; for Marcuse, see *Eros and Civilization*, e.g., 17. In *Eros and Civilization*, Marcuse argues that Freud made the mistake of rationalizing and hypostatizing the struggle for existence and questions whether a civilized society as such *must* be repressive. Like Dewey and Adorno, discussed in the previous chapter, Marcuse believes that we live in a society where scarcity is artificially maintained as a means of societal domination. Still, even in his most radical criticism of Freud, Marcuse remains his

disciple in practicing disclosing critique and suggesting a gradualist politics. In the first part of his book on Freud, he shows, following Freud, how the current adaptive pressures maintain a reality principle, which he famously calls the "performance principle," and constitute a vicious circle that produces surplus repression. He then shows how the very progress of civilization has attained a level of productivity at which the repressive demands of society, the instinctual energy expended on alienated labor, could be considerably reduced. This discloses that "the continued repressive organization of the instincts seems to be necessitated less by the 'struggle for existence' than by the interest in prolonging this struggle—by the interest in domination." This decentering disclosure raises the recentering question of "whether the performance principle has perhaps created the preconditions for a qualitatively different, non-repressive reality principle." That recentering disclosure is the task of the second part of his book. And here he remains a gradualist: what is to be investigated is "the real possibility of a gradual elimination of surplus-repression," the "historical possibility of a gradual decontrolling of the instinctual development." See Marcuse, *Eros and Civilization*, 130, 129, 131, 134. Marcuse, then, follows Freud's project of disclosing critique by radicalizing and substantializing the recentering disclosure: the objective possibility of a nonrepressive civilization is taken seriously, and a much more detailed program of its gradual realization is sketched. Along with Dewey and Adorno, he believes that the continuation of the state of nature in society is rendered unnecessary by technological progress, wherefore a more radical gradual organizational and educational effort to overcome suffering is possible than the more compromised gradualism of Freud makes seem plausible. For a historical and systematic account of the utopian aspects of this debate, see Whitebook, *Perversion and Utopia*.

23. Marcuse, *Eros and Civilization*; J. Benjamin, *Bonds of Love*; Gregoratto, *Love Troubles*.

24. The late Michel Foucault has, in a way, continued this method of drawing a line, but he related it to power rather than social suffering by putting the question of the *limits of governing* on the forefront of "critique"; see Foucault, "What Is Critique?"

25. See, e.g., the direct reference to it in Horkheimer and Adorno, *Dialectic of Enlightenment*, 149n1.

26. Adorno, "On the Logic," 113.

27. Blumenberg, *Paradigms for a Metaphorology*, 4.

28. Goodman, *Ways of Worldmaking*, chap. 1. On the relation of Goodman's "worldmaking" to the idea of disclosure, see Seel, "Über Richtigkeit und Wahrheit."

29. Goodman, *Ways of Worldmaking*, 7–10.

30. Goodman, *Ways of Worldmaking*, 10–12.

31. See, e.g., Horkheimer, "Traditional and Critical Theory"; Habermas, *Knowledge and Human Interests*.

32. Goodman, *Ways of Worldmaking*, 12–14.

33. Goodman, *Ways of Worldmaking*, 14–16.

34. See, e.g., Anderson, *Considerations on Western Marxism*.
35. Goodman, *Ways of Worldmaking*, 16.
36. *MI*, §§ 82, 128; see also Renault, "Mise au jour et exagération"; Andreev, "Thinking as Exaggeration."
37. The question of ego integration is, I believe, a very difficult problem for critical theory still today. For a state-of-the-art review of the issue and a very interesting suggestion for resolution, see Allen, *Critique on the Couch*, chap. 2. Although formulated as a reconstruction of Kleinian psychoanalysis, Amy Allen opts for a path that seems to lie closer to the Deweyan than the Freudian position here. While retaining a deep sensibility for the foreignness of the unconscious, she seeks to sketch a nonrepressive model of ego integration as "ego expansion": the enrichment of the ego through incorporation of ever more unconscious and preconscious impulses. See Allen, *Critique on the Couch*, 74–81. This seems to me to come very close to Dewey's account of creative habituation as presented in the previous chapter: it encompasses and directs itself by a greater number of impulses and thereby enables the individual to actualize more of her potential, making her less unfree and unhappy.
38. Adorno, "Sociology and Psychology," pt. 1, 70.
39. In contemporary critical theory, Allen has taken this problem seriously by introducing the phenomenon of transference into the analogy between psychoanalytic therapy and social critique; see Allen, *Critique on the Couch*, chap. 5. Even if I tend toward sharing Marcuse's and Adorno's skepticism about the analogies between therapy and critique, Allen's suggestion is surely important in liberating contemporary critical theory from some of the most dangerous illusions of the juridical picture of critique.
40. Marcuse, *Eros and Civilization*, 245.
41. *OP*, 177; see also Adorno, "Sociology and Psychology," pt. 1, 78; Fromm, "Die gesellschaftliche Bedingtheit"; Kotkavirta, "Adorno ja psykoanalyysi."
42. This whole discussion and problem complex belongs to a technical area where psychoanalysis and disclosing critical theory overlap: that of *caring for transference*. The topic of critique and transference is unsettlingly underdiscussed in critical theory. Allen has recently thankfully illuminated it; see Allen, *Critique on the Couch*, chap. 5.
43. Marcuse, *Eros and Civilization*, 262–63.
44. Horkheimer and Adorno, *Dialectic of Enlightenment*, 43.

Chapter 7
1. Marcuse, *Eros and Civilization*, 57.
2. Habermas, *Postmetaphysical Thinking*, pt. 1; Honneth, *Freedom's Right*, 56–58; Jaeggi, *Critique of Forms*, chap. 8, sec. 1.
3. Blumenberg, *Paradigms for a Metaphorology*, 118.
4. Geuss, "Adorno's Gaps," 246–47.
5. Blumenberg, *Paradigms for a Metaphorology*, 3.
6. Because of this reflexive use of metaphors for disclosure, Emerson is, on my

reading, not the *philosopher of nature* that Michael Hampe portrays him to be in his *Die Wildnis, die Seele, das Nichts*. Instead, I read him as using metaphorical and metaphysical language, with a deep awareness of the dynamics of projection, not to present nature as friendly and homely but to learn to live on *sliding ground*.

7. Rorty, "Dewey's Metaphysics"; Putnam, *Ethics Without Ontology*, chap. 1; Habermas, *Postmetaphysical Thinking*, chap. 3.

8. Latour, *Reassembling the Social*, esp. 110–11; see also Latour, "Why Has Critique Run Out of Steam?"; Latour, *Inquiry into Modes of Existence*.

9. Hook, *Metaphysics of Pragmatism*; Randall, *Nature and Historical Experience*.

10. Adorno, "Idea of Natural-History."

11. Marx, *Capital*, chap. 9, sec. 1.

12. For a contemporary, much richer account of the role of the concept of exploitation in critical theory of society, see Renault, *Abolir l'exploitation*.

13. *AE*, 34; emphasis added. The first chapter of *The Communist Manifesto* famously begins with the following sentence: "The history of all hitherto existing society is the history of class struggles." Marx and Engels, *Communist Manifesto*, 74.

14. Dewey, "Construction and Criticism," 137.

15. Dewey, "What I Believe," 274–75.

16. Horkheimer and Adorno, *Dialectic of Enlightenment*, 27.

17. Dewey, *Quest for Certainty*, 4–5.

18. Marcuse, *Eros and Civilization*, chaps. 8–9.

19. Dewey, *Logic*, 30.

20. See, e.g., Latour, *Reassembling the Social*, 13–16.

21. An interesting exception to the silence over Tarde in critical theory is, however, Adorno, who—in his introductory lecture to sociology—expresses curiosity toward Tarde's conception of imitation and recommends his students to write dissertations about the topic: "The sociology of Tarde . . . relates essentially to the category of 'imitation,' and thus raised the question of mimesis, as we then called it, for sociology for the first time. Discussion of this problem has withered in the most remarkable way in current sociology, and could be re-awakened by an intensive study of Tarde. I consider that work on Tarde would be a very rewarding subject for degree dissertations and suchlike tasks." Adorno, *Introduction to Sociology*, 97. I have not found any dissertation to have come out of this encouragement.

22. See, e.g., Dewey, "Need for Social Psychology."

23. For a helpful reconstruction and contextualization of how Tarde combines ontological monism and modal pluralism, see Debaise, "Dynamics of Possession."

24. Spinoza, *Ethics*, pt. 1, prop. 11.

25. Spinoza, *Ethics*, pt. 1, prop. 10, pt. 2, prop. 13, pt. 3, prop. 7.

26. Spinoza, *Ethics*, bk. 5.

27. *EN*, chap. 2; see also Hartmann and Särkelä, "Eine Metaphysik der 'lebendigen Mischung.'"

28. In contemporary metaphysics, this is the precise assumption of assemblage theory; see Deleuze, *Difference and Repetition*, 163. For further systematizations in social ontology, see DeLanda, *New Philosophy of Society*; and, more generally, see DeLanda, *Assemblage Theory*.

29. *MS*, 51; see also Debaise, "Dynamics of Possession."

30. On the Leibnizian roots of Tarde's metaphysics of possession, see Debaise, "Dynamics of Possession." On the Hegelian roots of Dewey's metaphysics of association, see Särkelä, *Immanente Kritik*, pt. 2; Levine, "Hegel's Place."

31. Lorenc, "Tarde's Pansocial Ontology," 80.

32. Dewey, "Need for Social Psychology," 53.

33. Särkelä, "Das andere Leben." For a different Deweyan alternative to contemporary intentionalism in social ontology, see Testa, "Dewey's Social Ontology."

34. Dewey, "Half-Hearted Naturalism," 76.

35. *IPI*, 44. For a more recent systematic attempt at distinguishing types of processes in this spirit, see Emmet, *Passage of Nature*, esp. chaps. 4, 6, 7, 8.

36. *IPI*, 44; *MS*, 47. Neither Dewey nor Tarde is particularly consistent in their typology of special modes: sometimes there are three, sometimes four, five, or six. The reason for this inconsistency is that, like Spinoza, they believe that one could, in principle, go on to identify an infinite number of modes because anything that can be conceptually constructed as a thing depends ontologically on its "infinitesimal." The question is, To what aim? Dewey's and Tarde's aim is to provide a ground map of the province of social critique or social science. And for this, they seem to agree that three associational fields demand special attention.

37. Dewey, *Quest for Certainty*, 179.

38. Dewey, *Quest for Certainty*, 179.

39. Whitehead, *Function of Reason*, 4.

40. For an illuminating historical account of the idea of *scala naturae* in Dewey's time, see Lovejoy, *Great Chain of Being*.

41. *EN*, chap. 7. For a detailed reconstruction of Dewey's view, see Särkelä, *Immanente Kritik*, chap. 6.

42. Spinoza, *Ethics*, pt. 3, prop. 7.

43. Peirce, "Evolutionary Love," sec. 1.

44. Bergson, *Les deux sources*, 264.

45. Dewey, "Influence of Darwinism"; Dewey, "Need for a Recovery"; see also Särkelä, "Der Einfluss."

46. Perhaps the two views can be reconciled. Let's assume that all life on our planet is based on DNA. One could speculate that there must have initially been several alternative inheritance-enabling substances next to DNA. We do not, however, know these substances today; they seem not to exist on our planet anymore. The reason for this, one could further assume, is that DNA defeated the alternatives. It was "selected," although the process cannot have been "fully" organic in the sense of inheritance as what was selected was the mechanism of inheritance itself.

Now, by analogy to this sort of preorganic selection, perhaps a universal desire, agape, conatus, etc. could be conceived as having been "selected." Then Tarde could be an agapist and a selectionist at the same time.

47. Although most readers of Tarde ignore the cosmological hierarchy in his metaphysics, Tarde has, ironically, better conceptual means than Dewey to grasp the asymmetrical relation between ontological modes—namely, his distinction between reciprocal and unilateral possessions. As we saw above, in Tarde, chemical associations unilaterally possess subchemical physical associations, organic associations unilaterally possess chemical associations, and social associations unilaterally possess organic and physical associations. Dewey does, however, often imply the idea of unilateral possession—e.g., when he conceptualizes "structure" as a slow process possessing other processes. *EN*, chap. 2.

48. For a Deweyan critique of the intentionalist paradigm in social ontology, see Testa, "Ontology."

49. McDowell, *Mind and World*, 34–36; *EF*, 21–22.

50. Hampe, *Erkenntnis und Praxis*, 20; my translation.

51. Dewey, "Influence of Darwinism."

52. Latour, *Facing Gaia*, 25.

53. MGH, 215; see also Adorno, "Free Time."

54. Adorno, "Working Through the Past," 100.

Chapter 8

1. Wittgenstein, *Philosophical Investigations*, § 69.
2. Geuss, "Genealogy as Critique," 154.
3. Geuss, "Genealogy as Critique," 257; Saar, "Genealogy and Subjectivity," 239–40.
4. Saar, "Genealogy and Subjectivity"; see also Geuss, "Genealogy as Critique," 157–59; Owen, "Criticism and Captivity," 216.
5. Guess, "Genealogy as Critique," 157.
6. Each of these four disclosing critics has, indeed, been a source of inspiration for genealogical critiques. On Nietzsche, see Foucault, "Nietzsche, Genealogy, History"; Saar, *Genealogie als Kritik*, chaps. 1–2; on Freud, see Greer, "Freud's 'Bad Conscience'"; on Dewey, see Koopman, "Genealogical Pragmatism"; Santarelli, "Between Problematization and Evaluation"; and on Adorno, see Menke, "Genealogy and Critique."
7. Guess, *Philosophy and Real Politics*, 52.
8. Rorty, "Feminism and Pragmatism," 232, 239; see also Lovibond, "Feminism and Pragmatism."
9. I thank Frederick Neuhouser for pushing me on these issues.
10. See, e.g., Losurdo, *Nietzsche, the Aristocratic Rebel*; Lovibond, "Selflessness"; Lovibond, "Nietzsche on Distance."
11. Wittgenstein, *Zettel*, § 160.
12. Brown, *In the Ruins*.

13. Stiegler, *"Il faut s'adapter."*

14. For particularly insightful studies in this direction, see Le Blanc, *Philosophie comme contre-culture* ; Stiegler, *"Il faut s'adapter."*

15. Adorno interestingly observed this exact contradiction but with reference to nuclear weapons. MGH, 210. This prompted me to think of global warming as a decentralized and slowly detonating atom bomb; see Särkelä, "Anpassung und Erschließung."

16. Gregoratto et al., "Critical Naturalism."

17. Fischbach, *Pour la Théorie critique*, 36; my translation.

18. Adorno, "Kultur und Culture," 156.

19. See, e.g., Latour, *Inquiry into Modes of Existence*; Latour, *Facing Gaia*.

Bibliography

Adorno, Theodor W. *Aesthetics*. Edited by Eberhard Ortland, translated by Wieland Hoban. Polity Press, 2017.
Adorno, Theodor W. *Aesthetic Theory*. Edited by Gretel Adorno and Rolf Tiedemann, translated by Robert Hullot-Kentor. 1970. Continuum, 2002.
Adorno, Theodor W. "Aldous Huxley and Utopia." In Adorno, *Prisms*, translated by Samuel Weber and Shierry Weber. 1955. MIT Press, 1997.
Adorno, Theodor W. "Aspects of Hegel's Philosophy." In Adorno, *Hegel: Three Studies*, translated by Shierry Weber Nicholsen. 1957. MIT Press, 1993.
Adorno, Theodor W. "Die Aktualität der Philosophie." In Adorno, *Gesammelte Schriften*, edited by Rolf Tiedemann. Vol. 1. 1931. Suhrkamp Verlag, 2003.
Adorno, Theodor W. "Die menschliche Gesellschaft heute." In Adorno, *Nachgelassene Schriften*. Sec. 5, vol. 1, edited by Michael Schwarz. 1957. Suhrkamp Verlag, 2019.
Adorno, Theodor W. "Die revidierte Psychoanalyse." In Adorno, *Gesammelte Schriften*, edited by Rolf Tiedemann. Vol. 8. 1952. Suhrkamp Verlag, 2003.
Adorno, Theodor W. "Education after Auschwitz." In Adorno, *Critical Models: Interventions and Catchwords*, translated by Henry W. Pickford. 1966. Columbia University Press, 2005.
Adorno, Theodor W. "Einleitung." In Émile Durkheim, *Philosophie und Soziologie*. 1967. Suhrkamp Verlag, 1976.
Adorno, Theodor W. "Free Time." In Adorno, *The Culture Industry: Selected Essays on Mass Culture*, edited by J. M. Bernstein. 1955. Routledge, 2001.
Adorno, Theodor W. *History and Freedom: Lectures 1964–1965*. Edited by Rolf Tiedemann, translated by Rodney Livingstone. Polity Press, 2006.
Adorno, Theodor W. "The Idea of Natural-History." In Adorno, *Things Beyond Resemblance: Collected Essays on Adorno*, edited and translated by Robert Hullot-Kentor. 1932. Columbia University Press, 2006.

Adorno, Theodor W. "Individuum und Organisation." In Adorno, *Gesammelte Schriften*, edited by Rolf Tiedemann. Vol. 8. 1953. Suhrkamp Verlag, 2003.
Adorno, Theodor W. *An Introduction to Dialectics*. Edited by Christoph Ziermann, translated by Nicholas Walker. Polity Press, 2017.
Adorno, Theodor W. *Introduction to Sociology*. Edited by Christoph Gödde, translated by Edmund Jephcott. Stanford University Press, 2000.
Adorno, Theodor W. "Kulturkritik und Gesellschaft." In Adorno, *Gesammelte Schriften*, edited by Rolf Tiedemann. Vol. 10. 1955. Suhrkamp Verlag, 2003.
Adorno, Theodor W. "Kultur und Culture." In Adorno, *Nachgelassene Schriften*. Sec. 5, vol. 1, edited by Michael Schwarz. 1958. Suhrkamp Verlag, 2019.
Adorno, Theodor W. "The Meaning of Working Through the Past." In Adorno, *Critical Models: Interventions and Catchwords*, translated by Henry W. Pickford. 1963. Columbia University Press, 2005.
Adorno, Theodor W. *Minima Moralia: Reflections from Damaged Life*. Translated by Edmund Jephcott. 1951. New Left Books, 1974.
Adorno, Theodor W. *Negative Dialectics*. Translated by E. B. Ashton. 1966. Routledge, 1973.
Adorno, Theodor W. "On the Logic of the Social Sciences." In Adorno, Hans Albert, Ralf Dahrendorf, et al., *The Positivist Dispute in German Sociology*, translated by Glyn Adey and David Frisby. 1962. Heinemann, 1977.
Adorno, Theodor W. *Philosophical Elements of a Theory of Society: 1964*. Edited by Tobias ten Brink and Marc Phillip Nogueira, translated by Wieland Hoban. Polity Press, 2019.
Adorno, Theodor W. *Philosophie und Soziologie*. In Adorno, *Nachgelassene Schriften*. Sec. 4, vol. 6, edited by Dirk Braunstein. Suhrkamp Verlag, 2011.
Adorno, Theodor W. *Philosophy of New Music*. Edited and translated by Robert Hullot-Kentor. 1949. University of Minnesota Press, 2006.
Adorno, Theodor W. "Society." Translated by Frederic Jameson. *Salmagundi* 10–11 ([1965] 1969): 144–53.
Adorno, Theodor W. "Sociology and Psychology (Part I)." Translated by Irving N. Wohlfarth. *New Left Review* 46 ([1955] 1967): 67–80.
Adorno, Theodor W. "Sociology and Psychology (Part II)." Translated by Irving N. Wohlfarth. *New Left Review* 47 ([1955] 1968): 79–97.
Adorno, Theodor W. "Spätkapitalismus oder Industriegesellschaft?" In Adorno, *Gesammelte Schriften*, edited by Rolf Tiedemann. Vol. 8. 1968. Suhrkamp Verlag, 2003.
Adorno, Theodor W. Theodor W. Adorno to Max Horkheimer, August 21, 1941. In *Gesammelte Schriften*, by Max Horkheimer, edited by Alfred Schmidt and Gunzelin Schmid Noerr. Vol. 17. Fischer Verlag, 1985.
Adorno, Theodor W. "Theorie der Halbbildung." In Adorno, *Gesammelte Schriften*, edited by Rolf Tiedemann. Vol. 8. 1959. Suhrkamp Verlag, 2003.
Adorno, Theodor W. "Thesen über Bedürfnis." In Adorno, *Gesammelte Schriften*, edited by Rolf Tiedemann. Vol. 8. 1942. Suhrkamp Verlag, 2003.

Adorno, Theodor W. "Über Statik und Dynamik als soziologische Kategorien." In Adorno, *Gesammelte Schriften*, edited by Rolf Tiedemann. Vol. 8. 1961. Suhrkamp Verlag, 2003.

Adorno, Theodor W. "Veblen's Attack on Culture." In Adorno, *Prisms*, translated by Samuel Weber and Shierry Weber. 1955. MIT Press, 1997.

Adorno, Theodor W. "Zur Demokratisierung der deutschen Universitäten." In Adorno, *Gesammelte Schriften*, edited by Rolf Tiedemann. Vol. 20, bk. 1. 1959. Suhrkamp Verlag, 2003.

Allen, Amy. *Critique on the Couch: Why Critical Theory Needs Psychoanalysis*. Columbia University Press, 2021.

Anderson, Perry. *Considerations on Western Marxism*. 1976. Verso, 1989.

Andreev, Plamen. "Thinking as Exaggeration." *Berlin Journal of Critical Theory* 9, no. 2 (2025): 157–84.

Aristotle. *History of Animals*. In Aristotle, *Generation of Animals and History of Animals I, Parts of Animals I*, translated by C. D. C. Reeve. Hackett, 2019.

Aristotle. *Nicomachean Ethics*. Edited and translated by Roger Crisp. Cambridge University Press, 2004.

Ásta. *Categories We Live By: The Construction of Sex, Gender, Race, and Other Social Categories*. Oxford University Press, 2018.

Benjamin, Jessica. *The Bonds of Love: Psychoanalysis, Feminism, and the Problem of Domination*. Pantheon Books, 1988.

Benjamin, Walter. *The Concept of Criticism in German Romanticism*. In Benjamin, *Selected Writings*, edited by Michael W. Jennings. Vol. 1, *1913–1926*, edited by Marcus Bullock and Jennings. 1920. Belknap Press of Harvard University Press, 2004.

Benjamin, Walter. "Critique of Violence." In Benjamin, *Selected Writings*, edited by Michael W. Jennings. Vol. 1, *1913–1926*, edited by Marcus Bullock and Jennings. 1921. Belknap Press of Harvard University Press, 2004.

Benjamin, Walter. "Goethe's Elective Affinities." In Benjamin, *Selected Writings*, edited by Michael W. Jennings. Vol. 1, *1913–1926*, edited by Marcus Bullock and Jennings. 1925. Belknap Press of Harvard University Press, 2004.

Benjamin, Walter. "On the Concept of History." In Benjamin, *Selected Writings*, edited by Michael W. Jennings. Vol. 4, *1938–1940*, edited by Marcus Bullock, Howard Eiland, and Gary Smith. 1940. Belknap Press of Harvard University Press, 2006.

Benjamin, Walter. *Origin of the German Trauerspiel*. Translated by Howard Eiland. 1928. Belknap Press of Harvard University Press, 2019.

Bergson, Henri. *Les deux sources de la morale et de la religion*. Presses Universitaires de France, 1932.

Bernstein, Jay. "'Our Amphibian Problem': Nature in History in Adorno's Hegelian Critique of Hegel." In *Hegel on Philosophy in History*, edited by Rachel Zuckert and James Kreines. Cambridge University Press, 2017.

Black, Max. "Metaphor." *Proceedings of the Aristotelian Society*, n.s., vol. 55 (1954–1955): 273–94.

Blili-Hamelin, Borhane. "Topography of the Splintered World: Hegel and the Disagreements of Right." PhD diss., Columbia University, 2019.

Blili-Hamelin, Borhane, and Arvi Särkelä. "Unsocial Society: Adorno, Hegel, and Social Antagonisms." In *Hegel and the Frankfurt School*, edited by Paul Giladi. Routledge, 2020.

Blumenberg, Hans. *Paradigms for a Metaphorology*. Translated by Robert Savage. 1960. Cornell University Press, 2010.

Blumenberg, Hans. *Shipwreck with Spectator: Paradigm of a Metaphor for Existence*. Translated by Steven Rendall. 1979. MIT Press, 1997.

Bohman, James. "Welterschließung und radikale Kritik." *Deutsche Zeitschrift für Philosophie* 41, no. 3 (1993): 563–74.

Boltanski, Luc. *On Critique: A Sociology of Emancipation*. Polity Press, 2011.

Brown, Wendy. *In the Ruins of Neoliberalism: The Rise of Antidemocratic Politics in the West*. Columbia University Press, 2019.

Butler, Judith. *The Psychic Life of Power: Theories in Subjection*. Stanford University Press, 1997.

Carré, Louis. "From Naturalism to Social Vitalism: Revisiting the Durkheim-Bergson Debate on Moral Obligations." In *Naturalism and Social Philosophy: Contemporary Perspectives*, edited by Martin Hartmann and Arvi Särkelä. Rowman and Littlefield, 2023.

Cavell, Stanley. *Cities of Words: Pedagogical Letters on a Register of the Moral Life*. Belknap Press of Harvard University Press, 2004.

Cavell, Stanley. *Conditions Handsome and Unhandsome: The Constitution of Emersonian Perfectionism*. University of Chicago Press, 1990.

Cavell, Stanley. *Emerson's Transcendental Etudes*. Stanford University Press, 2003.

Cavell, Stanley. *In Quest of the Ordinary: Lines of Skepticism and Romanticism*. University of Chicago Press, 1988.

Celikates, Robin. *Critique as Social Practice: Critical Theory and Social Self-Understanding*. Translated by Naomi van Steenbergen. 2009. Rowman and Littlefield, 2018.

Christ, Julia. "Critique of Politics: Adorno on Durkheim." *Journal of Classical Sociology* 17, no. 4 (2017): 331–41.

Conant, James. *Friedrich Nietzsche: Perfektionismus und Perspektivismus*. Konstanz University Press, 2014.

Conant, James. "Nietzsche's Perfectionism: A Reading of 'Schopenhauer as Educator.'" In *Nietzsche's Postmoralism: Essays on Nietzsche's Prelude to Philosophy's Future*, edited by Richard Schacht. Cambridge University Press, 2001.

Danto, Arthur. *Nietzsche as Philosopher*. Columbia University Press, 1965.

Davis, Angela Y. *Women, Race and Class*. Vintage Books, 1983.

Dawkins, Richard. *The Selfish Gene*. 1976. Oxford University Press, 2006.

Debaise, Didier. "The Dynamics of Possession: An Introduction to the Sociology of Gabriel Tarde." In *Mind That Abides: Panpsychism in the New Millennium*, edited by David Skrbina. John Benjamins, 2008.

DeLanda, Manuel. *Assemblage Theory*. Edinburgh University Press, 2016.
DeLanda, Manuel. *A New Philosophy of Society: Assemblage Theory and Social Complexity*. Continuum, 2006.
Deleuze, Gilles. *Difference and Repetition*. 1968. Columbia University Press, 1994.
Deleuze, Gilles. *Nietzsche and Philosophy*. 1962. Columbia University Press, 1983.
Deleuze, Gilles, and Félix Guattari. *Kafka: Pour une littérature mineure*. Les Éditions de Minuit, 1975.
Dewey, John. "America's Public Ownership Program." In Dewey, *The Later Works, 1925–1953*, edited by Jo Ann Boydston. Vol. 9. 1934. Southern Illinois University Press, 2008.
Dewey, John. *Art as Experience*. In Dewey, *The Later Works, 1925–1953*, edited by Jo Ann Boydston. Vol. 10. 1934. Southern Illinois University Press, 2008.
Dewey, John. "Construction and Criticism." In Dewey, *The Later Works, 1925–1953*, edited by Jo Ann Boydston. Vol. 5. 1930. Southern Illinois University Press, 2008.
Dewey, John. *Democracy and Education*. In Dewey, *The Middle Works, 1899–1924*, edited by Jo Ann Boydston. Vol. 9. 1916. Southern Illinois University Press, 2008.
Dewey, John. *Experience and Nature*. In Dewey, *The Later Works, 1925–1953*, edited by Jo Ann Boydston. Vol. 1. 1925. Southern Illinois University Press, 2008.
Dewey, John. "Half-Hearted Naturalism." In Dewey, *The Later Works, 1925–1953*, edited by Jo Ann Boydston. Vol. 3. 1927. Southern Illinois University Press, 2008.
Dewey, John. *Human Nature and Conduct*. In Dewey, *The Middle Works, 1899–1924*, edited by Jo Ann Boydston. Vol. 14. 1922. Southern Illinois University Press, 2008.
Dewey, John. "The Inclusive Philosophic Idea." In Dewey, *The Later Works, 1925–1953*, edited by Jo Ann Boydston. Vol. 3. 1928. Southern Illinois University Press, 2008.
Dewey, John. "The Influence of Darwinism on Philosophy." In Dewey, *The Middle Works, 1899–1924*, edited by Jo Ann Boydston. Vol. 4. 1907. Southern Illinois University Press, 2008.
Dewey, John. "Introduction to *Problems of Men*." In Dewey, *The Later Works, 1925–1953*, edited by Jo Ann Boydston. Vol. 15. 1946. Southern Illinois University Press, 2008.
Dewey, John. *Lectures in China 1919–1920*. Translated by Robert W. Clopton and Tsuin-Chen Ou. University Press of Hawai'i, 1973.
Dewey, John. "Lectures in Social and Political Philosophy" (notes for the lectures in China). *European Journal of Pragmatism and American Philosophy* 7, no. 2 (2015): 7–44.
Dewey, John. *Liberalism and Social Action*. In Dewey, *The Later Works, 1925–1953*, edited by Jo Ann Boydston. Vol. 11. 1935. Southern Illinois University Press, 2008.

Dewey, John. *Logic: The Theory of Inquiry*. In Dewey, *The Later Works, 1925–1953*, edited by Jo Ann Boydston. Vol. 12. 1938. Southern Illinois University Press, 2008.

Dewey, John. "The Need for a Recovery of Philosophy." In Dewey, *The Middle Works, 1899–1924*, edited by Jo Ann Boydston. Vol. 10. 1917. Southern Illinois University Press, 2008.

Dewey, John. "The Need for Social Psychology." In Dewey, *The Middle Works, 1899–1924*, edited by Jo Ann Boydston. Vol. 10. 1917. Southern Illinois University Press, 2008.

Dewey, John. "Philosophies of Freedom." In Dewey, *The Later Works, 1925–1953*, edited by Jo Ann Boydston. Vol. 3. 1928. Southern Illinois University Press, 2008.

Dewey, John. *The Public and Its Problems*. In Dewey, *The Later Works, 1925–1953*, edited by Jo Ann Boydston. Vol. 2. 1927. Southern Illinois University Press, 2008.

Dewey, John. *The Quest for Certainty: A Study of the Relation of Knowledge and Action*. In Dewey, *The Later Works, 1925–1953*, edited by Jo Ann Boydston. Vol. 4. 1929. Southern Illinois University Press, 2008.

Dewey, John. *Unmodern Philosophy and Modern Philosophy*. Edited by Philip Deen. Southern Illinois University Press, 2012.

Dewey, John. "What I Believe." In Dewey, *The Later Works, 1925–1953*, edited by Jo Ann Boydston. Vol. 5. 1930. Southern Illinois University Press, 2008.

Dewey, John, and James H. Tufts. *Ethics*. In Dewey, *The Middle Works, 1899–1924*, edited by Jo Ann Boydston. Vol. 5. 1908. Southern Illinois University Press, 2003.

Diamond, Cora. *The Realistic Spirit: Wittgenstein, Philosophy and the Mind*. MIT Press, 1991.

Durkheim, Émile. *The Rules of the Sociological Method and Selected Texts on Sociology and Its Method*. Edited by Steven Lukes, translated by W. D. Halls. 1895. Palgrave Macmillan, 2013.

Durkheim, Émile. *Sociology and Philosophy*. Translated by D. F. Pocock. 1951. Routledge, 2010.

Emerson, Ralph Waldo. "The American Scholar." In Emerson, *Essays and Lectures*, edited by Joel Porte. 1837. Library of America, 1983.

Emerson, Ralph Waldo. "Circles." In Emerson, *Essays and Lectures*, edited by Joel Porte. 1841. Library of America, 1983.

Emerson, Ralph Waldo. "Experience." In Emerson, *Essays and Lectures*, edited by Joel Porte. 1844. Library of America, 1983.

Emerson, Ralph Waldo. "History." In Emerson, *Essays and Lectures*, edited by Joel Porte. 1841. Library of America, 1983.

Emerson, Ralph Waldo. *Nature*. In Emerson, *Essays and Lectures*, edited by Joel Porte. 1936. Library of America, 1983.

Emerson, Ralph Waldo. "The Over-Soul." In Emerson, *Essays and Lectures*, edited by Joel Porte. 1841. Library of America, 1983.

Emerson, Ralph Waldo. "The Poet." In Emerson, *Essays and Lectures*, edited by Joel Porte. 1844. Library of America, 1983.
Emerson, Ralph Waldo. "Self-Reliance." In Emerson, *Essays and Lectures*, edited by Joel Porte. 1841. Library of America, 1983.
Emmet, Dorothy. *The Passage of Nature*. Macmillan, 1992.
Ferenczi, Sándor. "Confusion of the Tongues Between the Adults and the Child—(the Language of Tenderness and Passion)." *International Journal of Psychoanalysis* 30 ([1932] 1949): 225–30.
Ferrara, Alessandro. *The Force of the Example: Exploration in the Paradigm of Judgment*. Columbia University Press, 2008.
Finlayson, Gordon. "Hegel, Adorno and the Origins of Immanent Criticism." *British Journal for the History of Philosophy* 22, no. 6 (2014): 1142–66.
Fischbach, Franck. *Pour la Théorie critique: Raison, nature et societé*. Vrin, 2024.
Foley, Duncan. *Adam's Fallacy: A Guide to Economic Theology*. Belknap Press of Harvard University Press, 2006.
Fong, Benjamin Y. *Death and Mastery: Psychoanalytic Drive Theory and the Subject of Late Capitalism*. Columbia University Press, 2016.
Forrester, John. "If p, Then What? Thinking in Cases." *History of the Human Sciences* 9, no. 3 (1996): 1–25.
Forster, Fabienne, and Michael Hampe. "Classes as Clusters: Peirce on Evolution and Classification in Biology." *Nóema* 1, no. 15 (2024): 11–24.
Foucault, Michel. "Nietzsche, Genealogy, History." In *Nietzsche*, edited by John Richardson and Brian Leiter. Oxford Readings in Philosophy. 1971. Oxford University Press, 2001.
Foucault, Michel. "What Is Critique?" In *What Is Enlightenment? Eighteenth Century Answers and Twentieth Century Questions*, edited by James Schmidt. 1978. University of California Press, 1996.
Foucault, Michel. "What Is Enlightenment?" In *The Foucault Reader*, edited by Paul Rainbow. 1983. Penguin, 1986.
Freud, Anna. *The Ego and the Mechanisms of Defence*. Translated by Cecil Baines. 1936. Karnac, 1993.
Freud, Sigmund. *Beyond the Pleasure Principle*. In Freud, *The Standard Edition of the Complete Psychological Works of Sigmund Freud*, edited by James Strachey and Anna Freud. Vol. 18. 1920. Vintage Books, 2001.
Freud, Sigmund. *Civilization and Its Discontents*. In Freud, *The Standard Edition of the Complete Psychological Works of Sigmund Freud*, edited by James Strachey and Anna Freud. Vol. 21. 1930. Vintage Books, 2001.
Freud, Sigmund. *The Ego and the Id*. In Freud, *The Standard Edition of the Complete Psychological Works of Sigmund Freud*, edited by James Strachey and Anna Freud. Vol. 19. 1923. Vintage Books, 2001.
Freud, Sigmund. "Formulations on the Two Principles of Mental Functioning." In Freud, *The Standard Edition of the Complete Psychological Works of Sigmund*

Freud, edited by James Strachey and Anna Freud. Vol. 12. 1911. Vintage Books, 2001.

Freud, Sigmund. *Group Psychology and the Analysis of the Ego*. In Freud, *The Standard Edition of the Complete Psychological Works of Sigmund Freud*, edited by James Strachey and Anna Freud. Vol. 18. 1922. Vintage Books, 2001.

Freud, Sigmund. "Mourning and Melancholia." In Freud, *The Standard Edition of the Complete Psychological Works of Sigmund Freud*, edited by James Strachey and Anna Freud. Vol. 14. 1915. Vintage Books, 2001.

Freud, Sigmund. *An Outline of Psycho-Analysis*. In Freud, *The Standard Edition of the Complete Psychological Works of Sigmund Freud*, edited by James Strachey and Anna Freud. Vol. 23. 1940. Vintage Books, 2001.

Freud, Sigmund. "Remembering, Repeating, Working-Through." In Freud, *The Standard Edition of the Complete Psychological Works of Sigmund Freud*, edited by James Strachey and Anna Freud. Vol. 12. Vintage Books, 2001.

Freud, Sigmund. "The Uncanny." In Freud, *The Standard Edition of the Complete Psychological Works of Sigmund Freud*, edited by James Strachey and Anna Freud. Vol. 17. 1919. Vintage Books, 2001.

Freyenhagen, Fabian. "Adorno's Politics: Theory and Praxis in Germany's 1960s." *Philosophy and Social Criticism* 40, no. 9 (2014): 867–93.

Freyenhagen, Fabian. *Adorno's Practical Philosophy: Living Less Wrongly*. Cambridge University Press, 2013.

Freyenhagen, Fabian. "Honneth on Social Pathologies: A Critique." *Critical Horizons* 16, no. 2 (2015): 131–52.

Freyenhagen, Fabian. "Objective Reason, Ethical Naturalism, and Social Pathology: The Case of Horkheimer and Adorno." In *Naturalism and Social Philosophy: Contemporary Perspectives*, edited by Martin Hartmann and Arvi Särkelä. Rowman and Littlefield, 2023.

Freyenhagen, Fabian. "Why Professor Habermas Would Fail a Class on *Dialectic of Enlightenment*." *Res Philosophica* 101, no. 2 (2024): 245–69.

Fromm, Erich. "Die gesellschaftliche Bedingtheit der psychoanalytischen Therapie." *Zeitschrift für Sozialforschung* 4, no. 3 (1935): 365–97.

Gandesha, Samir. "'Identifying with the Aggressor': From the Authoritarian to Neoliberal Personality." *Constellations* 25, no. 1 (2018): 147–64.

Geuss, Raymond. "Adorno's Gaps." In Geuss, *Outside Ethics*. Princeton University Press, 2005.

Geuss, Raymond. "Art and Criticism in Adorno's Aesthetics." In Geuss, *Outside Ethics*. Princeton University Press, 2005.

Geuss, Raymond. *Changing the Subject: Philosophy from Socrates to Adorno*. Harvard University Press, 2017.

Geuss, Raymond. "Genealogy as Critique." In Geuss, *Outside Ethics*. Princeton University Press, 2005.

Geuss, Raymond. "Must Criticism Be Constructive?" In Geuss, *A World Without Why*. Princeton University Press, 2014.

Geuss, Raymond. *Not Thinking Like a Liberal.* Belknap Press of Harvard University Press, 2022.
Geuss, Raymond. *Philosophy and Real Politics.* Princeton University Press, 2008.
Glaude, Eddie S. *In a Shade of Blue: Pragmatism and the Politics of Black America.* University of Chicago Press, 2007.
Glock, Hans-Johann. "Wittgensteinian Anti-Anti-Realism: One 'Anti' Too Many?" In *Ethics After Wittgenstein: Contemplation and Critique,* edited by Richard Aimesbury and Hartmut von Sass. 2015. Bloomsbury, 2021.
Goodman, Nelson. *Ways of Worldmaking.* Hackett, 1978.
Gould, Steven Jay. *The Structure of Evolutionary Theory.* Belknap Press of Harvard University Press, 2002.
Greer, Scott. "Freud's 'Bad Conscience': The Case of Nietzsche's *Genealogy.*" *Journal of the History of the Behavioral Sciences* 38, no. 3 (2002): 303–15.
Gregoratto, Federica. *Love Troubles: Philosophy of Eros.* Columbia University Press, 2024.
Gregoratto, Federica, Heikki Ikäheimo, Emmanuel Renault, Arvi Särkelä, and Italo Testa. "Critical Naturalism: A Manifesto." *Krisis: Journal for Contemporary Philosophy* 42, no. 1 (2022): 108–24.
Gregoratto, Federica, and Arvi Särkelä. "Social Reproduction Feminism and Deweyan Habit Ontology." In *Habits: Pragmatist Approaches from Cognitive Science, Neurosciences and Social Theory,* edited by Fausto Caruana and Italo Testa. Cambridge University Press, 2020.
Guggenheim, Josef Zwi, Michael Hampe, Peter Schneider, and Daniel Strassberg. *Im Medium des Unbewussten: Zur Theorie der Psychoanalyse.* Kohlhammer, 2016.
Habermas, Jürgen. *Knowledge and Human Interests.* Translated by Jeremy J. Shapiro. 1968. Beacon Press, 1971.
Habermas, Jürgen. *Postmetaphysical Thinking.* Translated by William Mark Hohengarten. 1988. MIT Press, 1992.
Habermas, Jürgen. *The Theory of Communicative Action.* Vol. 1, *Reason and Rationalization of Society.* Translated by Thomas McCarthy. 1981. Beacon Press, 1985.
Hampe, Michael. *Die Dritte Aufklärung.* Nicolai, 2018.
Hampe, Michael. *Die Wildnis, die Seele, das Nichts: Über das wirkliche Leben.* Hanser Verlag, 2020.
Hampe, Michael. *Erkenntnis und Praxis: Zur Philosophie des Pragmatismus.* Suhrkamp Verlag, 2006.
Hampe, Michael. *What Philosophy Is For.* 2014. University of Chicago Press, 2018.
Hartmann, Martin. "Vertiefung der Erfahrung: John Dewey in der deutschsprachigen Rezeption." *Allgemeine Zeitschrift für Philosophie* 34, no. 3 (2009): 415–40.
Hartmann, Martin. "Why the Biblical Prophets Would Have Appreciated (Critical) Theory: Continuing Michael Walzer's Debate with the Frankfurt School." In *Exodus, Exilpolitik und Revolution: Zur Politischen Theologie Michael Walzers,* edited by Michael Kühlein. Mohr Siebeck, 2017.

Hartmann, Martin, and Arvi Särkelä. "Eine Metaphysik der 'lebendigen Mischung.'" In *John Dewey: Erfahrung und Natur*, edited by Michael Hampe. Klassiker Auslegen 66. De Gruyter, 2017.

Haslanger, Sally. "Racism, Ideology, and Social Movements." *Res Philosophica* 94, no. 1 (2017): 1–22.

Haslanger, Sally. *Resisting Reality: Social Construction and Social Critique*. Oxford University Press, 2012.

Hegel, G. W. F. *Outlines of the Philosophy of Right*. Edited by Stephen Houlgate, translated by T. M. Knox. 1820. Oxford University Press, 2008.

Hegel, G. W. F. *The Phenomenology of Spirit*. Translated by A. V. Miller. 1807. Oxford University Press, 1977.

Hirvonen, Onni. "On the Ontology of Social Pathologies." *Studies in Social and Political Thought* 28 (2018): 9–14.

Hogh, Philip, and Julia König. "Bestimmte Unbestimmbarkeit: Über die zweite Natur in der ersten und die erste Natur in der zweiten." *Deutsche Zeitschrift für Philosophie* 59, no. 3 (2011): 419–38.

Honneth, Axel. *The Critique of Power: Reflective Stages in a Critical Social Theory*. Translated by Kenneth Baynes. 1985. MIT Press, 1993.

Honneth, Axel. "The Diseases of Society: Approaching a Nearly Impossible Concept." Translated by Arvi Särkelä. *Social Research* 81, no. 3 (2014): 683–703.

Honneth, Axel. "Facetten des vorsozialen Selbst: Eine Erwiderung auf Joel Whitebook." *Psyche* 55, no. 8 (2001): 790–802.

Honneth, Axel. *Freedom's Right: The Social Foundations of Democratic Life*. Translated by Joseph Ganahl. 2012. Polity Press, 2014.

Honneth, Axel. *The Idea of Socialism: Towards a Renewal*. Translated by Joseph Ganahl. 2015. Polity Press, 2017.

Honneth, Axel. "Pathologies of the Social: The Past and Present of Social Philosophy." In Honneth, *Disrespect: The Normative Foundations of Critical Theory*, translated by J. Ganahl. 2000. Polity Press, 2007.

Honneth, Axel. "A Physiognomy of the Capitalist Form of Life: A Sketch of Adorno's Social Theory." In Honneth, *Pathologies of Reason: On the Legacy of Critical Theory*, translated by James Ingram et al. 2005. Columbia University Press, 2009.

Honneth, Axel. "The Possibility of a Disclosing Critique of Society: The Dialectic of Enlightenment in Light of Current Debates in Social Criticism." In Honneth, *Disrespect: The Normative Foundations of Critical Theory*, translated by J. Ganahl. 2000. Polity Press, 2007.

Honneth, Axel. "Reconstructive Social Criticism with a Genealogical Proviso: On the Idea of Critique in the Frankfurt School." In Honneth, *Pathologies of Reason: On the Legacy of Critical Theory*, translated by James Ingram et al. 2002. Columbia University Press, 2009.

Honneth, Axel, and Arvi Särkelä. "Anerkennung als assoziiertes Leben: Aktualität und Aufgabe von Deweys Vorlesungen in China." In *Sozialphilosophie: Vorle-*

sungen in China 1919/20, edited by Honneth and Särkelä, translated by Martin Suhr. Suhrkamp Verlag, 2019.
Hook, Sidney. *The Metaphysics of Pragmatism*. Open Court, 1927.
Horkheimer, Max. "Traditional and Critical Theory." In Horkheimer, *Critical Theory: Selected Essays*, translated by Matthew J. O'Connell. 1937. Continuum, 2002.
Horkheimer, Max, and Theodor W. Adorno. *Dialectic of Enlightenment: Philosophical Fragments*. Edited by Gunzelin Schmid Noerr, translated by Edmund Jephcott. 1947. Stanford University Press, 2002.
Huxley, Aldous. *Brave New World*. 1932. Vintage, 1994.
Institut für Sozialforschung. *Soziologische Exkurse*. Europäische Verlagsanstalt, 1956.
Jaeggi, Rahel. *Critique of Forms of Life*. Translated by Ciaran Cronin. 2013. Columbia University Press, 2018.
Joas, Hans. *The Creativity of Action*. Translated by Jeremy Gaines and Paul Keast. 1992. Polity Press, 1996.
Kant, Immanuel. *Critique of Pure Reason*. Edited and translated by Paul Guyer and Allen W. Wood. 1787. Cambridge University Press, 1998.
Kompridis, Nikolas. *Critique and Disclosure: Critical Theory Between Past and Future*. MIT Press, 2006.
Kompridis, Nikolas. "Über Welterschließung: Heidegger, Habermas, Dewey." *Deutsche Zeitschrift für Philosophie* 41, no. 3 (1993): 525–38.
Koopman, Colin. "Genealogical Pragmatism: How History Matters for Foucault and Dewey." *Journal of the Philosophy of History* 5, no. 3 (2011): 533–61.
Kotkavirta, Jussi. "Adorno ja psykoanalyysi." In Kotkavirta, *Tuhkaa ja timanttia I: Kirjoituksia filosofiasta ja psykoanalyysistä*. Ntamo, 2015.
Laitinen, Arto. "Social Pathologies, Reflexive Pathologies, and the Idea of Higher-Order Disorders." *Studies in Social and Political Thought* 25, no. 2 (2015): 44–65.
Laitinen, Arto, and Arvi Särkelä. "Analyzing Conceptions of Social Pathology: Eight Questions." *Studies in Social and Political Thought* 28 (2018): 21–30.
Laitinen, Arto, and Arvi Särkelä. "Four Conceptions of Social Pathology." *European Journal of Social Theory* 22, no. 1 (2019): 80–102.
Lara, Maria Pia. *The Politics of Disclosure: Struggles over the Semantics of Secularization*. Columbia University Press, 2013.
Latour, Bruno. *Facing Gaia: Eight Lectures on the New Climatic Regime*. Translated by Catherine Porter. 2015. Polity Press, 2017.
Latour, Bruno. *An Inquiry into Modes of Existence: An Anthropology of the Moderns*. Harvard University Press, 2013.
Latour Bruno. *Reassembling the Social: An Introduction to Actor-Network-Theory*. Oxford University Press, 2005.
Latour, Bruno. "Why Has Critique Run Out of Steam? From Matters of Fact to Matters of Concern." *Critical Inquiry* 30, no. 2 (2004): 225–48.
Lear, Jonathan. *Freud*. Routledge, 2015.

Le Blanc, Guillaume. *Philosophie comme contre-culture*. Presses Universitaires de France, 2014.

Leibniz, Gottfried. *Monadology*. In Leibniz, *Monadology and Other Philosophical Essays*, translated by Paul Schrecker and Anne Martin Schrecker. 1714. Bobbs-Merrill, 1965.

Lemm, Vanessa. "Is Nietzsche a Perfectionist? Rawls, Cavell, and the Politics of Culture in Nietzsche's *'Schopenhauer as Educator.'*" *Journal of Nietzsche Studies* 34 (Autumn 2007): 5–27.

Levine, Steven. "Hegel, Dewey and Habits." *British Journal for the History of Philosophy* 23, no. 4 (2015): 632–56.

Levine, Steven. "Hegel's Place in Dewey's Naturalistic Metaphysics: Causality, History, and Teleology." Unpublished manuscript, August 11, 2022.

Loick, Daniel. *Die Überlegenheit der Unterlegenen: Eine Theorie der Gegengemeinschaften*. Suhrkamp Verlag, 2024.

Loick, Daniel. *Juridismus: Konturen einer kritischen Theorie des Rechts*. Suhrkamp Verlag, 2017.

Lorenc, Theo. "Tarde's Pansocial Ontology." In Gabriel Tarde, *Monadology and Sociology*, edited and translated by Lorenc. Re.press, 2012.

Losurdo, Domenico. *Nietzsche, the Aristocratic Rebel: Intellectual Biography and Critical Balance-Sheet*. Translated by Gregor Benton. 2002. Haymarket Books, 2021.

Lovejoy, Arthur O. *The Great Chain of Being: A Study of the History of an Idea*. 1936. Harvard University Press, 2001.

Lovibond, Sabina. "Between Tradition and Criticism: The 'Uncodifiability' of the Normative." In Lovibond, *Essays on Ethics and Culture*. 2019. Oxford University Press, 2022.

Lovibond, Sabina. *Ethical Formation*. Harvard University Press, 2002.

Lovibond, Sabina. "Ethical Upbringing: From Connivance to Cognition." In Lovibond, *Essays on Ethics and Feminism*. 1996. Oxford University Press, 2015.

Lovibond, Sabina. "Feminism and Postmodernism." In Lovibond, *Essays on Ethics and Feminism*. 1989. Oxford University Press, 2015.

Lovibond, Sabina. "Feminism and Pragmatism: A Reply to Richard Rorty." In Lovibond, *Essays on Ethics and Feminism*. 1992. Oxford University Press, 2015.

Lovibond, Sabina. Introduction to *Essays on Ethics and Feminism*, by Lovibond. Oxford University Press, 2015.

Lovibond, Sabina. "Nietzsche on Distance, Beauty, and Truth." In Lovibond, *Essays on Ethics and Feminism*. 2014. Oxford University Press, 2015.

Lovibond, Sabina. "Practical Reason and Character Formation." In Lovibond, *Essays on Ethics and Culture*. 2015. Oxford University Press, 2022.

Lovibond, Sabina. "Selflessness and Other Moral Baggage." In Lovibond, *Essays on Ethics and Feminism*. 2012. Oxford University Press, 2015.

Lovibond, Sabina. "'The Sickness of a Time': Social Pathology and Therapeutic Philosophy." In Lovibond, *Essays on Ethics and Culture*. Oxford University Press, 2022.

Lovibond, Sabina. "Wittgenstein and Moral Realism: The Debate Continues." In Lovibond, *Essays on Ethics and Culture*. 2021. Oxford University Press, 2022.
Lovibond, Sabina. "Wittgenstein, Tolstoy, and the 'Apocalyptic View.'" In Lovibond, *Essays on Ethics and Culture*. 2016. Oxford University Press, 2022.
Marcuse, Herbert. *Eros and Civilization: A Philosophical Inquiry into Freud*. 1955. Beacon Press, 1974.
Marcuse, Herbert. "John Dewey, *Logic: The Theory of Inquiry*." *Zeitschrift für Sozialforschung* 8, no. 1 (1940): 221–28.
Marx, Karl. *Capital: A Critique of Political Economy*. Vol. 1. Marx and Engels: Collected Works 35. 1867. Progress, 1996.
Marx, Karl. Karl Marx to Arnold Ruge, September 1843. In *Writings of the Young Marx on Philosophy and Society*, by Marx, edited and translated by Loyd D. Easton and Kurt H. Guddat. 1843. Hackett, 1997.
Marx, Karl, and Friedrich Engels. *The Communist Manifesto*. Edited by Jeffrey C. Isaac. 1848. Yale University Press, 2012.
McDowell, John. *Mind and World*. Harvard University Press, 1994.
McDowell, John. "Virtue and Reason." In McDowell, *Mind, Value, and Reality*. 1979. Harvard University Press, 1998.
Menke, Christoph. "Genealogy and Critique: Two Forms of Ethical Questioning of Morality." In *The Cambridge Companion to Adorno*, edited by Thomas Huhn. Cambridge University Press, 2004.
Mercier, Hugo, and Dan Sperber. *The Enigma of Reason*. Harvard University Press, 2017.
Mill, John Stuart. *On Liberty*. 1859. Yale University Press, 2003.
Miyasaki, Donovan. "The Will to Power as Naturalist Critical Ontology." *History of Philosophy Quarterly* 30, no. 3 (2013): 251–69.
Moir, Cat. "Speculation, Dialectic and Critique: Hegel and Critical Theory in Germany After 1945." *Hegel Bulletin* 38, no. 2 (2017): 199–220.
Montaigne, Michel de. "Of Cruelty." In Montaigne, *The Complete Works: Essays, Travel Journal, Letters*, translated by Donald A. Frame. 1595. Alfred A. Knopf, 2003.
Müller-Doohm, Stefan. *Adorno: Eine Biographie*. Suhrkamp Verlag, 2011.
Nelson, Maggie. *Shiner*. Zed Books, 2001.
Neuhouser, Frederick. *Diagnosing Social Pathologies: Rousseau, Hegel, Marx, and Durkheim*. Cambridge University Press, 2022.
Neuhouser, Frederick. *Foundations of Hegel's Social Theory: Actualizing Freedom*. Harvard University Press, 2003.
Neuhouser, Frederick. "Hegel on Social Ontology and the Possibility of Pathology." In *I That Is We, We That Is I: Perspectives on Contemporary Hegel*, edited by Italo Testa and Luigi Ruggiu. Brill, 2016.
Neuhouser, Frederick. "Nietzsche on Spiritual Illness and Its Promise." *Journal of Nietzsche Studies* 45, no. 3 (2014): 293–314.
Neurath, Otto. "Anti-Spengler." In Neurath, *Empiricism and Sociology*, edited by Marie Neurath and Robert S. Cohen. 1921. D. Reidel, 1973.

Nietzsche, Friedrich. *"The Birth of Tragedy" and Other Writings*. Edited by Raymond Geuss and Ronald Speirs, translated by Ronald Speirs. 1872. Cambridge University Press, 1999.

Nietzsche, Friedrich. *On the Genealogy of Morality*. Edited by Keith Ansell-Pearson, translated by Carol Diethe. 1887. Cambridge University Press, 1997.

Nietzsche, Friedrich. *On the Uses and Disadvantages of History for Life*. In Nietzsche, *Untimely Meditations*, edited by Daniel Breazeale, translated by R. J. Hollingdale. 1874. Cambridge University Press, 2007.

Nietzsche, Friedrich. *Schopenhauer as Educator*. In Nietzsche, *Untimely Meditations*, edited by Daniel Breazeale, translated by R. J. Hollingdale. 1874. Cambridge University Press, 2007.

Nietzsche, Friedrich. *Twilight of the Idols, or How to Philosophize with a Hammer*. In *"The Anti-Christ," "Ecce Homo," "Twilight of the Idols," and Other Writings*, edited by Aaron Ridley and Judith Norman, translated by Judith Norman. 1889. Cambridge University Press, 2005.

Nietzsche, Friedrich. *Untimely Meditations*. Edited by Daniel Breazeale, translated by R. J. Hollingdale. 1873–1876. Cambridge University Press, 2007.

O'Connor, Brian. "Adorno's Reconception of the Dialectic." In *A Cambridge Companion to Hegel*, edited by Stephen Houlgate and Michael Baur. Wiley-Blackwell, 2011.

Owen, David. "Criticism and Captivity: On Genealogy and Critical Theory." *European Journal of Philosophy* 10, no. 2 (2002): 216–30.

Pearce, Trevor. *Pragmatism's Evolution: Organism and Environment in American Philosophy*. University of Chicago Press, 2020.

Peirce, Charles Sanders. "Evolutionary Love." In Peirce, *Collected Papers of Charles Sanders Peirce*. Vol. 6, *Pragmatism and Pragmaticism and Scientific Metaphysics*, edited by Charles Hartshorne and Paul Weiss. 1893. Harvard University Press, 1935.

Pensky, Max. "Natural History: The Life and Afterlife of a Concept in Adorno." *Critical Horizons* 5, no. 1 (2004): 227–58.

Putnam, Hilary. *Ethics Without Ontology*. Harvard University Press, 2004.

Randall, John Herman. *Nature and Historical Experience: Essays in Naturalism and in the Theory of History*. Columbia University Press, 1958.

Rawls, John. *A Theory of Justice*. Rev. ed. 1971. Belknap Press of Harvard University Press, 1999.

Renault, Emmanuel. *Abolir l'exploitation: Expériences, théories, strategies*. La Découverte, 2023.

Renault, Emmanuel. "Critical Theory and Processual Social Ontology." *Journal of Social Ontology* 2, no.1 (2016): 17–32.

Renault, Emmanuel. "Critical Theory, Social Critique and Knowledge." *Critical Horizons* 21, no. 3 (2020): 189–204.

Renault, Emmanuel. "Événement, processus historique et politique chez John Dewey." *Pragmata* 6 (2023): 744–68.

Renault, Emmanuel. "Mise au jour et exagération dans la phénoménologie adornienne des expériences négatives." *Alter: Revue de phénoménologie* 29, no. 1 (2021): 171–88.
Renault, Emmanuel. *Social Suffering: Sociology, Psychology, Politics.* Rowman and Littlefield, 2017.
Richardson, John. *Nietzsche's New Darwinism.* Oxford University Press, 2004.
Richardson, John. *Nietzsche's System.* Oxford University Press, 1996.
Rorty, Richard. "Dewey Between Hegel and Darwin." In Rorty, *Truth and Progress.* Cambridge University Press, 1998.
Rorty, Richard. "Dewey's Metaphysics." In Rorty, *Consequences of Pragmatism (Essays: 1972–1980).* University of Minnesota Press, 1982.
Rorty, Richard. "Feminism and Pragmatism." *Michigan Quarterly Review* 30, no. 2 (1991): 231–58.
Rorty, Richard. *Philosophy and the Mirror of Nature.* 1978. Princeton University Press, 2009.
Ros, Arno. *Begründung und Begriff: Wandlungen des Verständnisses begrifflicher Argumentationen.* 3 vols. Meiner Verlag, 1990.
Rose, Gillian. *The Melancholy Science: An Introduction to the Thought of Theodor W. Adorno.* 1978. Verso, 2014.
Saar, Martin. *Die Immanenz der Macht: Politische Theorie nach Spinoza.* Suhrkamp Verlag, 2013.
Saar, Martin. *Genealogie als Kritik: Geschichte und Theorie des Subjekts nach Nietzsche und Foucault.* Campus Verlag, 2007.
Saar, Martin. "Genealogy and Subjectivity." *European Journal of Philosophy* 10, no. 2 (2002): 231–45.
Saar, Martin. "Understanding Genealogy: History, Power, and the Self." *Journal of the Philosophy of History* 2, no. 3 (2008): 295–314.
Saito, Naoko. *The Gleam of Light: Moral Perfectionism and Education in Dewey and Emerson.* Fordham University Press, 2005.
Santarelli, Matteo. "Between Problematization and Evaluation: Some Remarks on Pragmatism and Genealogy." *European Journal of Pragmatism and American Philosophy* 8, no. 2 (2021): 1–18.
Särkelä, Arvi. "American Pragmatism and Frankfurt School Critical Theory: A Family Drama." In *Pragmatism and Social Philosophy: Exploring a Stream of Ideas from America to Europe*, edited by Michael Festl. Routledge, 2020.
Särkelä, Arvi. "Anpassung und Erschließung: Naturgeschichte als kritische Geste." *Allgemeine Zeitschrift für Philosophie* 47, no. 2 (2022): 201–22.
Särkelä, Arvi. "Das andere Leben: Deweys naturalistische Sozialontologie und ihre kritische Aufgabe." In *Pragmatistische Sozialforschung: Für eine praktische Wissenschaft gesellschaftlichen Fortschritts*, edited by Hauke Brunkhorst, Felix Petersen, and Martin Seeliger. Metzler, 2021.
Särkelä, Arvi. "Degeneration of Associated Life: Dewey's Naturalism About Social Criticism." *Transactions of the Charles S. Peirce Society* 53, no. 1 (2017): 107–26.

Särkelä, Arvi. "Der Einfluss des Darwinismus auf Dewey: Metaphysik als Hypothese." *Deutsche Zeitschrift für Philosophie* 63, no. 6 (2015): 1099–123.

Särkelä, Arvi. "Ein Drama in drei Akten: Der Kampf um öffentliche Anerkennung nach Dewey und Hegel." *Deutsche Zeitschrift für Philosophie* 61, no. 5–6 (2013): 681–96.

Särkelä, Arvi. *Immanente Kritik und soziales Leben: Selbsttransformative Praxis nach Hegel und Dewey.* Klostermann Verlag, 2018.

Särkelä, Arvi. "Negative Organicism: Adorno, Emerson, and the Idea of a Disclosing Critique of Society." *Critical Horizons* 21, no. 3 (2020): 222–39.

Särkelä, Arvi, and Arto Laitinen. "Between Normativism and Naturalism: Honneth on Social Pathology." *Constellations* 26, no. 2 (2019): 286–300.

Schacht, Richard. *Nietzsche: The Arguments of the Philosophers.* Routledge, 1983.

Schaub, Jörg. "The Incompleteness of Ideal Theory." *Res Publica* 20, no. 4 (2014): 413–39.

Scheman, Naomi. "Forms of Life: Mapping the Rough Ground." In Scheman, *Shifting Ground: Knowledge and Reality, Transgression and Trustworthiness.* Oxford University Press, 2011.

Seel, Martin. "Über Richtigkeit und Wahrheit: Erläuterungen zum Begriff der Welterschließung." *Deutsche Zeitschrift für Philosophie* 41, no. 3 (1993): 509–24.

Serrano Zamora, Justo. *Democratization and Struggles Against Injustice: A Pragmatist Approach to the Epistemic Practices of Social Movements.* Rowman and Littlefield, 2021.

Sloman, Steven, and Philip Fernbach. *The Knowledge Illusion: Why We Never Think Alone.* Riverhead, 2017.

Sommer, Marc Nicolas. *Das Konzept einer negativen Dialektik: Adorno und Hegel.* Mohr Siebeck, 2016.

Spinoza, Baruch de. *Ethics.* In Spinoza, *Complete Works*, edited by Michael L. Morgan, translated by Samuel Shirley. 1677. Hackett, 2003.

Stahl, Titus. *Immanente Kritik: Elemente einer Theorie sozialer Praktiken.* Campus Verlag, 2013.

Stiegler, Barbara. "1880: First Philosophical Critique of Adaptationism; Nietzsche, Reader of Herbert Spencer." In *Naturalism and Social Philosophy: Contemporary Perspectives*, edited by Martin Hartmann and Arvi Särkelä. Rowman and Littlefield, 2023.

Stiegler, Barbara. *"Il faut s'adapter": Sur un nouvel impératif politique.* Gallimard, 2019.

Stiegler, Barbara. *Nietzsche et la biologie.* Presses Universitaires de France, 2001.

Strawson, Peter F. *Individuals: An Essay in Descriptive Metaphysics.* 1959. Routledge, 2003.

Tarde, Gabriel. *Les lois de l'imitation: Étude sociologique.* In Tarde, *Œuvres de Gabriel Tarde*, edited by Éric Alliez. Sec. 2, vol. 1. 1890. Seuil, 2001.

Tarde, Gabriel. *Les lois sociales: Esquisse d'une sociologie.* In Tarde, *Œuvre de Gabriel Tarde*, edited by Éric Alliez. Vol. 4. 1895. Presses Universitaires de France, 1999.

Tarde, Gabriel. *Monadology and Sociology*. Edited and translated by Theo Lorenc. 1893. Re.press, 2012.
Testa, Italo. "Criticism from Within Nature: The Dialectic Between First and Second Nature from McDowell to Adorno." *Philosophy and Social Criticism* 33, no. 4 (2007): 473–97.
Testa, Italo. "Dewey, Second Nature, Social Criticism, and the Hegelian Heritage." *European Journal of Pragmatism and American Philosophy* 9, no. 1 (2017): 1–23.
Testa, Italo. "Dewey's Social Ontology: A Pragmatist Alternative to Searle's Approach to Social Reality." *International Journal of Philosophical Studies* 25, no. 1 (2017): 40–62.
Testa, Italo. "Ontology of the False State: On the Relation Between Critical Theory, Social Philosophy, and Social Ontology." *Journal of Social Ontology* 1, no. 2 (2016): 271–300.
Thomä, Dieter. "'Falling in Love with Becoming': Remarks on Nietzsche and Emerson." In *Nietzsche and the Becoming of Life*, edited Vanessa Lemm. Fordham University Press, 2015.
Thomä, Dieter. *Warum Demokratien Helden brauchen: Plädoyer für einen zeitgemäßen Heroismus*. Ullstein, 2019.
Vogelmann, Frieder. "Measuring, Disrupting, Emancipating: Three Pictures of Critique." *Constellations* 24, no. 1 (2016): 101–12.
Vuillerod, Jean-Baptiste. *Theodor W. Adorno: La domination de la nature*. Éditions Amsterdam, 2021.
Wagner, Richard. *Opera and Drama*. 1852. University of Nebraska Press, 1995.
Walzer, Michael. *Interpretation and Social Criticism*. Harvard University Press, 1987.
Walzer, Michael. *The Company of Critics: Social Criticism and Political Commitment in the Twentieth Century*. Basic Books, 2002.
Whitebook, Joel. "First and Second Nature in Hegel and Psychoanalysis." *Constellations* 15, no. 3 (2008): 382–89.
Whitebook, Joel. *Perversion and Utopia: A Study in Psychoanalysis and Critical Theory*. MIT Press, 1995.
Whitebook, Joel. "Wechselseitige Anerkennung und die Arbeit des Negativen." *Psyche* 55, no. 8 (2001): 755–89.
Whitehead, Alfred North. *The Function of Reason*. 1929. Beacon Press, 1971.
Wittgenstein, Ludwig. *Culture and Value: A Selection from the Posthumous Remains*. Edited by G. H. von Wright, translated by Peter Winch. 1977. Blackwell, 1998.
Wittgenstein, Ludwig. *On Certainty*. Edited by G. E. M. Anscombe and G. H. von Wright. Blackwell, 1969.
Wittgenstein, Ludwig. *Philosophical Investigations*. Translated by G. E. M. Anscombe, P. M. S. Hacker, and Joachim Schulte. 1953. Blackwell, 2007.
Wittgenstein, Ludwig. *Remarks on the Foundations of Mathematics*. Edited and translated by G. E. M. Anscombe. MIT Press, 1978.

Wittgenstein, Ludwig. *Tractatus logico-philosophicus*. Translated by D. F. Pears and B. F. McGuinness. 1922. Routledge, 2002.
Wittgenstein, Ludwig. *Zettel*. Edited by G. E. M. Anscombe and G. H. von Wright. 1967. University of California Press, 2007.
Zaretsky, Eli. *Political Freud: A History*. Columbia University Press, 2015.
Zurn, Christopher. "Social Pathologies as Second-Order Disorders." In *Axel Honneth: Critical Essays; With a Reply by Axel Honneth*, edited by Danielle Petherbridge. Brill, 2011.

Index

absolute metaphor, 13, 19, 20, 194–195, 209, 240; negative, 19, 20, 67, 195–196, 224, 237–240
action, 4, 10–11, 20, 23–28, 33, 40, 91, 93, 96–98, 109, 112–123, 127–134, 137–140, 149–150, 160, 168–169, 179–182, 189, 194, 204, 217, 226, 231, 233, 252
adaptate, 213–217, 220, 223, 225, 227, 233, 237, 250, 252
adaptation, 1–4, 7, 10, 23, 25, 33–36, 41, 50, 67, 74–76, 80–81, 87, 91, 95–97, 100, 109–113, 117–127, 132–133, 137, 141, 146–147, 156, 159–160, 164, 168–173, 178, 180, 186–187, 191, 198, 208, 213–215, 220, 224–225, 228, 231, 235, 239, 243–244, 247–250
adjustment, 10, 75, 76, 80–81, 95, 100, 109, 113, 116–117, 121, 124, 127, 129, 132–138, 156, 189, 228, 233
Adorno, Theodor W., 6, 15, 16, 17, 19, 37, chapter 3 passim, 71–73, 78, 86, 91, 94, 98–102, chapter 5 passim, 140–151, 158, 161, 164–175, 178–179, 184–187, 190, 195, 198, 201, 214, 229, 231–234, 238–251

affect, 41, 64, 66, 68, 91, 93, 99, 123, 126, 144–145, 163, 171–172, 175–177, 190, 191, 225, 227
aggregate, 54, 209–213, 216. *See also* adaptate
aggression, 3, 161, 180–182, 237, 269
alienation, 20, 39, 43, 47, 51, 53, 64–68, 72, 83, 111, 127–129, 137–38, 142, 145, 152, 172, 185, 190, 193–196, 224, 227, 232–233, 245, 247, 249
ambivalence, 142, 146, 154–158, 167, 169, 175, 242
antagonism, 4, 52–57, 60, 71, 106–107, 110, 114, 118–119, 131–132, 149, 179, 190, 214, 249, 258. *See also* conflict
Anthropocene, 251
anxiety, 144–145, 152, 182, 190, 251
archaic, 126, 158–159, 168, 173, 180, 205, 225, 241
Archimedean point, 15, 60, 104
Archimedes, 115
Aristotle, 18, 23, 26, 78, 79, 197, 219
aspect perception, 30, 43
association, 1–4, 12, 68, 72, 118–119, 130, 151, 157, 178–180, 194–195, 209–232, 247, 249

295

associational field, 215–222, 224, 228, 273
atomism, 211–212
attitude, 4, 27, 31, 107, 211, 242–243
autonomy, 53, 60, 109, 129, 186, 192, 193, 235

Bannkreis, 15–16, 45, 50, 56–64, 67, 71–72, 86, 91, 101, 106–112, 119, 123–128, 137, 148–149, 161, 190, 244
Beckett, Samuel, 50
behavior, 9–10, 25–28, 60, 109, 125, 130, 147, 162, 209, 213, 216–220, 228, 246
belief, 4, 29, 31, 87, 137, 141, 145–155, 161, 168–170, 188, 190, 218, 222, 229, 231, 242–243
Benjamin, Jessica, 167
Benjamin, Walter, 6, 14, 16n37, 52, 59, 254, 255, 258,
Bergson, Henri, 221
Black, Max, 20, 69n48
Blumenberg, Hans, 12–13, 18n40, 19, 38, 151, 173, 194–195, 209, 239–240
body, 77, 84, 153, 158, 198, 202, 204, 208, 214, 218, 223
Boltanski, Luc, 7, 87n24
Brecht, Bertolt, 43

capitalism, 54, 67, 114, 118, 128, 132–136, 200–203, 239, 251
care, 4, 8, 36, 39, 133, 136–138, 146, 152, 156, 158, 161, 179, 185–188, 238, 245, 250, 251, 252
catastrophe, 4–5, 38, 51–52, 55, 57, 102, 106, 108, 136, 231, 249–252
Cavell, Stanley, 87, 69n46, 95n35
Celan, Paul, 6
Celikates, Robin, 68
chain of beings, 207, 219, 222–223. *See also* scala naturae
childhood, 125, 145, 146, 151, 153, 157, 163–164, 169, 172–173, 181, 190, 205, 225

childlikeness, 191, 220, 226
codification, 2, 12, 17, 19, 23–24, 107, 195, 220, 225, 240, 259
cognition, 4, 12, 43, 152, 165, 186
Comte, Auguste, 47
Conant, James, 87, 79n16, 95n35
concretism, 91, 120–126, 129–130, 132, 147, 171, 214, 243
conditioning, 27–28, 40–44, 50, 52, 56, 110, 125, 134, 184
conflict, 5, 53–56, 69, 73, 78, 109–110, 117–118, 125, 138, 141, 156–159, 179, 190, 205, 229–231, 239
constellation, 16, 35, 127–128, 235, 250
cosmology, 73–74, 87, 192–194, 199, 206–207, 219–224, 274; critical, 87, 89, 102, 104, 194, 197, 204–207, 224–227, 238, 251
countercommunity, 94–102
countereducation. *See* counterformation
counterformation, 39, 69, 73, 82, 95, 96, 100–111, 117, 127–129, 133, 140, 167, 187, 227, 233, 237
counterteleology, 8, 22, 30, 34–44, 55–57, 71–72, 78, 96, 158, 166, 204; naturalized, 39–44, 46
crisis, 4, 5, 106, 134, 157, 251
critical skill(s), 11, 17, 119, 237, 238
critical social ontology, 6, 9
cruelty, 161–168, 175, 178, 185
custom, 1–2, 5–6, 23–25, 31, 60–61, 65, 78–81, 98, 112–117, 121, 130–134, 138, 163–164, 181, 198–199, 203, 214, 219, 226–229, 233, 248–249, 252

Darwin, Charles, 78n13, 89, 102, 109, 113, 222, 230, 231, 232
Davis, Angela Y., 6
debunking, 6, 8, 204, 209, 252
decentering, 64–67, 72, 82–87, 94, 97–98, 102, 111, 128–131, 165–167, 187, 224, 237–245
deception, 169–175

denaturalization, 5–7, 204
Despentes, Virginie, 171
Destiny's Child, 212
determinate negation, 65
deviation, 3, 5, 34, 36, 48, 62, 78, 81–82, 88–97, 101, 116–117, 147, 175, 226, 230
Dewey, John, 12, 15–16, 18–19, 70, 78n13, 102, chapter 5 passim, 140–143, 145–151, 158, 161, 164, 166–168, 173, 178–179, 186, 192, chapter 7 passim, 238–243, 246–251
disclosing critical theory, chapter 5 passim, 140, 170–176, 186–190, 225, 239, 242, 244, 247–248
disposition, 4, 25, 27, 40, 109, 112, 133, 180, 228
dissociation, 94, 151, 226–227
domination, 6–7, 32, 49–54, 117–118, 126–127, 130, 140, 160, 190, 197–205, 219–224, 227, 230–231, 243–244
Dostoevsky, Fyodor, 170
dualism, 52, 198–205, 211, 242
Durkheim, Émile, 47–55, 69n48, 214
dystopia, 49–53, 85, 151

education, 23–29, 35, 39, 44, 61, 69, 78–87, 95–104, 109–111, 114–116, 120, 123, 126–129, 132–142, 147, 172, 176, 185–187, 196, 203, 206, 220, 225, 228, 234, 237–238, 245–251
ego, 151–161, 175–182, 185–186, 191
ego ideal. *See* superego
elitism, 246–248
embodiment, 7, 79, 89, 92, 112, 130, 133, 154, 199, 203, 206, 217–218, 225, 230, 233, 243
Emerson, Ralph Waldo, 15–21, chapter 3 passim, 71–78, 83–84, 87–105, 108, 111, 114–117, 124, 134, 139–148, 151–157, 175, 178–180, 184, 188, 191–197, 204, 206, 208, 219, 225, 227, 229, 232, 236, 239–240, 246, 250
Engels, Friedrich, 91, 200

enjoyment, 132, 163, 164, 167–168, 196, 200, 201, 204–206, 217–220, 227
evolution, 2–3, 76–78, 87–89, 109, 230–232. *See also* Darwin, Charles
exaggeration, 63, 67, 175
exemplarity, 11, 82, 92, 95, 116–117, 217
exemplary reconstruction, 10, 11, 239, 250
exploitation, 32, 163–167, 181, 185, 200, 203–204
external critique, 5, 67, 84–86, 93

fear, 63, 114, 125–126, 139, 144–147, 152, 169, 175, 181–182, 188, 190, 201
figurative speech, 12–13, 19–20, 195
first nature, 25–31, 35, 39, 41, 44, 46, 49–50, 53–62, 71, 78–87, 94–101, 110, 112, 125, 133, 158–159, 192, 198–199, 242; individual, 56, 81–82, 86, 98, 110–112, 125, 133; inner, 50, 54, 57–58, 189
Fischbach, Franck, 251
form of life, 1–11, 15, 23–45, 60–130, 133, 136–141, 166–168, 185, 189, 192, 195, 199–206, 216, 225–227, 230–231, 237, 242–253
Foucault, Michel, 30, 36n19, 168n24
free will, 193, 227, 235
freedom, 6, 24, 29, 50–51, 55, 63, 77, 107–110, 121, 123, 129, 135, 148, 149, 151, 157, 160, 163, 172, 186, 191, 193, 204–205, 208, 215–216, 220–221, 224, 227, 233, 235, 243, 252
Freud, Anna, 56, 63, 125
Freud, Sigmund, 16, 18, 19, 51, 70, 102, chapter 6 passim, 192, 195, 205, 229, 238–242, 246, 251

genealogical critique, 7, 73, 227, 241–242, 245
genius, 63, 66, 68, 90, 92, 96, 98–102, 124, 127, 140–142, 147, 152–159, 162, 167, 175–180, 185, 188–189, 229, 235, 237

gesture: critical, 9, 40, 51, 58, 68, 110–111, 140–141, 165, 186, 237, 241; disclosing, 44, 55, 60, 64, 68, 72, 96, 111, 124, 127–129, 134, 138, 141, 150–152, 163, 166–170, 175–176, 180, 183–186, 224, 227, 232–243, 247, 249, 250; speculative, 39–41
Geuss, Raymond, 13–14, 95n35, 131, 137, 241–242
Goodman, Nelson, 173–175
Gould, Steven Jay, 78n13, 232
gradualism, 135–136, 166
Gregoratto, Federica, 167

Habermas, Jürgen, 136, 196
habit, 1–2, 4, 6–7, 23, 25, 27, 31, 57, 60–61, 65–68, 78–79, 86, 90, 97–99, 111–119, 122, 129, 133, 136, 138, 150–151, 160, 165, 180, 199, 202–204, 214, 217–218, 225, 228–235, 244, 248, 252; reflective, 23, 233–235
habituation, 23, 27, 78, 80, 97, 99, 112–113, 122, 126–127, 233
habitus, 23
Hampe, Michael, 14n34, 150n6, 226
happiness, 21, 50–52, 59, 86, 88, 107, 110, 124, 129, 133, 148–150, 157, 160–165, 181, 186, 190–191, 194, 201, 204–205, 215, 224–225, 233, 243, 252
Hegel, G. W. F., 47, 53–55, 58–59, 65, 83, 107, 131, 149, 158n13, 211, 229
hesitation, 228, 231–235, 247
heterochrony, 159, 173, 225
heteronomy, 147
hierarchy, 32, 44, 174, 213, 219, 220–223, 231
higher self. *See* genius
historicism, 29
Honneth, Axel, 8, 18, 46, 95, 159n14
Hook, Sidney, 196
Horkheimer, Max, 6, 56, 58n44, 59, 106, 135, 137, 201

Huxley, Aldous, 6, 27, 47, 49, 50, 51, 52, 53, 54, 55, 72, 185
Hyperbole. *See* exaggeration

id, 155–161, 173–175, 177, 185–186, 189, 191
idealization, 177–180, 188
identification, 56–57, 63, 108–114, 120, 125–126, 130, 155–160, 177–180, 185, 190–191, 215; with the aggressor, 56–57, 120, 125–132
ideology critique, 7, 198, 201–202, 241–245, 248
imitation, 27–28, 125, 151, 156, 195, 209, 217, 221–222, 228–235
imitational beam, 151, 195, 217–218, 228–235, 243
imitational radiation, 228–235, 249
immanence, 24, 41, 62, 67–69, 98, 100
immanent critique, 5, 8, 9, 12
impulse, 1–2, 35, 97, 112–116, 119, 125, 129, 133–134, 146–149, 156, 158, 161, 180, 182, 188, 214, 225, 237
individuality, 29, 110, 118, 126, 187, 197
instinct, 37, 78–82, 97, 112, 149, 180–183, 223
institution, 2, 23–25, 31, 34, 60–61, 86, 97–98, 112, 114, 130–134, 138, 164, 175, 181, 198–199, 203, 214, 229, 250
internal critique, 5, 8, 31–33, 38, 81, 95–99
internalization, 26–28, 57, 110, 158, 180–182, 186, 220

Jansson, Tove, 169
juridical metaphor of critique, 13–14, 20, 128, 193, 241–242, 246
justification, 4, 9, 64, 198, 244

Kafka, Franz, 90n28, 229
Kant, Immanuel, 13–14, 193
Knowles, Beyoncé, 41, 212, 223
Kraus, Karl, 229

language game, 6, 19, 24–25, 28, 43, 138, 198, 202–204, 225, 237, 242, 243, 248
Latour, Bruno, 196, 231
Lear, Jonathan, 157
Leibniz, Gottfried, 75, 211–212
Leviathan, 3, 4, 132, 249
libido, 156, 158, 160, 166
Lippmann, Walter, 249
Lovibond, Sabina, 8–10, chapter 2 passim, 46, 78, 82, 96, 101, 158
Lutz, Frank, 231
Mahler, Gustav, 229
Maistre, Joseph de, 47
maladaptation, 9, 159
Marcuse, Herbert, 106–107, 159, 160, 166–167, 186–188, 192–193, 205
market, 4, 214, 249
Marx, Karl, 67, 91, 193, 194, 200, 205, 229, 245,
McDowell, John, 31, 79, 81
mechanism, 3, 56, 61, 74, 114, 125, 158, 198, 202, 216, 218, 231
melancholia, 150–152
memory, 74–75, 116, 186, 191, 205, 225
metaphor history. *See* metaphorology
metaphorology, chapter 1 passim, 107, 148, 151, 173, 189, 195, 239–240
metaphysics, 19–20, 53–54, 70, 73, 76, 87–89, 92, 94, 101–104, 107, 117, 132, chapter 7 passim, 238, 242, 252,
mimetic impulse, 28, 30, 35, 96, 102
mind, 21, 40, 63, 77, 102, 114, 142, 145, –149, 154, 159, 198, 201–202, 204, 208–209, 225,
models of critique, 5–8, 11–15, 17, 22, 68–69, 73, 100, 128, 191, 193, 224, 246
monism, 76, 206–211, 214–216
morality, 8, 9, 32, 42, 161–166, 175
mourning, 151–152

natural history, 18, 23, 29, 109, 116, 130, 153
naturalism, 22, 29, 43, 46, 74, 76, 206, 208, 214
naturalization, 23, 26, 39, 40–46, 56, 117, 141–142, 158, 205, 219
Nelson, Maggie, 150–151
neoliberalism, 249–250
Neuhouser, Frederick, 46, 78n12
Neurath, Otto, 8, 31, 34, 38, 80
Nietzsche, Friedrich, 15–19, 27, 36n19, 58–60, 69, chapter 4 passim, 105, 108, 110–111, 114–117, 121, 124, 127, 129, 132, 136–137, 140–142, 147, 151–155, 158, 161, 165, 167, 186, 193–197, 204–208, 217–221, 226, 229–230, 238–242, 246–247, 251
nonrepressive self-control, 160, 191, 205, 220, 223–224, 227
nonrepressive thinking, 194
norm, 2, 14, 24, 240
normative critical theory, 18, 22, 37, 39, 44, 68, 171–172, 176, 247. *See also* normative model of critique
normative judgment, 5–7, 10, 13, 31–33, 36, 39, 73, 94, 100, 140, 237, 245
normative model of critique, 5–8, 12, 14, 69, 191, 193, 224. *See also* juridical metaphor of critique
normativism, 5–8, 12, 14, 32, 69, 191, 193, 224
normativity, 5–10, 13, 18, 22–23, 26–27, 31–41, 44, 55, 59, 62, 68, 73, 81, 85, 89, 92–95, 98, 100, 140, 160, 164–165, 171–172, 176, 191, 197, 217, 224, 237, 244–248, 252

objectification, 61, 184
objective possibility, 51, 61–63, 66–69, 107, 111, 123–124, 129, 132, 135–137, 165–167, 182, 186, 220, 233, 245, 249, 252

Oedipus complex, 147, 157–160
ordinary language, 14, 108, 225–226, 243, 252
organicism, 46–55, 61–62, 65, 72, 214; affirmative, 49, 53; negative, 49–50, 53–55
organization, 4, 61, 69, 80, 85, 95, 99, 102, 112, 124, 130–137, 234, 237, 248–251

pain, 4, 91, 123, 126, 139, 148, 156, 163, 194
pattern, 1–4, 23, 27–28, 44, 48, 109, 159, 173, 198, 237
Peirce, Charles Sanders, 221
Pessoa, Fernando, 192–193
phantasy, 1, 145, 172, 186, 196, 224; making, 172–173, 196, 199, 220, 223, 225, chapter 7 passim
physician of culture, chapter 4 passim, 111, 151, 165, 205, 251
plastic power, 75–81, 85, 87–89, 92–94, 98, 100, 104, 165, 208, 221, 238
Plato, 26, 32
pleasure principle, 148–149, 156–157, 172–173, 186, 189, 220
pluralism, 76–77, 119, 131, 178, 179, 206–208, 211, 215, 238
poetic metaphor of critique, 14–16, 18, 193, 238
poetic redescription, 15, 62, 72, 76, 93
poetry, 4, 66, 69, 73, 225, 236, 246
possession, 198, 201, 209–212, 218, 221–224, 272–274; reciprocal, 210–212, 216, 222, 224, 274; unilateral, 210, 212, 216, 221–223, 224, 274
postcritique, 196, 206
pragmatic, 85, 98, 100, 142–143, 196
pragmatism, 106, 113
preemptive silencing, 3, 6
pressure, 2, 23, 33, 35, 51–52, 91, 109–110, 114, 117, 119–126, 147, 160, 197, 201, 214, 215, 224, 241, 243, 244
Putnam, Hilary, 196

quietism, 9, 31, 40

Randall, John Herman, 196
rationality, 4, 7, 9–10, 23, 32–37, 43, 65, 95, 106, 114, 118, 123, 136–140, 149–151, 166, 173, 179, 186, 191, 194, 198, 204, 225, 239, 244, 246–249, 252; disclosing reason, 10, 107, 116–117, 133, 137–142, 173, 178–179, 185–186, 205, 233–235, 238, 251
Rawls, John, 136
reality, 31, 41, 48–49, 52, 54, 56, 59, 64–65, 67, 114, 135, 145–146, 155–160, 169–173, 185–186, 189, 193, 204, 207–211, 214–215, 220, 225, 228, 230, 240, 243–244, 247–248
reality principle, 156–157, 160, 172–173, 186, 189, 220, 225
reality testing, 146, 155, 169, 171–173, 185, 189, 225
real possibility. See objective possibility
recalcitrance, 2–11, 15, 20, 22, 30–42, 46, 48, 57, 60–64, 67–69, 78, 82, 86–104, 116–117, 119, 124–127, 132–142, 147, 160, 172, 178–181, 184, 186–187, 190–191, 196, 203, 209, 212, 223–227, 231–237, 241, 246–252; creative, 224, 225; speculative, 82
recentering, 64–67, 72, 82–87, 94, 97–102, 111, 134–135, 165–167, 186–189, 194, 224, 228, 237–238, 245–246
reconciliation, 55, 63, 91, 156, 191, 211, 251
reflection, 8, 19, 25, 30, 32, 39, 43, 53, 73, 91, 112, 121, 128, 194, 197, 204, 218, 247
regression, 147–148, 220, 241
reification, 61, 64, 124, 173, 220
renaturalization, 7
repetition compulsion, 148–150, 187, 205
repression, 5, 125–126, 144–149, 152, 157, 167–169, 173, 175, 180–184, 188–191, 200, 202, 224, 251
resemblance. See similarity

Rolland, Romain, 176
Rorty, Richard, 14n34, 36n19, 196, 244–245

Saint Phalle, Niki de, 6
saying/showing distinction, 4, 12, 247–248
scala naturae, 206–207, 219–224, 273
Schelling, Friedrich Wilhelm Joseph, 144, 149
Schönberg, Arnold, 50, 229
second nature, 7, 18, 25–35, 39–41, 44–50, 53–61, 64–65, 69, 71, 78–94, 97–101, 110, 112, 121–125, 131, 133–135, 158–159, 189, 192, 198–202, 214, 226, 228, 230, 233, 241–244; individual, 60, 97, 110, 122, 133; objective, 56; outer, 47, 50, 54–61, 65, 189; social, 81–82, 86, 98, 110–112, 121–125, 134, 192, 201, 214, 228, 230, 233
selection, 17, 43, 89, 90, 101, 221–222, 230–231
selectionism, 221–222
sense of guilt, 161, 180–185, 188–191
senseless suffering. *See* social suffering
sexuality, 157, 160–167, 180, 237
shame, 66, 68, 142, 144–147, 152, 175, 188
shock, 34, 146–147, 172, 175, 189–190, 227, 232–234
similarity class, 17
skepticism, 39, 69, 113, 124, 179, 233, 238
social construction, 6
social environment, 2–3, 10–11, 23–24, 27–30, 35, 41, 79–82, 85, 91–94, 97, 109–117, 121–129, 132–135, 142, 146–147, 152, 159–167, 173, 179–191, 213, 215, 229, 231, 244, 250. *See also* societal environment
social group, 2–4, 11, 82, 109–124, 127, 131–133, 137–138, 141–142, 162, 177–181, 203, 212–214, 228–230, 233, 239, 246; crowd, 32, 86, 177–180, 185

social movements, 7, 175
social ontology, 20, 45, 47, 49, 65, 72, 133, 206–207, 213–217, 224–226, 251; fractal, 115, 133, 213, 214, 226
social organism, 46–55, 61
social pathology, 46, 49, 74, 77, 85, 101, 121, 187
social reproduction, 7, 26, 29, 49–54, 60, 62, 69, 89–90, 110–112, 118, 123, 126, 133–134, 148, 151, 159, 164, 166, 175, 177, 180, 187, 190, 198, 214, 219, 229, 243
social suffering, 3, 4, 66, 88, 92–93, 111, 163–168, 176, 187, 189, 196, 200, 202–205, 214, 227, 238, 252
socialization, 23, 26, 30, 39, 41, 44, 48, 115–117, 126–127, 178–179, 201, 204, 237
societal environment, 2, 4, 115–121, 125, 133, 173, 186, 190, 230, 244
societal exaptation, 3, 6, 57
speculation, 20, 64, 66, 72–73, 87, 92–95, 99, 152, chapter 7 passim
Spencer, Herbert, 47, 113
Spinoza, Baruch de, 76–77, 208–211, 215, 221
spontaneity, 57, 108, 110, 126–127, 235, 237
state of nature, 3, 4, 132, 249,
Stiegler, Barbara, 78n13, 90n27, 249
substance, 1, 25, 46–49, 52–54, 62, 77, 120, 208, 222–223
superego, 125, 153–162, 166–167, 175–182, 185–189
suppression, 5, 57, 66, 94, 147, 175, 180, 225, 251

Tarde, Gabriel, 48, 70, chapter 7 passim, 238, 240, 243, 247, 250
teleology, 26, 34–39, 46–47, 111, 219; social, 26, 32–40, 45–49, 54–57, 60, 65, 71, 78, 95, 110, 158, 161
Testa, Italo, 61, 69n48

therapy, 186–188
totality, 53–56, 67, 194, 196, 228; antagonistic, 54–56; organic, 53–55, 58

uncanny, 3, 15, 16, 28–29, 34, 36, 40–45, 49–52, 55, 63, 69–70, 114, 129, chapter 6 passim, 226, 232, 234, 239, 245, 249; fictional, 168–171, 173–175; ordinary, 168, 170–171; theoretical, 170–175
uncodifiability, 19, 23–24
unconscious, 19, 56, 145–149, 155, 158, 161, 186, 188, 240
uncovering, 167, 186, 189
unhappiness, 57, 108, 111, 160, 163–167
utopia, 49–55, 62–65, 103, 151, 191, 205; negative, 50–51, 55, 63, 65

variation, 17, 25, 47–48, 62, 71, 90, 92, 101, 111, 116, 131, 133, 136, 147, 207, 209, 217, 218, 220, 222, 225, 228–232
violence, 29, 36, 39, 40, 56–57, 132, 147, 191, 199, 202, 226, 243, 248, 249
virtue, 11, 24, 27, 184, 237
virtue ethics, 22–23, 26, 30, 39

Walzer, Michael, 18, 81
Whitehead, Alfred North, 78n13, 217
Wittgenstein, Ludwig, 7, 9, 10, 22n1, 23–25, 42–43, 80, 90n28, 236, 248, 254, 256, 257, 262, 263, 274
world making, 173–175, 196, 220

youth, 32, 80, 115

Cultural Memory in the Present

Gilah Kletenik, *Sovereignty Disrupted: Spinoza and the Disparity of Reality*

Eyal Peretz, *American Medium: A New Film Philosophy*

Jensen Suther, *True Materialism: Hegelian Marxism and the Modernist Struggle for Freedom*

Jean-Luc Marion, *Cartesian Questions III: Descartes Beneath the Mask of Cartesianism*

Walter Benjamin, *On Goethe*

Elliot R. Wolfson, *Nocturnal Seeing: Hopelessness of Hope and Philosophical Gnosis in Susan Taubes, Gillian Rose, and Edith Wyschogrod*

Severo Sarduy, *Barroco and Other Writings*

David D. Kim, *Arendt's Solidarity: Anti-Semitism and Racism in the Atlantic World*

Hans Joas, *Why the Church?: Self-Optimization or Community of Faith*

Jean-Luc Marion, *Revelation Comes from Elsewhere*

Peter Sloterdijk, *Out of the World*

Christopher J. Wild, *Descartes' Meditative Turn: Cartesian Thought as Spiritual Practice*

Eli Friedlander, *Walter Benjamin and the Idea of Natural History*

Helmut Puff, *The Antechamber: Toward a History of Waiting*

Raúl E. Zegarra, *A Revolutionary Faith: Liberation Theology Between Public Religion and Public Reason*

David Simpson, *Engaging Violence: Civility and the Reach of Literature*

Michael Steinberg, *The Afterlife of Moses: Exile, Democracy, Renewal*

Alain Badiou, *Badiou by Badiou*, translated by Bruno Bosteels

Eric Song, *Love against Substitution: Seventeenth-Century English Literature and the Meaning of Marriage*

Niklaus Largier, *Figures of Possibility: Aesthetic Experience, Mysticism, and the Play of the Senses*

Mihaela Mihai, *Political Memory and the Aesthetics of Care: The Art of Complicity and Resistance*

Ethan Kleinberg, *Emmanuel Levinas's Talmudic Turn: Philosophy and Jewish Thought*

Willemien Otten, *Thinking Nature and the Nature of Thinking: From Eriugena to Emerson*

Michael Rothberg, *The Implicated Subject: Beyond Victims and Perpetrators*

Hans Ruin, *Being with the Dead: Burial, Ancestral Politics, and the Roots of Historical Consciousness*

Eric Oberle, *Theodor Adorno and the Century of Negative Identity*

David Marriott, *Whither Fanon? Studies in the Blackness of Being*

Reinhart Koselleck, *Sediments of Time: On Possible Histories*, translated
    and edited by Sean Franzel and Stefan-Ludwig Hoffmann
Devin Singh, *Divine Currency: The Theological Power of Money in the West*
Stefanos Geroulanos, *Transparency in Postwar France: A Critical History of the Present*
Sari Nusseibeh, *The Story of Reason in Islam*
Olivia C. Harrison, *Transcolonial Maghreb: Imagining
    Palestine in the Era of Decolonialization*
Barbara Vinken, *Flaubert Postsecular: Modernity Crossed Out*
Aishwary Kumar, *Radical Equality: Ambedkar, Gandhi, and the Problem of Democracy*
Simona Forti, *New Demons: Rethinking Power and Evil Today*
Joseph Vogl, *The Specter of Capital*
Hans Joas, *Faith as an Option*
Michael Gubser, *The Far Reaches: Ethics, Phenomenology, and the Call
    for Social Renewal in Twentieth-Century Central Europe*
Françoise Davoine, *Mother Folly: A Tale*
Knox Peden, *Spinoza Contra Phenomenology: French Rationalism from Cavaillès to Deleuze*
Elizabeth A. Pritchard, *Locke's Political Theology: Public Religion and Sacred Rights*
Ankhi Mukherjee, *What Is a Classic? Postcolonial Rewriting and Invention of the Canon*
Jean-Pierre Dupuy, *The Mark of the Sacred*
Henri Atlan, *Fraud: The World of Ona'ah*
Niklas Luhmann, *Theory of Society, Volume 2*
Ilit Ferber, *Philosophy and Melancholy: Benjamin's Early
    Reflections on Theater and Language*
Alexandre Lefebvre, *Human Rights as a Way of Life: On Bergson's Political Philosophy*
Theodore W. Jennings, Jr., *Outlaw Justice: The Messianic Politics of Paul*
Alexander Etkind, *Warped Mourning: Stories of the Undead in the Land of the Unburied*
Denis Guénoun, *About Europe: Philosophical Hypotheses*
Maria Boletsi, *Barbarism and Its Discontents*
Sigrid Weigel, *Walter Benjamin: Images, the Creaturely, and the Holy*
Roberto Esposito, *Living Thought: The Origins and Actuality of Italian Philosophy*
Henri Atlan, *The Sparks of Randomness, Volume 2: The Atheism of Scripture*
Rüdiger Campe, *The Game of Probability: Literature and Calculation from Pascal to Kleist*
Niklas Luhmann, *A Systems Theory of Religion*
Jean-Luc Marion, *In the Self's Place: The Approach of Saint Augustine*
Rodolphe Gasché, *Georges Bataille: Phenomenology and Phantasmatology*
Niklas Luhmann, *Theory of Society, Volume 1*
Alessia Ricciardi, *After La Dolce Vita: A Cultural Prehistory of Berlusconi's Italy*
Daniel Innerarity, *The Future and Its Enemies: In Defense of Political Hope*

*For a complete listing of titles in this series, visit the
Stanford University Press website, www.sup.org.*

www.ingramcontent.com/pod-product-compliance
Lightning Source LLC
Jackson TN
JSHW022231110126
96596JS00001B/1